Praise for

VANGUARD

Winner of the 2021 L.A. Times Book Prize for History

Finalist for the 2021 Mark Lynton History Prize

A 2021 MAAH Stone Book Award Short List Selection

A 2021 Cundill History Prize Short List Selection

Named a Best Book of the Year by

Ms. • *Time* • *Foreign Affairs* • *Black Perspectives* •
Undefeated • *Smithsonian*

"Jones has written an elegant and expansive history of Black women who sought to build political power where they could.... Jones is an assiduous scholar and an absorbing writer, turning to the archives to unearth the stories of Black women who worked alongside white suffragists only to be marginalized."
—*New York Times*

"In her important new book, Jones shows how African American women waged their own fight for the vote, and why their achievements speak mightily to our present moment as voters, regardless of gender or race." —*Washington Post*

"If you read no other book on suffrage this centennial of the Nineteenth Amendment, read this one. Let the incomparable historian Martha S. Jones take you to school." —*Ms.*

"Thanks to Martha Jones's *Vanguard*, Black women's rightful place in this history has been restored." —*Foreign Affairs*

"In her forceful and compelling history, Johns Hopkins professor Jones corrects and enriches the conventional narrative of the noble suffrage crusade led overwhelmingly by white women with the determined and strategic efforts by Black women to build their own movement to win the rights that had been denied them." —*National Book Review*

"Jones' book is a welcome addition to the spate of books on woman suffrage that have been published this year in honor of the Centennial of the Nineteenth Amendment. Through her rigorous scholarship and out-of-the-box perspective, she sheds new and important light on the crucial role of Black women in winning and ensuring the right to vote....Jones' scholarship addresses a gaping hole in suffrage literature." —*New York Journal of Books*

"A necessary, insightful book that shines light on Black women underexplored in history. Jones writes narrative nonfiction at its best." —*Library Journal*

"Highly charged, absorbing reading and most timely in the era of renewed advocacy for civil rights." —*Kirkus*

"Martha Jones is *the* political historian of African American women. And this book is *the* commanding history of the remarkable struggle of African American women for political power. The more power they accumulated, the more equality they wrought. All Americans would be better off learning this history and grasping just how much we owe equality's vanguard." —Ibram X. Kendi, National Book Award–winning author of *Stamped from the Beginning* and *How to Be an Antiracist*

"In her inspiring new book, *Vanguard*, renowned historian Martha S. Jones gives us a sweeping narrative for our times, grounded in the multi-generational struggle of black women for a freedom and equality that would not only fulfill their rights but galvanize a broader, redemptive movement for human rights everywhere. Through the carefully interwoven stories of famous and forgotten African American women, together representing two hundred years of history, Jones shows how this core of our society—so key to winning elections today—also gave us 'the nation's original feminists and antiracists.' From organizers and institution builders to preachers and writers, journalists and activists, black women found ways to rise up through the twin cracks of race and sex discrimination to elevate democracy as a whole. At a moment when that very democracy is under assault, *Vanguard* reminds us to look for hope in those most denied it."

—Henry Louis Gates, Jr.

"Bold, ambitious, and beautifully crafted, *Vanguard* represents more than two hundred years of Black women's political history. From Jarena Lee to Stacey Abrams, Martha S. Jones reminds her readers that Black women stand as America's original feminists—women who continue to remind America that it must make good on its promises."

—Erica Armstrong Dunbar, author of
Never Caught and *She Came to Slay*

"You cannot tell the history of modern democracy without the history of Black women, and vibrating through Martha Jones's prose, argument, and evidence is analysis that takes Black women seriously. *Vanguard* brilliantly lays bare how a full accounting of Black women as powerful political actors is both past and prologue. Martha Jones has given us a gift we do not deserve. In that way she is as bold and necessary to our understanding of ourselves as the women in this important work."

—Tressie McMillan Cottom, author of
Thick: And Other Essays

VANGUARD

VANGUARD

*How Black Women Broke Barriers,
Won the Vote, and Insisted on
Equality for All*

MARTHA S. JONES

BASIC BOOKS
New York

Basic Books
Hachette Book Group
1290 Avenue of the Americas, New York, NY 10104
www.basicbooks.com

Printed in the United States of America

First Edition: September 2020
First Trade Paperback Edition: December 2021

Published by Basic Books, an imprint of Perseus Books, LLC, a subsidiary of Hachette Book Group, Inc. The Basic Books name and logo is a trademark of the Hachette Book Group.

The Hachette Speakers Bureau provides a wide range of authors for speaking events. To find out more, go to www.hachettespeakersbureau.com or call (866) 376-6591.

The publisher is not responsible for websites (or their content) that are not owned by the publisher.

Print book interior design by Jeff Williams

Library of Congress Cataloging-in-Publication Data
Names: Jones, Martha S., author.
Title: Vanguard : how black women broke barriers, won the vote, and insisted on equality for all / Martha S. Jones.
Description: First edition. | New York : Basic Books, 2020. | Includes bibliographical references and index.
Identifiers: LCCN 2020006087 | ISBN 9781541618619 (hardcover) | ISBN 9781541618602 (ebook)
Subjects: LCSH: African Americans—Suffrage—History. | Women—Suffrage—United States—History. | African American women suffragists—History. | African American women social reformers—History.
Classification: LCC JK1924.J66 2020 | DDC 323.3/4092396073—dc23
LC record available at https://lccn.loc.gov/2020006087

ISBNs: 978-1-5416-1861-9 (hardcover), 978-1-5416-1860-2 (ebook), 978-1-5416-0025-6 (paperback)

LSC-C

Printing 1, 2021

For Nancy Belle Graves,
and all of us who are her daughters.

CONTENTS

PREFACE TO THE PAPERBACK EDITION

As I finished the last pages of *Vanguard* in early 2020, I knew I was *writing* a work of Black women's history. The timing was important because it was a momentous year, one that marked one hundred years since the 19th Amendment added women's votes to the Constitution. I aimed to ensure, amidst celebrations and commemorations, that the parts Black women played in the story of American voting rights would not be overlooked. I knew there was a lot to say about their politics that would be new to many readers. I did not anticipate how, before the year's end, we'd all be *living* through an unparalleled chapter in that story.

By summer 2020, I understood that we were seeing history in the making. I felt this at my core on the evening of August 19 when, like many millions of Americans, I sat in front of my television ready to watch Kamala Harris accept the Democratic Party's nomination for vice president of the United States. By every account, the moment would go down in the record books. Harris could claim another first in her journey from a start as a prosecutor in gritty Oakland, California, courthouses all the way to a campaign that aimed to place her just one heartbeat from the presidency.[1]

I tuned in to see Harris's moment at the podium. I knew there'd be lots of social media chatter about what she wore. (A deep plum pant suit and pearls, for those of you who missed it!) Mostly, I wanted to hear what then senator Harris would *say*. I expected that she'd take the occasion to tell the nation, and the world, how her rise to power fit into the story of American democracy. Black women before her—from Shirley Chisholm in 1968 to Michelle Obama in 2008—had deftly inserted themselves into histories not written for them. And still, Harris's moment was unprecedented. We'd never before seen a woman of color—one of Black and South Asian descent—represent a major party in a run for the vice presidency. Harris bore the distinct burden of telling a story that only she could write. Her challenge that evening was to explain how she came to stand at the pinnacle of a political culture that for many generations was defined only through the lives of men, nearly all of them white.[2]

Kamala Harris was not, of course, the first Black woman to vie for high office in the US, even if those earlier stories are not well known by many Americans. In 1952 activist-journalist Charlotta Bass ran for vice president on the Progressive Party ticket. Bass was a far-left outsider vis-à-vis the major parties, but she was a candidate nonetheless. Twenty years later, in 1972, Shirley Chisholm ran to win the Democratic Party's nomination for president. Her slogan was "Unbought and Unbossed." Chisholm first made history as the first Black woman elected to Congress in 1968 and, still, odds were stacked against her run for the presidency. Chisholm ran on principle and forever changed the nation's thinking about who could run, be elected, and lead.[3]

On that August evening in 2020, I waited to hear Kamala Harris write her own story. Could she insert herself into our national narrative? Yes; and she did not disappoint. The woman poised to become Joe Biden's running mate began by paying tribute to those women, as she put it, on whose shoulders we all stand. Among them Harris included her own mother, Shaymala Gopalan Harris, an immigrant to the United States from India, a cancer researcher, and a single mother who raised her daughters, Kamala and Maya, to be "proud" and to believe that "the fight for justice is a shared responsibility." Harris credited her political ascent to her family, its values and its legacies.[4]

Harris also introduced a new set of characters, Black women whose stories spanned more than one hundred years of strivings for power. She honored those political leaders who came before her. But Harris did not invoke Thomas Jefferson or George Washington, so-called founders. She did not pay tribute to Elizabeth Cady Stanton or Susan B. Anthony, women often lauded for their early work for women's rights. She did not credit the scions of the civil rights movement, leaving out names like Martin Luther King Jr. and Thurgood Marshall. Instead, Harris explained, the political tradition out of which she emerged by naming six Black women: Mary Church Terrell, Mary McLeod Bethune, Diane Nash, Fannie Lou Hamer, Constance Baker Motley, and Shirley Chisholm.[5]

These are women that I term the "Vanguard," Black women from our past who paved Harris's way to the national stage in 2020. Harris told how she emerged from more than a century of Black women's work as suffragists, educators, party operatives, organizers, strategists, lawyers, voters, journalists, candidates, office holders, and more. Harris positioned herself as the product of a distinctly Black women's journey through histories of enslavement, freedom, and Jim Crow and on to citizenship and voting rights, all the while battling against the twin scourges of racism and sexism.

Listening to Harris's acceptance speech, I suspected that the six names she dropped were not familiar to everyone. Likely, many viewers fired up Google searches in real time to keep up with the candidate and discover who the women she invoked were. Many Americans did not learn their names in school. Still, as Harris told it, these women are no mere sidebars to a main story about American politics. They *are* the main story. And anyone aiming to work with Harris would need to bone up. If elected, I was sure, understanding Harris's perspective would demand careful study and carry new, real-world consequences in the highest echelons of law, governance, and diplomacy. Doing business in Washington would never be quite the same.

That night kicked the 2020 election season into high gear. Kamala Harris's run, we'd soon see, made up one part of the outsized role that Black women would play. The story Harris told of Black women's rising influence on American politics turned out to determine more than who sat at the top of the ticket. Black women, as organizers, operatives, and at the ballot box, made the difference in tight races in states like Georgia, where their power tipped the balance at the Electoral College and sent Kamala Harris, along with Joe Biden, to Washington as vice president and president of the United States.[6]

Georgia's leader Stacey Abrams is the best known among the scores of organizers who got voters to the polls—despite a pandemic, long lines, and rampant voter suppression—and delivered Kamala Harris to Washington as vice president. Their continued efforts on the ground changed the course of American democracy when they rallied again during Georgia's January 2021 run-off and sent two Democrats—Jewish American Jon Ossoff and Black American Rafael Warnock—to the US Senate. These women organizers worked the grueling ground game of American politics in an old tradition. Since Black women began voting in the early twentieth century, they mobilized voters, cast ballots as a bloc, and made the difference on election day.[7]

Black women appeared like a force to be reckoned with. Suddenly, dubbing women like Vice President Harris as mere "firsts" felt less than adequate. Harris did not arrive as a singular or token candidate. She was one among six formidable Black women contenders who vied for a spot on the Biden ticket. On ballots across the country, alongside Harris a record-shattering 130 Black women vied for seats in Congress in 2020. In Missouri, minister, health care worker, and veteran organizer of the 2014 Ferguson uprisings Cori Bush ran to represent her state's 1st congressional district. In Atlanta, Georgia, Democrat Nikemia

Williams vied with Republican Angela Stanton-King for the House seat left vacant by the passing of Representative John Lewis. In Massachusetts, the incumbent Ayanna Pressley looked to return to Congress. Together, these women aimed to exercise outsized influence in Washington.[8]

Black women exercised unrivaled collective power at the polls. Exit surveys reported that 90 percent of Black women cast their ballots for the Biden-Harris ticket, voting as a bloc. Their nearest rivals in 2020 were Black men, 79 percent of whom supported the Democratic ticket. White American women, in contrast, split between the parties: 44 percent for Biden-Harris versus 55 percent for Trump-Pence. Behind the scenes, Black women ran things as highly-placed strategists, communicators, and surrogates. Karine Jean-Pierre gave up her seat as a television commentator to serve as chief of staff for the Democrat's veep candidate, Harris. After working as press secretary for Vermont senator Bernie Sanders and as a CNN commentator, Symone Sanders signed on as a senior advisor to Joe Biden. Collectively, nearly twenty Black women leaders brought hope, skill, joy, and a fierce commitment to change to the Biden-Harris campaign.[9]

Simply put, Black women were no longer "firsts" in 2020. They were a full-on force. When, many wondered, would this voting power translate to power in high office? In just over half a century of vying for political power, Black women moved to the front. Harris is not merely a barrier-breaker on the ballot; she's part of a generation of Black women leaders who are changing politics—and our collective future.

In 2020, many Americans got this lesson and calls to thank Black women went out. Sometimes these generated faint praise. While Black women received due credit, too few commentators acknowledged what a regrettable burden they bore while saving the nation from its worst self. Black women did not pick up that weight for the first time in 2020. They carried it for two centuries, season after season, challenging this country to jettison its most costly sins: slavery, Jim Crow, and the denial of human rights. Having paid with their health and well-being, Black women also gave their lives to challenge injustice and insist upon a democracy for all. It is a role no American should envy.[10]

Still, it looked like 2020 might be the year in which Black women received wide recognition for their efforts. Twitter lit up with accolades condensed into 280 characters. As upper Manhattan's New York State Senator Brian Benjamin put it, "I want to thank Black women for saving the Democratic Party once again." T-shirts broadcast "Thank Black women," and some of the sales supported organizations like the NAACP Legal Defense and Educational Fund, which is headed by a Black woman. Venmo details went up alongside calls to treat your favorite Black woman shero to a drink via the cash app Venmo.[11]

Black women clapped back, insisting that ephemeral expressions of thanks were not enough. Real appreciation needed teeth, and sincere admiration needed legs. Quickly, Black women urged California's Governor Gavin Newsom to fill Kamala Harris's US Senate seat with another Black woman. Massachusetts Representative Ayanna Pressley put it this way: "We absolutely cannot go backwards . . . must prioritize this leadership, perspective & representation in the vacated U.S. Senate seat & appoint a Black woman." Newsom instead appointed his secretary of state, Alex Padilla, to the post. That disappointment underscored a critical question: As Black women showed up—at City Hall, in Congress, at the White House—would Americans follow? The most sincere form of thanks should take the form of supporting Black women's leadership.[12]

When inauguration day 2021 finally arrived, as tradition dictates, Vice President Harris provided no formal remarks. Instead, the afternoon's featured poet, Amanda Gorman, best signaled how the story of Black women in American politics is still being written. Her inaugural poem, "The Hill We Climb," slowed the fast-turning world of that January for a few brief moments. A young, slight Black woman, clad in bright yellow and royal red, called a just future into being with the lyricism of her words and gestures. She issued a gentle but insistent call to action: "The new dawn blooms as we free it. For there is always light, if only we're brave enough to see it. If only we're brave enough to be it."[13]

Even before stepping onto the inauguration platform in front of Kamala Harris, Gorman made plain how she fits into that historical tradition built by Black women who came before her. "I am the daughter of Black writers," she once explained. Historically, Black poets always mixed word-craft with politics, Gorman insists, despite criticism from those who'd prefer a strict division between an otherworldly realm of allusion and allegory and the muck of campaign stump speeches. Blending the two has been the work of Black women poets for more than two centuries, pleasing the ear while aiming to change the world.[14]

Gorman entered the wake of Black women inaugural poets of our own time. In 1993, Maya Angelou graced the proceedings of Bill Clinton's first swearing in with "On the Pulse of Morning." She urged the nation to move forward, beyond its troubled past: "History, despite its wrenching pain, cannot be unlived, but if faced with courage, need not be lived again." Elizabeth Alexander delivered her "Praise Song for the Day" during Barack Obama's first inauguration in 2009, a tribute to those who labored to make the nation and its first Black president possible: "Say it plain: that many have died for this day. Sing the names of the dead who brought us here. . . . Praise song for struggle, praise song for the day."[15]

Seeing Gorman at the inaugural podium also brought to my mind our earliest Black women poets. Lucy Terry Prince interrogated the violence of colonialism. Born in Africa, Prince became a captive later enslaved in New England. Her only surviving poem—"The Bar's Fight"—was composed in 1746 and reflected upon a brutal confrontation between European colonizers and Native Americans at Deerfield, Massachusetts. Enslavers captured Phillis Wheatley in Senegambia on Africa's West Coast and then sold her to a family in the city of Boston. Though prolific, many who encountered her work doubted Wheatley's authorship. Her collection—*Poems on Various Subjects, Religious and Moral*, published in 1773—includes elegies to notable political figures and commentary on the American Revolution and how it might bring freedom to Black Americans. During the Civil War era, Frances Ellen Watkins Harper was a poet, teacher, and antislavery lecturer. Her first collection—*Poems on Miscellaneous Subjects*—came out in 1854 when she was thirty-one years old. Harper initially used poetry to decry slavery and to make a case for the participation of women in antislavery politics. Her talent with words permitted Harper, when she took the political stage, to hold listeners' attention with a distinctly persuasive style.[16]

These Black women poets took up politics as their subject. Amanda Gorman has explained that politics is also her *purpose*. She is a woman wholly of the twenty-first century—working in the long currents of movements for emancipation and civil rights, and at the very moment that a woman of African and South Asian descent holds the office of Vice President. Not to be outdone by Kamala Harris's ascendancy, Amanda Gorman explains that she carries with her the urging of her sixth-grade teacher, a woman sure that Gorman was destined to be president of the United States. Stay tuned for the 2036 election cycle, when the young poet reaches the age of thirty-five and is finally eligible to hold that office.

In the chapters that follow, *Vanguard* tells the story of how we got to the remarkable events of 2020. It is an epic story, one that stretches back two hundred years to early Black women thinkers who asked out loud what it would mean for them to speak in public, take part in politics, and to lead. For most of the last two centuries, Black women remained without voting rights, even after the so-called women's suffrage amendment became part of the Constitution in 1920. Still, they discovered how to influence law and policy and to claim their power by any and every means available. Their organizing, so effective in 2020, began a very long time ago. Throughout their struggles, Black women set the high bar for American democracy, insisting that neither racism nor sexism should bear on the body politic. The women of *Vanguard* knew that when they influenced parties, platforms, and the results on election day, all Americans would get there with them.

Introduction

OUR MOTHERS' GARDENS

I started writing *Vanguard* by collecting stories of the women in my own family. These begin, as far back as I can trace, with Nancy Belle Graves, who was born enslaved in 1808 in Danville, Kentucky. I wondered what it had been like for Nancy's daughters and granddaughters when, in 1920, the Nineteenth Amendment opened a door to women's votes. That year, three generations of women in my family—from my grandmother to her mother to her mother's mother—faced the same question: Could they vote and, if so, what would they do with their ballots? And though I knew lots of family tales, I'd never heard any about how we fit into the story of American women's rise to power. I knew that Black women had won the vote unevenly in a struggle that took more than a century. They'd fought for their rights, hoping to change the lives of all Black Americans. They confronted an ugly mix of racism and sexism that stunted their aspirations. Still, I knew that I came from women who had always found a way to gather their strength and then promote the well-being of their community, the nation, and the world.

My great-great-grandmother, Susan Davis, was Nancy's oldest daughter, and when she said that she wanted to vote, it was a radical idea. Born enslaved in 1840, twenty years before the

*Nancy Belle
Graves
(1808–1889)*
MARTHA S. JONES

Civil War, Susan was a young woman when slavery was abolished in 1865. Her husband, Sam, had fought for the Union and against slavery as a private with the 114th US Colored Infantry. Sam's valor gave him a claim to political rights. Susan celebrated when, with adoption of the Fifteenth Amendment, he won the ballot in 1870. But disappointment soon followed when local laws such as poll taxes along with intimidation and violence kept her Sam from the ballot box.[1]

Susan learned a critical lesson in those years: without the vote, Black Americans had to build other routes to political power. Racism kept Black Kentuckians to the sidelines on Election Day, but Susan got busy. She banded together with friends and neighbors to form a Black women's club that linked them to thousands of women across the country, in a movement that would use political power to ensure the dignity of all humanity. When the Nineteenth Amendment was adopted in 1920, Susan knew it was a new chance for her and women like her. I can't say precisely what she did in that moment, though I like to think that she steered her buggy from her home on the edge of Danville to the voting precinct office. White commentators in Kentucky certainly worried that she would do just that. Black women, they feared, might outnumber white women at the polls and tip the balance in favor of the Republican Party. Likely Susan didn't worry about that one bit. The potential for an upset would have been just what she had in mind.[2]

Susan's daughter, Fannie, was settled in St. Louis, Missouri, by 1920, when the Nineteenth Amendment became law. Susan had given Fannie every advantage she could manage. Above all else, that meant an education. As a teen, Fannie had left her mother's home in Danville and spent a preparatory year at western Pennsylvania's Allegheny College. Then she enrolled in the Classics course at Berea College, a place that taught Kentucky's poor, Black and white. Fannie received her bachelor's degree in 1888 and married her Berea schoolmate, Frank Williams, three years later. They began teaching careers and raised four children in Covington, Kentucky, before settling in Missouri's largest city. Frank rose to prominence as head of St. Louis's fabled Sumner High School.[3]

When it came to politics, Fannie borrowed a page from her mother's book. While barred from voting, she built power where she could. She proved to be a talented organizer and fundraiser and spearheaded construction of the first African American YWCA in St. Louis—named for the enslaved eighteenth-century poet Phillis Wheatley. Its rooms gave Black women a toehold in Fannie's city, a base from which they built skills and influence. In 1919, Missouri became the eleventh state to approve the Nineteenth Amendment, but it would take the approval of fifteen more states to make it law.[4]

In the meantime, there was work to do. Fannie spent the months before the Nineteenth Amendment was adopted preparing the city's Black women for the literacy and understanding tests that officials would use to keep them from joining voters' rolls. When Election Day 1920 came around, Fannie knew what was at stake. Perhaps she even cast a ballot. If so, she would have taken special care in dressing for the occasion, putting on a tailored dress, modest pumps, the right piece of jewelry, and a smart hat. The day of the first vote felt as special as any wedding, graduation, or public ceremony.[5]

Even when they could cast ballots, the work of winning voting rights was not complete for Black women. The Nineteenth Amendment cracked open a door, and some entered into the heart of American politics. Small numbers of those in northern and western cities exercised new political rights. But the daughters of Nancy Graves held no illusions. Even if some of them may have maneuvered past poll officials and cast ballots, the door remained closed to too many African American women. The same poll taxes, literacy tests, understanding clauses, and violence that hampered their husbands, fathers, and sons now beset Black women's lives.[6]

Susan Davis passed away in 1925. The women of Danville's Domestic Economy Club carried her vision forward for decades to come, raising student scholarship funds with poetry readings, concerts, and lectures. In St. Louis, Susan's daughter, Fannie, picked up her mother's mantle and poured her commitment to women's power into the College Club of St. Louis. She led nationally as a member of the YWCA's inaugural Council on Colored Work. When she boarded a train east to Baltimore in 1936, Fannie represented her state at the annual National Association for the Advancement of Colored People (NAACP) convention, where delegates resolved: "We insist upon the right to vote and denounce the methods used in some states to deprive Negro citizens of their suffrage." Fannie—the schoolteacher turned activist—believed that getting Black women to the polls was a goal that all Americans should work toward.[7]

In 1926, Fannie's daughter, Susie, settled into her own life's work. She and her husband, David Jones, arrived in Greensboro, North Carolina, that year to do some building of their own. Four children in tow, they set down their bags in David's hometown, charged with establishing a new liberal arts school for Black women, Bennett College. Since the end of the Civil War, David's family had called Greensboro home. There, his father, Dallas, discovered that politics fit his ambitions. He, along with his uncle William Holley, became county Republican Party leaders in the 1880s and 1890s.

Dallas promoted his party—responsible for slavery's abolition and the guarantee of Black citizenship after the Civil War—as having done more for African Americans than had Democrats. His brash style earned him enemies who aimed to purge Black men from state politics. It was dangerous business. Still, Dallas managed to hold on

The following is a correct list of the COLORED VOTERS registered at Greensboro,—Gilmer and Morehead Townships. If any of them are on your book let us know AT ONCE, through a letter from *your Registrar*, that we may chalenge them here and we may urge you to do so at your place ; *but don't challenge until the day of election.*

Albright, Charles; Adams, Alfred; Alston, Nathan; Albright, Anderson; Albright, Rufus; Ash, George; Alston, Joseph; Alston, David; Alston, Natt; Alston, Sam; Albright, Lamb; Alston, Wash; Albright, Johnson; Ashe, Charles; Allen, Gaston; Anderson, Aaron; Adams, Nelson; Adams, John; Boon, Elisha; Bowman, Nat B; Blount, Willis; Brown, Robert; Byers, Mitchell; Butler, Ed; Bain, Alex; Bass, Charley; Blackburn, Chas; Bass, Jno; Brooks, Samuel; Byras, Jno; Bethel, William; Bowman, Joseph; Bobbitt, H; Bird, Robt; Bland, Wm E; Bird, Warren; Barton, Robt; Barringer, General; Bailey, Ben; Bruce, James; Booker, Henry; Bailey, Thos; Bitting, Anthony; Brown, Spence; Bland, Alfred; Barnes, Daniel; Bethel, John; Burton, Henry; Billings, John W; Bevil, Martin; Barringer, Henry; Banting, B C; Bennett, Henry; Black, Ferd; Bass, Preston; Bevil, Daniel; Bitting, Winston; Bailey, George; Brittin, Louis; Bullock, Samuel; Caldwell, Nelson; Causey, Jacob; Caldwell, Cornelius; Caldwell, Jesse; Caldwell, Madison; Clayborn, Squire; Clark, Henry; Clark, Abram; Chambers, Miles; Cullin, William; Crawford, Robert; Conner, David; Caldwell, Thomas; Conner, Charles; Coltrane, Philip; Crutchfield, Samuel; Crump, Moses; Colbert, Albert; Coleman, Thomas; Caldwell, Wm; Clapp, James; Conrad, Jasper; Chrisfield, J A

Carter, Miles; Cannon, Martin; Caldwell, James; Carter, J W; Climer, J; Caldwell, H; Climer, Emanuel; Climer, C; Coltrain, Phillip; Chavis, William; Clark, Anderson; Day, Ed; Donnell, Henry; Davidson, Joe; Doggett, Lindsay; Dick, Shad; Dick, Elisha; Doak, Alex; Dorsey, Henry; Donnell, Aaron; Doak, Elijah; Dick, Gaston; Dick, B; Dotuell, Jno; Dick, Henry; Dick, Charles; Dorsey, William; Doak, Jasper; Donnell, Isp; Donnell, Calvin; Dick, Joseph; Donnell, Martin; Donnell, Jarney; Dean, James; Dick, Wilson; Donnell, Fenton Sr; Denny, Nathan; Donnell, Prince; Dick, T; Dick, Aaron; Donnell, Geo W; Dickey, Alfred; Dick, Harlan; Donnell, Adolphus; Dillard, Barney; Dodson, Daniel; Dunn, Albert; Donnell, Lee; Davis, Solomon; Dancy, J B; Donnell, John; Dick, Turner; Donnell, Daniel; Doak, Arthur; Davis, Isham; Donnell, Joseph; Davis, Ed; Donnell, Y; Estee, Christopher; Edwell, Anderson; Edwell, Hezekiah; Eckel, Louis; Edwards, Barry; Edwards, Henry; Eccles, Frank; Eckel, George; Edwell, James; Elliot, Pomroy; Evans, Shed; Edwell, S; Edwards, Alfred, Sr; Edwards, Alfred, Jr; Evans, Chas; Edwell, Jno; Edwell, Harrison; Ellis, Charles; Frazier, George; Freeland, Edward; Foster, Harry; Freeland, James; Foust, Michael

Foulken, Jno; Fries, Lewis; Farabee, Jack; Fries, Giles; Fries, Frank; Foust, Calvin; Field, Charles; Foust, Franklin; Fries, James; Freeman, Jacob; Gilmer, Robt; Gorrell, Nelson; Gorrell, Tom; Graves, Jiles; Graves, Freeny; Graves, T m; Galloway, George; Gilmer, Henry; Galloway, D; Galloway, Lewis; Gilmer, Calvin; Garrett, Yancey; Graves, Sidney; Gering, Mack; Gorrell, Jesse; Galloway, Jno; Galloway, A; Galloway, Greene; Gorrell, Calvin; Gilmer, Lucius; Galloway, Chalmers; Gorrell, Allen; Graham, H H; Gorrell, Abram; Gray, Harper, Jr; Gray, Frank; Gibson, Lewis B; Gleadgint, Lewis; Gibson, Yancey; Garrett, George; Graves, Weldon; Gilmer, Madison; Gorrell, Washington; Gillaspie, Loton; Gray, W M; Gossett, Calvin A; Galloway, Isaac; Garrett, Frank; Gilmer, Tobias; Gorrell, Isham; Griffis, John M; Gladson, Albert B; Gant, James; Gray, Thomas; Gray, Henry; Gibson, Joseph; Galloway, Jesse; Gibson, David; Garrett, John; Gorrell, Richmond; Graston, Jere; Gibbs, Anthony; Garves, Horace; Hill, Harvey; Harrison, Bart; Houston, Cumings; Hopkins, Jas; Hudson, Jno; Hill, Edward; Hargrave, Alfred; Houston, Lindsay; Holmes, Wilson; Houston, Jerry; Houston, Joe; Holmes, Henry; Hendricks, Andy; Hargrave, Robert; Hodge, Tom; Herbin, Joe; Harris, Isaac; Hughes, Carl; Houston, Jesse; Houston, Hugh

Hill, Lewis; Harden, Sarry; Hiatt, Richard; Hiatt, Martin; Hoskins, Charles; Hiatt, William; Hopper, Jack; Hairston, Allen; Houston, Madison; Hill, Edward; Hall, Austin; Headen, Orren; Hunter, Jordan; Harris, Hope; Harris, Bartlett; Headen, James; Howell, James; Holt, Mike; Harrold, Abram; Hairston, Jno; Hairston, Allen; Hiatt, Fount; Hill, John W; Hanner, Madison; Haywood, Wm; Jordan, Frank; Jones, Dallas; Jones, Seborn; Jordan, Thomas; Jones, Pinkney; Jones, Nelson; Jordan, Samuel; Jacobs, Stan l; Jordan, Isaac; Jones, Henry; James, William; Johnson, Squire; Jordan, Jno; Jordan, Charles; McElhenney, Chester; Joyce, James; Joyce, Sam; Joyce, Edward; Jones, Lemuel; Jackson, Thomas; Jones, Daniel; Jones, Joseph; Jonakin, Jno; Jones, Jesse; Kelly, Jno A; Kirkpatrick, Sam l; Kirkpatrick, Lindsay; Kirkpatrick, Branson; Kerr, John W; Kelley, John A; Kelley, Allen; Kirkpatrick, Andrew; Lindsay, Hiram; Lindsay, Greene; Lindsay, Caesar; Lane, Albert; Lindsay, Wesley; Logan, Stewart; Lewis, Mid; Lindsay, Pinkney; Lindsay, Jerry; Law, Jeff; Lovick, Wade; Logan Park; Lytell, Jesse; La h, Isaac; Lindsay, William S; Lindsay, Green; Lindsay, Henry

Milton, Sim; McMichael, Green; Melvy, Yancey; Morehead, Jas J; Morehead, Pinkney; Morehead, Caesar; Mendenhall, Sam; Mendenhall, Tyler; Mattock, Chas; McAdoo, Benton; Morehead, George; McAdoo, Milton; Morehead, Sidney; Mabry, H C; McLean, Bedford; Montgomery, Jos; McConnell, W H; McConnell, Wm; Maxwell, J C; McClintock, Mart; Minor, Joe; McKinzie, Ed; McAdoo, Sandy; Mendenhall, M M; Mendenhall, J B; Mans, Spencer; McAdoo, J W; Minor, Shad; Martin, Turner; McMurray, Geo; McConnell, Andrew; Mitchell, Henry; Miller, Wash; Miller, Milton; Melaane, Albert; Mendenhall, Harry; McAdoo, Orpheus; McAdoo, John W; Mumford, Carter; Morehead, Thomas; Mebane, Richard; McElhenney, Chester; Morehead, Sandy; Morehead, Warren; Morrow, Marcus; Morehead, Thenis; McAdoo, Samuel; Mendenhall, Alex; Mace, Nathan; Moody, Jas; Morehead, Robt; Mitchell, Turner; Mebane, Peter; Mendenhall, Darrel; McAdams, Hill; Moses, John; McIver, George; Moody, Andrew; McCallam, Robt; Morehead, Thisis; Mendenhall, Thomas; Mebane, Henry; Mendenhall, Lewis; Morehead, Wash; Mizea, W A; Morton, Rev E; McCallam, Albert; McLean, John; Morehead, Abram; Mendenhall, W; Mendenhall, Geo W; Nelson, Anderson; Nocho, J R; Nelson, Jno; Nelson, A P; Nelson, Jeb, son; Orrell, Ben; Patello, N H; Picket, Joe; Phillips, Amos; Pleasants, Cyrus; Powell, A A; Pleasants, B; Phillips, Wm; Payne, Frank; Pritchett, Floyd; Phillips, O; Parker, Gilbert; Permar, Thos; Powell, D; Pimix, W K; Pleasants, Giles

Patterson, Jno W; Pleasants, Hardy; Payne, James; Paisley, George; Payne, Burton; Putyear, John; Payne, Wm H; Puryear, Seymour; Pass, H P; Pass, P Y; Peoples, Isaac; Rankin, Dary; Reid, Major; Reynolds, Martin; Houston, James A; Roan, Rufus; Rhodes, Pet y; Eneum, Ahijah; Rogers, Warren; Rogers, James; Reynolds, Peter; Roberts, Joseph; Richmond, Henry; Revels, Lindsay; Rankin, Jno l; Roan, George W; Roberson, Edward; Rich, Jno; Rice, Benj; Reid, Wyat; Russell, C; Rankin, Aaron; Rankin, Sam; Russell, David; Robertson, Aaron; Rankin, Thomas; Rankin, Jno J; Sloan, Wilson; Simpson, Elisha; Scott, Jack; Simmons, Peter; Stelton, George; Stephens, George; Scales, Jno; Sloan, Jerry; Swaim, Henry; Stanfield, Sol; Shaw, Lewis; Sellars, Jno; Sellars, James; Singleton, Jeff; Sloan, Wm; Sloan, Isaac; Sullivan, D; Smith, Albert; Smith, Claborn; Sloan, H case; Sherwood, Isham; Sloan, Sampson; Sherwood, George; Steele, Mose; Sharp, Berry; Stipes, Archer; Stephens, Romeo; Sloan, Alfred; Sloan, Randall; Smith, Calvin; Sloan, Calvin; Spites, Anderson; Simpson, Calvin; Saunders, Alex; Swinson, Berry; Smith, Isaac; Swift, Sheppard; Simpson, Samuel; Slade, Ben; Shelton, Squire; Sloan, Wilson, jr; Sloan, James; Singleton, Alex; Smith, Caeto; Simpson, Alfred; Steele, Anderson; Sandridge, Charles; Stewart, Barney; Thacker, Samuel; Thacker, Thomas; Tatum, Barry; Tinnin, Radin; Tatum, David; Troy, Geo W; Thomas, James; Turner, Abner

Terry, Ed; Thompson, Hilliard; Thom, Ralph; Thompson, Anderson; Thomas, Sidney; Thacker, Caswell; Thompson, W C; Tatum, Henry; Thompson, J G; Unthank, Harmon; Unthank, Jasper; Unthank, Jasper A; Vanstory, Ceasar; Walker, William; Weatherly, Raper; Wharton, Thomas; Weatherley, Ed; Weir, Silas; Williams, Solomon; Walker, Mangum; Whitlee, Edmund; Whitfield, Henry; Wilson, Henry; Weatherley, Jno; Woods, Jacob; Wormack, Jacob; Whitlee, Abram; Williams, John; Williams, Zach; Wiley, Samuel; Wright, Alfred; William, Jno s N; Whitfield, Lee; Weatherley, Bob; Wharton, Henry; Wharton, Gaston; Weatherley, J; Winslow, Henderson; Wilson, George; Whitle, William; Wheeler, Joseph; Whitle, James; White, Cornelius; Wood, James; Wharton, Ben Sr; Wagstaff, Peter; Whitloe, Epl; Ware, Sam; Washington, Ed; Wharton, Joe; Wharton, Andy; Whitloe, James; Wharton, Wash; Wilson, Sam; Whitlee, Henry; Wharton, Milton; Wharton, Ben Jr; Witherspoon, Harry; Wharton, John; Wharton, Seth; Wharton, Joseph; Wiley, Robert; Williams, H; Ward, Alfred; Wharton, C; Williamson, Moore; Watkins, Hanibal; Whitloe, Dabney; Wallis, Henry; Wilson, George; Ware, S B; Watkins, Anderson; Windsor, Oliver; Wharton, Sam l C; Wiley, Haywood; Yates, William; Young, Jno; Yancy, Isaac; Yancey, Clevis; Young, Jas F.

Colored voters registered at Greensboro, ca. 1890

to power in central North Carolina as part of a coalition of Black and white Republicans.[8]

Sometime around 1890, the hammer dropped on Dallas's political career. In advance of an election, anonymous men circulated a printed notice that urged election officials to refuse Dallas and nearly four hundred other Black men from Greensboro at the polls. Each of the city's Black voters was identified by name: "The following is a correct list of the COLORED VOTERS registered at Greensboro....If any of them are on your book let us know AT ONCE, through a letter from your *Registrar*, that we may challenge them here and we may urge you to do so at your place: *but don't challenge until the day of the election*."[9] The surviving records don't say whether Dallas or any other Black man voted that year, but that episode marked the end of his political career.

This was the family history of voting rights that greeted Susie and David Jones when they arrived in 1926. David would be Bennett's president, and Susie acted as his partner at each turn. Together they undertook to build a college devoted to Black women's higher education. Every task Susie took on—cutting the ribbon on a new building, registering a new Bennett Belle for classes, depositing a check in the endowment fund—reflected her conviction that Black women were headed toward lives of leadership. She carried this view into the early civil rights years, raising the funds for a young Black activist and lawyer, Pauli Murray, who was documenting how Jim Crow laws blanketed the US South. Susie, a member of the Methodist Church's Women's Division of Christian Service, Board of Missions and Church Extension, underwrote and then published Murray's *States' Laws on Race and Color*. Theirs was a quiet alliance across generations. When, in 1960, Bennett College students organized a local Operation Doorknock, registering Black voters in Greensboro, Susie's support for their efforts came easily. When those same students sat-in at the city's Woolworth's lunch counter, Susie endorsed how young women used nonviolent resistance to win human rights.[10]

These women's stories—of Susan Davis, Fannie Williams, and Susie Jones—mark a starting place for the history that *Vanguard* tells. Their shared foremother, Nancy Graves, persisted even as she had endured enslavement, sexual violence, war, segregation, and the denial of her political rights. Nancy had kept the homes, cradled the children, and laundered the dirty linens of white Americans, people who thought that she and her daughters were worth little more than meager shelter or paltry wages. Still, by 1920, Nancy's daughters were women of learning, status, and enough savvy to navigate the maze that led to the ballot box. They were not typical, in that their education, homes in Upper South cities, and membership in middle-class circles shaped their journeys to the vote. Still, their stories teach lessons about African American women's politics. To them, power always mattered. They supported women's suffrage, in their states and in a federal constitutional amendment. They prepared themselves and the women around them to overcome hurdles that might otherwise have kept them from voting. Still, the vote was never their only strategy or goal. The women of my family, like so many Black women, constructed their political power with one eye on the polls and the other on organizing, lobbying, and institution building. They dreamed big about women's rights and aimed high, committed to using their power to win the dignity of all people.

VANGUARD GATHERS UP Black women's stories in the spirit of Alice Walker's 1983 essay collection, *In Search of Our Mothers' Gardens.* There, Walker uncovered, waded through, and immersed herself in the lives of the women who came before her. Many of them were unknown and too few of them had been celebrated. But Walker believed that in recovering their art, their activism, their joy, and their troubles she could help us know the worlds that Black women alone had created. She went in search of how they survived and thrived in a world not always of their making. Walker discovered what she termed Black women's distinct "womanist" worldview, one that took seriously their strivings for self-possession and for power and honored their capacity for making the whole world over in an embrace of all that is human.[11]

This book turns to the archives of Black women's political pasts to rediscover the worlds they made there. It recounts how, in their search for power, Black women built their own many-faceted and two-centuries-long women's movement. Their voices come through in the pages of tracts, newspapers, books, court transcripts, and memoirs. Yes, they struggled against racism and sexism from nearly every direction. Yet they never allowed doubters or opponents to define them. They looked out from their own positions and then devised a shared mission: winning women's power that would serve all humanity. Their grand, visionary ambition rebuked those who confined the nation's political culture to small, parochial, and exclusionary terms. *Vanguard* illuminates our own time, charting out how Black women—their values and their votes—came to sit today at the center of twenty-first-century American politics.[12]

Vanguard begins with a first generation of women who broke barriers in the 1820s, stepping up to the podium and the pulpit to insist upon having a voice in churches, antislavery societies, and mutual aid associations. By the 1860s, in the wake of slavery's abolition and with a guarantee of citizenship, Black women spoke the language of equality, dignity, and humanity and insisted on political rights. They won some battles. Black women witnessed the adoption of two constitutional amendments—the Fifteenth in 1870 and the Nineteenth in 1920—that promised them the vote. But lawmakers did not keep these promises, leaving many women to make their way in the face of rampant voter suppression: poll taxes, literacy tests, and intimidation. The long road to the 1965 Voting Rights Act was paved with Black women's organizing and courage. The result brought Black Americans, men and women, fully into the nation's political culture for the first time. That victory set the stage for how Black women today have assumed leadership: casting ballots, driving voter turnout, holding public office, and laboring in the trenches of precincts and parties.[13]

The women of *Vanguard* built a movement for political rights that was never separate or for women only. Its foundation lay instead in the institutions they shared with men. Their politics unsettled these spaces with debates over what sorts of power women could exercise, and women placed real value on electing a bishop, sitting as a convention delegate, controlling finances, interpreting the Bible, running for a board, or commanding the podium. These same contests provided a training ground. Women honed their ideas while practicing leadership, the art of persuasion, and the necessity of compromise. They shouldered responsibility for the collective. They stood up to men and also won them as allies. Some women did go on to take part in suffrage associations and women's clubs. But Black women never limited their work to a single issue. Winning the vote was one goal, but it was a companion to securing civil rights, prison reform, juvenile justice, and international human rights.[14]

Living at a crossroads, Black women developed their own perspective on politics and power. Their view was always intersectional. They could not support any movement that separated out matters of racism from sexism, at least not for long. Associations that asked Black women to set aside or subordinate one interest for another were never a good fit. They insisted, for example, that antislavery and women's rights were parts of one movement, and that civil rights included demands for women's liberty. Black women advocated for their interests as people doubly burdened by racism and sexism, and they reasoned that when society lifted them up as equals, everyone would rise. These insights led to a political philosophy rooted in a broad quest for freedom and dignity that extended to all of humanity.[15]

The trouble of racism is one facet of this story, but for the women of *Vanguard*, their encounters with slights, exclusion, derision, and even violence were not the whole of their politics. Racism was a given, a constant. Some women risked being rebuffed in the interest of working in coalition with white women. Other women had no choice but to sustain the wounds of prejudice when their work or travel forced degrading confrontations. But oftentimes, Black women, with plenty of work to do in their own communities with one another, stepped around or turned their backs on racism. If white Americans too often cast a jaundiced eye upon Black women, it was not a look that they needed to return. Remaining at a careful distance from racism was essential to personal dignity and a self-defined approach to women's power.

The stories in *Vanguard* have often been overlooked. But not wholly so. Historians over the last half century have dug deep into African American women's pasts to recover their ideas, their organizations, and their distinct brand of politics. These efforts correct a record made more than a century ago by Susan B. Anthony, Elizabeth Cady Stanton, Matilda Joslyn Gage, and Ida Husted Harper, who dubbed themselves *the* historians of the early women's movement. Between 1881 and 1922, they published the six-volume, fifty-seven-hundred-page *History of Woman Suffrage*. But they told only one part of the story and in that relegated Black women to the margins. Later historians relied upon these same volumes, producing new studies that, regretfully, repeated old omissions.[16]

Vanguard corrects that record by retelling two hundred years of Black women's political history. It does not tell every story; no history can do quite that. But by recounting the lives of some of the many Black women who engaged in political fights, the picture of a whole comes into view. In some eras, Black women pursued power as singular, cutting-edge figures. At other times, they joined coalitions that included white women and Black men. Most often, Black women built political power in their own circles. There are as many stories as there are women, but those recounted in this book represent Black women's varied political lives and their many routes to the vote and beyond.

Black women left their own record, and *Vanguard* tells their stories from the traces they bequeathed to us. Their essays, speeches, letters, and testimonies provide a fresh vantage point. In these stories, the familiar may also be strange. Black women did not attend the 1848 women's convention at Seneca Falls, but at the same moment in church conferences, they demanded rights equal to those of men. Black women did not join the new women's suffrage associations founded after the Civil

War. Instead, they came together in churchwomen's societies to demand the vote and office holding in religious communities. Black women campaigned for the Nineteenth Amendment, but they did not celebrate long once it was ratified. They understood it was only a slim guarantee, and thus redoubled their efforts in a campaign that took them down a long road to the 1965 Voting Rights Act. It was another women's movement, one that reflected Black women's distinct point of view.[17]

Terming Black women the "Vanguard" has a double meaning. Despite the burdens of racism, they blazed trails across the whole of two centuries. In public speaking, journalism, banking, and education, Black women led American women, showing the way forward. Some "first" Black women leapt out front because nothing less would get them where they aimed to go. Black women emerged from brutal encounters with enslavement, sexual violence, economic exploitation, and cultural denigration as visionaries prepared to remedy their own circumstances and, by doing so, cure the world.

As the vanguard, Black women also pointed the nation toward its best ideals. They were the first to reject arbitrary distinctions, including racism and sexism, as rooted in outdated and disproved fictions. They were the nation's original feminists and antiracists, and they built a movement on these core principles. They raised the bar high for all Americans and showed allies, among men and women, Black and white, how to work in coalition. Too often, they experienced disappointment. But undeterred, the women of *Vanguard* continued to reach for political power that was redemptive, transformative, and a means toward realizing the equality and the dignity of all persons.

ONE MORE STORY about Fannie Williams, my great-grandmother, remained untold in my family. I discovered it among some old newspaper clippings. Fannie completed her studies at Berea College in 1888, nothing short of a triumph. During commencement, President Edward Henry Fairchild remarked of Fannie:

*Fannie
Miller Williams
(1864–1956)*
MARTHA S. JONES

"In all of my experience of teaching for thirty-eight years, I have never had a better student than you. Remember that you are admitted to the circle of all those who have attained the title of Bachelor of Arts, and you will everywhere be welcomed within that circle by all, except a very few who are blinded by an ungodly prejudice." With that, she was on her way to make good use of the talent and ambition that Berea had encouraged. Fannie soon headed her own classroom, assuming duties as a teacher, with fresh pedagogy and bright polish.[18]

Fannie also had acquired a taste for entertainment, or at least aimed to develop one. In 1889 she set off on a January evening to the local theater in Pulaski, Kentucky, just south of Berea. The schedule included a "free Indian show," an evening of lectures on the history, culture, and medicines of Native Americans. Admission was gratis; the company earned its dollars by the sale of ointments, pills, and other remedies. Fannie entered the hall without trouble. She surveyed the room and spied a seat that was to her liking. Perhaps she was feeling a sense of equality that her recent triumph at Berea had fueled. Maybe her mood was contrary, leading her to challenge the rules that told her she was less than. Fannie crossed the theater, approached a row designated for white patrons only and quietly took a seat. I can imagine her there as she smoothed her skirt, placed down her purse, folded her hands in her lap, and waited.[19]

Even before segregation became baked into the laws of Kentucky, theater operators patrolled the color line, on alert for those who might cross it. First, an usher noticed Fannie. He approached and, as Fannie explained, "went to her in a gruff manner and ordered her to move." Immediately, a contest of wills flared: Fannie, with her sense of dignity and entitlement, on one side, and the usher on the other, adamant that a Black woman, even a respectable one, must be put in her place. Fannie ignored him and remained firmly seated, with her back erect and her eyes fixed straight ahead, until a local marshal arrived. He repeated the usher's admonition. Fannie retorted: "She asked him politely to tell her why she was not allowed to sit where she was as she did not think she was harming anyone by sitting there." Her words were both a query and a challenge.[20]

What happened next might suggest that Fannie had studied law rather than classics at Berea. The marshal repeated his order: she was to move across the aisle to the "colored" section. Why was she being ordered to move? By what authority? By whose power? Papers later reported that Fannie denounced the marshal in "strong terms," though she never devolved into the use of "indecent or profane language." A confrontation of words turned physical when the marshal, fed up with Fannie's challenge to his authority, "caught her roughly by the arm and led her to the door." In the days that followed, officials charged her with disorderly conduct, a mark that might have threaten her future as a teacher. She sought advice from friends, who counseled that she pay the fine and costs to resolve the dispute. And she did, though all the while maintaining that the blame lay with the men whose gruffness had provoked her flash of temper.[21]

Even today, my own temper boils when I imagine Fannie, fresh from her triumph at Berea College, being manhandled for taking her preferred seat in a theater. She might have believed that education, including the mastery of Greek and Latin, could exempt her from the color line. She may have hoped that class—her dress, deportment, and taste in popular entertainment—would insulate her from the degradations of Jim Crow. If she did, Fannie was wrong. Did she have a right to be a lady? Did she have a right in 1889 Pulaski, Kentucky, to don a fine dress, stroll the blocks to a public venue, take the seat of her choosing, and then be treated to an evening of learning and leisure? Could she expect an usher to offer her his arm or sweep her seat free of dust? Could she turn to a marshal as a safeguard against other men's gruffness? No. Racism was a brutal leveler that transformed a young woman's evening out into a contest over what rights Black women had, if indeed they had any at all.

This encounter fueled Fannie's work in the years to come. As a Black woman, her dignity and her survival depended upon securing political power. Fannie would endure many indignities across her lifetime, those that threatened her body as well as her soul. She would build for herself and other Black women the sorts of spaces in which they could learn, teach, organize, and be safe. She would link arms with white women when they shared her sense that American women, even after the Nineteenth Amendment, had a distance to go before they realized their full influence upon politics and policy. She shared with Black men a commitment to crushing racism—it was a burden that both sexes bore—even as the ways in which it undercut the fullness of womanhood were distinct. These were lonely and terrifying contests when they sprung up without warning in the aisles of a theater. But Fannie had friends, allies, confidantes, and advisors who shared her concerns and her aims. Yes, she was a suffragist. But such a label, ambitious as it might sound to our twenty-first-century ears, was far too narrow to capture her concerns, her activism, and her vision.

Chapter 1

DAUGHTERS OF AFRICA, AWAKE!

In 1827, any Black woman who considered stepping into the limelight of politics was on notice. She risked family, friends, and reputation. As the editors of the African American weekly *Freedom's Journal* put it: "A woman who would attempt to thunder with her tongue, would not find her eloquence increase her domestic happiness. A man, in a furious passion, is terrible to his enemies; but a woman, in a passion, is disgusting to her friends; she loses all that respect due to her sex, and she has not masculine strength and courage to enforce any other kind of respect."[1]

For all the fury that ran through their writing, the men who ran the country's first Black newspaper knew that their words were too little and too late. In their midst were women who were coming out of slavery and servitude and into their own. Some felt called by God; others were raised to serve the collective good. All of them were prepared to push back against anyone who deemed them merely men's helpmeets. The daughters of Africa were awake and ready to break new ground.

THE AMERICAN REVOLUTION ushered in an antislavery moment in the United States. This war that transformed slaves into soldiers also promoted revolutionary ideals about the equality of all. The conflict settled in 1783 with the signing of the Treaty of Paris and an affirmation that the new United States was independent of British rule. Black Americans already aimed to test the principles so eloquently set forth in the Declaration of Independence. The wartime troubling of slavery's bonds meant that newly free Black people could claim a place in American political culture. Men and women of African descent, at liberty to work, build families, and chart their collective futures, posed the most vexed questions the young nation would have to answer.[2]

Abolition was not a distant aspiration. When Northern states began to make slavery illegal, African Americans did their part to encourage the change. In Massachusetts during the 1780s, for example, Quok Walker and Elizabeth Freeman were among those enslaved people who challenged their bonds in court, arguing that the state constitution guaranteed equal rights to all. They won; slavery in Massachusetts was abolished through a cluster of court decisions. In other states, notably Pennsylvania and New York, legislators adopted abolition laws that planned for slavery's demise gradually over time: abolition was achieved in 1838 in Pennsylvania and in 1827 in New York.[3]

Communities of free people grew out of this northern abolition. However, the meaning of freedom was not settled. Some political leaders foresaw a future in which the United States was a white man's country. They promoted *colonization*, schemes that aimed to remove or relocate former slaves from the United States to the Caribbean, West Africa, or elsewhere. Beginning in 1816, the American Colonization Society and its local affiliates raised funds, dispatched recruiters, outfitted ships, and founded colonies such as Liberia. They offered land and political rights to those Black Americans who agreed to leave the country. Few people accepted colonizationists' enticements. Instead, free men and women insisted upon staying in the United States to make their lives in the place of their birth.[4]

With freedom came mobility, at least as far as a coach, ferry, or simply two legs might go. Those who up and went often headed toward something: a job, a loved one, or the streets of a fabled city. Others fled, leaving behind the lash, patrols, and men who believed them free in name only. Chance at a better life might have come in the form of another farm across the county, better wages at a workshop across town, possession of a small patch of dirt, or the warmth of a basement room with a door that shut out the world. For many former slaves, the best opportunities were in cities. In the growing urban spaces of the late eighteenth century lay the possibility of work for wages, a hard-knocks education, and, above all else, the safety offered by numbers.[5]

It is remarkable how quickly Black migrants began to remake cities in their own visions. Their food, clothes, ways of speaking, styles of dance, music, and general sociability became part of what Americans expected of cities. They became Bostonians, New Yorkers, and Baltimoreans, though often with a qualifier—Black, African, or colored—affixed. They began to build, first families and then quickly institutions that made up a new African American public culture. Churches, fraternal orders, mutual aid societies, political clubs, libraries, and guilds sprung up and took root in a way that signaled Black Americans were here to stay. They intended to be fully American.[6]

These beginnings were uneasy. Law and custom mixed with intimidation and violence to promote the racism that had been woven into the nation's fabric long before the heady years of the Revolution. City leaders closed doors, drew lines, and erected barriers that they hoped would lead free Black Americans to leave the country altogether. A debate brewed, one in which Americans sharply disagreed about the status of former slaves: If they were free, were they also equal? If they were citizens, did they also possess rights? How deeply and indelibly would the color line be etched into the life of the nation? Everyone heard these questions as clear as a church bell and as regular as hoof-beats on cobblestones. Black Americans set out to answer them, in word and in deed.[7]

The birth of Black political culture was linked to the troubles wrought by racism. The weight of discrimination was counterbalanced by the pride of self-making. Black institutions boasted of their superior commitment to ideals such as equality. They held themselves up as beacons of the new nation's potential: it could reject the holding of persons as property and erase the color line from the landscape of freedom. Racism met its first endings among these communities of former slaves.[8]

Winning broader freedoms demanded backbreaking effort. Money was scarce, political power slight, and the visibility that came with public life attracted danger and even retribution from villains who hoped to keep former slaves subordinate. The effort required the contributions of all—men, women, and children—and their labors extended from digging trenches and laying bricks to raising preachers' salaries and teaching young pupils with too few primers or slates. Tensions within Black communities developed along lines of education, class, and status and most acutely between those who remained committed to demanding rights in the United States and those who took off for new lands—Haiti, Liberia, and Canada West—where they might find fewer obstacles on their road to freedom.

Political rights—the vote, jury service, office holding—were one key to winning lasting equality. Unable to make the laws that regulated their communities, Black Americans faced a disadvantage. Sometimes white lawmakers might favor them out of benevolence or self-interest. But African Americans did not write the laws that governed their lives. They had little say about how taxes were allocated, and struggled in courts to protect their property and persons. By the 1820s, local memories of the days when Black men had once voted had faded. States like New Jersey, Maryland, and New York had cut Black men's access to the polls, and new states like Ohio and Missouri made "white" a prerequisite for voting in their founding constitutions. The injustice of this shift was underscored when, at the same moment, more and more white men were voting than ever before: states lifted the property qualifications and literacy tests that had once kept many of them from the polls.[9]

Though marginalized, Black Americans did not abandon politics. By the 1830s, activists built a "colored" convention movement, and though the term "colored" may strike twenty-first-century ears as racist, in the nineteenth century it was a preferred term among Black activists. The conventions brought together Black men and some women to debate the issues of the day and organize. The first gathering met in 1830 Philadelphia, where delegates from Maine to Maryland started a tradition that would continue for decades. Convention goers discussed big questions, including civil rights, the building of schools, and the value of every person's labor. Nearby, in Black churches, faith blended with politics when congregations turned their sanctuaries into convention halls, debated church politics, and organized against second-class treatment in white-led houses of worship. These were the earliest years of radical abolitionism and Black Americans worked alongside white allies to bring about the immediate end to human bondage.[10]

Black women participated in this new public culture, but they faced narrow ideas about who they could be and what they could do. Most men expected women to assist with building the community while also remaining subordinate. Men welcomed women as helpmeets who saw to the material needs of ministers, delegates, and lecturers. They encouraged women to raise funds that built houses of worship, published meeting minutes, and kept newspapers afloat. Men also expected women to take charge of families, and ensure the well-being of children, elders, and the vulnerable. All the while, most Black women also worked, as laundresses, housekeepers, nannies, boardinghouse keepers, nurses, and seamstresses. They brought home critically necessary dollars and cents. Among them were women who yearned for more, women who wanted to lead.[11]

Some women, at first just a few, began to question the limits imposed upon them, testing the waters. They did not aim to upset a fragile world, one in which everyone—men, women, and children—were bound together in the same struggle for spiritual, material, and political well-being. It was not yet time to speak about women's rights, or anything as distant as the vote, when even few Black men were able to cast ballots. Still, some women promoted the idea that their talents, their ambitions, and the needs of the community demanded that they also take control of podiums, pamphlets, and meeting halls.[12]

BLACK WOMEN'S SUGGESTION that they were more than help-meets did not go over easily. People sparred verbally in church sanctuaries and meeting halls. Discussions erupted on street corners and at family meals. On the pages of Black newspapers, editors ensured that competing views about women, their purpose, and their power got a good airing. The printed word, whether read silently or out loud, knit together communities of Black Americans across far-flung towns and cities, and it reached the most rural outposts, even if that took a bit longer. Starting in 1827, the pages of *Freedom's Journal* served as a virtual town hall. There, African Americans discovered women who believed they should be part of community building and the quest for the equality and dignity that citizenship promised. They also learned that some leading men opposed any such change.

Anxiety about women leapt from the paper's columns as former slaves from Maine to Maryland and from New York to Pittsburgh opened *Freedom's Journal*. From their desks in New York City, the editors promoted literacy and civic education while condemning slavery and racism. The timing of its debut, spring 1827, was auspicious. New York planned to abolish slavery on July 4 of that year. The paper fancied itself a primer on many things, including how women should contribute to life in freedom. At least, that's what its editors hoped. Their views were conventional. In its earliest articles, *Freedom's Journal* painted a portrait of a well-ordered Black society in which men and women were guided by their so-called innate and differing qualities. The paper deemed women helpmeets who possessed grace, piousness, virtue, modesty, gentility, and peaceableness, qualities that the editors urged would counterbalance the wild excesses of men. In all things, however, women should remain subservient companions.[13]

The editors hoped that their words—set with the authority of type, printed with ink, and circulated on the pages of a respected newspaper—would carry weight. Women might then accept limits imposed upon them in streets, salons, and sanctuaries. Sometimes it worked. In 1828, men and women founded the African Dorcas Society to promote the education of New York City's poorest Black schoolchildren. They named the society for a woman, Dorcas, who in the New Testament is celebrated for her good works and acts of love for the poor. But the founders put in charge an advisory board made up exclusively of men, including ministers and *Freedom's Journal* editor Samuel Cornish. These men encouraged women's work, but not their leadership.[14]

Just as often, however, Black women demonstrated how old ideas would not curb their public lives. Women zealously pursued educational opportunities. Among pupils at the New York African Mutual Instruction Society in 1828, for example, young women outnumbered men. Women also turned out at political meetings. At a New Haven, Connecticut, anticolonization meeting—organized to oppose migration to Liberia—Black women made up the majority of the crowd and even earned praise for their "spirit of enquiry." But these same scenes dismayed others: If women dominated school desks or church pews, might they want to also command the podium and the pulpit?[15]

Women's activism made the editors of *Freedom's Journal* uneasy. It upset their vision for a male-led society. Studiously, they itemized for readers examples how women openly defied limits, discomfortingly so. Many offenders were white women, such as Frances Wright, the Scottish-born journalist, utopian, and antislavery figure; Harriet Livermore, the first woman to preach in the House of Representatives chamber; and a Mrs. Miler, who was noted as a Methodist preacher and "but 22 years of age." The trouble extended beyond the United States. One report noted that as many as sixty Canadian women had voted in the fall of 1827, an alarmingly high number, according to *Freedom's*

Journal. The paper overstated the quantity of ballots cast by women in Lower Canada—it was likely no more than three— but the exaggeration underscored how the specter of women at the polls unsettled the editors. Women gave men reason to patrol the boundaries of public authority.[16]

Suspicion surrounded Black women who rejected conventional roles. Commentators derided breaches of propriety, while praising those women who remained "modest and unpresuming" and committed to the "gentler virtues" of their sex. *Freedom's Journal* openly chastised its women readers, wagging a finger at those who risked sacrificing the privileges of womanhood. The editors' words revealed an awkward truth. As Black communities faced the burdens of freedom, they depended on women's work: Women raised funds and distributed essential goods. They built structures and paid salaries. They filled pews and benches and purchased newspapers and tracts. But what if women were not restricted to these roles? They might also upset a social order that men expected to govern.[17]

Women's passions troubled men. So too did their words. When a correspondent to *Freedom's Journal* we know only as Matilda took up a pen to write on women's education, her tone was mocking and confrontational. She explained that the paper's editors had overlooked this important subject and she challenged: "I hope you are not to be classed with those, who think that [women's] mathematical knowledge should be limited to 'fathoming the dish-kettle,' and that we have acquired enough of history, if we know that our grandfather's father lived and died." Such thinking, Matilda asserted, was past its time: "We have minds that are capable and deserving of culture." Women's responsibilities included the raising of boys into men and shouldering a "duty to store their daughters' minds with useful learning." The editors offered no retort, leaving Matilda's voice to stand alone.[18]

BLACK CHURCHES WERE places of spiritual refuge and sustenance, but organizing them involved politics. Church law structured religious leadership. It set the terms of decision-making and detailed rituals. But even among those who shared a faith, disputes were common. Black Americans got caught up in disagreements over property, money, music, and who should hold the keys to the sanctuary. Always, these troubles revolved around power. They generated factions, schisms, and splits and exposed differences over what made Black churches distinct and necessary. Women also created friction when they made noise about how the role of helpmeet unfairly limited their power.

Jarena Lee, as she later came to be known, did not initially intend to upend power in her church. As a young woman, she first asked questions about her spiritual mission: the genuineness of her calling, the correctness of her biblical interpretation, and her capacity to convert souls. And yet she could not pose such questions without also bumping into the limits that womanhood placed on her purpose. Young Jarena, whose family name we do not know, came of age in a Christian world that believed in the perfectibility of human beings and the rejection of man-made distinctions between people. She underwent a conversion and arrived at a life-defining insight: she would give in to a calling from God and preach. Trouble arose, of course, when that divine purpose led Jarena to speak with authority on spiritual matters and do so in public. Since the 1760s, Black women who preached had provoked alarm about religious and sexual "disorder," but generally these women did not challenge their formal subordination. When Jarena rejected all limits placed upon her work, she introduced something altogether new.[19]

Jarena lived a humble early life. She was born in Cape May, New Jersey, in 1783, just at the end of the American Revolution. As best we can know, she was born free, even as slavery remained legal and not uncommon in the southern part of the state. Situated between New York and Delaware, New Jersey did not begin to abolish slavery until 1804, and some people would remain enslaved there until the post–Civil War abolition of 1865. For Jarena, being free did not mean that she was wholly at liberty. She was bound out as a servant at a young age, just seven years old, robbing her of a childhood. Her liberation story began years later, at the age of twenty-one, when Jarena converted to Christianity. As an adult, she was excused from the harsh obligations of apprenticeship, and she was free, as an eager new Christian, to experiment with what it meant to be spiritually unbound.[20]

Jarena struggled, and her troubles centered on the condition of her soul rather than on the status of her womanhood. Her religious journey went from self-doubt, despair, and contemplation of suicide to time spent searching for a home in the Presbyterian, Catholic, and Anglican faiths. Finally, she was moved to conversion in Philadelphia's young African Methodist Episcopal (AME) Church. Signs that Jarena would not be a conventional adherent to the faith surfaced early on, first in her exuberant worship style—one that mixed prayer with passionate tears and even fevers—and then in her striving for sanctification, a perfection on earth that went beyond traditional Methodist teachings. Jarena was, from the start, ambitious, even excessive.[21]

In 1811, four or five years after joining the AME Church, Jarena "distinctly heard, and most certainly understood" a voice that insisted that she "go preach the Gospel." She was being called, though she was not certain by whom. Perhaps it was Satan. She asked God for a sign, and witnessing a vision convinced Jarena that she was on a righteous path. Even while sleeping, she practiced, waking herself and her household with late-night preaching. Jarena wrestled with an urge to tell her local minister, Richard Allen, of her calling but then hesitated, a sign of just how inflammatory her ambition was. Not the first woman to speak publicly about the scriptures, she was among the very first to seek the formal approval of her church.[22]

Thus began a many-decades-long fight for Jarena. And the stakes were high. The AME Church was navigating a delicate separation from the white-led Methodist Episcopal Church, which would not ordain Black ministers and bishops and refused to transfer the ownership of church property to Black congregations. The movement for an independent Black church was centered in Philadelphia. It galvanized the city's growing free Black community that included veterans of the Revolutionary War and many people who had gained their freedom through gradual abolition laws. Allen, leader of Jarena's congregation, would go on to become the sect's head bishop. He was an experienced minister committed to safeguarding the future of his religious community.

Was Jarena, a preaching woman, an asset or a threat to this new Black Methodism? Allen initially tried to duck the question, doubting that Jarena's calling was genuine. The two went back and forth privately. Allen knew of another case, that of a Mrs. Cook of the Methodist Church, who had similar ambitions. Cook had been an effective exhorter—a religious speaker who did not interpret the scriptures—and had led class meetings during which new converts studied the Bible. Allen valued the talents of women like Cook and Jarena, but he doubted that church law permitted him to license them as preachers. He hoped that Jarena would accept a more limited role in which she preached occasionally with the permission of her local minister.[23]

Jarena tried to live within the bounds of this compromise. She married AME minister Joseph Lee, whom she followed to his parish in Snow Hill, New Jersey. The town was not a good fit for the new Mrs. Lee, and she mourned the loss of her Philadelphia friends, who now lived ten miles away across the Delaware River. Lee was generally ill, and whether the cause was her body or her mind, or both, is hard to say. She bore two children and endured the loneliness and frustration that life as a minister's wife imposed. Then, six years into their marriage, Lee's husband died. Although she suffered, as she later recalled, she was also free to return to the spiritual "fire" that had been suppressed when she played the ill-suited role of minister's wife.[24]

Lee returned to Philadelphia and Bishop Allen's sanctuary, which had become the leading house of worship in the new AME denomination. There, she hoped to find a middle ground that might fulfill her calling and at the same time keep the denomination from veering too far from the limits that

Methodists—Black and white—placed upon women's authority. All that changed, though not exactly by design, when Lee attended the sermon of a guest minister, a Rev. Richard Williams. She followed along as Williams preached "Salvation is of the Lord." At one moment, the minister "seemed to have lost the spirit." He faltered. Lee in turn "sprang" to action, moved by a "supernatural impulse, to her feet." She then, standing in her pew, delivered an impromptu sermon that explained how she, like the Bible's Jonah, had been kept away from her true calling. It was nothing short of an audition. As Lee sat down, Allen rose and declared that her call to preach was as genuine as that of any minister present.[25]

That day launched Lee's preaching career. Over the next thirty years, she measured her efforts by miles traveled and sermons delivered. In 1827, she covered 2,325 miles and delivered 178 sermons. Ten years later, in 1837, she preached 146 times and rode just shy of 1,000 miles. She was nothing short of tireless, but she also had to be fearless, especially when journeying alone or in the company of other women. She attracted converts, old and new, from Maine to Virginia and from Long Island to Ohio. She spoke to Black Americans, enslaved and free, and to white audiences that included doubters, the curious, nonbelievers, and even slaveholders. Lee stood up in camp meetings, in small Black houses of worship, and many times in a town's largest hall. She regularly accompanied Bishop Allen and the AME Church leadership to conferences, where she preached to those who might have doubted her right to do so but who nevertheless could not deny her power.[26]

Lee regularly provoked a question: Did a woman have the right to preach? "Troubles" surfaced in Salem, West Jersey, "from the elder, who like many others, was averse to a woman's preaching." In nearby Woodstown, a church elder "said he did not believe that ever a soul was converted under the preaching of a woman." And yet, when Lee's visit finished, the two shook hands in a concession of sorts. In Milford, Maryland, she arrived by invitation, knowing that preaching women had already generated objections there. In Reading, Pennsylvania, Lee encountered Rev. James Ward, who was "so prejudiced" that he would not "let me in his pulpit to speak." Ward was later, according to Lee, rightly "turned out" of the church. In Princeton, New Jersey, local ministers banded together to stop her from preaching there at all.[27]

Bishop Allen's support mattered. Anticipating Lee's arrival in Pittsburgh, for example, a local minister sent a letter ahead that aimed to stop her from preaching. In response, Lee waved her "License from the Bishop, with his own signature," as her authority. She ultimately succeeded, converting souls while also changing minds. A local church activist in Chillicothe, Ohio, started out opposing Lee's visit, but witnessing her preach led him to conclude that "God was no respecter of persons, and that a woman as well as a man, when called of God, had a right to preach." Sometimes ministers closed church doors to her, but Lee was resourceful and willing to speak in market houses, barns, private homes, and courthouses. But back in Philadelphia, when Bishop Allen proposed she take the pulpit in their home congregation, "opposition arose among the people against the propriety of female preaching."[28]

A woman's right to preach turned out to be more than incidental to Lee's work. Her rights as a woman fused with her divine calling. Lee briefly stepped away from the pulpit in the 1830s, just long enough to put pen to paper. What emerged was one part hard-learned lessons and one part manifesto on churchwomen's power. In 1836, the first edition of her spiritual memoir *Religious Experience and Journal of Mrs. Jarena Lee* appeared: a thousand self-published pamphlets formed a new front in Lee's campaign for rights. She put the question plainly: "Why should it be thought impossible, heterodox, or improper, for a woman to preach?" The answer, in her view, lay not with men but instead with the wonder of the divine and in the unequivocal authority of the Bible: "For as unseemly as it may appear now a days for a woman to preach, it should be remembered that nothing is impossible with God…did not Mary, a woman, preach the Gospel?"[29]

Doubters needed only to witness her at work to be convinced. Lee explained: "I have frequently found families who told me that they had not for several years been to a meeting, and yet, while listening to hear what God would say by his poor coloured female instrument, have believed with trembling—tears rolling down their cheeks, the signs of contrition and repentance towards God." Lee's moving successes demonstrated that women could transform the lives of individual believers. Did they also have the power to alter the institutions they called home? The framing of Lee's tract suggested yes, and its pages circulated along with their author, from churches to revivals and camp meetings. The rights of women preachers were women's rights.[30]

THE PULPIT AND the podium were companion venues in the early nineteenth century, and many Black men moved easily between the two. To command the podium, same as the pulpit, was to wield the power of persuasion. Orators stood in meeting halls and open groves, their voices booming, reaching the ears of hundreds and thousands for whom public oratory served as news, entertainment, and politics—all wrapped up in soaring speeches. Audiences did not always act orderly or attentive. Public speakers, especially reformers, could expect hecklers, lobbed tomatoes, and even rowdy mobs. Words mattered, but so did the person giving them voice. Speakers were sized up for their style of elocution, demeanor, dress, and experience, all of which contributed to how seriously their audiences took them. Listeners also judged orators by the company they kept and the venues that welcomed them. If a person of ideas hoped to influence others, they would sooner or later have to step to a platform or up on a box and project their voice. What might happen next no one could say with certainty.

Maria Miller Stewart discovered how risky taking the podium could be. Her outward appearance and her inner force did not match up. Abolitionist and editor William Lloyd Garrison described Stewart on the eve of her debut as a public speaker: "You....were in not the flush and promise of a ripening womanhood, with a graceful form and a pleasing countenance." This modest portrait was at odds with the fiery prose that burned on Stewart's pages: "I am sensible of exposing myself to calumny and reproach; but shall I, for fear of scoffs and frowns, refrain my tongue? Ah, no!" Stewart and Garrison struck a deal, and he agreed to publish her first book, *Religion and the Pure Principles of Morality*. Stewart's ideas, like those of the men who edited *Freedom's Journal*, would soon circulate in print.[31]

Politics ran high in Stewart's hometown of Boston by the late 1820s. The city was a wellspring of radical antislavery activism and a crossroads for writers, orators, organizers, and agitators, all committed to converting Americans to the slave's cause. Within this group, Stewart forged her public identity, starting in print and then moving to the podium. She was the first American woman to address an audience of both men and women on politics. Long before women's conventions became regular occasions, Stewart broke that barrier. But she paid the price for doing so.[32]

Nothing about her early life destined Stewart to make her mark as a lecturer. Hardship had defined her younger years. At five, in Hartford, Connecticut, Maria Miller lost her parents, which left her vulnerable to exploitation, kidnapping, and sale into a domestic slave trade that trafficked people between the free North and the slaveholding South. She was "bound out" to the family of a local minister and lived a quasi-freedom in which, by necessity, she was coerced to give up her labor.[33]

She learned a hard lesson about racism and inequality. So-called indenture contracts formalized tough bargains. Children without guardians or means of support traded their labor for food, shelter, clothing, and the promise of training or some education. Maria's work, at a tender age, involved attending to the needs of her contract holder and his household. She might have aided her mistress or the staff in the everyday tasks of cleaning and cooking. In a city like Hartford, she may have run errands or helped tend a small, urban garden plot. Perhaps she was a companion to white children. In contrast, Maria would have seen her own youth quickly wither and harden into early adulthood while her companions enjoyed the privilege of innocence and play.[34]

At twenty-three, Maria stood before Rev. Thomas Paul to be married. Liberated from her indenture contract, she had migrated from Hartford north and east to Boston. There, she met and agreed to wed James W. Stewart, a somewhat older man who, after serving in the US Navy and being held as a prisoner during the War of 1812, had succeeded as a shipping agent at Boston's bustling port. The two stood together in the African Meeting House, a building that symbolized the aspirations of the city's Black Baptist community. The skilled hands of Black Bostonians had raised the church frame and the funds to complete the project, and the meeting hall had opened in 1806. Its elegant façade incorporated the townhouse design of the Boston architect Asher Benjamin. And though it began as a place for educational and religious activities such as the Stewarts' wedding, it also hosted public celebrations, political conventions, and antislavery meetings. As Maria and James wove together their lives, a bigger community wove the two into its fabric.[35]

Black Bostonians earned notoriety with their organizing at the African Meeting House. In 1829, David Walker, a member of the Massachusetts General Colored Association and an agent for *Freedom's Journal*, published an incendiary pamphlet: *Walker's Appeal, in Four Articles, Together with Preamble, to the Colored Citizens of the World*. A used clothing dealer by day, by night Walker honed a manifesto that condemned slavery, upbraided Christians who supported bondage, railed against white supremacy, and, most provocatively, advocated open rebellion against slavery with the refrain "kill or be killed." Southern states labeled Walker's pamphlet so dangerous that they suppressed its distribution, arresting sailors who carried it into port. They condemned the text as seditious and even offered a reward for the delivery of Walker, dead or alive.[36]

Stewart likely knew Walker and had read his *Appeal*. But in those same months of 1829, she focused her concerns elsewhere. Her husband of just three years had died suddenly. He had provided for her, leaving Stewart and his children with cash, property, and household goods that should have sustained them. But, one after another, James Stewart's business associates filed suits that claimed debts unpaid and contracts unfulfilled. They brought their claims before sympathetic courts and pressed them against a widow who was inexperienced and without counsel. They targeted a young grieving woman, aiming to wrest control of James Stewart's estate using subterfuge and persistence. After a two-year legal battle, which she lost, Stewart slowly pieced together a new life.[37]

It was not easy: "For several years my heart was in continual sorrow," Stewart wrote. First, she needed work. She began to teach, a vocation that would sustain her for years to come. She also turned to the church, where she found consolation through a newly discovered faith: "I found that religion was full of benevolence; I found there was joy and peace in believing." Then Stewart did the unexpected. She stepped out from the shadows of home life and picked up where David Walker had left off after his own untimely death. She commanded a quill and inscribed hot words onto paper, awakening the consciousness of men and women, Black and white, to the evils of racism. She must have written by candlelight, in the late hours after her workday ended. If she confided her ambition to anyone, no record of it exists. Stewart channeled her grief and anger into prose that rocked Black Boston, and she immediately became a household name.[38]

Stewart wrote expressly to Black Americans, former slaves who faced the challenges that racism imposed in Boston and beyond. She rebuked them, making the case that they would never rise to their best if they did not reform: "Never, no, never will the chains of slavery and ignorance burst, till we become united as one, and cultivate among ourselves the pure principles of piety, morality, and virtue." She issued a steep challenge. Her readers, she urged, held the future of Black America in their hands. On the front lines of their liberation Black Americans must master themselves.[39]

Stewart did not spare Black women from criticism, even though she knew that sexism multiplied their burdens: "Oh, ye daughters of Africa, awake! Awake! Arise! No longer sleep nor slumber, but distinguish yourselves." Women had to do their share of the work if Black Americans would ever see true equality. Women had long played a special role, Stewart believed. Black mothers held one key to real freedom: their children, who in next generations would steer Black Americans forward. Stewart insisted that women take pride in their contributions to the political future. They should not shy away from the challenge, and she chided: "Shall it any longer be said of the daughters of Africa, they have no ambition, they have no force? By no means."[40]

Stewart dared to go further, calling for women to play a part in politics, well beyond the domestic sphere. Anything less was to waste women's skills and experience in a community that needed all the resources it could muster: "How long shall the fair daughters of Africa be compelled to bury their minds and talents beneath a load of iron pots and kettles?" Black women needed to lead despite the distinct degradations that marred their lives. She pointed the finger at white Bostonians, and by implication all white Americans, for the sexual debasement of Black women. They had "caused the daughters of Africa to commit whoredoms and fornications." This would end, Stewart insisted, only when Black women seized their own power and resisted assault, coercion, and compromise.

When the invitations to speak in public arrived, Stewart did not see controversy coming. She dwelled, after all, in the bosom of Black Boston. She carefully crafted her remarks, and the heat of her ideas burned. With great courage, Stewart made her way first to Franklin Hall and then to the African Masonic Hall to face curious crowds. She took a deep breath and spoke. How long did it take before people began to squirm uncomfortably, glance around skeptically, or clear their throats to unsettle Stewart just a little? Did some talk back or heckle? Stewart never reported precisely how she knew that her ideas were unwelcome and that her audacious challenge to the authority of men was out of bounds. We only know that she felt the rebuke strongly enough that she quit.[41]

On a September day in 1833, Stewart got ready for her very last appearance at a public podium. Did she select just the right dress, don a piece of jewelry that made her feel powerful, or carry a special trinket for luck? It would not be an easy time. Her critics had driven Stewart to speak yet again, but only to say goodbye. She had long known contempt: "It was contempt for my moral and religious opinions in private that drove me thus before a public." Though opposition to Stewart had surfaced, she did not simply fold. Instead, Stewart used her last speech to make a record of what it meant to be a woman who broke barriers. She echoed Jarena Lee: "What if I am a woman; is not the God of ancient times the God of these modern days? Did he not raise up Deborah...queen Esther...Mary Magdalene...the women of Samaria...holy women [who] ministered unto Christ and the apostles?" God sanctioned women like Stewart even if men did not: "God at this eventful period should raise up your own females to strive, by their example both in public and private, to assist those who are endeavoring to stop the strong current of prejudice that flows so profusely against us at present." She warned those who had been against her to be wary of deriding other women. "No longer ridicule their efforts," she said, "it will be counted for sin."[42]

Stewart retired from public life. Although *retired* is too strong a word. She did not retreat, nor did she abandon her pathbreaking ideas. She did take a new approach. In the decades following her final speech in Boston, Stewart continued as a teacher. In her classrooms—from Boston to New York and Washington, DC— Stewart trained new generations of young African American women in public speaking. She dispensed formal lessons in the art of elocution, how to use breath and voice, posture and gesture, tenor and tone to move and to persuade audiences. Her experience there, alone at Boston's podiums, was its own lesson: women who stepped out of bounds could expect trouble when they put their bodies on the line.[43]

SOME WOMEN CHOSE the pen instead of the podium or pulpit. Appearing in print, their challenges to men's authority have survived. Cloistered at home, by candlelight, women found that penning a letter to the editor constituted another way to enter politics. At the same time, the written word promised to go far and last a long time. Readers shared newspapers, clipped notable pieces, and returned to them later, long after spoken words had evaporated. Though no one would boo them on the pages of a newspaper, women still risked their reputations when they published, especially when they vied with men for power. It was a risky business that led some women to use pseudonyms when they wrote for the press.

Sarah Mapps Douglass and Philadelphia's Female Literary Association used their pens as weapons when they gently rivaled the city's men. In 1834, the women planned to celebrate the First of August, the marking of what would become known as West Indian Emancipation Day. That day, Britain's Slavery Abolition Act of 1833 went into force. When the day arrived, Philadelphia's leading men turned out for a dinner that included a long series of toasts. When the women presented a satin banner that hailed the "birth day of British emancipation," they never spoke a word, reduced to little more than symbols. Douglass rightly anticipated that, despite extensive speechifying, women would be muzzled. But she had a plan.[44]

For Douglass, how to also mark the occasion was a delicate matter, requiring the women to plan carefully or be overshadowed by their fathers, husbands, and brothers. They chose the following night, August 2, to gather for their own commemoration, and then staged a different type of affair. Women chaired the event, setting the agenda and directing the proceedings, with precision. Members read aloud essays selected especially for the occasion and presided over men who attended by invitation only. Journalist Benjamin Lundy offered a brief address, while Presbyterian minister Stephen Gloucester said a few prayers. But the women remained in charge. *The Liberator*'s headline read:

Sarah Mapps Douglass, *"A token of love from me to thee."*
Amy Matilda Cassey Album. Watercolor
LIBRARY COMPANY OF PHILADELPHIA

"Female Celebration of the First of August." The event stood apart and alone.[45]

Douglass was born into public life. Her parents, Cyrus and Grace, esteemed members of Philadelphia's Black activist circles, raised their daughter to take on the burdens of her community and her conscience. But her road would not be smooth. Born at the dawn of the nineteenth century, Douglass confronted an unprecedented set of questions about her place as a woman. It's not likely that she met Maria Stewart, but certainly she read Stewart's speeches in the pages of *The Liberator*. She may not have witnessed Jarena Lee's preaching—but in spirit the two women were close. Douglass's home sanctuary, the Quaker Arch Street Meeting House, was just a short, twenty-minute walk from the AME Church's Mother Bethel, where Lee was a member. The generation of women to which Lee, Stewart, and Douglass belonged served the public good while honoring the sense that they must also break with stereotypes about womanhood.[46]

Douglass spent her entire life as a teacher. She was formally educated in Philadelphia, preparing to assume responsibility for her own classroom. She might have continued in that vein had not the abolitionist cause called to her, as it did to so many free African Americans. In Philadelphia, she linked arms with other women to form the city's Female Literary Association in 1831. Black women led the society, one that expanded their intellectual ambitions through meditation, conversation, reading, and speaking. A robust sympathy with enslaved people infused all their work, and they built up their political acumen by hearing one another's voices and testing new ideas.[47]

Women's literary associations became increasingly common in the 1830s. Women—Black and white—who aspired to better education, skilled jobs, and the ability to engage in political debates banded together in cities and towns throughout the northern United States. Some women built upon very limited schooling, while others moved beyond their study of literature and the arts. Douglass and her friends distinguished their association by insisting that it be highly visible to the public. They set out to make a statement and, under Douglass's leadership, the Female Literary Association broadcast its existence, joining the confluence of activists who published their ideas and their proceedings in *The Liberator*.[48]

The first challenge that Douglass and her associates confronted was setting the rules that would govern their collaboration. The women gathered for self-improvement, and they adopted structures similar to those of antislavery societies, church conventions, and political gatherings. They drafted a constitution that gave the group a legal identity and put on paper a provocative idea: men's leadership was unnecessary because women knew how to convene and preside over their own associations. The constitution provided for officers, elections, prescribed duties, membership, and the ongoing operation, all of which ensured the women's independence. Douglass and her friends also hoped to spark a broader movement, one not confined to their city. They came together to "induce our colored sisters in other places to imitate their example." Black women's public work could be widespread and collective.[49]

Alongside the association's constitution, Douglass published a letter, signed with her pen name, Zillah, a Hebrew word for "shadow," likely borrowed from Genesis. Douglass revealed her commitment to influencing the course of politics. She commented on a bill pending before the Pennsylvania legislature that proposed restricting the travel of free people of color into and out of the state. Douglass jumped in, both measured and confident: "I do not despair on account of the Bill," she began. Douglass recommended a way forward that began with the study of historical figures, such Barbara Blaugdon, the seventeenth-century Quaker preacher. Douglass found inspiration and example in women's humility, fortitude, and faith in God. She called it an "invisible power." Douglass also offered her own observations. She was encouraged by seeing in Philadelphia Black and white Americans "mingling together...without a shadow of disgust." Her piece illustrated a distinctly Black woman's approach to law and politics that built upon women's history and women's insights above all else.[50]

Imagine Douglass, intently reading the pages of *The Liberator*, carefully dissecting various positions before penning her response. As she wrote, candles burned down and quill nibs wore out. The newspaper's pages gave Douglass an opportunity to engage in open debate before an audience. She weighed in, for example, on the troubled prospect of Black Americans emigrating away from the United States. She knew that pressures, such as colonization and Black laws, tempted some to consider self-deportation. Douglass also saw how emissaries from Haiti—the only independent Black Republic in the Americas—toured major cities and enticed Black migrants to the Caribbean nation. Douglass did not mince words when she sparred in the pages of *The Liberator*. Dispensing with pleasantries and ritual politeness, she countered a correspondent who went by the name of "Woodby" as having been "entirely mistaken" in their understanding of Douglass's position on emigration. And then, Douglass mocked Woodby as unprepared for a serious debate: "I wish you would read what is said on emigration."[51]

Douglass never spoke expressly about how it felt to depart from the role of helpmeet. What she did, however, revealed what she thought. Her work with the Female Literary Association demonstrated shrewd leadership that used a women's platform to enter political debates. Was she thinking about rights? Did she believe herself to be specially oppressed as a woman? Whatever her private thoughts, as Douglass pressed up against conventions—especially by creating vehicles for women's organization—she became a peer to women like Jarena Lee and Maria Stewart.

In cities like Philadelphia and Boston, Black women did not go unnoticed. They gathered in church sanctuaries and meeting halls. They exchanged ideas in pamphlets and newspapers. They met one another and broader audiences when they stood at podiums and pulpits. But they also lived their lives on the streets, in shops, and as audience members in the entertainment venues of the nation's towns and cities. Daily rhythms and habits changed in the 1820s. Social life moved from the privacy of parlors out into parks, sidewalks, and shops. African American women joined these teeming crowds, where the people of

Edward W. Clay, Life in Philadelphia, *Plate 8, "Miss Chloe and Mr. Cesar," ca. 1827*

American cities mixed like never before. Women like Jarena Lee, Maria Stewart, and Sarah Mapps Douglass moved freely through their cities and learned the pleasure of the public gatherings they frequented. They also assumed risks. As they became more visible, Black women opened themselves to a new brand of racism, one that critiqued their aspirations, daily lives, and their very bodies. Blackness, some proposed, excluded them from middle-class, urban culture.

Images served as powerful weapons in a war against Black women. In the windows of print shops, on the walls of coffee houses and saloons, and on parlor tables, pictures—accessible even to those who could not read—derided Black women. In the late 1820s, a series of fourteen lithographs titled Life in Philadelphia appeared, with eleven of the images featuring African Americans. The artist, Edward Clay, portrayed women like Lee, Stewart, and Douglass as women shopping for luxury goods, strolling in parks, hosting tea parties, attending balls, and bantering with the opposite sex—all in the public eye.[52]

Clay used his lithographs to denigrate Black women. He caricatured them, had them uttering malapropisms, wearing clothing of exaggerated proportions, and adopting ungraceful postures. His depictions promoted the idea that Black women were less-than-respectably middle class, they only *pretended* to be so by adopting the mores and customs of that class. Clay's parodies suggested that Black women, despite great efforts, could never be more than amusingly inadequate imitations of white ladies.

Clay's ideas spread far from Philadelphia. The racism he promoted found audiences beyond a local scene. The Life in Philadelphia series circulated widely. Print shops from Philadelphia and New York to Baltimore and New Orleans sold and reprinted it. It spawned a parallel series titled Life in New York and even found salience in London, where printmakers issued elaborate reproductions for British audiences. Eventually, Clay's images adorned illustrated books, newspapers, broadsides, sheet

*Jarena Lee
(b. 1783).
Frontispiece,*
Religious
Experience
and Journal of
Mrs. Jarena Lee
*(Philadelphia,
1849)*
LIBRARY COMPANY OF
PHILADELPHIA

music, and fine French wallpaper. Black women might step into
the public spotlight, but once there they would have to fight
against an arsenal of cruel and demeaning stereotypes.[53]

Surely, Jarena Lee had these demeaning images in mind
when she commissioned a portrait. The face of this inspired
and learned woman greets readers of her memoir, *The Life and
Religious Experience of Mrs. Jarena Lee.* Lee posed carefully,
sitting in an elegant curved back chair, one elbow resting on
a table laden with books. "What is she reading?" the portrait
invites viewers to wonder. She is dressed carefully, a fine but
plain bonnet tied under her chin, a shawl of white gauze drap-
ing her shoulders and torso. Though her hands are modestly at

rest, the gesture should not be misunderstood, nor should the woman. In her right hand Lee holds a quill, a reminder that she is the author of her own text, a woman accustomed to handling fine writing instruments and to firing off the ideas they produced.[54]

Chapter 2

THE CAUSE OF THE SLAVE, AS WELL AS OF WOMEN

When they gathered, Black women often did so to serve the needs of everyone. In antislavery societies, benevolent associations, literary clubs, and vigilance auxiliaries, they tended to their communities and to one another. As Elizabeth Wicks put it in an address to the African Female Benevolent Society in Troy, New York: "For are we not a company of sisters united to support and assist each other?" The answer was yes. But to "support and assist" one another also entailed taking risks. For abolitionism, above all other causes, Black women linked arms, reached across the color line, and took their chances. When male leaders rejected their efforts, women began to speak about their rights.[1]

OPPOSITION TO SLAVERY had always lived in the minds and souls of people of African descent. When the radical abolitionist movement was born in the early 1830s, Black people across the diaspora had been living their own antislavery politics of resistance for at least three hundred years. Eighteenth-century Americans had organized against slavery's most flagrant abuses, insisting that as long as human bondage persisted it should do so by the rule of law. These early antislavery societies demanded that rules about manumission and suppression of the international slave trade be strictly enforced. Slavery might legitimately continue, these early activists admitted. When it did finally end, in years or even decades, many of them proposed that all former slaves should be colonized, or removed from the United States to the Caribbean or West Africa. The first decades of antislavery activism conceded that slavery would likely continue for decades and left anti-Black racism unchallenged.[2]

It was something new, then, when Americans, Black and white, began to call for slavery's immediate, unequivocal, and irredeemable abolition. It assumed the equality of Black and white Americans. These ideas sounded radical, but their justifications ran deeper than mere sensation. Abolitionists drew upon Christian ideals that viewed all humans as equal in the eyes of God. They embraced the natural rights tenets expressed in the Declaration of Independence. Inequality rooted in racism ran contrary to higher principles. They rejected the Constitution and state laws that grew out of proslavery and illegitimate impulses that no righteously minded person was bound to respect. Radical abolitionists committed to changing the hearts and minds of Americans by "moral suasion," prepared to lecture, publish, and preach until the national tide turned forever against slavery.[3]

The movement began with ideas, but it also required tactics and strategies if it was to succeed. Abolitionists had only a small number of committed members, but they multiplied their reach many times over by investing in print culture. Presses, paper, and ink turned into weapons in the hands of typesetters, editors, and scores of agents who distributed newspaper weeklies, such as William Lloyd Garrison's *The Liberator*, far and wide. The same presses churned out tracts, pamphlets, and convention minutes that widely spread the movement's ideas, making them tools of persuasion. Speechifying was equally important. During countless appearances at podiums, open air groves, and salons, abolitionist lecturers used their individual style and personal testimony to introduce crowds to slavery's many ills. Trekking across New England, along the Atlantic seaboard and west to the Mississippi, abolitionists put the best of the oratory arts on display. They enraptured audiences, by weaving drama and pathos with polemic and facts and figures. Crowds, filled with the converted, the curious, and combatants, thronged.[4]

Abolitionism was a dangerous business from the very start. Crowds turned into mobs, and opponents, into assassins. Early martyrs included Presbyterian minister and journalist Elijah Lovejoy, who was killed in Illinois in a melee that also destroyed his press and abolitionist materials. Few antislavery lecturers could avoid the swarm of an angry crowd or the harrowing words of a heckler. Violence occurred as a regular part of the movement, requiring that activists take care with how they traveled and with whom. State authorities also meted out punishments. Abolitionists could expect to face charges of sedition for the mere possession of antislavery materials, especially in Southern states. Lending direct aid to a fugitive slave promised criminal prosecution. Risk ran in many directions.[5]

Free African Americans living in Northern states endorsed the radical abolitionist critique of slavery. They saw their own interests in the antislavery cause, but it was not a crude or distant self-interest. Though they generally lived beyond slavery's reach, the threat of kidnapping was ever present. And the discrimination they faced was rooted in the enduring association of Blackness with enslavement. They reasoned that free Black people would be barred from full equality as long as slavery persisted. Many in the Free States had once been held as property. Their liberty was new, and fragile. Many others had loved ones who remained against their will in slaveholding states. To oppose slavery, to fight for its downfall, was to protect one's freedom and work for the liberty of family and friends.[6]

Abolitionist advocacy especially targeted white American women. Editors and speechmakers alike thought middle-class women to be particularly susceptible to pleas grounded in slavery's immorality—its corruption of women and scuttling of family ties. These tactics converted many to the antislavery cause. But the movement resonated even more deeply. White women saw their own oppression in the plight of the enslaved. As persons who were legally disabled by laws of marriage, property holding, and inheritance, they saw slavery as analogous to their own condition: Women were, in this view, owned by men, without rights or the capacity to act by way of individual will. They suffered under the slavery of sex. These women joined the abolitionist movement, lecturing, writing, and raising funds. They learned the political sophistication that later fueled calls for women's rights.

Women on the antislavery lecture circuit generated unease, but they also drew large audiences and attention. Sisters Angelina and Sarah Grimké unsettled their fellow Quakers and abolitionist circles when they began to write and then speak out publicly against human bondage. Daughters of a South Carolina planter and slaveholder, the two had fled to New England, where they openly denounced their family's way of life and testified to what they knew about slavery's inhumanity. They did so at great risk. Not only did the sisters sacrifice family ties, they faced ridicule and violence on the antislavery circuit. Notoriously, they spoke openly about politics and cast off the privileges of white Southern womanhood, becoming permanent insiders-outsiders. Still, the sisters converted people who arrived curious about unorthodox women into antislavery supporters passionate about ending human bondage.[7]

Free Black women wrestled with where they fit in the new antislavery politics. Enslaved people's experiences resonated with their own plight: They suffered anti-Black discrimination, and had family and friends who remained in bondage. They clashed with men, Black and white, in their efforts to champion the antislavery cause. They also strained against narrow prescription of their public roles. But their circumstances were distinct. Black women generally did not experience the troubles related to property holding and inheritance that concerned white women of the propertied middle class. And the growing political circles built by white women often did not welcome them. When they organized, Black women increasingly created their own associations, spaces from which they began to tell their own stories of what it meant to call for women's rights.[8]

IT TOOK COURAGE to be an antislavery woman. Some risked their reputations, challenging those who thought the politics of abolitionism was men's business. Others risked the charge of overstepping by fueling the national strife over slavery's future. Those who left the confines of their homes, churches, or women's circles encountered ridicule. Women also faced violence. Their opponents rarely made exceptions for women when they meted out recrimination. Black women abolitionists endured a litany of risks, and racist violence marred their public lives, even as teachers or churchgoing women.

At home in Boston, Susan Paul readied her valise for a trip to Philadelphia and a meeting of the Anti-Slavery Convention of American Women in 1838. Among the things she had to pack was her courage. Paul knew that the days at the convention would spark with urgency, as Black and white women mingled in meeting halls and at podiums. For only the second time, radical women had dared to announce their cause and meet openly in front of a doubtful public. Paul could not wholly foresee the troubles that would threaten this budding sisterhood. In the coming days, they planned to walk the city streets, arm in arm without regard for the color line. Living their principles would demand a price on the rocky terrain of antislavery politics.[9]

Paul came equipped with courage that she inherited from the first generation of Boston's brave Black abolitionists. Her father, the Reverend Thomas Paul, raised his daughter in a Baptist community that included the incendiary antislavery pamphleteer David Walker. Rev. Paul's congregants included Maria Stewart, the writer and speaker whose public career had been cut short when she championed the political ambitions of Black women. Stewart had proposed placing the future of slavery's demise and the future of free Black Americans into women's hands. It was a promise that Susan Paul sought to keep.[10]

Paul entered public life as a teacher at Boston's Primary School Number 6. She followed in the footsteps of her mother, Catherine Waterhouse Paul, also an educator. But Paul did more, and soon transformed her schoolroom into a platform for antislavery work. This began when Paul authored a book that featured the life story of a remarkable student. Her *Memoir of James Jackson* broke new ground, the first Black biography published in United States and the first evangelical children's text about an African American child that was not fiction. Its publication was controversial, and Paul struggled to get the memoir published after being rejected by Baptist Church publishers that were reluctant to be associated with a text themed on slavery and racism.[11]

Not content to stay cloistered in classrooms or at her writing desk, Paul organized her pupils into the Juvenile Choir of Boston and traveled with them on the road throughout New England. On stage, the choir performed a repertoire that condemned slavery and colonization with songs such as "Ye Who Are in Bondage Pine" and "Home, This Is Our Home." It was a test of New England's commitment to racial equality and Paul exposed its fault lines. Though Massachusetts had abolished slavery decades earlier and led the abolitionist movement, racism plagued the work of Paul and her young charges. After a performance in Salem, coach drivers refused to shuttle the choir back to Boston. Paul found the group another way home, remaining steely and resourceful throughout the ordeal. She later remarked: "We were not surprised at our treatment from these persons. This is but a faint picture of that spirit which persecutes us on account of our color—that cruel prejudice which deprives us of every privilege whereby we might elevate ourselves—and then absurdly condemns us because we are not more refined and intelligent."[12]

The urgent efforts of radical antislavery societies drew Paul to politics. She saw Black women playing pathbreaking roles in that movement. The Black women of Salem, Massachusetts, took the trouble to advise William Lloyd Garrison that he had wrongly accused Black Americans of failing to establish antislavery societies. The women published their constitution in *The Liberator*, evidence that the Female Anti-Slavery Society of Salem, led by Black women, had been founded in February 1832. They lit a spark. Paul joined antislavery societies—first the New England Anti-Slavery Society and then its women's auxiliary, the Boston Female Anti-Slavery Society—and was immediately out in front of a movement. It did not take long for her to learn that women could not maintain middle-class comportment at antislavery meetings.

Paul soon witnessed firsthand how opponents did not hesitate to place women in the crosshairs of the contest over slavery during the October 1835 meeting of the Boston Female Anti-Slavery Society. A mob disrupted the proceedings, descending upon the delegates and attempting to capture the women's guest speaker, British abolitionist George Thompson. Eventually, the crowd let the women escape. But they took William Lloyd Garrison into their hands and nearly lynched him on the streets of Boston. Paul weathered the melee and remained steadfast in her antislavery commitments.[13]

WOMEN ANTISLAVERY ORGANIZERS acted upon a new ambition. Though their local meetings remained important, and they still attended men's meetings, in 1837, American women called for their own national convention. It was time, the call explained, for women to lead the movement, much in the way that women antislavery activists in Britain did. Not everyone welcomed the opportunity, and some women stayed home, reluctant to challenge the men who had steered the radical opposition to slavery through its early years. Those who packed their bags and set out for women's gatherings were building something altogether new.

In 1838, Paul joined this new wave. She traveled by coach from Boston, part of a delegation that included two Black members, Paul and Martha Ball. A shared commitment to the cause moved these antislavery women—Black and white—to welcome one another across the color line. They were allies in a women-led foray into national politics, yet the alliance was not easy or untroubled. Antislavery women walked together on Philadelphia's streets, but they did not travel in the same shoes. Racism divided their experiences, casting a shadow over women's conventions, both outside and inside the meeting halls. When the women pledged to meet for politics, in public, together—Black and white—everyone had reason to be uneasy.[14]

Among the women who greeted Susan Paul in Philadelphia was Sarah Mapps Douglass. They knew one another from the antislavery press. Both women had been featured in Garrison's *The Liberator*. But at the convention, they met face-to-face, among the few Black women who made the trip to Philadelphia. Though small in number, this handful quickly assumed leadership, contributing their political acumen. Their presence was also symbolic for the women's antislavery movement. The visibility of women like Paul and Douglass testified to the convention's antiracist ideals. The delegates endorsed Susan Paul as a vice president, Sarah Mapps Douglass as treasurer and business committee member, and Martha Ball as secretary. These Black women then assumed seats within the convention's inner circle, steering toward a political platform and a distinctly women's agenda. It was a promising start. But it also proved to be as close as Black women would ever get to national leadership in the antislavery movement.[15]

The warmth of sisterhood had greeted the visitors to Philadelphia. So too had warning signs. Placards hanging on the city's walls and lampposts encouraged opponents to disrupt the proceedings. The convention's second afternoon ended peaceably, with the women retiring to their rooms and taking meals without trouble. By evening, the mood was changed. Delegates returned to Pennsylvania Hall to join a crowd of three thousand who hoped to hear antislavery lectures from William Lloyd Garrison and Angelina Grimké Weld. A mob outside threatened, and the speakers delivered their remarks against a backdrop of breaking glass and shouting. When the meeting finally broke up around ten that night, the women confronted the truest danger as they stepped out of the relative safety of the hall and onto the streets. They clutched one another, trying to avoid the menacing crowd. Not everyone escaped unassailed, and before it was all over, several African Americans endured assaults and sustained severe injuries.[16]

Threats did not discourage the leaders of the women's convention and they stuck to their meeting plans. Authorities tried to convince them otherwise. The next day, Pennsylvania Hall's managers and city authorities conferred about how to ensure the safety and free speech rights of antislavery speakers. Mayor Jonathan Swift put his finger on the problem: the mob was especially provoked by the presence of Black women. Swift proposed

J. C. Wild, Destruction by Fire of Pennsylvania Hall. On the Night of the 17th May, 1838

a compromise in which the women would continue to meet, but without Black women in attendance. The women's convention refused. They had the backing of Pennsylvania Hall's managers, for whom open rather than segregated accommodations were a principle: "We are accused of allowing our colored fellow-citizens to sit without molestation in the different parts of the Saloon:—in other words, of having no particular place or gallery assigned to colored men and women. We freely admit this; we should have been false to our principles if we had refused to admit men of every sect, rank, and color, on terms of equality, to witness our proceedings."[17]

This failure to reach a compromise proved fatal. The women's daytime meeting went forward, but the mayor canceled the evening's antislavery speeches. Even that was not enough to quell the mob's bloodthirst. After dark, the horde reassembled, larger and even more determined to do damage. Things reached a fever pitch, and then city officials, including fire fighters, stood by as the mob torched Pennsylvania Hall. They lit fire to piles of furniture and then fueled the flames with gas jets torn from the walls and aimed at the open blaze. City officials tacitly condoned this when they did nothing at all. No human life was lost that night, but the point was made. A women's antislavery meeting—one that mixed Black and white activists—should expect to confront terror. Pennsylvania Hall, a brick-and-mortar symbol of women's ambitions, was reduced to little more than rubble and ash.[18]

Commentators offered many explanations for the burning of Pennsylvania Hall, most of which had to do with the economic and political anxieties of white men, some of whom were outsiders who had journeyed to Philadelphia just to harass antislavery proponents. Still, women like Sarah Mapps Douglass and Susan Paul could not avoid another lesson. Just being at women's political gatherings could expose them to violence that no one—neither antislavery activists nor municipal officials—stood ready to prevent. In the days that followed the burning of Pennsylvania Hall, the mob shrank, but it did not wholly end its attacks. African American women remained its special targets. Their bodies were at risk. So too were the institutions they helped to build. The same crowd attacked a structure slated to house a new shelter for "colored orphans." They set upon and damaged Bethel Church, home to Black worshipers, including Jarena Lee. Few women risked more—from their respectability to their very lives—than women like Paul and Douglass.[19]

BLACK WOMEN WANTED to lead antislavery societies, and perhaps they had earned that much. In this, they were not unlike white antislavery women who also aspired to sit on the boards and business committees that defined principles and set strategies for the movement. Experience in the women's conventions of the 1830s suggested that Black and white women might move forward in tandem, parlaying their skills and savvy into seats at the table. They even had allies, men within the American Anti-Slavery Society who acknowledged their capacities and endorsed their quest for power. But when talk of women's rights in the abolitionist movement surfaced, leaders were deeply divided and Black women got the rawest end of the deal

Hester Lane never faced a mob, but she did face opposition from national antislavery leaders. She had been born enslaved in Maryland, the records suggest. Whatever her origins, by the 1820s, Lane was a free woman, settled in New York City, and thriving. Some termed her a whitewasher. She might have preferred calling herself a decorator. In any case, New Yorkers recognized Lane for having devised a novel technique for coloring the walls of homes. As an entrepreneur who operated her own business and owned her own home, Lane stood out in a city in which most Black women labored as domestics and laundresses.[20]

Though she settled in New York, and mixed with civic leaders, visiting notables, and a growing community of Black women activists, Lane never forgot Maryland or the enslaved people she had left behind. By the 1820s, she was earning enough to buy the freedom of others. It was costly, daring work. But Lane had a gift for subterfuge, entering and then exiting the South undetected after bargaining for the purchase of people whose lives demanded a price. She bid at auctions and negotiated with reluctant and greedy slaveholders. One report credited her with freeing eleven people, from Maryland to South Carolina, a story Lane did not deny. She was moved by humanitarianism and secured the freedom of entire families, even when that required more than one foray into slaveholding territory. Still, even in this work, Lane operated as a businessperson. She expected those she liberated to repay the cost of their freedom.[21]

Lane planted deep roots in New York. She was a builder, and her commitment to the antislavery cause led her to organize with other women and support the New York Committee of Vigilance. The committee's principal concern was the safety of Black people living in New York City—those already free and fugitives seeking liberty. Led by Black men—journalists, ministers, and teachers—the committee defended the freedom of Black Americans, which brought on confrontations with kidnappers, slave hunters, and local officials, all of whom aided the interests of slaveholders. In the vigilance committee, women like Lane found a home for their political interests.

Women's vigilance committee work mixed with ideas about their rights. A poem published in the committee's newspaper, *Mirror of Liberty*, provides one glimpse into how those in Lane's circle thought about women. David Ruggles, the committee's head, suggested that "woman's rights" could extend even to enslaved women.[22] Ruggles wrote: "Woman's Rights.... Was woman formed to be a slave—To sink in thralldom to the grave, And freedom never know! Say, must she toil and sweat, and bleed, A pampered lordling's pride to feed, And every joy forego?...But, Tyrant King, avaunt, I pray; Humanity demands thy stay 'Till she address the nation: And plead the cause of woman's right, By urging on in Pharaoh's spite INSTANT EMANCIPATION." Ruggles cast the end of slavery as a fulfillment of the rights of Black women.[23]

Ruggles' endorsement of women's rights may have been limited to his poetry. In the everyday of vigilance committee work, men in the leadership saw women like Lane as helpmeets and rarely put them out front. Still, Lane slowly built a reputation. Heading the aptly named "Effective Committee," for example, she led a "penny program" that financed the work of the always fiscally strapped committee. Lane led the work of the African Dorcas Society, another group that had formed under the watchful eye of men, but which soon operated independent of their gaze. Its purpose was to ensure that children had proper clothing to attend the city's African American–run schools. Women like Lane generally moved in the spaces reserved for them, such as schoolrooms and parlors. But not always. In at least one instance, "men and women" of the vigilance committee came together and opposed the seizure of an alleged fugitive, openly resisting his detention on the city's streets.[24]

Like many women who assumed a public profile, Lane's community tested her and she faced a curious mix of denigration and admiration. It was a difficult line to walk. On one occasion, Lane was caught up in a scandal that arose out of her associations with a former slave, Martha Johnson, whom Lane had aided to come to New York. Sometime later, unnamed others alleged that Lane had threatened Johnson with sale into the slave markets of the South. It was a serious charge that, if proven, would undercut Lane's reputation as an antislavery leader. She might also have been prosecuted under New York law. Lane fired back, denying the accusation and then claiming to have been libeled; her character had been falsely maligned. The men of the vigilance committee convened a tribunal. Johnson appeared and admitted that she and Lane had gotten into a disagreement about overdue rent. Falsely charged, Lane fought and kept her reputation.[25]

Lane's ambition grew, and she aimed to join the highest ranks of the antislavery movement. Her money and fundraising for the American Anti-Slavery Society (AASS) laid a foundation. Sometimes Lane made cash contributions on behalf of "an association of ladies in New York," as was the case in 1835. Other times, Lane made personal contributions, such as in 1836 when the AASS acknowledged her for a donation of thirty dollars. Her earnings enabled Lane to join a small class of Black abolitionist-philanthropists. Money was an avenue to power, and Lane wanted to stand as a peer to the men who underwrote the antislavery movement.[26]

Leadership included steering the movement, especially through moments of conflict. The year 1839 was rife with tension in the American Anti-Slavery Society. Lane arrived at the annual meeting as a delegate for New York City. Trouble immediately surfaced over the future direction of the society, with some members advocating a decidedly political turn toward lobbying and litigation as strategies for change. Others urged the society to stay close to its roots in moral suasion—the changing of hearts and minds through public speaking and the written word. Lane not only occupied a front seat for these debates. She also voted on multiple resolutions, generally siding with the political abolitionists. The meeting minutes recorded "ayes" and "nays," and among them were the voices of Lane and a handful of other women casting their ballots.[27]

The women did not go unnoticed and their presence troubled the 1839 convention. How awkward it must have been for Lane to listen as the secretary included women's names on the delegates' roll only to have a debate erupt. Resolutions flew in an effort to control the woman question: "That the roll of this meeting be made by placing thereon the names of all persons, male and female, who are delegates from any auxiliary society or members of this society" and "That the term 'person' as used in the 4th Article of the Constitution of this society, is to be understood as including men and women and as entitling women to sit, speak, vote, hold office and exercise the same rights of membership as persons of the other sex." The exact nature of the dispute became clear: the delegates agreed that women could represent their local antislavery societies but were at odds over whether women should be elected to leadership roles.[28]

As Lane exited the meeting, she was left alone to think through the awkward note upon which the meeting had concluded. A faction of 123 men, her allies in the political wing of the society, had lodged a formal protest that opposed the intrusion of women's rights into the work of an antislavery society. Women might form "distinct societies of the female sex," but their incorporation into the leadership, it was argued, risked inviting "unnecessary reproach and embarrassment to the cause of the enslaved." It was a shot across the bow at antislavery women, and not one of them signed onto this dissenting report. Lane had risen in the ranks of the society, but there remained an open question about how far she, and women like her, might go.[29]

One year later, Lane was back. The following May, in 1840, she readied herself for the American Anti-Slavery Society's annual meeting. Again, the delegates convened in her hometown, New York City, ensuring that Lane and a large contingent from the Empire State would be present. Things felt uneasy, however. The intervening twelve months had not been a cooling-off period. Instead, delegates arrived prepared to lock horns over women's leadership, and nobody wasted time with niceties. In the meeting's earliest moments, the chair appointed a business committee that included a woman— Abby Kelley, a leader of the Lynn (Massachusetts) Female Anti-Slavery Society. Like Lane, Kelley had risen to leadership through fundraising for the national organization. The vote upon her appointment revealed a deep split among the more than one thousand delegates: 557 for and 451 against. Kelley's opponents—those who rejected women in leadership roles—resigned and then walked out, dividing the organization irreconcilably.[30]

The split, though costly, did open the way for women's leadership in what remained of the AASS. At the same meeting in 1840, women stepped into unprecedented roles as members of the Finance Committee and as delegates to the upcoming World's Anti-Slavery Convention in London. The Executive Committee of nine included three women: Lydia Maria Child, Lucretia Mott, and Maria Chapman. Nearly 120 women delegates from throughout the Northeast and New England joined them. The price had been high; it included the loss of an active faction of men who left to create their own society. But the split exiled fears that powerful women might undermine the work.[31]

Even as many of her old allies had exited, Lane stayed, maintaining her place among the delegates. Her friend Charles Ray, whose wife, Henrietta, had collaborated with Lane in New York's Ladies Literary Society and the African Dorcas Society also remained. Ray knew that Lane aspired to leadership. When time came for delegates to nominate members to the executive board, David Lee Childs nominated Lucretia Mott and his own wife, Lydia Maria. The two, both well-known white activists, won their seats. Ray's nomination of Lane did not fare as well, failing to win the votes that would seat her alongside Mott and Childs. It was an embittering turn of events. In the coming months, society members wrangled over what precisely had happened. Ray strongly intimated that Lane had been rejected because she was African American. Writing in the *Colored American*, he quipped: "The principle [of women's rights] could not carry her color—eh!" Others countered that Ray voluntarily withdrew Lane's nomination under a cloud: she was said to be loyal to the faction that had split from the society. It was even suggested that Lane herself was opposed to women's leadership in the movement, marking her as disqualified. "It is to be supposed that the Society would be guilty of this obvious impropriety of appointing to office a woman who denies her own right of membership?" retorted William Lloyd Garrison in *The Liberator*. The net result was that a total of four white women had been elevated to the society's highest ranks, while the sole Black woman candidate—Hester Lane—was not.[32]

Lane never went on record about what happened at the 1840 meeting, and she quickly disappeared from the antislavery scene. A bit of her did survive, but only as a symbol. Lewis Tappan, who had led the 1840 exodus from the American Anti-Slavery Society, spoke of Lane during the 1843 meeting of his new American and Foreign Anti-Slavery Society. In Tappan's telling, Lane's story was a convenient fable that reduced her to evidence for how former slaves deserved the society's benevolence. He described Lane as "a woman well known to myself and to many of my associates here." He lauded her heroic efforts to rescue those held in bondage, missions she herself financed. Lane, he said, was a woman of exceptional intelligence. But Tappan left out a fateful chapter in Lane's life. He never recounted her time as a philanthropist and aspiring leader within antislavery politics. He erased how she had been caught in the crosshairs of a debate over women's rights, one in which women's equality had lost out to a color line. An antislavery newspaper quietly noted her death in July 1849, when Lane succumbed, along with more than five thousand other New Yorkers, to that summer's epidemic of cholera.[33]

AT THE START of 1848, few Americans anticipated that the year would go down in history as a legendary one for women's rights. Only decades later would activists brand it as the start of a movement for women's suffrage. In that year, small communities of women began organizing around demands for rights. That spring in Philadelphia, for example, African American church-women insisted that they, like men, should have preaching licenses in the AME Church. Later that summer, a small band of white, mostly middle-class women in the Upstate New York village of Seneca Falls produced a manifesto that demanded equality with men. Women's rights saturated the air in 1848, though precisely what liberation looked like depended upon which air one breathed.[34]

In Black churches, the troubles over women's power paralleled those of antislavery societies. Women paid ministers, purchased lots, and erected sanctuaries. They filled pews, managed Sunday schools, attended class meetings, and made the church a regular part of daily life. Occasionally, women stood up to preach the scriptures. Together, these works started a women's movement in the Black church. Debate in white religious circles mirrored that in Black churches, but rarely did the two spheres of Christian politics intersect.[35]

By the 1840s, preaching women no longer toiled as solitary figures as had Jarena Lee. Around Lee grew up a sisterhood that

W. L. *Breton*, Bethel African Methodist Episcopal Church,
Philadelphia, 1829
LIBRARY COMPANY OF PHILADELPHIA

included a broader range of churchwomen, and her concerns
soon became theirs. Members of groups calling themselves the
Daughters of Zion and the Daughters of Conference came to
church politics by more conventional routes, starting out as
helpmeets to men who expected to steer religious life. Their circumstances would not remain conventional, however. Women—
whether fashioned as preachers or helpmeets—challenged the
limits placed upon them in Black Methodist circles. Their work
required organizing, subterfuge, and alliances with men sympathetic to their cause. Black churchwomen knew that when they
invoked rights, above all else they were aiming to break men's
monopoly on the pulpit.[36]

But in the spring of 1844, the Daughters of Zion faced a
problem. They planned to attend that year's AME Church general conference. It was an important occasion held only every
four years, where delegates elected church leaders and voted

on policy. The women knew that church rituals invited them in but also kept them silent. If they wanted to be heard in the proceedings, they needed a strategy. Perhaps they conspired beforehand, or maybe they hatched a plan only after arriving in Pittsburgh for the conference. Banded together, women in the AME Church prepared to fight for the right to have preaching licenses. The only question was how to accomplish that in the face of sixty-eight ministerial delegates who had no intention of listening to them at all.[37]

The challenge demanded ingenuity, and the women devised a scheme that promised to be controversial. They would win their own power through a strategic alliance with men. First, they needed to find a willing accomplice. The Daughters of Conference approached the Reverend Dr. Nathan Ward, a missionary delegate and founding member of the church's Indiana Conference. He heard them out. Ward, the women proposed, would act as their spokesperson, seizing the conference floor and putting forth an amendment to church law that would guarantee licenses to female preachers. They handed him ammunition: a petition.[38]

At the conference, Ward did as he promised. He rose before the dozens of men delegates and explained that on behalf of the forty church members who had signed the petition, he demanded preaching rights for churchwomen. Looking on was itinerant preacher Julia Foote, who later described the mayhem that erupted: "This caused quite a sensation, bringing many members to their feet at once. They all talked and screamed to the bishop, who could scarcely keep order. The Conference was so incensed at the brother who offered the petition that they threatened to take action against him." The women's demands were explosive and the resolution failed. Still, the churchwomen put the leadership on notice that they had organized as a sisterhood that included laywomen helpmeets and controversial preaching women. They expected to shape church politics by way of a new collective point of view that linked the struggles of extraordinary women, like Jarena Lee and Julia Foote, to the aspirations of all churchwomen.[39]

If the results of the 1844 meeting discouraged them, the Daughters of Conference gave no sign of it. Over the next four years, they prepared to continue the battle. By 1848, the general conference scene had grown only more intimidating. Women gathered in the hallways and on the periphery of the conference chamber. There, they observed men—the leadership—of a burgeoning denomination that came from fourteen states: 175 officials and 375 lay leaders. The formal agenda was ambitious, including electing a second bishop, structuring the church missionary society, establishing a book depository, planning for commons schools, and enacting sanctions for divorce and remarriage.[40]

To get on the agenda, the Daughters again needed an ally. Perhaps it was Eliza Ann Bias who suggested that her husband, J. J. Gould Bias, could be trusted to speak for the women. He had a track record of supporting women's leadership. Bias did the women's bidding, putting their resolution on the conference floor. The deliberations that followed have not survived. But the record does show that the Daughters scored a victory: the leadership agreed to their demand for women's preaching licenses. Going forward, women like Jarena Lee would not need to broker special deals before commanding the pulpit.[41]

There had been opposition, it seems, and a rebuttal later surfaced, making clear that the war over churchwomen's power wasn't over. Daniel Payne, a brilliant and ambitious Baltimore-based minister, protested the women's victory. He began with the proposition that women's roles should conform to the ideals of respectability and domesticity. The licensing of women preachers was, he warned, "calculated to break up the sacred relations which women bear to their husbands and children," leading to the "utter neglect of their household duties and obligations." Payne played upon concerns about how slavery already threatened the sanctity of African American family life. Just as the consumption of alcohol led men to neglect their families, Payne urged, women might also abandon their home duties if they bore the responsibilities of a licensed preacher. Payne exploited real tensions in the lives of preaching women, who did feel a pull between religious responsibilities and domestic obligations. Payne made a record of his objections. But in 1848, churchwomen's rights moved forward.[42]

Only a few months after AME Church women scored a victory for their rights, women in Seneca Falls, New York, also set forth a demand for churchwomen's rights. The Declaration of Sentiments, a document drafted during the July 1848 convention, criticized thinking that deprived women of preaching licenses: "He allows her in Church, as well as State, but in a subordinate position, claiming Apostolic authority for her exclusion from the ministry, and, with some exceptions, from any public participation in the affairs of the Church." The meeting's final resolutions included a demand that spoke to the right to preach from the pulpit: "*Resolved,* . . . it is pre-eminently his duty to encourage her to speak and teach, as she has an opportunity, in all religious assemblies."[43]

Black women did not attend the Seneca Falls convention. They were not barred or excluded. Still, only white women took part in the proceedings. On those meeting days in July, the Black women of Seneca Falls were elsewhere. Even those who were members of the meeting place, the Wesleyan Methodist Church, did not attend. Certainly, Sarah James knew that women planned to gather in her village to discuss their rights. Her home on State Street sat just two blocks from the Wesleyan Methodist Church. The notice appeared in the Seneca Falls *Courier* and in Douglass's *North Star*. A stream of delegates passing along the streets of her village would have been hard for James to miss. James ran an activist household. Her husband, barber Thomas James, participated in antislavery and Free Soil Party politics. Sarah herself did not work outside the home, or at least she did not report doing so two years later when the census taker visited. Perhaps she spent her days in July caring for her daughter Martha and attending to household duties.

Samantha Wright's husband, Joshua, also served on the board of the Wesleyan Methodist Church. Their home stood on Troy Street, three short blocks from the women's convention. Still, Wright did not join the proceedings. The same was true for the many other Black women in Seneca Falls. Julia Ann Dillsworth, like Sarah James, was likely at her home on Walnut Street, overseeing the day-to-day demands of her small family and the boarders whose rent supplemented her family income. Harder to place on those summer days are women like Nabby Anderson. More than seventy years old, Anderson perhaps was too frail or infirm to attend a political gathering. Louise Hill was Anderson's peer, an elderly woman who lived in a white household headed by Elias Wayman. She may have been obligated to work that day, despite her advanced age.[44]

Abby Gomor should have been there. Perhaps she was hard pressed to join a midweek meeting of women. She labored in a farming household headed by Richard Gay that was situated toward the outskirts of town on Cayuga Road. Gomor was not, however, a stranger to the women who drafted the Declaration of Sentiments. She was a member of Seneca Falls' Trinity Episcopal Church, where she worshipped with Elizabeth Cady Stanton, one of the meeting's organizers. The two knew one another, and Stanton later told one version of Gomor's story in the *History of Woman Suffrage*, though it was more like myth. Stanton wrote about Gomor as an object of pity, a Black woman who, as a property holder and taxpayer, should have been entitled to her vote in New York. But her sex, Stanton decried, kept Gomor from the polls. Stanton never explained why, then, Gomor did not join her and other women of Seneca Falls women's convention to demand that right.[45]

FOR BLACK WOMEN, the "cause of the slave, as well as of women" were two parts of a whole. On the floor of colored conventions in 1848, this proposition unsettled the deliberations. The conventions began with Black activists organizing against colonization, but the agenda quickly expanded to include a sweeping range of issues. Foremost was slavery, and convention delegates—who included former slaves—banded together to secure the freedom of their brothers and sisters in bondage. Delegates also took up civil rights, believing that their status as free people would be compromised as long as slavery persisted. They also put questions about freedom on the table: What social, political, and economic rights should former slaves have in a world that doubted they were citizens at all? In 1848, the issue of women's rights was added to convention agendas, though it was not an easy fit.[46]

Even when unbidden, women made their way to the conventions. In early September when the weather was mild, Sydna Francis and her husband, Abner, boarded a steamboat in western New York destined for the 1848 National Convention of Colored Citizens in Cleveland, Ohio. He was a delegate, elected to represent Black Buffalo, and his words were recorded in the minutes published later that year. Sydna carried her own credentials as head of Buffalo's Female Dorcas Society, where she advocated for women's education. She was among the women that supported the newspapers and conventions headed by men; she raised the money and paid the bills. This was not enough, however, to give her a voice at the convention. Still, Francis's presence could generate a debate.[47]

Francis listened in as Frederick Douglass used his authority as president to introduce women's rights onto the convention agenda. It is likely her ears perked up. Those who knew Douglass were not surprised. He was known as a woman's rights man. The previous year, 1847, Douglass had begun publishing his new weekly, the *North Star*, by proclaiming: "Right Is of No Sex, Truth Is of No Color." He had been present at the Seneca Falls women's convention and had acted as an ally to a white delegate, Elizabeth Cady Stanton, when she proposed to include women's vote among that meeting's demands.

Francis quickly learned that inserting women's rights on the agenda of an African American convention invited controversy. It became clear that she and the other women present at the national convention were causing trouble when the words of

Resolution 33 rang through the convention hall: "Whereas, we fully believe in the equality of the sexes, therefore, Resolved, That we hereby invite females hereafter to take part in our deliberations." It was a modest proposal, one that declared women equal but extended to them no power. Instead, men would usher in women and, although they might "take part" in "deliberations," it was unclear whether they could vote. In short order, the matter was squelched when the proposition was "indefinitely postponed." The affirmation of women's authority had not been defeated, at least not yet. But it was surely not a victory. Resolutions indefinitely postponed often remained in limbo, put off and never voted upon.[48]

Douglass was not done and he enlisted the aid of a woman. Her name was Rebecca Sanford. Perhaps Francis noticed Sanford as she entered the meeting hall, the only white woman recorded as taking part in the convention—indeed, as the only woman mentioned by name. Sanford stood out. Her words might be important. But even before she spoke, Sanford's presence was symbolic of what Douglass hoped to incorporate into the convention. Sanford was passing through the city on her way farther west, after having taken part in the August women's rights meeting in Rochester, New York. For Douglass, Sanford embodied women's rights.[49]

Sanford did indeed speak, but not for all women. It was late in the day, early evening, in fact, when Douglass suspended the regular deliberations to introduce "a lady who wished to say something on the subject of the Rights of Woman." He turned the podium over to Sanford. She explained the issues that had concerned the white women who had convened at Seneca Falls and Rochester that summer: the right to vote, rights to marital property, and a role in "making the laws." If Sanford knew that just hours earlier the convention had tabled a debate over the rights of Black women, she did not let on. She never acknowledged Francis or women like her, never suggested how her interests fit with those of Black women. Sisterhood never surfaced in Cleveland. A white woman—a guest permitted to speak from the podium—appeared unaware of what freedom meant for the Black women who sat before her.[50]

Douglass's concern was not Francis. Instead, he was interested in a principle, and he used Sanford's remarks to revive his resolution. After speaking in clumsy terms about the interests of women, Sanford stepped down, and things got even more complicated. Delegates traded resolutions that parsed words rather than the rights of women. Some argued that when the convention had deemed "all colored persons present, delegates to this Convention," women had been made delegates because they "considered women persons." Others sought to clarify: "The word persons used in the resolution designating delegates [should] be understood to include woman." A resolution finally carried and a shout went up: "Three cheers for woman's rights." And still, not one Black woman had spoken.[51]

Francis had just witnessed the convention arrive at a resolution that endorsed her right to serve as a delegate and take part in convention proceedings. But it was an awkward series of events that got her there. Men claimed to be allies with Black women. Sanford ignored Black women altogether. If anyone conferred with Francis, there is no evidence of it. And this is how the meeting concluded. Francis and her husband shared the steamship ride across Lake Erie, back to Buffalo, with Douglass himself. Likely each of them had a distinct view of what it meant for women to win "three cheers."[52]

Francis left Cleveland shrouded in questions. Unclear was whether she could claim allies in white women or in Black men. But she knew, at least, that Black women could be counted upon to band together, that they might collectively make a case for their rights in political culture. These earliest efforts may have been awkward, but these years were the start of a new, persistent questioning about the degree to which African American political leaders would incorporate women and their rights into their platforms. Others, it seemed, still spoke for them. But Black women could also speak for themselves—taking the opportunity that their fundraising provided to insert themselves and their interests onto the agenda. They were satisfied, it appeared, to do this work from the inside and to combine their challenges to the inequality of sexism with a defiance of racism.

BLACK WOMEN LAID the groundwork for their movement in the rocky soil of women's antislavery conventions, Black Methodist conferences, and the heart of Black politics: the colored convention movement. Their counterparts among white middle-class women were at the start of their own movement, one that insisted upon building power within discrete women's spaces. These differences, though not stark or all-defining, suggest how American women charted divergent routes to power and political rights going forward. These differences were not only structural or strategic. And they cannot be reduced to the effects of racism. Black women would never sever their political power from the movements and organizations that sat at the heart of their communities. At times, their drive to power led them to convene as women. But all roads brought them back to the needs of the African American public culture in which they had been formed.

Chapter 3

TO BE BLACK AND FEMALE

By the 1850s, when they stepped out into public Black women were accustomed to being read. Observers—finding them at the market or in a carriage, tending a garden or soothing a child, traversing a park or entering church on Sunday—sized up women. Edmund Burke, whose words Frederick Douglass reprinted in his newspaper, expressed a gentler version of such encounters: "To describe her body describes her mind; one is the transcript of the other." Burke found in his ideal woman (likely his Irish Catholic wife) a harmony that Black women, too, aimed to embody. Too often, they were taken for one quality or another, as a woman or as an African American. Their task was to develop self-awareness and then put to words what it meant to live at an incongruous crossroads. In solving this puzzle, Black women established a distinct and enduring touchstone for how their vision of rights might begin.

IN 1850, BLACK Americans looked out across the nation's political landscape and saw that it had taken a troubled turn. Fissures opened everywhere, dividing the old movements and giving birth to the new. The geography of Black life expanded, with important settlements taking hold as far west as San Francisco and Sacramento in California. Black communities strained under the labor strife that arose in the many cities that welcomed immigrants from places like Ireland and Germany. Whiteness as a political identity had calcified, reinforcing how racism organized politics, the economy, and the social world.[1]

The abolitionist movement persisted, but only as an array of awkward allies. Those who worked by moral suasion persevered, but activists who viewed political advocacy as the most effective way forward operated in a rival antislavery society. Some abolitionists, particularly African Americans, embraced violence: direct and admittedly illegal resistance to slavery employed especially in the rescue of fugitives. William Lloyd Garrison and Frederick Douglass ended their long alliance, thus severing one of the movement's most powerful partnerships. Their differences were, in part, ideological—with Garrison still committed to moral suasion and Douglass drawn to politics. When Douglass began publishing his own newspaper, the *North Star*, one that competed with Garrison's *Liberator*, it signaled that Black abolitionists would be demanding increased control in a movement that spoke for their interests.[2]

By the early 1850s, the Black-led colored conventions had hit their stride. Black leaders regularly met in their home states and in national gatherings that provided an independent political platform for men excluded from state legislatures and national political parties. The delegates came out of local, grassroots organizations that conventions knit together. Print culture served as a powerful instrument for organizing. Those who missed meetings read newsweeklies like *Frederick Douglass's Paper* (formerly known as the *North Star*) along with pamphlets that recorded proceedings and broadcast them to remote locales. Increasingly, the perspectives of enslaved people influenced Black politics. Fugitive slave narratives put firsthand testimony at the center of political deliberations. The genre reached its high point with the 1855 publication of Frederick Douglass's second narrative and the stories of William Wells Brown, Solomon Northup, and Jermain Loguen. Sojourner Truth released her narrative in 1850, adding a distinct woman's perspective to these tales about the journey from slavery to freedom.[3]

Activists recommitted to Black politics in response to the Compromise of 1850. Congress had passed a series of bills by which it hoped to settle tensions generated by slavery's expansion west into new lands seized at the end of the Mexican-American War. The act permitted newly added territories to decide whether they would permit slavery. California was admitted as a Free State, and the domestic slave trade was banned in the District of Columbia. But it remained to be seen whether this—or, indeed, the Compromise itself—would calm the tension between pro- and antislavery factions. A final provision of the Compromise, a new and onerous Fugitive Slave Act, especially troubled Black Americans. It promised that slaveholders could demand the help of federal and state officials in capturing fugitive slaves. Those fleeing bondage were no longer entitled to due process protections, such as a jury trial or the right to testify, even if state law said otherwise. In the face of this national edict, thousands of Black Northerners fled farther north to Canada, seeking refuge on free soil. Those left behind exercised new vigilance and radicalism as they defended themselves and their communities.[4]

Those who left the United States after 1850 did not act merely on impulse. A new movement was gaining momentum, an unprecedented Black-led emigration movement. Its leaders encouraged African Americans to reconsider their place in the world. Perhaps they could make a better home in West Africa, Canada, or the Caribbean. It was time, emigrationists urged, to go after a chance for full citizenship in their own lifetimes. Opponents of emigration bitterly denounced such schemes and reiterated the fact that Black Americans had paid many times over for citizenship's full privileges in the United States. Emigration opened yet another fissure within Black politics, one in which old allies faced off across a divide that went to the core of their political identities.[5]

Women also aimed to remake the decade's politics. Beginning in 1850, they convened the first national women's conventions and made plain that a new movement, a *women's* movement, was part of the political landscape. It had originated in the antislavery meetings of the 1830s, and local gatherings such as those in Seneca Falls and Rochester, New York, in 1848. But the meetings of the 1850s were neither incidental to another cause, nor were they local or impromptu. Organizers intended to build and sustain the women's conventions over many years. They wanted to attract broad attention. They wanted political rights. And they brought a broad array of concerns to the floor. The first meeting in 1850, at Worcester, Massachusetts, included demands for property rights, access to education and employment opportunities, and a general insistence upon women's "political, legal, and social equality with man." The convention even acknowledged enslaved women, whom the delegates deemed worthy of "natural and civil rights."[6]

Everywhere across this fractured political landscape, Black women took advantage of the cracks. They were newly strategic and took every chance to make inroads. Rarely did African American conventions recognize their claims on politics—many still insisted that race and gender were separate concerns to be addressed by separate movements. But, in spite of the opposition, Black women found their voices standing at the podium or with pen in hand. They spoke with the same courage that had emboldened Maria Stewart two decades before. They surrounded themselves with like-minded women just as Jarena Lee found support in the Daughters of Conference. Stepping into the political spotlight, Black women preached, taught, and demanded to be heard on their own terms.

FOUNDING A NEWSPAPER might sound like little more than a gentle knock on the doors of power. Since the 1820s, Black editors, wielding bold pens, had exercised outsized influence on public opinion. Nineteenth-century journalism rested to an important degree upon the borrowing between papers, which emphasized an editor's ability to curate his pages. Rather than producing a mash-up of thought, editors assembled a distinct point of view using their own writing, that of regular correspondents, and pieces borrowed from far-flung news outlets. This exhibited power of the first order. Black women aimed to seize it.

Mary Ann Shadd's career as a journalist is a testament to her sense of herself as a person with rights. Born free, to parents Abraham and Harriet Shadd, she started out life in the slave-holding state of Delaware but was educated in Pennsylvania, where her family moved to avoid the Southern bans against educating children of color. She worked as a teacher and then, in 1853, migrated to the city of Windsor in Canada West, today's Ontario. There, Shadd joined a growing community of Black Americans who had fled—or, in the language of the day, emigrated from—the United States in search of free soil. A deep despair underlay the decision to relocate; many migrants doubted that the United States would ever abolish slavery and then acknowledge them as full citizens. Shadd settled down in a new country and, with a little bit more freedom, soon emerged as one of the era's most insightful commentators. She lived in exile, but Shadd's heart and mind remained fixed on the past, present, and future of America's former slaves, especially women.[7]

She had, from the beginning, been an upstart. In 1849, at twenty-six, Shadd wrote a long letter to Frederick Douglass, responding to his request for suggestions on how to improve the "wretched conditions" of free Black Americans in the North. Shadd did not couch her comments in a timid or deferential tone and, instead, she claimed authority based in her "ten years of teaching Black children in all Black schools." But she was unwilling to let an editor impose his whims and put out her own twelve-page pamphlet, *Hints to the Colored People of the North*. It was an openly political tract published to "arouse her readers with a direct analysis of the condition of northern Blacks, regardless of whether it might offend." Some men were admittedly uncomfortable. A supporter chided: "What think you of the language of this young sister...does she tell the truth or not! As one man I am sorry that I have to answer in the affirmative." Perhaps her words contained "too much truth!" another observed. Martin Delany, a former slave, journalist, abolitionist, and emigration proponent, mixed praise for Shadd's pamphlet with doubt about her character, branding her "a very intelligent young lady, and peculiarly eccentric."[8]

Settling in Canada West meant starting over just beyond the shadows cast by eminent men like Douglass and Delany. How Shadd decided to publish a newspaper, it is difficult to say with certainty, but the idea must have been brewing for some time. Canada provided her just enough of an opening to realize her dream. Shadd built a team, one that included her future husband, barber Thomas Cary. Some men helped with the writing and editing, while others set type, rolled ink, and operated the printing press. She was a new publisher who, while the pages dried, traveled to promote the paper to subscribers across Canada and the United States. She was soon at the helm of a brand-new weekly, the *Provincial Freeman*. By publishing her own paper, Shadd joined the ranks of "first" women on the day the inaugural issue left the office. With the next issue due in just seven days, she did not have much time to boast.[9]

Instead, Shadd worried. The *Provincial Freeman* needed committed subscribers to stay afloat. She hoped to win readers with relevance, timeliness, and a voice that guided the lives and the political culture of Black people. This required, Shadd concluded, that she conceal the extent of her role at the *Provincial Freeman*—readers would be uncomfortable getting their news from a woman, she judged. She named two men, Samuel Ringgold Ward and Alexander McArthur, as editors and, masking her sex, instructed that letters to the paper be addressed to "M. A. Cary." Later that first year, Shadd was "promoted" to the role of publishing agent, which acknowledged that she traveled the United States and Canada to win subscribers. Of course, it was Shadd who had promoted herself. Not until May 1856, two-plus years later, did she list herself as an editor and by her full name, along with coeditors Henry Ford Douglass and her brother Isaac Shadd. By November that year, she had married, and the *Provincial Freeman*'s masthead reflected the name change: Mary A. S. Cary was now listed as among the paper's editors.[10]

Cary never spoke openly about the dilemmas she faced as an editor who was also a woman. Instead, she used her editor's prerogative to tell readers about the difficulties that women like her confronted. The paper chronicled the history and labors of women's rights leaders and explored married women's legal rights, the content of women's education, and avenues for women's work. She celebrated women's accomplishments, especially their firsts, and featured noted thinkers, such as Jane Swisshelm, who held forth on issues ranging from women's mission to men's sphere.[11]

Cary's *Provincial Freeman* read like an open forum, but as editor, she always determined which opinions made it into print. The paper advocated that women had the right to speak and write in public, control property, hold elective office, obtain an education, and enter the professions. In contrast, other columns reminded women about the demands of respectability and domesticity, criticized women who refused chivalrous gestures, encouraged refined manners, and warned against petty jealousies. It was a primer on the uneven terrain that women like Cary navigated. The *Freeman* shined a special light on African American women's achievements, from Cary's own grueling lecture schedule to the orations of the "eloquent and talented" poet Frances Ellen Watkins and "the fine literary and artistic attainments" of educator and emigration activist Amelia Freeman.[12]

Women came forward and used the paper to explain their own journeys through racism and sexism. "Henrietta W." responded to an article on education. Her letter begins with a cautious and apologetic tone: "I hope you will pardon the seeming boldness....I have ventured to address you, with the view of ascertaining whether you will receive communications coming from one of my sex....I have taken up my pen with a trembling hand and a fearful heart." Henrietta confessed that she did not possess even a "common school education," yet she offered her perspective, asserting that "the class of teachers under whom it has been our misfortune to be placed have been just a little better than none at all."[13]

In return, Henrietta received a lesson or two. In her reply to Henrietta, Dolly Bangs first admitted her own fears: "I belong to 'that class styled the weaker sex' and...I can sympathize with her in her state of anxiety." Bangs also offered reassurance: "A writer need never fear of bringing down anything like ridicule upon herself...the only danger would be in her extreme modesty." A woman need not hesitate to join the debate on education, or any other issue, for such a move was "hers by right." Bangs claimed for women rights equal to those of men: "Would it not be preposterous to ask of man that which he has not the power to give?—he like woman, is but a creature dependent upon his Creator for his own rights." She argued that to discourage women from asserting public leadership "now, in the afternoon of the nineteenth century...seems ridiculous." All her readers, she maintained, had an interest in encouraging women's public endeavors. To do otherwise was to squander the "vast amount of latent talent which might be used." Yet women themselves must be the guardians of their own fate: "It is her right, as her duty, to press boldly forward to her appointed task, otherwise who is guilty of burying her talent?"[14]

CARY SAW A bit of herself in Frances Ellen Watkins Harper, the poet and antislavery lecturer. Harper also had been born free in a slaveholding state, Maryland, and worked as a teacher before she entered politics. Both women had become teachers after receiving some of the best education that a young Black woman might expect. The two wrote poetry and prose, and shared interests: temperance and antislavery, though they differed on emigration. Cary published Harper's early work in the *Provincial*

Freeman: an essay titled "Christianity" and a poem, "Died of Starvation." By 1856, while Harper was lecturing on the anti-slavery circuit, Cary published a lengthy missive out of Bath, Maine, that praised her in broad terms. Cary, the editor, drew upon the words of a correspondent, "Humanitarian," who described Harper's speeches as "fervent," "eloquent," and "with almost superhuman force and power over the spell bound audience."[15]

By the winter of 1856, Cary was out to promote the work and the career of Harper. A reprint from the *Anti-Slavery Standard* noted the "talented young lady" had undertaken an ambitious schedule of lectures across Pennsylvania. It ended with an advertisement that encouraged those "desirous to have the services of Miss Watkins" to write to the abolitionist James Miller McKim in Philadelphia. It was part of Cary's effort to promote Black women. Watkins was an instrument in her overall effort to crush racism. She frankly compared white women such as "Miss E. T. Greenfield [and] Mrs. Webb" to "Miss F. Watkins." Watkins, "by competing successfully with the most celebrated white females, in their several professions, notwithstanding the superior advantage of white women, can be safely said to have removed from their class and sex the stigma of *natural* inferiority." Cary signed the note with her initials, "M.A.S.C.," claiming such thoughts as admittedly her own.[16]

AMONG THE WOMEN that Cary featured in the *Provincial Freeman* was Sojourner Truth. Cary reprinted a piece that quoted Truth as having gently mocked white Americans who mixed abolitionism with racism. Cary used Truth's words to level a critique that was at the root of Black women's political thought: in American politics, they set the bar high, such that commitment to a good cause did not excuse complicity with evil. The newspaper was likely the only place that Cary and Truth—two towering intellectuals and activists—ever met. And still, for Cary, the encounter was unforgettable.[17]

I Sell the Shadow to Support the Substance.
SOJOURNER TRUTH.

Sojourner Truth, "I Sell the Shadow to Support the Substance," 1864
LIBRARY COMPANY OF PHILADELPHIA

Few who met Sojourner Truth forgot the experience. She was an imposing presence, standing six feet tall and speaking with a Dutch accent she had acquired during her early life in Upstate New York. Truth attracted audiences as a former slave and advocate for abolition and women's equality, and she eventually commanded the podium with unrivaled frankness, humor, and personal testimony. She once told a story, for example, that included a struggle between her desire for freedom and the need to care for her children. She adorned herself in bonnets, shawls, and, later in life, dresses crafted from fine fabrics. Truth knew that audiences had questions about what kind of woman she was, and she became as deliberate as any woman of the 1850s about crafting her own image. Wasn't she a woman?[18]

Truth's early life had been unorthodox. Born enslaved, Truth had claimed her own freedom, endured separation from her children, spent years living in a utopian, free love community, and by the 1840s had finally settled in Northampton, Massachusetts, where she embraced antislavery activism. As she embarked on a political career, Truth hoped audiences would understand her point of view—and so she sat for a series of interviews with a white abolitionist, Olive Gilbert, to whom Truth dictated key episodes of her life story. The resulting *Narrative of Sojourner Truth*, published in 1850, became a peer to the era's best-known slave narrative, *Narrative of the Life of Frederick Douglass, a Slave*. It also became Truth's calling card, and she sold the pamphlet on the lecture circuit. But self-definition for a woman unable to read and write was not a straightforward task. Gilbert's desire to show white Americans the wrongs of slavery did not mesh with Truth's story about a Black woman's hardships, losses, and the irreconcilable choices she faced when enslaved. The problem of being spoken for and about by others would haunt Truth's entire public life.[19]

There was no precedent for the moments when Truth stepped to the podium at the women's conventions of the 1850s. On the antislavery circuit, Truth had kept the hospitable company of white Americans who evidenced little prejudice. She counted among her friends British antislavery lecturer George Thompson and radical Quakers Isaac and Amy Post of Rochester, New York. Though she never held office, Truth appears to have avoided the ambivalences that had troubled Hester Lane in the American Anti-Slavery Society a decade earlier. These associations, along with her ties to figures like Frederick Douglass and William Lloyd Garrison, buttressed Truth as she became the first Black woman to join the new national women's movement.[20]

Truth was indeed a first when she arrived in Worcester, Massachusetts, in October 1850—Black women had not attended the women's meetings of 1848 in Seneca Falls and Rochester, New York. She arrived, the sole delegate representing Northampton, Massachusetts, to face as large an audience as she had ever encountered. Over one thousand people filled Brinkley Hall to capacity, with others milling about outside after being turned away. In Worcester, women presided but shared leadership with men. And they dominated the podium. Others spoke about Truth long before it was her turn. Speakers expressed sympathy for the enslaved. They affirmed their commitments to the antislavery cause. One resolution strongly alluded to the distinct plight of enslaved women as targets of sexual assault: "The claim for woman of all her natural and civil rights, bids us remember the million and a half of slave women at the South, the most grossly wronged and foully outraged of all women." In Worcester, Truth alone embodied that memory. She finally took her turn and delivered a speech full of biblical allegory that lightly touched upon women's political rights.[21]

Ill-fitting for Truth was how speakers juxtaposed the condition of "women" against that of "the slave." President Paulina Davis drew a parallel between "Woman" and "the contented slave" as two figures who had not yet claimed their rights. Abby Price lamented how, in "many countries," women "were reduced to the condition of a slave" and decried how "the very being of a woman, like that of a slave, is absorbed in her master!" Price especially implored men: "Will you…dim the crown of [your sisters' and wives'] womanhood, and make them slaves?" Elizabeth Cady Stanton did not attend the Worcester meeting, but her letter to the convention echoed the sentiments of Davis and Price, warning men "so long as your women are mere slaves, you may throw your colleges to the wind." These deliberations left Truth alone to carve out her own space, as a woman who began life enslaved but who was now free, who stood alongside women in the North rather than enduring as a captive in the South. Truth was not a metaphor. She was alive, with presence, voice, and her own views about women's equality.[22]

In the following year, as plans for a next women's convention came together, organizers wondered whether including women like Truth posed a problem; Truth and others had introduced the issue of racism into meetings called to combat sexism.

Pittsburgh-based journalist Jane Swisshelm objected to how, during the 1850 meeting, delegates had introduced "the color question," what she deemed a sidebar and a distraction. "The convention was not called to discuss the rights of color; and we think it was altogether irrelevant and unwise to introduce the question." To succeed, women should not take on the "additional weight" of problems that concerned Black men. And Swisshelm doubted that Black women would expect to make gains through a women's movement: "As for colored women, all the interest they have in this reform is as women. All it can do for them is raise them to the level of men of their own class."[23]

Swisshelm published her thoughts in her newspaper, the *Saturday Visiter*. But if Truth had gotten wind of the suggestion that she might undercut the women's meeting, she did not take it to heart. In May 1851, she made her way to the Ohio Women's Rights Convention in Akron and took a seat among the scores of delegates. As she listened to the proceedings, once again Truth heard speakers compare the slave to the woman, much like she had in Worcester. This time, however, Truth responded. Her words were nearly lost for all time—the members of the Publishing Committee left Truth's words on an editing room floor when they published sixty pages of official proceedings.

But in the audience at Akron, journalists Marius and Emily Robinson made certain Truth's speech survived. The two were long-time antislavery activists, teachers of African American children, lecturers on the antislavery circuit, and, by spring 1851, editor and publishing agent of the Salem, Ohio, *Antislavery Bugle*. Witnesses to the entirety of the women's proceedings, the Robinsons published their own version of the deliberations, beginning with the keynote address delivered by Frances Dana Gage. When it came to Truth, the Robinsons aimed to do their best to convey her words and their force. They deemed her remarks "most unique and interesting" and admitted that it was difficult to capture the effect that Truth had had on the audience as a speaker who was Black, a woman, a former slave, and an exceptionally talented orator who mixed humor, colloquialism, and her own life experience to great effect.[24]

Truth had waited her turn in Akron, following women whose remarks showcased their high levels of education, status, and experience. She could not match such credentials. Still, during her years on the lecture circuit she had learned to riff off the remarks that preceded her own, and it paid off. Truth reframed the convention, resetting its goals as defined from the perspective of a Black woman. She began, "I want to say a few words about this matter. I am a woman's rights." There, as she was, unlettered and unrefined, Truth made the case that she was the truest embodiment of women's rights. Slavery was no mere metaphor and the labor it demanded had made Truth the equal of any man: "I have as much muscle as any man, and can do as much work as any man." This experience was also the philosophical foundation for a women's movement. She urged: "I have heard much about the sexes being equal; I can carry as much as any man, and can eat as much too, if I can get it." Truth then spoke to the men in the room, turning to the Bible, the book that blamed women for humankind's earthly woes, for a perspective on justice: "I have heard the Bible and have learned that Eve caused man to sin. Well if woman upset the world, do give her a chance to set it right side up again."[25]

Truth never spoke the words most often attributed to her Akron speech—"Ain't I a woman?" That refrain was later put in print by Frances Dana Gage, who in 1863 used it to tell a sensationalized story about Truth that she hoped would rival another told by Harriet Beecher Stowe, "The Libyan Sibyl," published that same year. When she took the podium, Truth risked having her words misrepresented and mythologized. Unable to read, she did not write out her speeches nor could she correct the transcriptions produced by others. Still, she spoke plenty, always emphasizing that she was neither a symbol nor just like white women. In 1858, she bared her breasts before an Indiana audience, driving home the fact that she was capable of nursing children—her own and those of white women—the surest test of a woman. When Black women like Truth spoke of rights, they mixed their ideas with challenges to slavery and to racism. Truth told her own stories, ones that suggested that a women's movement might take another direction, one that championed the broad interests of all humanity.[26]

IN THE 1850S, a new generation of women entered public culture, young women who had been raised in the bosom of women's activism in antislavery societies, churches, and beyond. Sometimes the torch was passed from mother to daughter, but young women also found models in women preachers, lecturers, and writers. The first generation linked arms with the next to build a momentum that carried Black women forward. In the rough-and-tumble politics of the colored conventions movement, Black women provoked frank debates as they aimed to take seats alongside men. They met opponents who wanted to push them back into narrow roles and demanded women sacrifice their rights as women—the price of being made agents of antiracism. It was a bind.

The colored conventions exploded during the 1850s, and women seized upon the opportunity. As meetings sprung up locally, statewide, and nationally, women staked their claim. If they had once stood on the sidelines, now Black women arrived expecting to take part as delegates and members of the voting body. The door opened just wide enough for some to slip in during the 1855 National Convention of Colored Men. When it came time to call the roll, two women from Philadelphia took their seats as delegates. Then, Massachusetts abolitionist Charles Remond, whose own sister, Sarah, was a well-known abolitionist lecturer, proposed that Mary Ann Shadd Cary be admitted as a "corresponding member" of the convention, a member on paper rather than in person, who would represent those exiled in Canada. A full-blown debate ensued, with men speaking for and against Cary's admission. The final vote of 38 to 23 went in Cary's favor, but also admitted the matter was not

settled. Cary showed no gratitude and instead criticized the convention, writing in the *Provincial Freeman* that it "was quite a
disorderly body, and broke up without doing a great deal." Her
tone suggests one reason why her nomination may have been
controversial.[27]

Barbara Ann Steward was nineteen years old when she headed
to the 1855 Convention of the Colored People of the State of
New York, but she did not get there all on her own. Even at that
tender age, Steward had big ambitions and expected to be seated
as a delegate. Her confidence grew out of her upbringing as the
daughter of entrepreneur and antislavery activist Austin Steward. She was no stranger to the collision of issues and concerns
that confronted African American leaders. She also benefited
from the influence of spiritual mothers, including activist Mary
Jeffrey who helped open the door to Black politics for Steward.
Through Jeffrey's example, Steward saw up close how a woman
claimed her place in Black politics. Both battled for their chance
to vote and hold office.[28]

In the 1840s, Mary Jeffrey was a young mother in the upstate
town of Seneca, New York, who spent most of her days home
with her son and husband, both named Jason. The elder Jason
Jeffrey worked as a porter and later as a waiter. His political career preceded hers. In 1843, he attended the National Colored
Convention in Buffalo, New York, and by winter of 1848, he
was a member of the Western New-York Anti-Slavery Society.
Jason was part of a political community in which women and
men stood on equal footing, though no Black women had tried
to join this Upstate New York antislavery circle.[29]

In 1852, Mary Jeffrey entered politics, much like Hester Lane
had done in New York City a decade earlier. She donated mon-
ies to support Frederick Douglass's newspaper and took credit
for her financial contributions in her own name: "Jason Jeffrey
and Mrs. Jeffrey, 50 cents each." By the next year, something
had shifted. Jason Jeffrey attended the 1853 National Colored
Convention in nearby Rochester, but he did not go alone. Mary

Jeffrey made the trek with him, and not simply to serve meals or otherwise attends to men's needs. At the urging of Frederick Douglass, Mary Jeffrey was seated as a delegate—the only woman—and she did so while escaping ridicule.[30]

Later that same year, 1853, in December, young Barbara Ann Steward and Mary Jeffery met up at another convention, this one held in Geneva, New York. The convention not only seated both women as delegates, positioning them equals to the men. It also elected the women officers, with Jeffrey as a vice president and Steward as secretary. Steward took to the podium and delivered a formal address recorded as "able and eloquent." Frederick Douglass recognized Steward's potential as an antislavery speaker, and she was soon on tour through the small towns of Upstate New York: Hopwell Center, East Bloomfield, West Bloomfield, Victor, and Geneva.[31]

Jeffrey had paved the way for Steward's political career, and it made a difference. In 1855, Stewart attended a mass meeting of Black residents in Douglass's hometown of Rochester. The subject was voting rights, and much of the discussion concerned an odious property requirement that kept many Black men from the state's ballot boxes. Stewart was the featured speaker, a young woman spokesperson on men's voting rights. Her remarks on "the Rights and Wrongs of her suffering people" were "favorably received." The road ahead was not entirely smooth, however. In 1855, when Steward arrived in Troy, New York, to be seated at the Colored Men's State Convention of New York, she might have expected a cordial welcome. After all, among those hosting the meeting was her friend Frederick Douglass. Instead, delegates confronted Steward and did not mince words when they revoked her credentials and expelled her from the meeting for "no other reason than her sex." The presence of a woman, even a proven antislavery advocate, threatened to undercut or distract the deliberations. The pronouncement—"this is not a Woman's Rights Convention"—rang from podiums and rolled off printing presses so often that it was a familiar refrain in the

1850s. The sentiment was clear: women like Steward would not find an easy home in a political culture that associated women with the disruptive matter of their rights.[32]

ALONG WITH ENSLAVED men and children, women faced the demand that they labor without compensation as persons with a price. And so, enslaved women like their free counterparts also aspired to win liberty, equality, and dignity. Slavery exacted an especially high cost from women, who fought for the right to bodily integrity, in law and in life. Their bonds came in the form of shackles, ropes, pens, and the isolation of a small rural farm or a vast and remote plantation. Slavery weighed on the minds of people held in bondage through the threat of sale or the separation of family members. Their bodies endured torture meted out with a lash, a switch, the toes of a boot, or the back of a hand. Lawmakers drew boundaries that cut into enslaved people's personhood, from restrictions on reading, writing, and worship to the strict regulation of coming and going of all sorts. Amid this, enslaved women still managed to tell their stories, in their own ways. They expressed what they thought in what they did and in rare cases created a record of their lives with pen and paper. They had a distinct story to tell about what it was to be enslaved and what women's rights might mean. First and foremost, that meant being liberated from the threat of rape.

Though often far from convention halls, enslaved women put the problem of sexual violence before the public eye when they resisted. A woman named Celia, young and alone in central Missouri, earned notice when she killed her owner after years of being raped by him. Harriet Jacobs penned her fugitive slave narrative, one of the few written from a woman's perspective, recounting her harrowing escape from an owner's sexual advances. Their stories joined those of women like Sojourner Truth to make clear that control over their bodies and their intimate lives was, for enslaved women, a problem that a movement for women's rights should remedy. Delegates to the 1851 Akron women's convention recognized the issue, and they expressed sympathy for the "most grossly wronged" and "foully outraged of all women." Free women understood the stories that enslaved women needed to tell.

Too often, enslaved women's bodies were understood to be the property of slaveholders, men who claimed unlimited and unbridled authority over the women they held. In the notorious case of *State v. Mann*, North Carolina's highest court reviewed the shooting of an enslaved woman named Lydia. She had been shot from behind and wounded while running away from a punishment of whipping. It's difficult to say why Lydia believed she had a right to flee and avoid a harsh and perhaps unjust punishment. When she ran for her life, she gave judges an opportunity to impose limitations upon the man who had assaulted her. But they did not. In the words of Justice Thomas Ruffin: "The power of the master must be absolute, to render the submission of the slave perfect."[33]

Mary Ann Shadd Cary's *Provincial Freeman* took note of the fate of Celia, enslaved in central Missouri: "A colored woman, named Celia, was hanged on the 21st ult., at Fulton, [Missouri,] for the murder of Robert Newsom, whose slave she was in June last. The evening preceding her execution she made a full confession of her crime." It was a cryptic report and perhaps this is all Cary knew about Celia; her Canada West office was a long way away from Missouri. Cary likely picked up the story from another paper. She could not tell her readers the more detailed tale that Celia's trial record reveals: Celia had killed her owner in an act of self-defense after enduring years of his sexual abuse. Her owner, "the old man, had been having sexual intercourse with her....Her second child was his." He had first "forced her" years earlier, after purchasing Celia in a neighboring county. She had wanted to "hurt him, not to kill him" and had warned her owner "not to come," that she was "sick." The young woman had confessed that she struck him "twice on the head with a stick, and then put his body on the fire and burnt it nearly up....She took up the ashes and bones [and] emptied them on the right hand side of the path leading from my cabin to the stable."[34]

No one disputed Celia's story. But they did doubt that she was a woman, at least under Missouri state law. Instead, she was property. When Celia killed her abuser, she claimed ownership of her body as a woman and drew a boundary that ran contrary to her owner's desires, and perhaps his expectations: "He had told her he was coming down to her cabin that night. She told him not to come and that if he came she would hurt him." Her perspective was no secret; it was not a quiet objection held private and close. Everyone in the household—a small, slave-holding family that spanned three generations—knew of Celia's grievance: "She had told the (White) family. (She said she was threatened.)" The young woman did not harbor a silent complaint. Instead, Celia appealed to what she hoped was a shared sense of propriety: she warned "she would hurt him if he did not quit forcing her while she was sick."[35]

Celia's case began in the rooms of a rural farmstead, but the final judgment would take place in the county courthouse. What had once been family matters became public fare. Celia was repeatedly interrogated, once by a local attorney, and then again by a neighboring farmer. Both would testify at trial. Finally, she faced the Justice of the Peace, before whom she would swear to the truth of her story, affixing her mark, an "x," to a sworn statement: "She killed her master on the night of the 23rd of June 1855 about two hours after dark." The dispute presented to a Callaway County jury did not depend upon the proving of facts—no one disputed that her owner had habitually raped her and that, on the fateful night, Celia had refused his insistence with a warning and then a stick.[36]

Celia had her say, but in the courthouse her lawyers did the talking. They took her story and molded it into a defense that might save her from execution. Celia's lawyers presented the judge with their theory broken down into four critical parts. First, if Celia had killed to avoid rape she was not guilty: "If the Jury believes from the evidence that Celia did kill Newsom, but that the killing was necessary to protect herself against a forced sexual intercourse…they will not find her guilty of murder in the first degree." Second, rape was an offense against which a woman in Missouri may act in self-defense: "An attempt to compel a woman to be defiled by using force, menace, or duress, is a felony." Third, Missouri law prohibited the rape of enslaved women: "The using of a master's authority to compel a slave to be by him defiled, in using force, menace and duress." And fourth, the law made no distinction between women: "The words *any woman* in the first clause of the [law] embraces slave women, as well as free White women."[37]

Celia was entitled to lawfully defend herself against an owner's sexual aggression, her legal team argued. But the judge refused to let her lawyers put this theory to the jury. Instead, he ruled that Celia did not share in the rights held by other "women" in the state of Missouri. As a "slave" woman, she was not equal to "free white women" before the law. She could be brutalized and raped, and in legal terms she could not be "defiled by using force, menace, or duress." What her owner had done to her was not a crime, the trial judge concluded. In the months that followed, an appeals court agreed. Celia was executed in December 1855.[38]

Celia told her story under desperate circumstances: she was on trial for murder. The demands of the law squeezed this and other stories told by enslaved women into narrow forms such as testimony, causes of action, and statutes. Harriet Jacobs managed to defy such constraints and instead used her own pen and paper to tell her version. She too fought hard against the threat of sexual assault, and lived to tell a story that connected the rights of enslaved people to the rights of women. Jacobs had her own story to tell about years spent barely avoiding the sexual advances in her owner's household. She was enslaved in Edenton, North Carolina, where she lived proximate to free family members who attempted to shelter her as a young girl. They could not, and Jacobs was left to devise her own escape when faced with an impossible choice: give in to the man's demands, or be sold away far from her loved ones.[39]

Jacobs had no easy options. She launched a scheme of first entering into a sexual liaison with a white man, by whom she bore two children, believing that he might then aid the three to secure their freedom. Jacobs then turned to her family, a grand-mother nearby, who agreed to hide Jacobs from her owner. And there she remained, in a crawlspace under the roof of her grand-mother's home, for seven years. When the opportunity to flee finally came, Jacobs headed to free soil—Philadelphia, New York, and Boston, where she spent precarious years as a fugitive. Her acquaintances included sympathetic white people and radical antislavery activists. When others, including Harriet Beecher Stowe, expressed interest in penning her story, Jacobs decided to write it herself.[40]

By 1855, the same year that Celia was hanged in Missouri, Jacobs's freedom had been purchased, and she labored as a child's maid in a New York City family. She was also at work finding her voice and crafting her story, penning a memoir of slavery and freedom in the evenings. It was, as she told a friend, a risky—even compromising—undertaking. Jacobs feared that should she confess her personal history of near sexual assault and a liaison outside of marriage—though circumstances all too ordinary for an enslaved woman—the free women of the North would judge her, shame her. Perhaps it was out of bounds for Jacobs to expect that she might live free from sexual assault, choose her intimate partners, and resist unwelcome overtures, even to the degree that she might risk running away. Her circumstances were only hinted at during women's rights meetings in the North, and Jacobs ultimately told a hard truth about what it meant to grant that enslaved women too had rights.[41]

IN 1854, THE poet and antislavery lecturer Frances Ellen Watkins Harper arrived at Boston's African Meeting House, where Maria Stewart had faced down her critics twenty years before. Harper's visit was altogether different. She took command of the podium and delivered a lecture on Christianity followed by the reading of an original poem. Men followed her on the same stage, including local minister and Harper's mentor, the journalist and antislavery activist William Cooper Nell, who provided "a few words of encouragement." Not a word of criticism was uttered. A woman's magazine later noted that Harper's speech tore down barriers: "It would seem that the prejudice against female speaking, which prevails still in some sections, but which we think is every day becoming less, might be laid aside by everybody, so far as to hear a colored young lady plead eloquently and powerfully for the oppressed of her race."[42]

Harper did not effect the change alone, of course. She built on the work of the women before her who had been knocking on the doors of power for decades. Her approach was, however, self-styled, deploying a gloved hand and a gentle rap. She was raised in Baltimore under the watchful eye of an uncle, William Watkins, a newspaper correspondent, minister, teacher, and abolitionist. Her girlhood home had been abuzz with the goings-on of African American politics. Harper spent time as a schoolteacher in Pittsburgh, Pennsylvania, but that was not enough to satisfy her ambition. Like many of her generation who had been raised free, she deeply identified with those still in bondage. Her talents, she determined, would go to serving the slaves' cause and Harper joined the antislavery lecture circuit in 1853.[43]

Her success was one part style. Harper exhibited unassailably ladylike comportment even as her ideas were sharp and highly political. Audiences admired her "unassuming manners, graceful oratory, fervency, pathos, and truthfulness." She delivered "outbursts of eloquent indignation" in a "style of speaking, which is highly poetical [and] quite touching and effective." Listeners responded: "The address, coming from a gifted daughter of this despised and down-trodden race, possessed a freshness and reality which no other circumstance could so well impart. Her words fall on the hearts of those who hear her, in a manner that cannot fail to be appreciated."[44]

Harper avoided the vexed confrontations that many women before her had faced when they assumed power in public. Her peers still battled, meeting by meeting, to be included in the colored conventions. Harper appeared there, too, and then waited until she was "requested to take part," during the 1858 Ohio State Colored Convention. Harper remained close to her uncle William and their relationship taught her how to build alliances with the men who still dominated the antislavery circuit. Her mentor and traveling companion, William Cooper Nell, reported on her successes—even boasted about them: as "a colored American, and...a woman...[she] had attractions for and should be heard by the masses." Before the decade was over, Harper had shared the podium with many of the era's best-known antislavery speakers, men like H. Ford Douglass, Robert Purvis, Charles Remond, William Still, and William Howard Day. She also came to know white women lecturers such as Lucretia Mott and Josephine Griffing.[45]

Appearing on the antislavery stage was not easy. Harper generated controversy as audience members debated whether she, with all her talent and refinement, really was a woman equal to her white counterparts. In Randolph County, Indiana, the answer was no. Following Harper's appearance there, a commentator remarked that she was very welcome to a local school, the Farmers' Academy, as a speaker. However, "feelings of prejudice" meant that she and other Black women would be rejected as a matter of "principle" should they apply there to be students. The overriding "principle" was racism. Harper was parodied by Southern and antiabolitionist journalists. One dubbed her "a mulatto girl" that "argues that the surest and quickest way of placing the colored race in the position to live without labor, is, for the White folks to abandon the use of sugar and cotton, and other products of slave labor." *Mulatto* was a slur.[46]

Harper spent many months on the road, where threatening confrontations with drivers, conductors, and engineers loomed constantly. In 1858, Harper marked her fourth year on the lecture circuit and had seen a lot: "I have been insulted in several railroad cars." In these moments, her ladies' gloves came off: "The other day...the conductor came to me, and wanted me to go out on the platform. Now, was not that brave and noble? As a matter of course, I did not. Some one interfered, and asked or requested that I might be permitted to sit in a corner. I did not move, but kept the same seat. When I was about to leave, he refused my money, and I threw it down on the car floor, and got out, after I had ridden as far as I wish. Such impudence!"[47]

Assaults on her dignity accompanied the physical dangers. Harper left readers to imagine her fears when she remarked, "On the Carlisle road, I was interrupted and insulted several times. Two men came after me in one day." Recalling this confrontation for a friend, Harper was a bit more frank: "I hardly think that I shall be at your meeting after all. The distance is far, and the road most accessible that I know of, is proscriptive to colored persons. I was interrupted and insulted on it Monday this week—the Cincinnati and Carlisle road." No number of lace cuffs or carefully tailored dresses could protect Harper from violence. At a meeting in Cool Spring, Ohio, "an attempt was made to break up by rowdy violence, one of Miss Watkins' meeting." Her hosts had the offenders arrested.[48]

The root cause of the mob's objections came through during the court proceedings that followed. Yes, Harper sued. The attorney for the defendants asked one witness, a white man, "Are you a nigger worshiper?" Rather than sanctuaries, courtrooms permitted the insults to her dignity to continue. She stayed in town to testify against the men who had disrupted her remarks and threatened her harm. The court required Harper to repeat her lecture for the jury so that it might determine the "character of the meeting." The trial ended in favor of Harper and her right to lecture. But that victory did not mean she was safe. Harper continued to speak about politics willingly, and she influenced hearts and minds. And still, she had to endure a distinct mix of threat and danger. She may have not been boxed in, but neither was she free.[49]

BY THE END of the 1850s, when Black women exercised their power, they might have faced opposition, but no longer was anyone surprised. They had made themselves visible at public gatherings—church conferences, political conventions, benevolent society meetings. They still served meals or attended to the comfort of a speaker or delegate. But they also insisted on claiming their own time at the podium and during deliberations. Black women challenged the politics of the 1850s by what they did and by what they said. They were loyal to organizations in which they could battle against both racism and sexism. They crafted their own definition of women's rights, one drawn from their experiences with the indignity of forced labor, the scourge of sexual assault, and their rough handling on streetcars and trains. These critiques steered the course of a new women's movement, one with Black women at the helm.

Chapter 4

ONE GREAT BUNDLE OF HUMANITY

When Frances Ellen Watkins Harper stood up before the American Equal Rights Association in 1866, she did not mince words. She came to face down figures no less formidable than Elizabeth Cady Stanton and Susan B. Anthony, so she needed to be at her best. She was the only Black woman to speak in a gathering brimming with skilled orators. Most often quoted is her admonition that "we are all bound up together in one great bundle of humanity." It was a fierce reframing of American politics that rejected differences of race and of sex. What she did not say also mattered, and Harper did not speak about property rights or the ballot. Instead, her grievances emanated from the everyday indignities Black women endured on the nation's streetcars, where Harper had been roughed up, ridiculed, and refused service. All this, while white women watched. "You white women speak of rights. I speak of wrongs," she railed. No one dared talk back.[1]

EVEN AMONG THOSE who had followed the rising tensions of the 1850s closely, few anticipated the fury and scope of the Civil War. Yes, there were those in the North who feared they'd be

Frances Ellen Watkins Harper (1825–1911)
GETTY IMAGES

overrun by the South's slavocracy—the interlocking power that slaveholders exerted over politics, economics, and law. Southerners worried that a free soil–abolitionist alliance presided over by the newly elected President Abraham Lincoln would lead to slavery's demise. Some of the most defining disputes arose over how states and territories to the west would regard slavery.[2]

The war caused real disruptions. Trade, commerce, and the production and processing of staple crops—especially cotton—suffered. Filling military ranks and quotas, North and South, drew men away from farms, factories, plantations, and workshops toward enlistment, conscription, and the procurement of substitutes. Demands for foodstuffs and the depletion of the labor force made life on the home front bleak, especially in regions where troops practiced "scorched earth" policies and targeted civilians or co-opted their homes by billeting soldiers and establishing military outposts there. North and South, citizens questioned aloud who bore the costs of war. Working-class white people especially wondered whether they were risking their own lives to preserve the privileges of the planter and the industrialist. And why were they asked to pay the ultimate price to liberate the distant millions of Black Americans? Antidraft riots and desertion exacerbated the chaos of war. The conflict went on for months, and then years, longer than anyone had anticipated in 1860. It was a revolution.³

The future of slavery was at the heart of the conflict, no matter how politicians may have spun the Civil War to be about other matters. Some fought to preserve their own slaveholding privileges. Others assented to war to clear the way for a future in which slaveholding could expand, especially to the west. Free-soil principles led some to sign on to the conflict. They hoped to keep slavery from expanding into states and territories, leaving the way clear for economies built upon smaller farms, modest manufacturers, and wage labor. Those with abolitionist commitments took up arms as a next step in a campaign to end, unequivocally and irreversibly, holding persons as property. Notions such as "states' rights" and "preserving the Union" elided how everyone who contemplated the war did so through a lens that was clouded by their thinking about the future of slavery.⁴

Black Americans were of one mind when it came to war: after the discouraging years of the 1850s, they hoped it might provide a radical opportunity. Enslaved people watched and waited for the moment when disruptions—battles, destruction, and displacement—provided a chance to steal their liberty. Fugitives and refugees—people displaced by the movement of troops and the destruction of property—took to the road, hoping to land behind Union lines and in camps set up just out of harm's way. In the North, Black Americans clamored to serve the Union.

They could nearly taste the freedom and civil rights that their valor might win for everyone. They lobbied and voted with their feet, even though they faced unparalleled risk when Confederate officials treated Black prisoners of war as anything but that— capture meant enslavement or death.[5]

For women, the war presented new opportunities and new burdens. The absence of able-bodied men left women alone to run farms, workshops, and entire households. Women saw their work, even domestic duties, in political terms. When they maintained households and managed finances, trade, or commerce, women were doing their part for the war as well as for their families. And women stepped up their relief work when the Army showed that it was unprepared for the war's human demands. Here, the benevolent work that many women had done locally, in their neighborhoods and churches, became part of a national network of women who supported the war. Women's concerns extended to the well-being of sons and husbands, and in war these concerns became politicized. Love transformed mothers and wives into demanding members of political culture. They lobbied public officials—including the president—on the course of the war, for the support of soldiers, and for the needs on the home front, sometimes with raised voices. It was a delicate business for middle-class women, Black and white, who risked their status as ladies.[6]

The war loosened Black women's bonds. Enslaved women were more likely than their male counterparts to remain on plantations and farms and at urban homesteads. But many of them took their chances when they made it to Union camps, where they traded labor for a modicum of safety and a distance from servitude. Others, often with children and elderly persons to care for, arrived at refugee camps, where they set up, crude though they were, their first households as free people. Union officials did not anticipate how many women and children would seize freedom and be on the move, taking advantage of the cover offered by the chaos of war. Officers would absorb a small number of women into the domestic work that supported troops—cooks and laundresses were essential to sustaining the war effort. Still, the lives of many more refugeed women verged on the dangerous, and were shot through with brutality. They did not gain freedom merely by crossing a line; freedom's full promise remained unfulfilled.[7]

Free Black women shared the enthusiasms of their sons and fathers for the war. And they, too, began to put their principles into action. Some women adapted the networks of benevolence through which they had long provided poor relief, aid to widows and orphans, and burial funds to the needs of soldiers and refugees. Others left the relative calm and safety of Northern towns and cities to aid newly freed people in the South, serving as nurses, caretakers, and teachers. These women explained their work in expressly political terms. They even undertook work they had never done before. For the first time, women were building schools, carrying firearms, negotiating with laborers, masterminding fundraising campaigns, traveling alone and far from home, and risking their safety and reputations as they worked alongside soldiers and refugees. The war unsettled much of everyday life, and Black women stepped into the fray.[8]

When Confederate forces surrendered at Appomattox in spring 1865, the country was left with the monumental task of rebuilding. This required a reimagining of society. Reconstruction, the period immediately following the war's end, was the nation's first experiment in interracial democracy. Remaking a postconflict society demanded that lawmakers and citizens alike attend to production and trade, infrastructure and labor. No blueprint existed from which to plot points from total war to normalcy, not to mention prosperity. The emancipation of four million enslaved people required that the entire nation reformulate its economy. Those who had treated human property as assets saw their net worth give way to human liberation. The agriculture and industries that rested upon the extraction of free and forced labor had to wrestle with former slaves' demands for wages, compensation, and even shares of land into which they had been forced to pour their blood and sweat.[9]

Left alone, a world of modest, self-sufficient Black communities might have sprouted across the South after the Civil War. African Americans aspired to autonomy above all. But whether the demand came from Southern elites who aimed to reestablish their political supremacy or from public officials who saw in the labor of former slaves a way to fill their tills, Black Americans were never simply left alone to determine their futures. Federal officials—first the Army and then a newly created Bureau of Refugees, Freedmen and Abandoned Lands, often termed the Freedmen's Bureau—oversaw Reconstruction's earliest years. Former slaves got out ahead of bureaucrats, making what they needed out of very little and rebuilding: tilling soil, erecting schoolhouses, reuniting families, and convening congregations of faith. Their efforts would represent some of Reconstruction's most enduring successes. Former slaves partnered with Black Northerners who had migrated south, along with missionaries, Black and white, who committed to the well-being of the newly liberated. They debated politics in Union Leagues and traded ideas in pamphlets, tracts, and newspapers. Freed people set the terms for an African American public culture that would soon rival that which had long been part of Northern cities and towns.[10]

Despite that vibrancy, the old regime of the prewar era threatened to reinstall itself—only this time, with a thin veneer called "freedom" covering it. Onerous labor contracts aimed to bind Black Southerners—entire families—to the soil and to the rhythms of staple crop production. Legislators set in place Black Codes that marked former slaves as second-class citizens, with only a barebones capacity to protect their property and their persons. Organizations like the Knights of the White Camelia directed intimidation and violence at Black Americans, attempting to keep white men on top the new social order. What, then, was the meaning of freedom? former slaves and their allies asked.[11]

In Congress, lawmakers asked the same question. They set out to answer it by writing new laws and amending the Constitution, all in an effort to breathe meaning into *freedom* and to give it teeth. They designed three amendments with this in mind.

When it abolished slavery in 1865, the Thirteenth Amendment promised that no postwar re-enslavement scheme could gain a toehold in the United States. The Fourteenth Amendment of 1868 made formerly enslaved people—and all those born in the United States—citizens. It guaranteed equal protection under the law and due process—lofty principles, the meaning of which would only be worked out over time. And then in 1870, the Fifteenth Amendment barred the states from using race to deny voting rights—an important step toward ensuring that Black men would have access to the polls, jury service, and office holding. Civil rights acts complemented the amendments, spelling out what citizenship and equality meant, from the rights to sue and be sued to the rights to testify and make and enforce contracts. This constitutional revolution promised that Black Americans would always have a seat at the table of law and policy.[12]

EVEN BEFORE THE war's end, Americans wondered who former slaves would be in a world without their forced labor. Four million people, once claimed as the property of others, became members of political culture. Freedom did not guarantee political rights, but it was impossible to deny that if the country was to reunite after a brutal conflict over slavery, it must address who could vote and hold office going forward. The political rights of Black men came first to mind for many. But debates about the rights of women also arose. No one could say for certain in 1865 where those debates might lead. The years of Reconstruction opened a door, and many Americans who had long been excluded from polling places and legislative chambers vied for their chance at power.

A small-town newspaper like the *Rutland Weekly Herald* was not an obvious place to discover the suggestion that Black women should have the vote. The predominantly white city of Rutland had grown up around the marble quarries of southern Vermont. There, the *Herald*'s editors had long kept their readers tuned in to antislavery and women's rights politics. The town's residents had come to expect this. From time to time, Rutland had hosted radical reform meetings, most recently the Free Convention of 1858. That call had brought to Rutland advocates of free trade, education, labor and land reform, temperance, antislavery, and women's rights in one roiling gathering. Women's rights debates—from marriage and free love to property rights—dominated there.[13]

Still, when the *Herald*'s editors endorsed voting rights for Black women in 1865, it proved to be a bold and unexpected move. Black women had not taken part in the 1858 convention, nor were they spoken of there except as enslaved people. But the war had broadened the *Herald*'s perspective, and its editors looked toward a new future, saying out loud what some readers hoped for and others feared. The "terrible scourge" of war had rid the nation of the "inequality and wrong" of slavery. And though wounds were still fresh, there was reason to celebrate. The nation was on the road to ratifying the Thirteenth Amendment, and "the utter annihilation of that which has been denominated the sum of all villainies…African slavery."[14]

The *Herald* warned that slavery's abolition was just the beginning. The nation was starting a long process of righting itself. Granting enslaved people freedom was a first step, but it was not enough. Other blights remained, especially barriers to Black political rights, and the paper urged its readers to consider how these wrongs should be eradicated. What would it take to make former slaves into citizens and voters? The *Herald* counseled that even those Americans tucked away in the small corners of New England must face "the *dark* and *crying* evil of the present hour, the disenfranchisement of colored men and women." Enslavement and disfranchisement, twin evils, had to go.[15]

The editors continued on to the subject of Black women and the vote. Why they did so is hard to say. Words ascribed to Sojourner Truth clearly moved the *Herald*'s editors, who used a report on one of her speeches to craft a vision of how Black women fit into political culture. Black women had a capacity for hard work: "They can plough, hoe, pick cotton, and make the welkin ring with their songs as well as the men." Black women stood out for having shouldered the burdens of production and reproduction: "They can nurse their own children, as well as those of their mistresses, and work sixteen hours a day, which the men cannot do." The paper misrepresented Truth's actual words, but it was true to her spirit when it promoted the prospect that Black women would join men at the polls.[16]

The paper's final point would have won the agreement of Black women from Maria Stewart and Sojourner Truth to Mary Ann Shadd Cary. "WOMEN? Shall colored women be allowed to vote? Why not?" The *Herald*'s editors turned the table on readers who assumed that Black women were not suited to political rights. They encouraged new thinking about who should have access to the ballot and on what terms. They intended their words to be provocative and to stir up readers. But it was not a hollow gesture. Black women themselves were already demonstrating that they were entitled to rights: "They *know* as much," the paper pointed out, "and are as patriotic and as moral as the men."[17]

The remarks of a small-town Vermont newspaper alone would not take Black women far in the rough politics of Reconstruction. But that editorial was a sign that even some white Americans saw Black women coming. In the years that followed, anyone who was surprised, whether in rural Vermont or in the heart of the nation's capital, when a Black woman claimed her seat at the table would need to adjust. Those who thought such women out of bounds were behind the times and would have to abandon old assumptions. The *Herald* mocked those who might resist: "The idea of *women* and especially colored women voting, is altogether too radical. It is tearing up by the roots all the long-established usages and maxims of human society." The *Herald* thought it nearly laughable to discount their political rights, and so did many Black women.[18]

THE CIVIL WAR set people in motion: armies on the march, refugees displaced by war, and relief workers determined to repair the devastation. Many Americans, including Black women, faced circumstances they'd never known and traveled to locales they'd never before seen. For many, the journey was a literal one. Women exiled in Canada returned to the United States. Women in the North headed to the South, while others made a reverse migration. Across the country, Black women stepped up and then into the breaches of war, as teachers, nurses, and relief workers. The personal became undoubtedly political, as Black women did the same kinds of jobs they had long performed in local communities now as part of a broader national effort, one to end slavery and preserve the Union. It was a watershed moment for African American women's leadership.

With the start of the war, Mary Ann Shadd Cary changed her mind and became a Union loyalist. Cary was among those émigrés to Canada who, when conflict began between North and South, saw the world anew. It was not an easy transformation. Since leaving the United States, Cary had built family and community in a place where the air smelled a lot like freedom. She was a respected commentator and the first Black woman to be a news editor in Canada West. But the outbreak of war redirected her efforts when it appeared that Black men's military service could alter the course of the conflict. To clothe African American men in uniforms and to place firearms in their hands, she knew, were steps toward overturning an old order and opening new doors to political rights.[19] Cary's decision came at a time of personal turmoil. Her newspaper, the *Provincial Freeman*, was struggling to win subscribers and stay afloat. Her husband, Thomas, died in the fall of 1860, after four short years of marriage. She was the sole parent of a toddler, with another child on the way. She nearly withdrew from public life altogether, but fellow emigration advocate Martin Delany called upon Cary to assist him with recruiting Black soldiers to serve the Union.[20]

Cary could not write policy as one of Washington's elite, but she could pressure those who did. She signed on to recruit young men to the 29th Regiment Connecticut Volunteers. She went into the field, drawing upon her skills as a lecturer. Cary retraced familiar routes—by train, by coach, and on foot—with new purpose. She dodged dangers, especially threats leveled by those who opposed African Americans entering their states. She lobbied influential allies, including Indiana governor Oliver P. Morton, who eventually pledged protection for Delany and his agents, including Cary, as they worked to expand the Union's manpower. She won praise, though it is not clear that she needed it. Cary was, more than once, reappointed to recruit Black troops. She did this work in her own name, winning her distinction as yet another women's "first." But this time was different. Cary was trading in ideas and building an army that would fight for the cause of freedom and citizenship that had always been at the heart of her life's work.[21]

Wartime challenges demanded new policies for the relief of soldiers and refugees. Federal officials set up makeshift hospitals and refugee camps near Washington, DC. There, the devastating human cost of the war was evident. The Army opened Freedmen's Hospital and Asylum in 1862 on the grounds of the notoriously crowded and unhealthy Camp Barker. The camps were crude outposts of freedom, hard-won points of refuge for formerly enslaved people who left farms and plantations to claim liberty and a small respite behind Union lines. The women among them, first hundreds and then thousands, insisted upon slavery's demise with their feet and walked toward membership in a radically changing nation. They demanded from federal officials basic rights: food, shelter, and defense from those who regarded them as property or the fodder of war.[22]

Harriet Jacobs was among those women in the North to quickly recognize that the politics of freedom turned on the plight of refugees. In spring 1862, walking away from the North, with her daughter Louisa in tow, she returned to the South, first to Washington, DC, and then to Virginia. There, the two women—mother and daughter—rolled up their sleeves. Jacobs did not stop writing. She became one of the first correspondents to report on the plight of refugees for *The Liberator*. She signed her own name—Mrs. Jacobs—to those clear and confident letters.

In the politics of war, Jacobs discovered a new freedom and even joy away from the domestic labor that had previously dominated her life.[23]

Jacobs did not cut her ties to the North. Instead, she expanded her networks and won support for the refugees, who were the heart of her concern. She began to build links between Black women who had for too long been separated by the line between slavery and freedom. Other women were her allies. In spring 1863, Jacobs made her way back to New York to attend Susan Anthony's meeting of the Women's National Loyal League. Arriving at the rooms of the Cooper Institute, Jacobs became a peer to women such as Elizabeth Cady Stanton and Angelina Grimké Weld. Jacobs opened the league's inaugural meeting, making her debut as a political speaker with a prayer that called upon God to "save the nation and free the slave." She served on the league's executive board, and her mind turned toward politics as she, for example, called for constitutional amendments that would extend "liberty, justice, [and] equality" to former slaves. Winning women's power was on her mind in these years, showing up even in her work among refugees in Alexandria. There, Jacobs wrestled with men, Black and white, over control of a school for refugee children. By the time the dispute concluded, officials named the school for Jacobs and placed it in the hands of a new head teacher, a woman: her daughter, Louisa.[24]

Like Jacobs, Sojourner Truth responded to the call of the National Women's Loyal League and lectured to support the war. Along the way, she was met by the special dangers that accompanied appearing in meeting halls full of both sympathizers and the curious. For Truth to speak publicly about "the war," rather than about slavery or the rights of women, was especially risky. In Angola, Indiana, she stood her ground in the face of mobs that threatened "tar and feathers, eggs, rails, shooting and a general blowing up" and then shouted her down. Truth was a seasoned speaker. Still, she had to rely upon the protection of local constables and the area's "best men," who themselves were vilified for extending to a Black woman a platform and the right of free speech. Truth knew her message rankled, and that the sight of her enraged: "It seems that it take *my* black face to bring out *your* black heart; so it's well I came.... You are afraid of my black face, because it is a looking-glass in which you see yourselves."[25]

Truth took up relief work, first providing aid to Black soldiers who were enlisting in her home state of Michigan. There, word reached her that needs were most pressing in Washington, DC, and the same soldiers and refugees who also concerned Harriet Jacobs drew Truth away from her home in the Midwest. She soon headed east from Battle Creek, traveling in the company of her grandson Samuel Banks. She got quickly to work, accepting appointments with the National Freedmen's Relief Association and later the Freedmen's Bureau, sharing responsibilities with other women relief workers—Black and white—including Jacobs.[26]

Truth battled on another front line in the fight for freedom—that of civil rights—especially when she traveled. Back home in Michigan, in the cities of Kalamazoo and Coldwater, Truth had been denied passage while traveling. Arriving in Washington, she knew that she might be ignored or refused when she tried to use streetcars, as Black women and men frequently were in the nation's capital. Black life in Washington had until recently been regulated by laws that demanded passes and freedom papers. That climate made moving about risky. Each day, Truth uneasily made her way to and from the Freedmen's Hospital. On a fall afternoon in 1865, a conductor confirmed her worries when he confronted her, intent on keeping Truth off his streetcar.[27]

Truth was traveling with a white woman, Laura Haviland, who was also a relief worker from Michigan. Truth had permitted Haviland to flag down the streetcar; the women knew that it was unlikely to stop for Truth. As the car slowed, Truth moved to board, stepping up ahead of Haviland, only to have the conductor, John Weeden, roughly take hold of her shoulder, wrenching it to prevent her from boarding. Haviland spoke up in Truth's defense. But Weeden judged with his eyes, not his ears, and then demanded to know whether Truth "belonged" to Haviland. Haviland responded that Truth did not, that she belonged only to humanity. Despite their teamwork, neither Truth nor Haviland managed to board the streetcar. Instead, they walked to see a doctor and then filed a complaint.[28]

Truth tested the proposition that she and Haviland were equals—both entitled to board a city streetcar—in court. Her complaint brought Weeden before a Justice Thompson, where the conductor was charged with assault and battery. Truth sat by as Haviland testified that Weeden had seized Truth with "such violence as to injure her shoulder, and that it was done with unusual and unnecessary violence." The court also heard from Dr. W. B. Ellis, of the Freedmen's Hospital, who explained that Truth's "shoulder was very much swollen, and he had applied liniment." No, Ellis replied in response to the judge's question, Truth's injury "was not from rheumatic affection, but from the wrenching of her shoulder."[29]

Witnesses for Weeden pitted the conductor's comportment against that of the former slave, testifying to his "good character" and insisting that he had held back Truth merely "to prevent her from getting into the car, until the passengers, who were to get out at the junction had left the car." Courtesy rather than racism explained the assault, they claimed. Judge Thompson required Weeden to post bail and guarantee his appearance at court to defend against the charge of assault and battery upon Truth. It appears that Truth eventually won her case. What the precise cost to Weeden was is not known. But the victory for Truth was symbolic. In Washington, not only did she take part in remaking the nation through providing aid to refugees, she also pressed for equality before the law and in her daily life. Her suit against Weeden—there in the nation's capital—put the city on notice: Black women knew how strike back in the courts when others laid hands on them.[30]

Other women were drawn farther south. On the Sea Islands, off the South Carolina coast, some of the earliest work of Reconstruction was already under way by 1863. An incursion of

Union forces had caused the region's white residents, especially plantation owners, to flee the islands. Hundreds of people, now former slaves, were left behind—and army officials and missionaries, including Black women, offered their support. Many were drawn to Beaufort, South Carolina, where they saw the future being defined by the fate of these new communities of freed people. Black women returned to places like this. Harriet Tubman was already well known for her work leading to freedom those held as slaves in Maryland. By May 1862, Tubman was in Beaufort, where she worked to help freedwomen become self-supporting. She would go on to serve as a nurse in the local hospital, and as a spy and a scout for the Union Army. Tubman is not best remembered for having spoken about women's rights. But when she insisted, in a practical gesture, upon giving up her skirts in favor of the comfort and ease of a bloomer costume, she advertised a look that was synonymous with women's greater freedom.[31]

Other women let their work tell the story of their talents and skills but were not always rewarded. Formerly enslaved in Georgia, Susie King Taylor followed her husband and his band of Black soldiers—the First South Carolina Volunteers of African Descent (later the 33rd United States Colored Troops)—many of them newly free, to the Sea Islands. Taylor did the work she could, beginning as a laundress, a job that gave her enough flexibility to also see to the needs of the men in uniform. Taylor let on to army officials that she had attended school and could read and write. Soon they drafted her to teach soldiers and freed people. Her service earned her admiration and the station of nurse, a story she later told in her 1902 memoir, *Reminiscences of My Life in Camp with the 33rd United States Colored Troops, Late 1st S.C. Volunteers*. Because she was a woman, however, Taylor earned neither a salary nor a pension.[32]

Charlotte Forten left the comfort of New England for the adventure and purpose that the Sea Islands promised. In the pages of her diary, a young Forten described the climate in which young women activists in the North came of age. Between 1854 and 1862, while working as a schoolteacher in Salem, Massachusetts, she had attended scores of political gatherings. During antislavery meetings, Forten listened to luminaries such as Garrison, Phillips, Remond, and William Cooper Nell, among others. The era's women speakers, Black and white, especially inspired her ambition: "to be—an Anti-Slavery lecturer." Like Tubman, she donned a "Bloomer" costume, read newspapers published by women, and practiced her debating skills in a local women's literary society.[33]

By 1862, Forten joined the first wave of African American teachers to venture south and work with Black refugees behind Union Army lines. She was twenty-five years old. She carried with her the ambition of the women who had come before her: Forten's grandmother Charlotte, her mother, Mary Virginia Woods, and three of her aunts—Margaretta, Sarah, and Harriet—were founding members of the Philadelphia Female Antislavery Society in 1833. In Salem, Massachusetts, she had fallen under the influence of Sarah Parker Remond, a lecturer for the American Anti-Slavery Society. Forten admitted her admiration of Remond's activism in the pages of her diary: "Last night Miss R. entertained me with an account of her tour, and of the delightful day she spent with Mr. [Wendell] Phillips....I listened with most unwearied attention until the 'small hours of the morn' stole upon us."[34]

Secure in her classroom skills, Forten set out to teach among former slaves, of whose "sad...sufferings" she had heard moving accounts. Naive, Forten anticipated that the experience would offer the "delights of travel," while enabling her to find her "highest happiness" in doing her "duty." Through the auspices of the Port Royal Relief Association, she secured a position on St. Helena Island. To get there, Forten survived a treacherous sea voyage, and then she learned to defend herself with a gun, travel alone, and minister to the wounded. She knew that her presence, along with that of many other Northern women, raised questions about how former slaves might think about the rights of women. In a December 1862 letter to William Lloyd Garrison,

Forten related the events surrounding a Thanksgiving Day celebration during which women's rights activist "Mrs. Frances D.
Gage...spoke for a few moments very beautifully and earnestly."
Forten imagined the freed people's thoughts upon meeting Gage:
"It was something very novel and strange to them, I suppose, to
hear a woman speak in public, but they listened very attentively,
and seemed much moved by what she said."[35]

There, in the midst of war, women mixed politics with teaching and nursing. Black women found their footing on a rough
terrain that too often paid little mind to their status as ladies.
There was less room for the policing of their public authority when they worked in places where the urgency of war set
aside some notions of propriety. There was power to be earned
through the commitment, risk taking, and sheer effort that Reconstruction demanded. Black women would not finish the war
with a claim to military valor that propelled their sons and husbands into politics. But these women served on the front lines of
a revolution that had only just begun.

FOR FRANCES ELLEN Watkins Harper, the war years sharpened her thinking about how Black women's perspectives—and
their struggles against racism and sexism—should define the
nation's way forward. She waded into the war's roiling political waters in the fall of 1862 when she made a brave stand
against the shortcomings of President Lincoln's initial draft of
the Emancipation Proclamation. She read carefully. The president's proposed proclamation gave the rebel states one hundred
days to surrender. Should they refuse, the president promised
to order slavery's abolition in Confederate-controlled territories. This, Harper endorsed. But what came next troubled her.
The president also proposed to colonize—remove from the
United States—those persons freed by the proclamation, sending
them to Canada, Liberia, or elsewhere. Her resulting speech—
"The War and the President's Colonization Scheme"—decried
the president and put Harper on the road to becoming one of

the era's most sought-after political commentators. If she had any worries about challenging Lincoln on the eve of emancipation, it did not show.[36]

By the spring of 1864, Harper lectured regularly about the consequences of war and the hopes of Reconstruction. Not all her destinations were improbable—she traveled to Black communities near and far, though many of them were new to her. In May, for example, she journeyed to Indianapolis, Indiana, where she delivered a talk titled "Mission of War." Later that fall, she made her way to Providence, Rhode Island, Worcester and Boston in Massachusetts, and then New York City's Cooper Union. In crafting her speeches, Harper drew upon her own life story. She stood at the podium when it came time to celebrate the abolition of slavery in her home state of Maryland in November 1864. Harper, a daughter of the South who had long lived in exile, showed off her capacity for astute political analysis, and the day's cheers for a "free Maryland" touched her deeply.[37]

Harper was rarely allowed to forget that her place in politics was framed by her race and her sex. At the 1864 National Convention of Colored Men, it was her womanhood that set Harper apart. She was noted as present, but as "among the lady portion" of the delegates. She then watched as Edmonia Highgate, a twenty-year-old teacher from Norfolk, Virginia, gingerly addressed the meeting. Highgate took the podium in the shadow of experienced men such as Frederick Douglass. Remarking upon the upcoming presidential contest, she came down squarely in support of Lincoln's reelection and she urged other delegates to do the same. Highgate at the same time confessed her inner doubts, wondering aloud whether "she would not be quite in her place perhaps, if a girl as she is should tell the Convention what they ought to do." The news reports gently mocked her as "a strong Lincoln MAN," and noted that Highgate was "unwell and labored under a little difficulty speaking." But Harper's presence underscored that it was correct when any young woman, including Highgate, took her turn to speak.[38]

Theodore R. Davis, "The National Colored Convention in Session at Washington, D.C.," Harper's Weekly, *February 6, 1869*
LIBRARY OF CONGRESS

Black Americans already knew Harper as a poet and orator, whose words were dedicated to promoting antislavery politics. After the Civil War, she became a conscience for the entire country, instructing her listeners—Black and white, men and women—about what it meant to reconstruct the nation. Regardless of sex and color, all of humanity was, she said, bound up together. She believed that when Black women's dignity was respected, so too would be the dignity of all people. She expressed the hopes and despair of her audience members as she recited her poems, from "Moses" to "The Slave Auction," "To Mrs. Harriet Beecher Stowe," and "The Fifteenth Amendment." She returned to subjects such as the war and Reconstruction again and again, conditioning her listeners—from veteran Black activists to newly freed slaves—to expect that women would impart astute insights into politics.[39]

In early 1865, Harper set off on a schedule that was nothing short of grueling. Matter-of-fact newspaper notices of her appearances hid the stress and strain of travel. That year, Harper covered hundreds of miles between New York City, Indianapolis, and Philadelphia. She crisscrossed New England: Boston, Roxbury, Framingham, and Lowell in Massachusetts; Pawtucket and Providence in Rhode Island; and beyond. The year 1866 brought more of the same. Harper's primary audience was Black Americans, from the North and the South, for whom the future was urgent and fast becoming the present. She shared the bill and the podium with illustrious men, many of whom were her elders. In one speakers' series sponsored by Philadelphia's Social, Civic and Statistical Association, she delivered the fourth lecture, on the heels of presentations by William Lloyd Garrison and Frederick Douglass. She was uniformly praised for her elegance and poise. She headlined commemorations and celebrations, from those marking the Fourth of July to West Indian Emancipation Day and the life and death of the Black Revolutionary War martyr Crispus Attucks. She always brought a distinct woman's point of view, as suggested by the title of one speech: "A Colored Woman's Opinion of the Republic." Mary Ann Shadd Cary had remarked in 1858 that Harper was "the greatest female speaker ever." In the postwar years, Harper proved her right.[40]

Conceit was not one of Harper's qualities. By all accounts, her words were direct and incisive while her demeanor was modest and her tone soft-spoken. Harper had cultivated this persona over many years to deflect her critics, especially those who might accuse her of being less than ladylike. The strategy sometimes failed. Critics labeled her a member of a "tribe of female ranters," and especially deserving of rebuke as "a negress." She could do little when newspaper editors warned that women like her poisoned pro-Union circles: "We shall soon have a pythoness, white or black, among the 'properties' of every Loyal League in the country." Her appearances made headlines and exposed her to ridicule. One paper remarked that Harper—"a mixed Amazon with the high sounding title 'Right Rev. Hon. LLD Mrs. F.E.W. Harper'"—had been "haranguing the North

Carolina Blacks on suffrage." Harper encouraged former slaves to vote, and white men did not approve.[41]

When the first post–Civil War women's rights conventions met in May 1866, Harper was there. Elizabeth Cady Stanton and Susan Anthony called for delegates to gather for the Eleventh National Women's Rights Convention. Harper made the trip and met up with many other veterans of the movements against slavery and for women's rights, at New York City's Church of the Puritans. There, old and new allies together established a new American Equal Rights Association (AERA), committed to securing "equal rights to all American citizens, especially the right of suffrage, irrespective of race, color or sex." The delegates elected Quaker activist Lucretia Mott, a woman long associated with antislavery and women's equality, president. The same group recognized Harper's leadership and appointed her to the Finance Committee, charged with raising funds for "the cause."[42]

Harper came to express her solidarity with the interests of women: "justice is not fulfilled so long as woman is unequal before the law." She also championed a distinctly Black women's movement that emanated from the perils of travel that they were obliged to endure: "Going from Washington to Baltimore this Spring, they put me in the smoking car....Aye, in the capital of the nation, where the black man consecrated himself to the nation's defence, faithful when the white man was faithless, they put me in the smoking car! They did it once; but the next time they tried it, they failed; for I would not go in. I felt the fight in me; but I don't want to have to fight all the time." She pushed back against such indignities, even as they plagued her.[43]

What women's movement, Harper asked, would countenance brutality directed at Black women? "Have women nothing to do with this?" It was the strife of streetcars and railroads that were at the root of Harper's notions about women's rights. She continued: "Not long since, a colored woman took her seat in an Eleventh Street car in Philadelphia, and the conductor stopped the car, and told the rest of the passengers to get out, and left the

car with her in it alone, when they took it back to the station."
No measure of respectability was enough: "One day I took my
seat in a car, and the conductor came to me and told me to take
another seat. I just screamed 'murder.' The man said if I was
black I ought to behave myself. I knew that if he was white he
was not behaving himself. Are there no wrongs to be righted?"
This was the question Harper had come to ask of the American
Equal Rights Association: of white women, including Susan Anthony and Elizabeth Cady Stanton, and of white men, such as
Wendell Phillips and Henry Ward Beecher.[44]

Harper doubted that white American women would join her
in this movement, one that aimed to end the terror of the ladies' car. The vote for women would not be enough, she urged:
"I do not believe that giving the woman the ballot is immediately going to cure all the ills of life. I do not believe that white
women are dew-drops just exhaled from the skies. I think that
like men they may be divided into three classes, the good, the
bad, and the indifferent. The good would vote according to their
convictions and principles; the bad, as dictated by preju[d]ice
or malice; and the indifferent will vote on the strongest side of
the question, with the winning party.... You white women speak
here of rights. I speak of wrongs." Black women labored and
risked their lives, while white women hung back, waiting "to be
lifted of their airy nothings and selfishness."[45]

Harper set the bar high, warning that any movement that
would bear passive witness if not itself act to "trample upon
the weakest and feeblest" of society invited a "curse in its own
soul." Harper was not there merely to chastise. She had come
to advocate an approach that might keep the new coalition together through a demand for voting rights. "We are all bound up
together in one great bundle of humanity," she urged. Harper's
aspirations for the American Equal Rights Association extended
beyond the problem of race, beyond gender, and even beyond
class and nation. She implored others to join her.[46]

In 1869 Harper returned to the American Equal Rights Association (AERA) in one last effort to have delegates recognize

Black women as part of the postwar political culture. There, she endorsed a first step toward her voting rights, a Fifteenth Amendment that prohibited states from making race a bar to voting. It was a victory, but only a partial one. It was the final AERA meeting and in its wake the organization split into two: the American Woman Suffrage Association and the National Woman Suffrage Association. The division reflected how racism was powerful enough to cleave a great new voting rights organization down the middle. With their interests largely set aside, neither organization held much allure for Black women. They failed to realize their vision in the tumult of postwar women's conventions, but they were not defeated. For Harper and women like her, Black women who aspired to win political rights and with them secure the dignity of all humanity, it was time to look elsewhere. It was time to build their own movement.[47]

MARY ANN SHADD Cary did not join Harper at the AERA meetings of the 1860s. She was not, however, on the sidelines. Cary was still writing, and by the early 1870s she was aiming her pen directly at members of Congress. Black women were ready to assume political rights: "The colored women of this country though heretofore silent in great measure upon this question of the right to vote…have neither been indifferent to their own just claims under the amendments, in common with colored men, nor to the demand for political recognition so justly made every where throughout the land." Cary aimed to dispel any misunderstanding and warned others not to give in to petty divisions; she rejected attempts to distance Black women from Black men. She echoed Harper by carving out a position that was both in common with Black men's claim to political rights and part of white women's ardent cry for universal suffrage.[48]

The two women shared a point of view but had not arrived there by the same route. While Harper was standing up to delegates of the AERA, Cary was in Washington, DC, for the 1869 meeting of the Colored National Labor Union (CNLU). The gathering was crowded with 214 delegates, a who's who of national leaders, though Cary was the only woman officeholder. Her charge was heading the Committee on Female Suffrage, where she was paired with two white women, budding suffragists Belva Lockwood and Josephine Griffing. Now widowed, Cary supported herself and a young son by teaching public school in Washington, DC. After hours, she remained an activist and keen-eyed commentator. When Frederick Douglass called upon her to serve as an agent for his newsweekly, the *New National Era*, she grabbed the opportunity to return to the speakers' circuit. Her ambition only grew. In fall 1869, when Howard University Law School opened its doors, Cary was the only woman to enroll in the very first class.[49]

The bonds she made with women's suffrage activists at the CNLU endured. Cary soon joined national women's suffrage organizing, one of a small number of Black women who affiliated with Stanton and Anthony's new National Woman Suffrage Association. Despite how NWSA's founders had used anti-Black racism to win support for women's votes, Cary lauded the organization and attended its conventions. She did not, however, defer to the NWSA focus on a national campaign waged in courts and Congress. She actively worked a more local strategy: Congress should use its power to ensure the voting rights of women in the District of Columbia.[50]

Cary believed in direct action. On a Saturday in April 1871, dozens of women converged upon the District of Columbia's Board of Registration. Cary, Amanda Wall, and Mary Anderson were the three Black women in the crowd. Petition in hand, the women faced off with the board. When casually rebuffed, they held their position. Supporters soon appeared, including Frederick Douglass. The women insisted that they be given the opportunity to make their applications for a place on the voters' rolls. They won the point. Each woman formally presented herself, only to be refused. It was dramatic, but it was not merely political theater. Behind the scenes, some planned a test case that would challenge the District's requirement that voters be "male." Sarah Spencer, a local teacher, would later bring a suit that failed when a court concluded that the Constitution did not guarantee to any citizen, including a woman, a right to vote. Cary endorsed Spencer's move, believing it imperative that women push back against the view that neither the Fourteenth nor the Fifteenth Amendment guaranteed political rights. Overall, the effort in April at the Board of Registration netted little: "The refusal [to register the women] was and is a bitter pill to swallow."[51]

Cary seized upon her standing as a citizen governed by Congress rather than by an individual state legislature. In a message to a federal judiciary committee in 1872, she recommended a revision of existing laws: We "hope that the word male may be stricken out by Congress...without delay." Cary shifted away from constitutional claims to target local laws. Even though women were barred by the Board of Registration and the courts, the District's prohibition of women voters was still improper and Cary advocated for a small but potent change to the law. She objected to the "discrimination against [women] in the retention of the world *male*," and urged that instead women in the District would "vote as men do" before being further "taxed." They would be "governed by their own consent," a realization of the "principles of the *founders*."[52]

Cary was a "first" and a beacon among Black women who led the way into politics. She modeled how to challenge the limits imposed on their citizenship and sometimes overcome them. Still, Cary also demonstrated how to avoid political traps, including divisions such as local versus national concerns, legal versus political tactics, and Black- versus white-led organizations. These lines did not serve Black women's interests. Changing the language of law—striking words like *male*—was a route to women's power that resonated far beyond the District of Columbia. Churchwomen, too, were seizing upon this approach, believing small changes in the law—making its language gender neutral—was a starting point in a renewed campaign for rights. Women like Cary pursued voting rights in women's suffrage associations, while others headed to their churches, employing the same tactics with equal resolve.[53]

Chapter 5

MAKE US A POWER

When Black women spoke about power, they used a term that was as vague as it was blunt. They found it sometimes necessary to be that forceful, especially in contests with men who spoke in metaphors of war. Yes, battles ensued when Black women aimed to exert authority over men—in churches, at conventions, and at the ballot box. But that did not form the whole picture. Anna Julia Cooper offered a more nuanced portrait of what power looked like. It included self-governance: "Only the Black woman can say when and where I enter." It was driven by a quest for dignity: "The quiet, undisputed dignity of my womanhood." Her power would not come at the expense of others or by gamesmanship: "Without violence and without suing or special patronage." And her ultimate aim was dignity for men and women both. Cooper explained that when she as a Black woman took her seat or cast her ballot, "the whole Negro race enter[s] with me." Women's power was a route to dignity for all.[1]

RECONSTRUCTION OFFERED AN unprecedented set of promises to Black Americans. Southern states, as a condition of reentry into the Union, rewrote constitutions that fulfilled the purpose of the Fourteenth Amendment. Black Americans wasted no time and clamored to enter politics, at conventions, in legislative chambers, and in the streets. For the first time, Black Southerners acted as agents of their own governance—making laws and setting the terms for how power and resources would be shared. With the more than two thousand African Americans who held office during Reconstruction—from a US senator and Congress members to sheriffs and postmasters—the reality of a nation that was beyond slavery and white supremacy came into view. By the presidential contest of 1868, Black men in the North and South were at the polls, many of them casting their very first votes.[2]

Black women also played a part in this radically new scene. Black men may have been positioned to cast ballots, but women shaped all the deliberations that led up to Election Day. Black-led political meetings included women who helped to steer the future of their communities. Women's presence and their voices ensured that this new political culture was porous, informal, and alive with community spirit. Men would eventually serve as delegates, chairs, and spokespeople, but women prepared them to reflect the views of their families and their communities. When Election Day came, women went the polls and kept watch for those who might try to intimidate men who came out to cast their ballots.[3]

Black women knew the power of the vote and what it meant to use it. How to get there was the question. One way forward might have been joining the work of two new national women's suffrage associations: the National Woman Suffrage Association (NWSA) and the American Woman Suffrage Association (AWSA), where women were lobbyists and organizers and spearheaded litigation. But only a small number of Black women joined these new suffrage associations. The racism that persisted there often drove them out. And suffrage alone was too narrow a goal for Black women. They went on to seek the vote, but on their own terms and to reach cures for what ailed all humanity. The vision that Harper had promoted in the American Equal Rights Association showed Black women their own path.[4]

Too soon, Black women learned that the urgent interest of all of humanity included those very close to home: that of their husbands, sons, and fathers. The hard-won voting rights of Black men were under attack. Starting in 1877, federal authorities— Congress and the courts—made a devastating pullback from enforcement of Reconstruction's democratic promise. State by state, Southern lawmakers began to roll back the gains that new constitutions and civil rights acts had promised. This regime change took hold over the course of two decades, imposed by fits and starts, but from the start it was part of one movement that aimed to reimpose white supremacy. Violence and intimidation worked together with poll taxes, grandfather clauses, and literacy tests to keep Black men from the polls and office holding. The United States was on its way to a new political order, a new American apartheid regime built upon disfranchisement, segregation, and lynching, known colloquially as Jim Crow.

There was no reason to think that any constitution would protect Black women. Their rights were tested early on right where Frances Ellen Watkins Harper had told the AERA that they mattered most, in transportation. In 1872, Josephine DeCuir tested who she was before the law after a steamboat company refused her entry into a ladies' stateroom as she headed north, up the Mississippi from New Orleans. In protest, DeCuir spent the night in an anteroom intended for nursemaids and their charges rather than lay her head in the "bureau," short for the Freedmen's Bureau, the colloquial moniker that Southern ship operators gave to their quarters for Black passengers. DeCuir was not a newcomer to this dilemma. Captains and clerks later recounted the many instances in which she had groused, held fast to a white-only ladies' seat, and insisted on equal access. She spoke only through her lawyer during the lawsuit—in a complaint, during cross examination, through briefs—never submitting to questioning. That would only repeat the original offense.[5]

DeCuir relied upon Louisiana's 1868 Constitution, a text drafted by radical men, Black and white. Article XIII guaranteed: "All persons shall enjoy equal rights and privileges upon any conveyance of a public character…without distinction or discrimination on account of race or color." In the proceedings, DeCuir heard the steamboat's indignities now recrafted into words. She was curiously said to be like a white man—someone absolutely barred from the ladies' cabin. She was also compared to "repulsive and disagreeable" persons whom everyone agreed steamboat operators could exclude, segregate, and expulse at will. At the US Supreme Court, the state laws that guaranteed DeCuir's right to travel as she chose were said to violate the US Constitution's commerce clause, an impermissible regulation of trade between the states. It was a clinical conclusion that could not cool the hot indignity that DeCuir felt.[6]

The doors to courthouses and legislatures were closing on Black women who aspired to win their rights and preserve their dignity. There was, however, another opening. In their churches, Black women saw the chance to make a revolution that was all their own. There, debates over women's power had a long history and struggles in churches kept Black women close to the institution-building work in which they took pride. A church-women's movement kept them linked to men, children, and even those women who opted out of politics. Churches also insulated Black women from the worst that white supremacy had in store.[7]

THE EARLY YEARS of Reconstruction kept preaching women busy as their churches shifted their focus from the North to the South. The AME Church relocated its headquarters from Philadelphia to Tennessee, and the AME Zion Church similarly left New York for North Carolina. Church leaders—especially those among Black Methodists—called upon women to help fill new sanctuaries with new converts. The status of these women was, however, far from settled. Women worked in their churches holding only loose and even unorthodox understandings of how high they could rise. Even as they faced uncertainty and skepticism, these women widened their circles, preached across lines of

Supreme court

rhetoric today!

denominations and of color. They relied on a time-tested strategy: women's effectiveness would win them expanded power.

Amanda Berry Smith had success in the pulpit but never managed to breach the color line that divided her from white women
preachers. She had been born enslaved just outside of Baltimore.
Her father worked to liberate their family and relocated Smith
and her siblings to the Free State of Pennsylvania. Her parents
saw to it that Smith went to school, but too soon she was sent
out to work, earning her living as a domestic worker, a cook,
and a washerwoman. Her hardships only increased when Smith
lost first one and then a second husband, along with four of
her five children. She had long sensed that she was called to
preach, but widowhood gave Smith the freedom to learn precisely what that meant. Smith got her start at her local sanctuary, Philadelphia's Green Street AME Church. By 1869, she was
traveling regularly between churches and camp meetings, where
she became known as a powerful evangelist, a reputation that
eventually carried Smith and her ministry to England, India, and
Africa.[8]

Smith never felt limited by the obstacles that men placed in
her way. Many Christian leaders drew sharp lines between denominations. Smith did not. She paid little mind to whether her
hosts were Methodists, Baptists, or Presbyterians. She preached
to anyone who would listen. Though born in Maryland, Smith
never regarded herself as limited by her Southern roots or her
origins in the United States. She traveled the world and found
common ground with other Christians and candidates for conversion everywhere she went. Smith also did not defer to any
color line. Her greatest supporters were laywomen—Black and
white. Smith knew how some church leaders used women's
sex to limit their power. She pushed back, speaking out openly
in support of women's right to preach and be ordained to the
ministry.[9]

The racism Smith encountered marred her work. Often, white
women preachers kept her at the margins. She was disappointed

in more than one encounter with Sarah Smiley, a popular preacher who started life as a Quaker but spent her career preaching to a wide range of Christian sects. In 1870, Smith was invited to hear Smiley speak during a Bible reading at the Twenty-Fourth Street Methodist Church in Brooklyn, New York. Upon arrival, Smith was encouraged to sing a hymn prior to Smiley's taking the pulpit, and she obliged. Smith then stayed on to hear Smiley's Bible reading but was taken by surprise when she was inexplicably escorted out of the sanctuary. One of Smiley's confidantes explained that Smith was not welcome to share the venue with her white counterpart. Smith left, tearful and despondent.[10]

Smith and Smiley met a second time in another awkward encounter when both were touring Britain. Smiley offered Smith advice about her preaching schedule and, at first, her suggestion sounded generous. Smiley discouraged Smith from making a stop at Broadlands, where, Smiley advised, Smith would encounter ideas that would trouble her mind. Smith kept to her original schedule and only later discovered Smiley's true, self-serving intention. Smiley hoped to redirect Smith to where Smiley's associates hoped that Smith would draw large crowds to their events. Smiley did not mean to protect Smith from troubling ideas; she had meant to save her own supporters from the disappointment and embarrassment of small crowds. Smith only learned this later, a discovery that left her feeling exploited by another preaching woman.[11]

Smith was also slighted in print. She never met Phebe Hanaford, author of the 1877 book *Women of the Century*, published for the centennial of the United States to document the national debt owed to women. Hanaford was an ordained pastor in the Universalist Church, a suffragist allied with Elizabeth Cady Stanton and Susan Anthony and the American Equal Rights Association, and a prolific writer. Her 640-page tribute to American women included hundreds of biographical essays that highlighted women's "patriotism, intelligence, usefulness, and moral worth." Across twenty-seven chapters, Hanaford charted women's contributions to US history and culture. Somehow, she overlooked Amanda Berry Smith.[12]

Hanaford did mark the achievements of African American women, though only in a paternalistic and diminishing tone. She wrote of women like the eighteenth-century enslaved poet Phillis Wheatley, who demonstrated Black women's intellectual capacities: "Even African women, despised as they have been, have intellectual endowments." The part that Wheatley's "mistress" played in the poet's education further demonstrated the virtue of white slaveholding women: "Colonial women, though some of them slaveholders, were not destitute of a lively interest in those the custom of the times placed wholly in their charge." Mary Peake, a teacher of former slaves on the Sea Islands, evidenced the morality of the American Tract Society when it endorsed "Christian effort without regard to race or color." Frances Ellen Watkins Harper was "one of the colored women of whom white women may be proud." Why other women should take credit for the self-made Harper, Hanaford never explained. Among those noted under the heading "Women Lawyers," was Charlotte Ray, an 1872 graduate of Howard University Law School: "Ray...said to be a dusky mulatto, possess quite an intelligent countenance." She "doubtless has also a fine mind, and deserves success." Sculptor Edmonia Lewis was included among "Women Artists," a "waif" possessed of "perseverance, industry, genius, and naïveté," all of which had earned her the admiration of white Americans. In every instance, Hanford offered only backhanded praise when it came to Black women.[13]

Hanaford gave generous space to churchwomen activists of all sorts. Three chapters—"XIII. Women Preachers," "XIV. Women Missionaries," and "XIX. Women of Faith"—made up 15 percent of the book overall. Hanaford lauded the great contributions that American women had made to religious life. The same chapters were, however, remarkable for whom they left out. Not one African American woman nor one Black churchwomen's organization is mentioned. It is a notable omission.

Hanaford certainly was aware of Smith and women like her. The *Woman's Journal*, one of Hanaford's principal sources, along with the national press reported regularly on Smith's work. It was an awkward oversight and at worst it was an erasure of Smith and other Black women preachers.[14]

Critics subjected all preaching women to similar criticism. In turn, preaching women, Black and white, agreed that men regrettably monopolized the pulpit, leaving women unacknowledged and uncompensated for their talents and labors. All women faced skepticism when they stepped into the pulpit, and they defended themselves by claiming a true calling from God. Laywomen supported preaching women—as hosts during their visits, companions during their travels, and devoted listeners during their sermons. Still, a color line kept Smith from Smiley's meeting halls and Hanaford's pages. Not to be overlooked or forgotten, Smith wrote herself into the record in 1893 when she published her life story, *An Autobiography: The Story of the Lord's Dealings with Mrs. Amanda Smith, the Colored Evangelist.*[15]

As CHURCHWOMEN OF the 1870s prepared to make a full press for their rights, they renewed an old struggle. Boundaries of race and gender limited the work of women, from Jarena Lee in the 1820s to Amanda Berry Smith in the 1870s. Laywomen had consistently done the work—raising funds, staffing Sunday schools, attending to ministers, and filling the pews at each service. But something new arose in the years after the Civil War. Perhaps it was an accumulation of struggles over many decades, like a boiling over of women's demands. Debates in the secular realm certainly fueled it, when churchwomen heard Black women in political circles making claims to power. Black women were disappointed by the outcome of the preceding decade's debates over voting rights in the American Equal Rights Association. They had won a half victory only when some among that coalition endorsed the Fifteenth Amendment. But that compromise did not end their quest for political power. They brought those same aspirations to church.[16]

Eliza Ann Gardner led the way. She had come of age in Boston in the decades before the Civil War. During the day, her home life ran on the rhythms of work and school. Her father, James, labored as a stevedore and eventually became a modest entrepreneur in a busy port, where he hired "his own crew" and provided "the handcarts, blocks, tackles, and winches to load or unload vessels and to move cargo between ship and warehouse." Eliza spent days at school, where she excelled through a "keenness of her mind" and "retentiveness of her memory," though none of this excused her from lending a hand to everyday chores.[17]

Evenings and weekends were different. Whether she was eavesdropping while perched on the edge of a settee, pouring cups of tea, lost with her nose in the pages of *The Liberator*, or at attention during church or in a meeting hall, Eliza came to know many of the era's radical luminaries. Thinkers from William Lloyd Garrison, John Brown, and Frederick Douglass to Sojourner Truth and Charles Sumner stretched her horizons across the endless miles of the lecture circuits. These were lessons in politics that no primer taught.[18]

Gardner's home, 20 North Anderson Street, was set in Boston's West End. There, and in nearby Beacon Hill, Black Bostonians clustered around institutions such as the Baptist African

Officers of Convention of 1895 (Mrs. J. St. P. Ruffin, Mrs. Hannah Smith, Mrs. Florida R. Ridley, Miss Eliza Gardner). Historical Record of 1895–1896 of the Colored Women of America, 1902
NATIONAL PORTRAIT GALLERY

Meeting House and the Abiel Smith School, where, as a girl, Gardner attended the city's only public school for Black students. Her family's home was, however, no ordinary place. In the years before slavery's abolition, the Gardner home was known as a "Bethel" for fugitive slaves, a safe haven for those fleeing bondage and the grasp of fugitive hunters. After her parents' deaths, Gardner transformed it into a place of needles, thread, and fabrics, the tools of her trade as a dressmaker. Yet it remained a haven, as Gardner extended a caring hand to young women in need of work. She also took in boarders, men and women who traded coins for a warm and dry bed, which ensured that Gardner remained financially independent late into her ninth decade.[19]

When those who admired Gardner dubbed her the "Julia Ward Howe of her race," they complimented the strength of her commitments—antislavery and women's suffrage were interests Gardner shared with Howe, a white Bostonian. There, the similarities between the two parted ways. Gardner centered her activism in a spiritual home, the AME Zion Church. In 1858 she made her public debut when organizing a fundraiser for her local congregation, the Columbus Avenue AME Zion Church. It was a start at transforming women's church work. Gardner and three others titled themselves "managers," and then held a fair "for the laudable purpose of raising funds to enable them to build a more comfortable House for the Society to worship in." Gardner never aspired to be a helpmeet to those men who controlled her denomination. Instead, as a woman manager she was prepared to lead others for the good of the collective "society." Gardner discovered how to build women's power and it was a project that would last a lifetime.[20]

By the 1870s, Gardner was ready to directly address churchwomen's rights, and this turn was no happenstance. She was a student of history and knew that, since the 1840s, Black Methodist women had been demanding, and for a brief time had even won, the right to preaching licenses. Something new was in the air, however, and it was talk of women's suffrage. During the 1860s, Gardner had witnessed how abolitionists and women's rights allies had clashed over women's voting rights in the American Equal Rights Association. At home in Massachusetts, she had seen Black women activists, along with the Republican Party and statehouse leadership, put women's suffrage on the agenda, only to fail. There was more work to do.[21]

At the podium, Gardner never failed to put women's concerns first. "Our fathers and *mothers, too,* fought to secure that glorious boon of liberty," Gardner admonished those who assembled in Boston at the 1876 centennial celebration of the Declaration of Independence. The emphasis is hers. Women's fundraising, she believed, was a key to their power, and Gardner's remarks came along with a $100 contribution on behalf of the Ladies' Charitable Association, a "society composed of colored women." As if to underscore the women's political savvy, she emphasized that they had "voted" to assist the Centennial Committee—operating by political, even democratic, principles. Then came the bargain: "We have made this effort for more than one reason," Gardner explained. Black women had been among the nation's founders and "are American citizens, all attempts to waive our claims to that title to the contrary notwithstanding." Gardner hoped to be thanked for the women's gift, and then expected to be fully recognized as a rights-bearing citizen. Had they been listening, leaders in the AME Zion Church would have done well to take heed. Gardner was coming for them next.[22]

In 1868, the Sisters of Zion, women of Gardner's Boston congregation, turned to the matter of church law, the *Doctrines and Discipline.* They began by giving it a close, careful read. Sexism, they discovered, was baked into the foundation of their denomination. So, the women got to work, demanding that terms like *man* and *male* be purged from law. In anticipation of an upcoming general conference, they drafted a request that the church's governing body "remove all words, etc., from the *Discipline* of our church which prohibits females from having the same rights and privileges as male members." It was a request made "respectfully" but unequivocally. Women like Gardner expected to have the same rights as their fathers and husbands.[23]

The general conference did as asked, and the law changed, without a fight. For Gardner's and Zion's churchwomen, it was a first victory, but they were not done. The women formulated a next set of demands that included a call for their right to hold office. And again they won. The church created the Office of the Deaconess, a team of women lay leaders to be appointed within each congregation. Soon women began appearing in church conferences as delegates representing the men and women of their state or region. They took seats as decision makers—hundreds gathered to debate the church's future—engaged in lawmaking, and otherwise directed AME Zion's governance. It was a sea-change. Soon women preachers received licenses as part of ordinary business, and few objected when a woman stepped into the pulpit to interpret the scripture. Women petitioned for control of their missionary work and won a new Ladies' Home and Foreign Missionary Society, where they controlled the direction of benevolent work, including how the dollars and cents they raised were spent.[24]

Gardner led by a style that mixed directness with wit. She won over both men and women with an appeal to equality in AME Zion. The key to her success lay in the terms of a bargain in which women leveraged their labor to win power: "If you will try to do by us the best you can…you will strengthen our efforts and make us a power; but if you commence to talk about the superiority of men, if you persist in telling us that after the fall of man we were put under your feet and that we are intended to be subject to your will, we cannot help you." It seemed that the churchwomen's movement in AME Zion had won. Then, trouble surfaced. As women—those ordained to the ministry—stepped up to exercise power over men, Zion Church plunged into stormy waters.[25]

WHEN JULIA FOOTE and Mary Small became the first women ministers in the AME Zion Church, Emily Bird-Walters stepped in to defend them. Bird-Walters explained them as two facets of women's collective power in 1899. Foote and Small were not exceptional when they became equal to men, she explained. They were just two figures among a pantheon that included writer and lecturer Frances Ellen Watkins Harper, journalist and anti-lynching advocate Ida Wells-Barnett, artist Edmonia Lewis, and club leader Victoria Earle Matthews. The women ministers were in step with AME Zion's own Eliza Ann Gardner and the itinerant preacher Amanda Berry Smith. Such women, although their concerns and goals varied, Bird-Walters saw as parts of a whole: "While she shines as a star of greatest magnitude in the home...she can also when sufficient opportunity is given or circumstances demand, shine as brilliantly on the platform, in the halls of legislation and in the arenas of art, science, literature, philosophy and reform, as man."[26]

Bird-Walters wrote emphatically. She had to. A maelstrom had erupted when the two women—Foote and Small—rose to the pinnacle of ministerial authority, ordained as deacons with full rights to preach, preside, and participate in church governance. If this breakthrough was to survive its opponents, it would do so only if advocates and allies stepped into the fray. Women in AME Zion had been talking about their rights for decades. Their strides were evident. And still there were those who aimed to halt their progress and impose a ceiling, preserving the highest offices for men alone. Two women who had long labored for the church and, some argued, deserved their ordination by right, inspired the charge against sexism.[27]

Foote was the more seasoned of the two. Her career had a rough start when, in the 1830s, her minister expelled her from a Connecticut congregation for holding prayer meetings without his permission. Her response was to organize with other women and petition for a license. To prove her calling was genuine and her skills formidable, Foote held open-air meetings, where women demonstrated their capacity to attract converts. In 1879, Foote recounted this rocky beginning in a spiritual memoir, *A Brand Plucked from the Fire: An Autobiographical*

Sketch. With a book in hand, Foote's public work was newly launched. By the early 1880s, she was crisscrossing the country and logging thousands of miles as a much-sought-after evangelist, a featured speaker who drew the lapsed, reluctant, and curious into Methodism. She need not preach churchwomen's rights to endorse that cause; as one commentator in Topeka, Kansas, put it: Foote's presence "encourages our women; too many of them believe as the men do that a woman should not preach, nor occupy a public position in the church."[28]

Mary J. Small, born a generation after Foote, came late to her calling, joining the church in the 1870s after her marriage to minister John Small. Initially, she resisted the feeling that she was destined to preach, "being somewhat unfavorable to lady preachers." Her time was occupied with raising the two young nieces who lived with the Smalls. She finally gave in to "the call of the blessed master" in 1892 and began to interpret the word of God. Small stepped out from her husband's shadow, secured a license, and was soon sharing the Sunday pulpit with him in their local York, Pennsylvania, congregation. Unlike Foote, who built her reputation as a traveling itinerant, Small remained close to home until she was promoted to the intermediate post of Elder in 1896. With that, she extended her reach, headlining weeks-long revivals in major venues, while also directing the work of the Ladies' Home and Foreign Missionary Society. Critical to Small's rise—she was elevated to the office of Deacon in 1898—were her alliances with powerful men, including her husband, who would soon to be elected a bishop, and ministers, who saw up close her capacity to win converts to their congregations.[29]

Churchwomen broke through and became equals in AME Zion, and a firestorm erupted, one fueled by white supremacist forces from outside of the church that were robbing Black men of their political rights. The promise of Reconstruction's experiment in interracial democracy was being brutally crushed by the imposition of a new, racist regime, that became popularly termed Jim Crow. In courts, in legislatures on city streets and along rural lanes, violence, disenfranchisement, and segregation were changing the terms of Black life. Black men's brief but very real contributions to new, postwar lawmaking were being undone. Black churches and schools remained among the few institutions available to those men who aspired to leadership. In AME Zion, many men and some women experienced the suppression of their political and economic lives. Women were urged to step back and let men regain the lead.[30]

Foote and Small ducked below the crossfire as Zionites took to the pages of the church's newsweekly, *Star of Zion*, to debate the women's fates. Opinions flew as fast as the paper was delivered across the nation. Neither woman spoke publicly. Instead, their supporters spilled countless bottles of ink defending them. Some members of AME Zion clashed face-to-face in conferences, as happened in 1898 when Small was ordained an elder at the May meeting of the Baltimore Conference: "When it became known that she was a candidate a number of ministers protested and asked the bishop to give them a hearing." But most protests were delivered in print through exchanges so heated that even local papers noted the furor: Zionites were hurling "cannon balls" at "female preachers" and faced a "hot time" ahead as the "question of female elders in Zion Church is being fought and discussed from every point of the compass." For observers, the spectacle provoked one part concern and another part amusement. Everyone wondered: Would leaders strip Foote and Small of their ordinations?[31]

The debate consumed all of 1898. Men approached the matter of women's rights as if it were something to be worked out between them. They underestimated Zion's women, who refused to let men determine their fate. Their prior victories emboldened women who had tasted power by voting, holding office, and controlling the purse strings of missionary societies. They worked apart from men in the office of the deaconess. Churchwomen joined the debate, wielding words, lobbing opinions, and otherwise speaking out. They were being tested, and, in response, the women of Zion did not sit back and follow the debate but directed its course with the sharpness of their pens and tongues.[32]

Views on women's ordination paralleled controversies in politics. The question was put: Should the ideas about women's equality that were animating politics—including the suffrage movement—penetrate policy and practice in the church? Some argued that, whatever might be transpiring in the secular world, the church should remain independent and indifferent: "The 'New Woman' is becoming most too new. The next General Conference should toll the death knell of this petticoat ministry." Women preachers might be fine, even if women in politics were not. The Reverend Josie Mayes, herself an evangelist, supported women like Julia Foote. In the church, women's talents, Mayes admitted, were often superior to those of men. Still, Mayes could not endorse a "new woman" when she aspired to mount the rostrum and remodel politics. That would be going too far.[33]

For some, ordaining women was consistent with progress: "The nineteenth century is one of improvement in all lines, ecclesiastical, literary and scientific." Churches were like political parties, the argument went. All such institutions should expect to keep up with the "times," as Rev. B. J. Bolding put it. That meant supporting women like Foote and Small, whose status reflected an improvement. Sarah Dudley Petty, wife of a Bishop, addressed the matter with a poetic flourish: "Christian generosity, keeping pace with the advanced ideas of to-day, has overleaped the once insurmountable barriers, and to-day, to the called female church worker there is no majestic Shasta looming up before her, with sexual prejudicial peaks and impregnable sentimental buttes saying 'thus far shalt thou come and no farther.' " Sexism, then, should be relegated to the past.

When it came to women's equality, for Reverend Chambers the answer was obvious: "Woman is not man's equal, and the claim is simply ridiculous." Those who agreed with Chambers relied upon old stereotypes: "A woman is not physically able to pastor a church." The duties were beyond women's reach:

"She is too timid and fearful to get up at one or two o'clock in the night, unless some man is with her, and go across the city to see the sick or pray with some one ready to die." Women might compromise the dignity of church rituals: "She is not able and would be a pitiful looking object standing in the river trying to baptize a lot of heavy men and shouting women." No matter that women had long endured on the lecture circuit: "It would be too hot and dusty in the Summer and too cold and slushy in the Winter for her to walk ten, fifteen and twenty miles on a circuit in the country to try to preach the gospel." The demanding itineraries Foote and Small kept, effort witnessed firsthand by dozens of congregations, directly refuted charges of women's physical fragility.[34]

In contrast, others spoke of women as equal to men. "'In Christ Jesus there is neither male nor female,' Gal. 3:28, is the magna charta [*sic*] of women's rights in the church. If it means anything, it is that males and females stand on equal footing in Christ's Church." Bishop James Hood chided: "On the question of woman's rights I should like if possible, to be clearly understood." He pushed back against the view that "woman is the weaker vessel." "The test of strength is not what a thing is capable of doing once or for a little while," Hood explained, "but its capacity for endurance." Hood spoke as though he had seen women in action: "Put a woman in the sick room and let her be anxious respecting the recovery of a loved one, and where will you find a man possessing the staying qualities that are found in her?" The differences between men and women did not determine their fates: "It could be admitted that man is stronger physically, it must be remembered that we have a mental as well as a physical nature, and to find the strength of an individual you must consider the entire person, body, life and soul." Maggie Hood-Banks, a bishop's daughter, linked arms with Foote and Small: "Our idea has been to show to the world woman as she is, that she is equal in all respects and where the power of imagination, perception and emotion of the soul is the point of judgment, she is superior, in many respects, to man."[35]

Among church leaders were men who followed the lead of women, from Maria Stewart to Frances Ellen Watkins Harper, and condemned sexism and racism as equally wrong. AME Zion should dispense with both. Bishop Hood explained what equality meant in his church: "Christianity is destined to give, eventually, both to woman and to the Negro, the rights of which they have long been deprived. Both can fully rely upon that heaven-born system, and wait with confidence supreme." It was time to reject arbitrary lines of difference drawn by men, not God, and Eliza Gardner urged Zionites to view women ministers in the long history of their church: "It has been one hundred years of joy and sorrow, labor, conflict and triumph. The century has witnessed the emancipation of man and the almost severed bonds of woman. 'Tis glorious though that this grand old Church...is the first religious organization to accord to women...the same rights she accords to [men,] the sterner sex."[36]

The debate threatened to reveal that women were not merely equals but often outperformed men. Even commentators who opposed ordaining women managed to undercut men's leadership: "We have too much useless ordained male timber lying around in all of our conferences; why begin now on the women?" Mrs. Rev. Moore cut through much of the long-winded opposition: "Brother S. A. Chambers says there is no authority for the ordination of women. Our brother does not see through eyes of faith, but looks at Sister Small with eyes of jealousy." The church should avoid squandering women's distinct contributions: "Suppose God has a work for this sister to do which some of us men cannot or will not do, and we attempt to get into her way; what will be the consequence?"[37]

The debate over women's power went to the heart of Christianity. Mrs. Franklin Clinton, widow of a late minister explained: "Some of you brethren talk about women being unfit to deliver Christ's message. Christ commissioned them first Himself to carry the good news. While men were clamoring for his blood it was the women who pleaded at the cross to have His life spared. Where were His disciples when women rushed through that murderous crowd of soldiers to the very foot of the cross? Women embalmed his body and first greeted Him after the resurrection." Women had been most Christ-like, she chided: "If you brethren would listen more to women you would arouse the world....Why not arouse a missionary spirit and help these poor churches and ministers and not fret about who will be Bishop? Christ was the first missionary. Brethren, imitate him." Her tone was mocking, reflecting Mrs. Clinton's confidence, earned during many years of leadership in church missionary societies.[38]

Foote and Small were among the many women preachers who had already earned a track record of success. They converted one skeptic: "After hearing a number of these [women,] partly out of curiosity as most of us do for a time or two." Clarissa Betties, writing from Calvert, Texas, defended Reverend Small: "Let her alone; she is doing what you won't do. I will be glad when the time comes that those men will find something to do and let Rev. Mrs. Small alone." Women laid the church's foundation, sustained ministers, sanctuaries, and Sunday schools: "Methodist women...know well enough that we form a majority of the membership; that we furnish a large part of the spiritual life, and that we collect most of the money of the Church. We believe and know that this entitles us to share in the government of the Church; and whether the Church law provides for it or prohibits it, cuts no figure with us. We shall continue to claim our rights."[39]

Most difficult to refute was the view that Black Christianity rejected all bigotry: "The doctrine of equality, Christianity thunders against all wrong and seeks to breakdown every stronghold of oppression, blotting out the distinction of race, sex or caste. From this point of view there is neither Jew, Greek, bond nor free, male nor female, for all are one in Christ." If AME Zion fully committed to women's equality, it would stand above all other denominations. Changes to church law erased "the only discrimination against the rights of women found in our laws, blotting out that relic of a state of barbarism in which 'might makes right.'" This was a logical and even natural extension of an insistence upon racial equality: "For a hundred years we have been pleading for and demanding the equal rights of citizens, without regard to color. Is it any wonder that we recognized the fact that the same arguments which, as to equality of rights, abolish the sex line." History mattered. "As a rule where a white man was an abolitionist he was per consequence an advocate of women suffrage[.] Fred Douglass was consistently an ardent advocate of both Negro and of woman suffrage. These lines are from his pen: Right is of no sex, Truth is of no color, God is our common Father, And all mankind are brothers. To my mind they are not only epigrammatic, but immortal."[40]

Eliza Gardner watched from her "sick room" in Boston as opinions flew on the pages of the *Star of Zion*. Finally, she felt compelled to speak, and her words were harsh: "I have read with pain some of the articles that have been sent to the *Star* vilifying woman, for some of them were unworthy of the pen of a true woman. And as I read some of their bitterer passages, I wondered if mother, wife, and sister had inspired in these gentlemen no chivalry, and if so of what sort it could be." The bar was high, she conceded, for men, who must accommodate to the full effects of women's rights. It was also high for women, who would now bear the new burdens that power imposed. AME Zion was not alone and was instead part of a greater shift toward women's equality in all things. Zionites watched as white Methodists wrestled with similar questions when the head of the Women's Christian Temperance Movement, Frances Willard, tried to take a seat in their general conference: "Our Church has seen to it that…there should be no bar to place or position on account of sex," Gardner boasted.[41]

Churchwomen's rights were women's rights, and the values that promoted suffrage also supported the right to ordination. Bishop Small explained: "Two things caused [me] to become an American citizen—America's tenacious clinging to the Gospel of Jesus Christ, and her fearless and liberal recognition of her women. In [my] mind, these are the things which will make any nation great; and if this country perseveres in holding up these two principles, nothing can keep her from standing at the head of the nations of the world." A nation, like a church, only showed its weakness when it aimed to "baffle the success of a woman...to legislate her to the rear." Lay leader John Dancy confessed that "he believed in woman's rights as much as he did in man's," and urged that "woman's cause is man's; They rise or sink together Dwarfed or God-like, bond or free."[42]

In some moments, the debate over women's ordination clearly borrowed from ideas about the vote. Mrs. Holden, before writing to the *Star of Zion*, likely had read Anna Julia Cooper's words in *A Voice from the South*: "Should we ask what factor was most needed in taking the world for Christ, we would say woman, for a nation, as a river, cannot rise above its source. Neither can a nation rise above the virtue, intelligence, strength and character of its womanhood, for women are the mothers of men." The thinking of white women suffragists could also be heard. When Maggie Hood-Banks analogized the status of women to that of enslaved people, she was borrowing directly from Elizabeth Margaret Chandler, who in 1836 had likened the oppression of women to that of enslaved people: "If we confine our views to the female slaves, it is a restitution of our own right for which we ask—their cause is our cause—they are one with us in sex and nature." Coming from Hood-Banks, the analogy was all the more potent. If the position of AME Zion's women had been like that of enslaved people, those same women were descended from people who had actually been enslaved.[43]

The debate came to an end only as women drove a bargain that had been proposed long ago by Eliza Gardner. Women's work for AME Zion was dependent on men's support for their leadership. Hood-Banks explained, "For centuries woman was considered inferior to man, and in view of this fact had no rights man was bound to respect." It was a neat play on language from the notorious Dred Scott case. No African American wanted to be charged with bigotry analogous to that of Chief Justice Roger Taney, who in 1857 declared that no Black American could be a citizen of the United States. There was a way forward for her church, Hood-Banks suggested: "With the advance of Christianity she began to be more respected, more noticed, thus honored more, until now there is no place or position too great for her to hold." If women's possibilities were limitless, so was their bargaining power. Her tone turned stern: "I warn you that the women are not always going to submit to the second place. They are not always going to work hard to raise money unless they can have full control of all the facts connected with it. They are getting very tired of 'taxation without representation,' and equally tired of raising money for some of the men, who cannot raise their salaries."[44]

Hood-Banks's final quip—"Fair play, brethren"—put the men of her church on notice. And she was heard. Before the year was over, most had heeded her warning and the opposition to women's ordination quietly fell away.[45]

CHURCH ACTIVISM DEMANDED that women be armed with ideas and with stiff backs. It also demanded that they spend time on the road. Church conferences, local, regional, and national, were sprinkled throughout the year and across the nation's landscape. Meeting minutes did not reflect the many hours and multiple conveyances it took to get to the next city or a far-flung hamlet. Conference deliberations generated the collective will that was essential to the Methodist model of governance and could only be enhanced (but never replaced) by newspaper columns or pamphlets. Nothing was riskier for Black churchwomen than those hours in carriages, on the rails, and aboard streetcars. Whether traveling in the company of men, oftentimes their minister husbands, or alone, Black women faced a cruel and dangerous set of arrangements. More than any other travelers, they risked the indignity and danger of cars designed for men or the prospect of ejection from the ladies' cars set aside for women travelers and their companions.[46]

Selina Gray traveled with her husband, William, a minister, foremost concerned with the fragile health of their small child.

They were seasoned travelers headed, one day in 1881, between Cincinnati and their home in Lexington, Kentucky. The family had purchased first-class tickets and expected to ride in the ladies' car, where men were permitted to enter in the company of female travel companions. A judge explained his version of Gray's dilemma: "She had a right to say that she would not travel in the smoking-car. It is very unpleasant for gentlemen, sometimes, to sit in a car of that character. Not every man likes smoke; not every man likes tobacco. It is bad enough for them to force a gentleman…let alone forcing a lady there with a sick child." To this, Gray added, the "refusal was because she was a woman of color wholly." Gray never boarded the train. Instead, her family split up, with her husband heading home in the smoker while Gray waited behind with their child, returning later by another route that would accommodate them in the ladies' car.[47]

Little was sure as Black women, tickets in hand, exposed their lives to the whims of brakemen, conductors, and railway officials. Women were armed, if only with expectations borne of past travels, and they pressed on, trying to meet the urgent demands of sick and dying children or expectant and demanding employers. Risk taking—defiance in the face of those who aimed to regulate their travel—became part of the bargain, and the ladies' car was a proving ground. Entering coaches of plush seats and respectable comportment—or attempting to—was a defining encounter that, to see it through, might justify missing a workday, compromising health, or separating a family. Dignity and indignity fused as women invited ridicule, discomfort, disarray, and worse.[48]

Anna Julia Cooper had women like Selina Gray in mind when she penned her 1892 manifesto, *A Voice from the South*. Cooper had been born enslaved in North Carolina on the eve of the Civil War. She was trained first in the nearby Saint Augustine's Normal School and Collegiate Institute and later at Oberlin College. She would go on to earn her PhD from the Paris-Sorbonne University in 1925, when she was in her sixties. But in 1892, she was a founder of the Washington, DC, Colored Women's League. By day, Cooper taught Latin at Washington's M Street High School. During the evenings, she was at work on her book, which argued that it was time for Black women to claim political power.[49]

Cooper regretted that Black women were marginalized in churches. Her example was an 1886 gathering of Protestant Episcopal Church ministers. They, Cooper charged, had failed to win members among Black Americans in the South. Why? Black men and women had been overlooked. White church leaders had failed to invite Black men into the denomination's leadership, rendering its work "purely theoretical" and "devoid of soul." Their second error was the failure to develop "Negro womanhood." Black women's leadership was "fundamental to the elevation of the race," Cooper explained. The church had missed an opportunity when it failed to build upon their "agency in extending the work of the Church." The failure had been fatal: The "church training, protecting and uplifting our colored womanhood [is] indispensable to the evangelization of the race."[50]

Cooper also knew that women like Gray experienced cruel scrutiny on trains and streetcars. The choice that they faced— between the smoker and the ladies' car—captured the stakes that Black women had in winning power. Cooper's wit was her weapon when she wryly promised that Black women would comply with laws that demanded they sit somewhere other than the ladies' car. They would do so in a utopian world in which railroads provided to Black women cars that were equal in all other respects to those available to white women. It would be a marvel: "I might wonder at the expensive arrangements of the company and of the state in providing special and separate accommodations for the transportation of the various hues of humanity." Of course, such a turn was impossible.[51]

Cooper added her story to the many that women told about traveling while Black. Drawing upon a true experience, Cooper speculated that she might comply with a request to change her seat if a gentlemanly conductor asked that she move to a well-appointed car set aside for Black ladies. But anything less would win only her rebuke. She told how she resisted when "a great burly six feet of masculinity with sloping shoulders and unkempt beard swaggers in, and, throwing a roll of tobacco into one corner of his jaw, growls out at me over the papers I am reading, 'Here gurl,' (I am past thirty) 'you better git out 'n dis kyar 'f er don't, I'll put yer out.' " Cooper revealed her contempt for the man, an "American citizen who has been badly trained." And she did not give up her seat.[52]

Above all else, securing dignity most concerned Cooper: "There can be no true test of national courtesy without travel." It was the demands of her body and of her spirit that set the country's high bar. Travel invited vulnerability: "The Black Woman of the South has to do considerable traveling in this country, often unattended." She affirmed a collective tale of rough indignities, "personal violence to colored women traveling in less civilized sections of our country, where women have been forcibly ejected from cars, thrown out of seats, their garments rudely torn, their person wantonly and cruelly injured."[53]

Cooper had been wounded when the politics of respectability failed despite her efforts to be "quiet and unobtrusive in her manner, simple and inconspicuous in her dress." Still, "gentlemanly and efficient" railroad conductors failed to extend to Black women the same courtesies they eagerly provided to others. Black women lifted their own satchels and steadied themselves as they stepped down to the platform. They bore this "unnamable burden" silently, their discomfort quietly signaled by "the heaving bosom and tightly compressed lips." There were innumerable inconveniences and slights to be endured, but the truest burden was "the feeling of slighted womanhood [which] is unlike every other emotion of the soul."[54]

Black women aspired to freedom from the tyranny of conductors and brakemen, one dimension of their full liberation. Which car one rode in was a matter of equality: "When I ... apply for first-class accommodations on a railway train, I do so because my physical necessities are identical with those of other human beings." The "unique position" of Black women upset the same routine transactions. They were confronted "by both a woman question and a race problem," in Cooper's analysis, a dilemma that remained generally "unknown or...unacknowledged." It was not enough for Black women to fight their battles for the ladies' car, be it with wit, writs, or fisticuffs. They would also need to speak for themselves. No one else could: "Our Caucasian barristers are not to blame if they cannot *quite* put themselves in the dark man's place, neither should the dark man be wholly expected fully and adequately to reproduce the exact Voice of the Black Woman."[55]

Struggles over the ladies car inspired Cooper's battle for women's rights and the vote. When they confronted railroad officials and the passengers who witnessed their abuse, Black women joined the "great national and international movement...based on the inherent right of every soul to its own highest development, [a] movement making for woman's full, free, and complete emancipation." Black women's dignity would emerge through a movement that saw how "its own 'rights' are the rights of humanity": "Woman's cause is the cause of the weak; and when all the weak shall have received their due consideration, then woman will have her 'rights,' and the Indian will have his rights, and the Negro will have his rights, and all the strong will have learned to at least deal justly, to love mercy, and to walk humbly."[56]

CHURCHWOMEN HAD MANAGED a revolution in AME Zion. It reflected one dimension of the needs, concerns, and goals that Black women carried with them as they moved between sacred and secular spaces in the 1890s. Julia Foote, Mary Small, and Eliza Gardner led a women's movement in their church. They did not leave their politics in the sanctuaries of their denomination. Instead, they brought them along into emerging civil rights circles. Julia Foote accompanied Zion's Bishop Alexander Walters to gatherings of T. Thomas Fortune's new National Afro-American League, a precursor to the twentieth century's

NAACP. The league's New York City branch elected Walters a delegate to an upcoming convention. Foote made an impression strong enough to secure her place as an alternate delegate, empowered to speak on civil rights and church politics. When Mary Small was not attending church conferences, she could be found at Women's Christian Temperance Union (WCTU) gatherings. There, she provided opening "devotional exercises," a scriptural reading, which fit with her status as a minister. Also in the WCTU, Small linked arms with women working toward women's suffrage and passage of the Nineteenth Amendment.

In 1895, Eliza Ann Gardner was among the Black women leaders who convened a first meeting of the National Association of Colored Women. It was the birth of a movement that would mobilize Black women's power for many decades to come. Gardner was singled out for leadership, a recognition of her years championing women's rights in the church. The convention designated her its chaplain. Gardner provided the opening and closing prayers at the association's very first meeting. She was a force behind the founding of another Black women's movement, one that combined their energies to tackle national problems under the motto "lifting as we climb."[57]

When Eliza Ann Gardner signed an 1899 letter, "Yours for Zion and the complete redemption of women every where," she expressed a political philosophy in which the struggle for the rights of churchwomen was one facet of a fight for women's rights everywhere. AME Zion activist women moved nimbly between sacred and secular circles, cross-fertilizing each with ideas about their rights—including their capacities to vote and hold office. These were not women who made stark choices between the pulpit and a temperance hall, or between missionary society fundraising and a club movement convention. Just as political debates informed their religious deliberations, women's work in churches was a route to rights consciousness, an occasion for honing arguments, and a proving ground for their capacities for leadership, governance, and even political wrangling. In this there was power.[58]

Chapter 6

LIFTING AS WE CLIMB

Black women's politics did not start in a women's movement. But when it was time for them to organize independently, the principles were already understood. Josephine St. Pierre Ruffin, the head of the National Federation of Afro-American Women, boasted in 1895: "Our woman's movement is woman's in that it is led and directed by women." Not to be confused with organizations driven by a single interest or exclusive in its goals, she noted what made her organization stand out: It was "for the good of women and men, for the benefit of all humanity." The NACW would build upon the years Black women had spent in antislavery societies, churches, and civil rights organizations: "We want [and] we ask the active interest of our men, and, too, we are not drawing the color line; we are women, American women, as intensely interested in all that pertains to us as such as all other American women." The women of the NACW would not, however, take a back seat to anyone: "We are not alienating or withdrawing, we are only coming to the front, willing to join any others in the same work and cordially inviting and welcoming any others to join us." Who might accept their invitation, Ruffin did not speculate. Only time would tell.[1]

THE 1890S DEMANDED nothing less than visionary leadership. Times were tough for reformers who bore witness as Jim Crow thinking became enshrined in law and policy. The US Supreme Court gave its decisive stamp of approval to this view when it decided *Plessy v. Ferguson* in 1897. Separate was equal in the court's eyes. Women's suffrage work went ahead haltingly. It won small victories in the West, but the movement was stalled. In 1875, the US Supreme Court concluded in the case of *Minor v. Happersett* that the Constitution did not guarantee to women, or any American, a right to vote. The Senate refused to put forth a women's suffrage amendment to the Constitution in 1887.[2]

In the last gasp of the nineteenth century, the nation's future became wedded to white supremacy. Congress and the US Supreme Court lent succor and legitimacy to the countless Southern officials who ran roughshod over the rights and the lives of Black Americans. Often termed the nadir or the low point of American race relations, it was a period during which Reconstruction was turned upside down, like a feed sack, and all that had been built was scattered to the winds. Black Americans gathered the bits of Reconstruction that they could—their schools and churches—and held fast to them. Segregation was the order of the day, and it was far more than custom or personal preference. It was a way of life, in public and in private, and authorized by law. It broadcast how one race, a Black one, was subordinate to the other, white.[3]

Jim Crow was more than separation. Violence was its central pillar and it took public, ritual form in the practice of lynching. Kidnappings, torture, and barbaric killings were the hallmarks of this brutal brand of terrorism. Lynching was also spectacle, crowd-pleasing demonstrations of the absolute power of white over Black performed in front of dozens and even hundreds who gathered to gawk, encourage, and even grab a souvenir photo or artifact, including parts of a now dead victim's person. The state played its own role in these gruesome scenes. Local officials turned away, juries declined to convict, and even postmasters permitted the mail to extend the reach of lynching by circulating graphic images on postcards. The fate of any one victim scarred their family, friends, neighbors, and the entirety of Black America, as news reports warned of the worst that white supremacy was capable of.[4]

Lawmakers and mobs alike rendered the polls off limits to Black men. Not only did federal courts decline to protect their voting rights, they approved state laws that disqualified many Black Americans as voters. Local officials also worked their angle, letting discretion determine who was administered which literacy or understanding test, and then who passed. They combed voters' rolls, using discrepancies of names, addresses, or residency to strike Black men in anticipation of Election Day. They imposed grandfather clauses—meaning that a voter would have to prove that their ancestors had voted before 1867—knowing full well that no descendant of enslaved people could affirm their fathers had cast ballots before the Civil War. Poll taxes sat uncollected until a Black citizen had cleared all the other obstacles. Then, more like a fine than a reasonable demand for a tax, sums that had accumulated over many years were presented like a bill, the payment of which became one more hurdle to casting a ballot. Black voting rates plummeted, and few white Americans thought much of it.[5]

Black politics took a civil rights turn that mobilized political savvy, journalistic bite, probing research, and mass membership to challenge Jim Crow. The early organizations, such as the National Afro-American Council and the National Afro-American League, drew together leaders from education, religion, and politics to hone a critique and to strategize. By 1909, what had begun in 1905 as the Niagara Movement took hold, producing the National Association for the Advancement of Colored People, the leading civil rights organization of the twentieth century, known best for its long legal campaign against Jim Crow. Its founders included men such as W. E. B. DuBois and Archibald Grimké in partnership with Black women, including Ida B. Wells and Mary Church Terrell. It was impossible to position such women as mere helpmeets. That time had passed. Terrell was

the nation's most prominent Black suffragist, and Wells was unequivocally a brilliant journalist and the country's most effective
antilynching advocate, bar none.[6]

Women's suffrage associations had struggled enough that
leaders regrouped. The two parallel organizations merged into
the National American Woman Suffrage Association (NAWSA)
and committed to a campaign that would work state by state to
win American women access to the polls. Some western states
permitted women to vote, deeming suffrage an asset to state
building in territories that still looked to attract white residents.
Elsewhere, women voted in local elections. Still, most American
women remained disenfranchised by state law.[7]

Black women referred to the years after 1890 as "the wom-
en's era." Although the idea was in no way ironic, it was remarkable how at the very moment that Jim Crow's proponents
purged Black men from much of public life, Black women were
firming up their place in political culture. At the center of this
turn was the founding of the National Association of Colored Women (NACW). It built upon benevolent networks that
stretched back at least as far as the Civil War, a long view that
let Black women see what troubled the nation and fueled its
inequalities. By founding an independent organization, the new
pavestones on their road to political power were laid.[8]

The NACW spearheaded the conventions, newsletters, and
personal connections that knit together Black women—led
mostly by middle-class women but including many working
women active in their local clubs and associations. The leadership bore shared characteristics: descended from slaves, educated
at Oberlin or a historically black college or university (HBCU),
elocution training or a talent for public speaking, and a belief
that Black women would work in the interests of all humanity.
At its inception, the NACW joined together nearly two hundred
local clubs from across the country—North, South, West, and
Midwest—under its umbrella. Incorporated as the National Association of Colored Women's Clubs in 1905, by 1924, its membership totaled nearly a hundred thousand women.[9]

Clubwomen were of many hues, but all had to develop a thick skin. Jabs born of racism and sexism were the ordinary taxes they paid as they sought alliances and influence and built new hubs of power. Not unlike preaching women before them, clubwomen endured the indignities and dangers of travel aboard streetcars, trains, and ships. Their view of suffrage reflected club-women's histories and the political insight this accorded them. If neither Black churches nor the NAACP could contain them, neither could NAWSA or the later National Women's Party. Though they became increasingly independent, the women of the NACW did not abandon the struggles of Black men. Experience had taught them not to divide themselves between woman-hood and Blackness.[10]

THE NATIONAL ASSOCIATION of Colored Women gathered under the motto "Lifting as we climb." This philosophy brought thou-sands of Black women into politics and aimed to bring on board thousands more. Clubwomen were on the rise, and they intended to reach a hand out to pull all Black women up with them. Club work drew women beyond familiar settings like the schoolhouse and church, and their leadership consolidated at a national level. Their motto also admitted that the politics of the clubs was pre-mised on inequalities in a metaphor that posited some women above others, and some women in need of help and others in a position to provide it.[11]

James Jacks, then president of the Missouri Press Association, galvanized clubwomen when he publicly ridiculed Ida B. Wells and her antilynching campaign and then impugned all Black women, branding them prostitutes, thieves, and liars. Jacks's words ignited a "pressing…need of our banding together if only for our protection." The NACW was more than an emergency response. Its first president, Mary Church Terrell, in her speech "The Progress of Colored Women," explained how Black wom-en's politics grew out of a history that they shared, in part, with white women: "Elizabeth Cady Stanton, Lucy Stone and Susan B.

Anthony began that agitation" while millions of Black women remained enslaved, she explained. Black women had, however, come to create their own political organization "not because we are narrow and wish to lay special status upon the color of the skin....But we refer to the fact that this is our association of colored woman, because our peculiar status in this country seems to demand that we stand by our selves." Their needs and their ambitions could not be met elsewhere: "It was thought best to invite the attention of the world to the fact that colored women, as a unit realize their responsibility." First, they had to combat the "false characterization and salacious slanders [that] are circulated against us every day, both in the press and by the direct descendants of those who in years past were responsible for the moral degradations of their female slaves." In politics, Black women put themselves first, while also working for the interests

Mary Church Terrell
(1863–1954)
GETTY IMAGES

of all humanity. The rising tides of Jim Crow demanded nothing less.[12]

Terrell never hid her support for women's voting rights. She made clear her commitment to winning the ballot even when it put her at odds with other leaders. Terrell organized a distinct constituency, a national network of Black women to combat lynching, secure civil rights, and even work toward the vote. She and her husband shared a partnership of mutual cooperation and equality, an industrious partnership in which they were matched in ambition and savvy. Terrell never shied away from alliances with white women, especially when it suited her aims, and she traveled nationally and internationally in circles where she was often the only woman of color. She held public office, used her status to develop working relationships with members of Congress, and knew how to exploit them to her advantage.[13]

The belief that she was the equal of any—including white women, and men of all colors—ran deep in Terrell, and it had been instilled in her at an early age. She was a child of privilege, born in Tennessee to parents once enslaved who gave their daughter a cosmopolitan upbringing filled with travel, clothing, and ideas. At Oberlin College, where Anna Julia Cooper was her classmate, Terrell had taken the more demanding "gentleman's" course and thrived among students—Black and white, men and women—who, when they mingled, challenged conventions. As a student and later as an activist, Terrell traversed the United Kingdom and Europe, sometimes alone, where her mastery of languages, deft diplomacy, and an unflappable sureness won her many admirers. It wasn't always clear where Terrell's sense of confidence ended and her sense of superiority began. She was an elite, a woman of what W. E. B. DuBois termed the African American "talented tenth," who spoke earnestly for all women and still, sometimes, talked down to those who were "ignorant and poor."[14]

Washington, DC, was the place to be for a young woman of Terrell's experience and ambition; the city fueled her talent for politics. She arrived in 1890, taking a post in the Latin

Department at the city's fabled M. Street High School, where she came to know Robert Terrell, who would soon graduate from Howard University School of Law. When the two married in 1891, Terrell was already working as an activist and public speaker. When in 1892 Terrell was a speaker at the esteemed Bethel Literary and Historical Society, she was one of only two women among luminaries such as newspaper editor T. Thomas Fortune, US Supreme Court justice John M. Harlan, and minister Alexander Crummell. When her turn at the podium arrived, Terrell spoke of the subject that no one else dared broach: "The Ethics of Woman Suffrage."[15]

Terrell saw the problems of "race" and "sex" as intertwined, part of one great concern for humanity. She did not privilege the so-called rights of women over the rights of Black Americans. Her women's cause included the battle against lynching, for example. In 1893 at a Washington, DC, antilynching meeting, with Frederick Douglass presiding, Terrell introduced Ida B. Wells. The two women had known one another as friends from when they had shared time in Memphis, Tennessee. Terrell condemned what she termed "Southern Mob Rule" and lauded Wells "for her undaunted courage [and] zeal." Going forward, Terrell would follow Wells's lead and join a circle of activists who pressed Congress to act against lynching when state officials refused to do so. She accompanied Wells, Frederick Douglass, and others in urging the US Senate Judiciary Committee to hear them on the "lawless outrages" that "denied [Black Americans] the ordinary means of establishing their innocence by due process of law." The two women would maintain a long, though strained, alliance through their shared commitments.[16]

Terrell amassed a set of distinctions along the way. She became a household name among Black Americans. And she was a "first" when, in 1895, the DC board of commissioners appointed her to the Board of Trustees of Education for the District of Columbia. There, she pressed for innovations in early childhood education. That same year, Terrell was among those who launched an early civil rights organization, the National

Afro-American Council. She would go on to be elected vice president of the council's District of Columbia branch and later direct its national antilynching bureau. As a writer, Terrell's words won her followers among readers of the *Colored American* and the Black Methodist's *A.M.E. Church Review*; she also reached white audiences in the *Washington Post* and the *North American Review*. She was a powerhouse.

Each spring, Terrell was a commencement speaker—one sign of her national reputation. She gave these addresses at institutions that included North Carolina Agricultural and Mechanical College; the Normal School at Albany, Georgia; Georgia State Industrial College; Livingstone College; the State College at Savannah; the Agricultural and Normal School at Covington; and scores of high schools. Terrell took part in the eighth of W. E. B. DuBois's Atlanta Conferences of Negro Problems, giving a presentation titled "The Negro Woman and the Church." And in 1909, she attended the inaugural meeting of the NAACP, joining its board of directors, along with Carrie W. Clifford—they were two Black women helping to launch the newest civil rights organization. When in 1912 the women of Washington celebrated Terrell, a local paper dubbed her "the peerless queen of the platform, for her valiant and effective services in behalf of humanity, her race and sex."[17]

Terrell stood out and oftentimes stood alone when it came to women's suffrage. It was a risky subject for a middle-class woman who practiced the politics of respectability. Stumping for women's votes might have undercut Terrell's reputation as a paragon of Victorian comportment and sensibilities. At least this was the case in the eyes of editors at the *Colored American*. When Terrell spoke at Washington's Second Baptist Church Lyceum on suffrage, the paper felt the need to reassure readers: "Mrs. Terrell sacrifices not one iota of her womanly graciousness and her charming and stately attractiveness is not diminished one degree by the position she takes on this vital question." Her ability to express provocative ideas in conventional terms enabled Terrell to draw men to her way of thinking. After her remarks, the paper reported, the "discussion grew so interesting that when the time was all gone, President Thompson announced that a continuation would be granted at an early day [and] Mrs. Terrell was given an ovation." Terrell changed minds that weren't always open at the start of her remarks.[18]

Terrell's commitment to women's voting rights also earned her warm regard, and even outright affection. In a light-hearted Christmas Day feature in the *Indianapolis Freeman*, the editors printed a list of "Desirable Presents for Well-Known People." In Terrell's case, they imagined a gift suited specially to her: "A woman suffrage bill passed by Congress." It was a festive way of acknowledging how deep Terrell's women's suffrage commitments ran. The same editors made sure that Black women were not left in the movement's shadows. They observed, in 1912, that white women were engaged in a bit of political theater and "making up cabinets which they would like to have constructed to advise the President." The *Freeman*'s editors published their own African American slate and they nominated Mary Church Terrell for Secretary of the Interior. It was a flight of fancy that also revealed how Terrell inspired innovative thinking about Black women in politics.[19]

Racism ran through organizations like the National American Woman Suffrage Association (NAWSA), but Terrell never avoided the suffrage circles organized by white women. She publicly expressed admiration for Elizabeth Cady Stanton and especially Susan Anthony and explained that her own work for women's voting rights was part of a broad tradition of women's activism that had begun with women abolitionists and had consolidated in 1848 at Seneca Falls. Terrell did not dwell long on the problems of marginalization or exclusion that plagued the Black women in these organizations. Instead, she focused on promoting the insights and interests of Black women as equally important in the past and the present.

Terrell maintained a strategic distance, however, and her engagements with NAWSA's leaders often looked like ritual performances rather than deep collaborations. When the year 1898 marked fifty years since the women's meeting at Seneca Falls, New York, the anniversary gave Terrell a platform. She attended that year's NAWSA convention, and when her turn came, Terrell didn't just speak—she flipped the script. The year was a "double jubilee," she reminded her audience, and marked not only the anniversary of Seneca Falls. That same year marked three decades since ratification of the Fourteenth Amendment and "the emancipation of my race." The title of her talk, "The Justice of Woman Suffrage," called out the injustices that tainted suffrage work. Still, Terrell managed to keep her connections with white suffragists. In 1902, she represented the white-led Equal Suffrage Association at the Washington, DC, meeting of NAWSA. There, Terrell was welcomed and then elected a "life member" of the association.[20]

Terrell's work took her to Europe in 1904, where, in Berlin, she addressed the World's Conference of Women in a speech called "The Progress of the Colored Women in the United States." In many ways, this was a pinnacle of her early career. Still, her most important work in this period was with the National Association of Colored Women. Through their local clubs, Black women responded as Jim Crow drew their families, communities, and reputations as women into racism's fray. In 1896, Terrell's leadership had brokered a consolidation of Black women's clubs. It was a triumph of diplomacy and a model of leadership in troubled times.[21]

Though she led, Terrell did not always drive the NACW's agenda and in the earliest years her commitment to women's votes was relegated to the margins. After two terms as president, Terrell stepped away from the helm and was then free to openly press voting rights onto the NACW agenda. Women like Terrell and Rosetta Lawson, an education and church activist, urged clubwomen to take seriously winning the vote, "the pioneer force for woman's emancipation and progress." Local clubs mirrored this view, such as in the Women's Improvement Club of Louisville, Kentucky, where suffrage was among the topics debated at regular meetings.[22]

The NACW was slow to respond. The change finally came about thanks to the persistence of women like Adella Hunt Logan, an instructor at Booker T. Washington's Tuskegee Institute. Logan made a full-throated plea for the NACW to join the white-led National Council of Women of the United States. The move would be a "gainer" for the NACW, bringing Black women's politics closer to white-led organizations like the NAWSA: "Wonders have been wrought for humanity in general and woman in particular, by that grand band of women, under the leadership of the sainted Lucretia Mott, scholarly Lucy Stone, the sweet poetess, Julia Ward Howe, the brilliant Elizabeth Cady Stanton and...every woman's champion and friend, dear Susan B. Anthony." Logan's thinking was tempered by the realization that gaining political rights as women could not take Black women the full distance to equality. Racism would persist: "I do not claim that woman suffrage will set the whole catalogue of wrongs right. I do see that it is one thing that will go a great way toward removing injustice and oppression."[23]

Some within the NACW determined to keep their organization at a distance from the suffrage movement, especially its most radical factions. In 1906, Margaret Murray Washington, president of the NACW and wife of Tuskegee Institute's president Booker T. Washington, explained that Black women's politics were distinct from those of white women: "The Anglo-Saxon woman has found her status in the affairs of men and state by the effort of the pioneer women who worked and fought for woman's suffrage. The colored woman of the race has found her status in the home by the earnest labor of women of the race who, for the past ten years have been making a way,—raising standards for motherhood and home." Washington promoted Black women's right to be mothers and homemakers. This remained a valued privilege for women living just one generation from slavery. Murray was determined to defend the homes of NACW women from the indignities that their mothers and grandmothers had endured. This meant keeping Black women at a distance from radical suffrage politics.[24]

Washington challenged the efforts of women like Terrell, who inserted voting rights into the midst of NACW proceedings. Earlier in the same year, 1906, Terrell had taken the floor during the NACW convention just long enough to introduce a resolution in honor of Susan B. Anthony, who had died some months before. It was a heartfelt tribute to someone for whom Terrell had sincere affection. It was also a subtle effort to rally other clubwomen to Terrell's way of thinking about suffrage politics. By 1908, Terrell and other Black suffragists won a decisive victory when the NACW established a "woman suffrage department."[25]

Still, the distance between Black women's clubs and the white-led suffrage movement grew in these years. Terrell was often all alone when she attended NAWSA events. For her, keeping alive the memories of how Black and white suffrage advocates had once been allies had a symbolic value. In 1908, when the sixtieth anniversary of Seneca Falls came around, Terrell made a pilgrimage to that place as part of a group assembled to re-create the original gathering. Terrell had been invited to stand in for the late Frederick Douglass, who had been the sole Black American to go on the record in the 1848 women's convention. There was no small irony in how it had taken six decades for a Black woman to finally take part in the proceedings at Seneca Falls. Still, Terrell, who had been mentored by Douglass, was honored by this passing of the mantle to her, as an individual and as a suffragist.[26]

Terrell was increasingly on the offensive when it came to women and the vote. She continued to present "The Justice of Woman Suffrage" to audiences, but by 1912 her remarks reflected a new impatience with those Black Americans—men and women—who spoke against women's votes. She may have had Margaret Murray Washington in mind: "It is difficult to believe that any individual in the United States with one drop of African blood in his veins can oppose woman's suffrage. It is queer and curious enough to hear an intelligent colored woman argue against granting suffrage to her sex, but for woman's suffrage is the preposterous and ridiculous thing in the world." Terrell's primary targets were, however, Black men who stood for equal rights only until women claimed them, and she ridiculed them: "What could be more absurd than to see one group of human beings who are denied the rights which they are trying to secure for themselves working to prevent another group from obtaining the same rights?" She pointed out the parallels between voting rights for women and for men: "For very arguments that are advanced against granting the right of suffrage to women are offered by those who have disfranchised colored men." Critics of women's votes engaged in hypocrisy: "If I were a colored man, and were unfortunate enough not to grasp the absurdity of opposing suffrage because of the sex of a human being, I should at least be consistent enough never to raise my voice against those who have disfranchised my brothers and myself on account of race."[27]

Washington remained at odds with Terrell into the next decade. When news reached Washington that Alice Paul and the NAWSA were planning a 1913 women's march in Washington, DC, she did not remain silent for long. Washington lobbed another volley in an old debate with Terrell and others in the NACW. Marching in the streets, in Washington's view, was beyond the bounds of a clubwoman's correct comportment: "Our attitude toward the suffrage is the conservative kind. We have not blown any houses with dynamite nor have we been engaged in parading the streets in men's attire." She would not march for women's suffrage, and Washington hoped that other women would follow her lead. She was not indifferent to the question, however. Black women prepared for the likelihood that the polls would open to them: "Of one thing I am certain, we are reading and studying the great questions which are to make for the good of the country, and when the vote is given to women as it surely will be...we shall be ready to cast our votes intelligently." Both sides of the debate agreed that once they won the vote, Black women would use it. They differed on how to get there.

MARY CHURCH TERRELL was on the lecture circuit as Alice Paul and the NAWSA's Congressional Committee wrapped up their plans for a Washington, DC, suffrage parade in March 1913. Even in the last days, Terrell did not let on about whether she would attend. She spoke to the students of Wellesley College, just outside of Boston, on Wednesday evening, February 26. The next day, a Thursday, she had two events, back to back. In the afternoon, Terrell appeared at the Academy of Music and delivered "The Emancipation Proclamation and the Development of Christian Womanhood in the South" for the Brooklyn Institute for Arts and Sciences. She had just enough time for a quick meal before at eight joining proceedings at Brooklyn's Concord Baptist Church of Christ, where the North East Federation of Women's Clubs and its Department for Suppression of Lynching held a "large demonstration." The following afternoon, Friday, Terrell spoke to the New York Women's Missionary Society.[28]

Busy as she was, Terrell headed back to Washington. But it was more than the women's march that drew her there. Up ahead, she could see a political minefield. The time from 1913 to 1914 would test her political skills: Mississippi's senator-elect James K. Vardaman would soon arrive in Washington, riding on a campaign promise to repeal the Fifteenth Amendment. A new president, Woodrow Wilson, was moving into the White House and no one could predict his position on Black officeholders such as Terrell's husband, Judge Robert Terrell, of the Municipal Court of the District of Columbia. Terrell's pursuit of the vote was intensified by these challenges, ones that went to the well-being of Black men as well as women.[29]

The prospect of a parade tapped into Terrell's attraction to political theater. In African American politics, parades had a long history, starting with mid-eighteenth-century festivals, including Pinkster, a derivation of the Dutch holiday of Pentecost, and Negro Election Day, during which Black militias engaged in public drills. With the 1808 abolition of the international slave trade came a new set of public processions, marking a step forward in the overall movement to end human bondage. August 1, also known as West Indian Emancipation Day, honored the liberation of enslaved people in the British Empire. By the end of the Civil War, Black men and women punctuated major victories with parades, such as in 1870 when, in Baltimore, there was a national celebration of the Fifteenth Amendment. In many cities, the Fourth of July was an occasion for marches that filled city streets.[30]

Still, Paul's 1913 parade—planned and peopled by women—was something new. And the prospect of Black women participating unsettled the organizers. The NAWSA had long worked by way of a dirty compromise with white supremacy that put the interests of Southern white women above those of Black women, no matter where in the country they were from. Paul later recalled that she had deployed an organizer to encourage the "college woman" at Howard University to attend the parade, and she settled the matter of precisely where they would march by assigning them to the "college section," adjacent to a delegation of men, and where Paul herself would march. Objections to the Black women's participation poured in, and Paul nearly balked.[31]

The parade was tainted by the ambivalence that surrounded the prospect of Black women marchers. Terrell's NACW collaborator Carrie Clifford noted that the local suffrage committee had been "reluctant" to encourage Black women to join in. Black suffragists faced "conflicting rumors" that "disheartened many" who had good reason to stay away. NACW president Margaret Murray Washington worried that Black women would be discredited if they marched. They risked unsexing themselves by joining an event that she likened to civil unrest. Julius Taylor, editor of the *Broad Ax*, a Chicago weekly, mocked the women as unattractive, disorganized, and generally without a purpose.[32]

In the few days she had between lectures in New York, Terrell headed back to Washington. She made her way to the parade that morning along with dozens of Black women who shared education, vocations, and middle-class circles of philanthropy and sociability. There was Clifford, a poet and Terrell's ally in the NACW, the NAACP, and antilynching work. Sculptor May Howard Jackson, whose husband taught in the city's local schools, appeared. Director of the Washington Conservatory of Music Harriet Gibbs Marshall and Howard University–trained pharmacists and drug store owners Dr. Amanda Gray and Dr. Eva Ross joined the parade. There was a contingent of so-called college women that included Oberlin College graduate and advocate for early childhood education Anna Evans Murray, M. Street School French instructor Georgia Simpson, and Smith College graduate Harriet Shadd. Howard University students—sorority members—joined the procession decked out in caps and gowns. At least three Black women marched with their state delegations, a Mrs. McCoy with Michigan, a Mrs. Duffield with New York, and Ida B. Wells with Illinois: "Mrs. Ida B. Wells-Barnett, proudly marched with the head officials or with the head Ladies of the Illinois delegation showing that no Color line existed in any part of the first national parade of the noble women who are in favor of equal suffrage." After much strife within the Illinois delegation, Wells marched alongside the state's white women and ended the day satisfied with their joint presence.[33]

Some concluded their thinking about the march by sweeping the tensions under the rug. Looking back, Julius Taylor at the *Broad Ax* judged that racism had been kept at bay during the 1913 march: "No color line existed in any part of it. Afro-American women proudly marched right by the side of the white sisters." Black women warranted special credit, in Taylor's assessment. They had been present and, perhaps despite his fears, they "were accorded every courtesy and did nothing to reflect discredit on the race." It was an odd assessment given how much strife Black women had faced in the weeks before the march.[34]

Black men also had a role to play that day, especially when violence descended upon the marchers. Thousands of spectators confronted the five thousand women paraders, and the scene devolved into a near riot. The city police were charged with maintaining order, but while the crowd jeered at, spit upon, and assaulted the women, officers left the them to fend for themselves. Everyone acknowledged a small group of heroes: African

American police officers who stepped between the mob and the marchers. Elizabeth Balloch, a government stenographer and suffragist marcher, explained: "I observed the efforts of a colored policeman, which I thought were quite conspicuous....As I went along I noticed the policemen, as a rule, stood quietly. There was very little said or done. But the only efforts really actively made, as I happened to notice, were by this colored policeman."[35]

For Black Washingtonians, there was irony in the stories marchers later told about the efforts of Black officers during a Senate hearing. Committee members learned what Black women already knew: the presence of Black officers on the city's streets enhanced women's safety during parades and on any given day. Despite this, their appointments had fallen off in recent years, leading Black activists to call out city administrators who failed to make new appointments and promote rank-and-file officers. When Black men left their posts, white police replaced them, and when they arrested white suspects, Black officers risked being brought "up on charges" by Southern senators. The presence of Black officers on Washington's streets was a civil rights matter, a special concern for Black women who could not travel far without "being insulted by white men." Their safety and, it turned out, the safety of white suffragists depended upon it.[36]

Terrell hardly had time to catch her breath after the women's parade before she confronted the prospect of Black men losing federal protection for their voting rights. On his way to Washington was Mississippi's newest senator, James Vardaman, the state's former governor. Black news outlets did not avoid Vardaman's arrival, or its implications. The Democrat had been elected on a platform built almost exclusively on the promise that he would bring about the political death of African American men. His state had already gone a long way toward this end by using its authority over voter registration and the polls to exclude Black men from election days. As a newly elected member of Congress, Vardaman proposed to take disfranchisement to the national level and called on federal lawmakers to repeal the Fourteenth and Fifteenth Amendments and wipe away federal provisions for equal protection, due process, and voting rights. He aimed to stop the "Black peril."[37]

Vardaman's views had a history. As governor of Mississippi, he had, as far back as 1904, urged his party to repeal the Fourteenth and Fifteenth Amendments. Failing to persuade, Vardaman put the idea in his "pocket and returned to his home in Mississippi, at the same time vowing that at no distant date he would be elected [to the] US Senate and would introduce the same resolution and deliver the speech of his life against the Colored Race." With the start of the Sixty-Third Congress in March 1913, Vardaman's moment had arrived. And he had fellow travelers, Southern senators who promoted anti-Black legislation when exercising their power over the District of Columbia. Senator Thomas Hardwick of Georgia, for example, had recently introduced a bill to prohibit the "intermarriage of Whites with Negroes and Mongolians, etc., in the district."[38]

African Americans disagreed about how to regard Vardaman's threat. Some were sure that the new senator was little more than a man who had bamboozled white voters into thinking he could fulfill their dreams of unbridled white supremacy. From this perspective, Black Americans had so many friends and allies in Congress that Vardaman, although a distraction, was little more than that. Editors of the *Washington Bee* mocked the senator: "Vardaman stands as much chance of receiving a serious hearing on the 'issue' he represents as he would were he attempting to bring about the abrogation of the Declaration of Independence."[39]

Others were less sure. They counseled caution as Vardaman took his seat in the Senate chamber. He was not a lone radical white supremacist in Congress. Instead, Vardaman was part of a faction committed to building consensus around repeal of the Fifteenth Amendment, even if it was an uphill battle. St. Louis lawyer Walter M. Farmer spoke to Black activists at the Bethel Literary Society about men like Vardaman: "I owe no apology for calling these men the leading statesmen of the country. For no one will deny that these men have more influence in forcing their views of the Negro on the American people and on the world for that matter, than all the other statesmen North, West and East combined. The pendulum seems to have swung back, and it looks as if liberty was about to suffer defeat."[40]

It's not clear that suffragists saw it coming when, in March 1914, Vardaman stepped into the debate over a women's suffrage amendment. For months, the Senate had been back and forth over whether to put forward a new voting rights amendment to the Constitution. Those exchanges had always been influenced by fears that, if the law guaranteed women the vote, Black women might be enfranchised, strengthening the influence of African Americans and the Republican Party. When the issues stalled, Vardaman was among those who pressed forward with a compromise: the repeal of Black voting rights in exchange for women's suffrage. It was classic political horse trading and a crude attempt to exploit anti-Black racism to further white women's political empowerment. Vardaman promised that even Southerners, long known to be indifferent, if not hostile, to women's voting, could be brought on board in support of the so-called Anthony Amendment if it would win them unbridled white supremacy without federal interference. Vardaman was no feminist; he was not even a suffragist. But he was a dealmaker, and the prospect that he might carry the day set off alarms for women like Terrell.[41]

Rather than repeal the Fifteenth Amendment, Vardaman proposed that Congress enact an end run around it. He took the floor of the Senate on March 5, 1914, to promote the amendment drafted by Elizabeth Cady Stanton nearly forty years earlier. Yes, he conceded, the Constitution should provide that "the right of citizens of the United States shall not be denied or abridged by the United States or by any State on account of sex." To these words, he added a new clause: "but in all other respects the right of citizens to vote shall be controlled by the state wherein they reside." There was no question as to Vardaman's purpose. With this addendum, he aimed to empower the individual states to disenfranchise Black voters by whatever means they chose. Directly at odds with the Fifteenth Amendment and the rights of Black voters, Vardaman invited the Senate to join in a dirty alliance with those advocates of women's suffrage who had long been willing to sacrifice Black women's political power.[42]

Suffragists filled the Senate galleries during the debate, and at least one commentator was sure he could detect their astonishment when Vardaman proposed that women's votes might win at the expense of Black men. Vardaman had supporters and they were not limited to Southern representatives. Idaho senator William Borah took the floor in a twisted promotion of the Anthony Amendment. He advocated for women's votes, but then "declared it was impracticable and impossible to obtain through constitutional amendment so long as the fifteenth amendment remained unrepealed." Suffragists had "loaded themselves down with the color question, the Japanese question and a dozen other States' rights problems." Borah was an ally to white suffragists, and he was prepared to do business with Vardaman and "vote for the repeal of the fifteenth amendment, if only by so doing could equal suffrage be obtained." Vardaman chimed in: The Fifteenth Amendment had been "a blunder.... Time has not shown the colored man's capacity to participate in government or to rule the white man. While he has made some improvement, he is today as incompetent and unreliable as fifty years ago."[43]

Two weeks passed before a final vote and on that day Vardaman failed. He was, he told the Senate and the women who filled its galleries, planting a seed, staking a claim, and otherwise making one small step toward the political evisceration of Black men. At Vardaman's flank was his fellow senator from Mississippi, John Sharp Williams, who at the last moment proposed his own addendum to the women's suffrage amendment: the word *white*. That, too, failed. Still, when the clerk tallied the yeas and nays, "nineteen members of the United States Senate—all Democrats—voted to repeal the Fifteenth Amendment... and at the same time forty eight Senators—31 Republican, 15 Democrats, and 2 Progressives voted against the repeal of said amendment." It was a correct but hardly reassuring outcome for Black Americans.[44]

Black women had not missed one episode in this political drama. Its ins and outs revealed where Black men and women stood in political culture. Maggie Lena Walker—publisher of the *St. Luke Herald* and founder of the St. Luke Penny Savings Bank in Richmond, Virginia—let the facts speak for themselves: "This is interesting reading, and will doubtless cause some of us to stop and think a little while, if only for a moment. Our two U.S. Senators, Martin and Swanson voted to repeal the 15th Amendment." Walker placed a great deal of confidence in the view that if Black women built their economic power, they would control the destinies of their families and communities. Still, she knew that any attack on voting rights also did not bode well for Black women's political futures.[45]

Teacher and social worker Cecilia de Nellottz saw a bit more promise in Vardaman's defeat and doubled-down on the view that women's full political rights were in reach: "The voting strength of the world is about to be doubled and the new element is absolutely an unknown quantity. Does any one question that this is the most important political fact that the modern world has ever faced?" She put men like Vardaman on notice that Black women not only intended to vote but when they did they would use the ballot for their own ends: "The modern thinking, planning, self-governing woman came into a world which is losing faith in the commercial ideal and endeavoring to substitute in its place a social ideal. She became one with a nation which is weary of wars and hatreds, impatient with greed and privilege, sickened of poverty, disease and social injustice." The concerns of all humanity, an agenda pioneered by Frances Ellen Watkins Harper and Anna Julia Cooper, showed de Nellottz the way forward: "What will women do with their votes? The answer is simple: They will do with their votes precisely what they do, or try to do, without their votes....The Woman's cause is man's; they rise or sink together, dwarfed or godlike, bond or free. If she be small, slight-natured, miserable, how shall men grow?"[46]

Mary Church Terrell remained uncharacteristically quiet during the critical days when Vardaman's amendment was pending. There is, however, little doubt that she paid attention to every twist and turn of the Anthony Amendment—from its emergence from a Senate committee to its defeat by a floor vote. Why was the ordinarily forthright Terrell so circumspect? Her household was being hit by Vardaman's direct fire. Terrell's husband, Judge Robert Terrell, and his future had been caught up in the Mississippi senator's efforts to quash Black political power. Vardaman not only opposed Black voting—he also objected to office holding and aimed to use his power in the Senate to defeat Robert Terrell's reappointment to the bench. The Terrells together worked their connections to save Robert's career. While Vardaman was blustering in the Senate chamber, Mary Church Terrell went to work behind the scenes.

The Terrells had good reason to worry. Vardaman aspired to influence the new Wilson administration. The president and Southern senators had already clashed over the appointment of a Black American during summer 1913 when Adam Patterson was proposed as register of the US Treasury. Patterson, a Democrat, had been recommended by Senator Thomas Gore of Oklahoma and was Wilson's first African American nominee for a presidential appointment. Vardaman and his allies pounced. They were indifferent to Patterson's record as a Democratic Party loyalist and, some said, even an accommodationist on race relations. In a matter of days, support for his confirmation failed to materialize and Patterson withdrew. Wilson let it happen. The president was susceptible, if not sympathetic, to the color line that Vardaman sought to impose on federal office holding. Those commenters who had deemed Vardaman impotent had egg on their faces.[47]

Thus, when Vardaman aimed to put Robert Terrell off the bench, it was one part of a broader campaign to purge federal offices of Black men. That winter, Vardaman broadcast his plan to put forward a series of bills "the ultimate effect of which would be to expel Negroes from all government positions.... Holding of office is the symbol of sovereignty and the Negroes must not exercise sovereignty." Vardaman went public with his opposition to Terrell and preemptively "served notice on the President that he will oppose the appointment." Wilson was undeterred and, over Vardaman's objections, he moved to reappoint the judge, sending his name to the Senate for confirmation. This, of course, left Robert Terrell vulnerable to the senators who aimed to defeat him.[48]

Mary Church Terrell later recalled that she had "suffered much more than [her] husband" in this period. This she attributed in part to their differing personalities. Judge Terrell was "an optimist from the crown of his head to the soles of his feet," while she confessed to being sent to the "depths of despair." Terrell watched as Vardaman promoted an analogy between her husband and a fictional rapist. She witnessed a cruel caricature portray the judge as more animal than human. Privately she raged. But publicly Terrell composed herself and headed off to lobby men she had come to know through her work on education, women's suffrage, and lynching: "I would sometime go to the Senate and talk with the Senators who, I was sure, believed in a square deal. Without exception, they always received me cordially and pledged me their support."[49]

Terrell understood there were ties that might transcend the color line when it came to the judge's appointment. Her letter to Ohio senator Theodore Burton sheds light on how Terrell worked in Washington—building on commonalities and connections. Burton was, she knew, like her, an Oberlin graduate. In her letter to him, she put the judge's plight and her own despair on full display. Burton had an opportunity to oppose racism's arbitrary capacity to unseat a deserving professional and crush his spirit. The judge was an innocent, and still his case turned on a "great principle": opposition to the view promoted by Vardaman that African Americans "no matter how able, worthy or successful...shall receive no recognition [and] shall be driven from any position of honor or trust." Terrell also appealed for the assistance of "newspaper men," especially those for whom she had done "favors" by giving information.[50]

The Terrells quietly declared victory at the end of March 1914. As one headline put it: "Vardaman Gets a Very Rude Jolt. U.S. Senate Refuses to Regard His Anti-Negro Measures Seriously. Terrell to Be Confirmed...No Fifteenth Amendment Repeal." The Mississippi senator had been bested in a yearlong contest in which suffrage, civil rights, and the future of Terrell's family had all been violently tossed about. Terrell remained a deeply committed suffragist throughout. But the demands on her time and her politics extended well beyond any one cause. Terrell belonged to a world that demanded her politics be as multifaceted and nimble as they were ambitious.[51]

THE POLITICS OF clubwomen like Terrell were often hard edged—they lived at the podium, in newspaper columns, at congressional hearings, and in politicians' back rooms. At the same time, they operated within a world of Black women's history, enveloped in a cloak of decades-long movements. Clubwomen adopted naming practices that tell another story, one of how they derived from the women who came before them inspiration, strength, and sureness of purpose. Clubwomen gathered under the auspices of luminaries who had preceded them, an atmosphere that went beyond the podium or the pen.

For example, among the hundreds of clubs that affiliated with the NACW were the Sojourner Truth Club in Montgomery, Alabama; the St. Joseph, Missouri, Frances Ellen Watkins Harper League; and in St. Louis, the Phillis Wheatley Club. Pittsburg and Alleghany, Pennsylvania, combined, were home to the Frances Ellen Watkins Harper League, whereas Nashville, Tennessee, named its club for Phillis Wheatley. Adrian, Michigan, dedicated its club to Anna Murray Douglass, the wife of Frederick Douglass. Battle Creek, Michigan, her one-time home, named its club for Sojourner Truth. Fort Worth, Texas, was home to the Phillis Wheatley Club. Jacksonville, Florida, named its club the Phillis Wheatley Chautauqua Circle, and New Bedford, Massachusetts, deemed Josephine St. Pierre Ruffin its namesake. In February

1905, Terrell spoke to the Frances Ellen Watkins Harper Literary and Social Circle in Savannah, Georgia.[52]

Into the twentieth century, a crop of clubs named for Terrell herself flourished across the country: in St. Louis, Missouri; Albany, New York; Des Moines, Iowa; Los Angeles, California; Milwaukee, Wisconsin; New Orleans, Louisiana; Natchez, Mississippi; Pittsburgh, Pennsylvania; Nashville, Tennessee; Oakland, California; Marshall, Texas; Camden, New Jersey; and Akron, Ohio. These gestures were grand, weaving Terrell—her ideas and her activism—forever into Black women's political culture. She understood the impulse. Years before, Terrell had named her youngest daughter for the great eighteenth century poet Phillis Wheatley, ensuring that the young woman knew her place in the world was linked to the tradition of Black women's firsts. When her book *Poems on Various Subjects, Religious and Moral* debuted in 1773, Wheatley had been the first Black woman poet to be published. Their political history was written in the names Black women gave themselves and one another.

Chapter 7

AMENDMENT

By fall 1920, it looked as though Hallie Quinn Brown and the women of the National Association of Colored Women (NACW) had been left alone to drive the next phase of the fight for women's votes. Across the nation, they had appeared before registrars and clerks, but too many African American women had been rebuffed, rejected, and written out of the revolution that the Nineteenth Amendment promised. In winter 1921, Brown made one last effort to forge an alliance with Alice Paul and the National Women's Party, aiming to link forces and bring the promise of the new amendment to all women. Brown wrote to Paul about the upcoming unveiling of a monument to "our three pioneers of suffrage." The likenesses of three white women—Lucretia Mott, Susan B. Anthony, and Elizabeth Cady Stanton—were scheduled to be revealed at the US Capitol on February 15, the 101st anniversary of Anthony's birth. Brown's words admitted the strain she felt: "I am anxious," she wrote, "that the National Association of Colored Women's Clubs be represented on that occasion and shall appreciate *all* information bearing upon this matter."

Brown got what she sought in one sense. Paul made sure that Brown was there in the Capitol rotunda during the unveiling ceremony, representing the NACW in grand style. Accompanied by a flower girl, Brown posed before the statue while a royal purple banner proclaimed the presence of the National Association of Colored Women. Applause followed. Brown aimed to ride the celebration to full voting rights for all women. Behind the scenes, however, things did not go her way. A delegation of Black women called upon Paul just days before the National Women's Party Convention was set to begin. Their delegation aimed to win support for federal legislation that would give strong teeth to the amendment such that Black women could overcome the state laws that continued to disenfranchise them. The delegation was received. But before the NWP convention concluded, their aims had been rejected. Rather than continue to work toward women's full and free access to the polls, the organization declared its work completed and then folded. When Brown had reached out to Paul she had offered a slim olive branch by terming Mott, Anthony, and Stanton "our" pioneers. They might just be foremothers for Black and white women. Paul did not return the sentiment—no Black woman was included on the monument or her political agenda.[1]

THE 1912 ELECTION of President Woodrow Wilson set the stage for a major reordering of US political culture. The president quickly became an arbiter of who might be an American—and by what terms. He inherited the troubles of a country that had grown increasingly imperial in its scope, and his influence led to the 1916 Jones Act, which conceded the eventual liberation of the Philippines from US rule. He signed the 1917 Jones-Shafroth Act that recognized Puerto Ricans born after 1898 as US citizens. At the same time, Wilson asserted dominion over many in the hemisphere. In his years as president, the United States invaded the Dominican Republic and occupied Haiti. It made military incursions into Cuba, Panama, and Honduras. Wilson's administration purchased Denmark's Caribbean colonies and rechristened them the US Virgin Islands. And he encouraged laissez-faire immigration of people from Southern and Eastern Europe, believing that over time they would assimilate and become part of white America.[2]

Black Americans crossed party lines to vote for Wilson, the Democratic candidate, but soon regretted it. Only months into his first administration, Wilson signaled that African Americans would fare badly under his leadership. In spring 1913, Wilson concurred when the postmaster general segregated the Railway Mail Service. The president would then purge Black officials and separate Black and white workers within the federal government. Jim Crow became the official order in much of Washington on Wilson's watch. The nation's capital resembled its Southern neighbors, with segregation ordering labor, politics, and everyday life and putting power in the hand of white supremacy's proponents.[3]

Wilson was a lightning rod for protest, and a new phalanx of rights organizations joined the NAACP, building up an African American political culture that included the National Urban League, Marcus Garvey's United Negro Improvement Association, and the Association for Negro Life and History. The 1915 release of filmmaker D. W. Griffith's *Birth of a Nation* underscored the depth of Wilson's complicity with white rule. The film's epic telling of the Civil War and Reconstruction substituted the truth of African American valor and leadership with myths about ineptitude and avarice. It featured Wilson's onscreen endorsement of Griffith's telling of "history" and was screened at the White House. The NAACP fired back, spearheading a campaign that sought to suppress the film and expose its racist falsehoods.[4]

When, in 1917, Wilson led the United States into World War I, he recast domestic matters as essential to supporting the war on the home front. The administration soon introduced loyalty as yet another arbiter of who might be an American and by what terms. The Espionage Act of 1917 and the Sedition Act of 1918 aimed to suppress antiwar dissidents. Officials put recent immigrants on the receiving end of deportation proceedings. Those said to be anarchists, communists, labor organizers, and pacifists were especially targeted. A civil liberties movement was born in response to wartime repressions by federal agencies that had grown large and emboldened.[5]

The war effort needed workers, and Black Americans quickly moved to the factories and manufacturers that had expanded as a result of the unprecedented demand for armaments, supplies, and transport. The influx of African Americans into Northern towns and cities was often met with rioting and assault by white residents. In East Saint Louis, Illinois, for example, tensions boiled over and hundreds of white men, striking workers from the Aluminum Ore Company, attacked Black residents on the city's streets. The National Guard quelled the unrest. Months later, in July, gunfire exchanged between Black residents and white joy riders left two police officers dead. Thousands of white men descended, killing dozens of Black residents and leaving thousands more homeless. Local officials were indifferent, and some even joined in on the melee. The Wilson administration stood by, enacting a policy best described as "hands-off."[6]

State-level contests occupied suffrage activists, and the results were mixed. In the West, states including Arizona, California, Kansas, Montana, Nevada, and Oregon extended full political rights to women. But in the East, states including Massachusetts, New Jersey, New York, and Pennsylvania defeated ballots for women, in spirit-crushing losses. The South was conspicuously beyond the reach of these efforts. Since the 1890s, NAWSA had determined to recruit Southern women to its ranks. Though these branches were not especially strong, they still hoped to influence men from the region who sat in Congress. The so-called Southern strategy was a concession. Suffrage leaders accommodated the deep logic of Jim Crow, leading NAWSA to endorse the principle of state's rights, a thinly veiled commitment to permitting white supremacy to organize the movement and influence its goals. Black suffragists felt the force of this view; they were marginalized, rebuffed, and overlooked at conventions, at marches, and during behind-the-scenes strategizing.[7]

Women suffrage leaders all sought Wilson's support, knowing that his endorsement might loosen the tight refusals of lawmakers who held Congress back from submitting a constitutional amendment to ratification. Early on, the president would go no further than to say that ballots for women was a matter for the states to settle—leaning, again, on the state's rights principle. NAWSA's head, Carrie Chapman Catt, quietly nurtured an alliance with Wilson, hoping that over time the president would be persuaded to support her cause. Alice Paul and the women who would form the National Women's Party, meanwhile, came at the president head-on, upstaging his inauguration with the 1913 parade, opposing Democrats in the 1916 elections, and then picketing the White House until the administration transformed them into political prisoners. The president did succumb, and in a January 1918 speech, he finally endorsed what would become the Nineteenth Amendment. His pressure moved Congress to act.[8]

After Congress ratified the amendment, too little changed for Black women. For them, life on both sides of the Nineteenth Amendment was fraught. Racism led some Black women to turn away from voting rights struggles. Others refused to let racism get in the way of working toward ballots for women. But no matter which side Black women were on, the amendment's ratification left them all grappling with how its passage left too many disfranchised. Jim Crow still dominated in the South, while organizations like NAWSA and the National Women's Party considered their work on voting rights complete. They turned their attention to encouraging women's votes through the League of Women Voters. Alice Paul launched a campaign for an Equal Rights Amendment. None of this addressed the concerns of the country's 5.2 million Black women, 2.2 million of whom lived in the South. Black women knew that they were being left behind. They persisted, but with a sharp sense that they would need to act in their own interests, whomever they might hope to win over. Some Black women abandoned voting rights altogether, searching instead for approaches that let them avoid the racism in women's politics that appeared to be more immovable than ever.[9]

NEW YORK WOMEN won the vote just as the Nineteenth Amendment campaign was gaining momentum in Washington. To push their cause over the top, the state's suffragists met in Saratoga, New York, in fall 1917. With a reputation for spring waters that promoted health, the upstate village had been a fabled meeting place since the mid-nineteenth century, one popular with generations of New York's political leaders. In 1917, the New York City Women's Suffrage Party delegates might have taken time to drink in the salutary effects of the spas and they drew breath from the same air breathed by the state's most prominent powerbrokers.

The suffragists had every reason to think that they were on the verge of victory when they convened in Saratoga. After an extended campaign to win the vote for New York's women, Anne K. Lewis, who had presided over the Harlem delegation, boasted that "every distinguished speaker from the governor of the State down who was asked to address the delegates accepted...men who realize that woman suffrage is one of the vital issues of the day to be given serious consideration." Members of Harlem's Colored Woman's Suffrage Club were among those who made the journey to Saratoga in the early days of September. Although they were united under the auspices of their club, the women were not of one mind. The club was moving toward an affiliation with the Women's Suffrage Party and not everyone was comfortable with the change. Despite that unease, they packed their bags, boarded northbound trains, and took seats among the hundreds of women committed to pushing New York forward on women's voting rights.[10]

There was nothing new about Black Americans feeling uneasy when it came to the politics of suffrage. In New York it was, by September 1917, a familiar story. In 1821, as the state opened the polls to all white men, it had imposed a new property qualification upon Black men—$250, a formidable threshold. In 1848 at Seneca Falls, Frederick Douglass had supported Elizabeth Cady Stanton, even as most Black men in their home state of New York remained disenfranchised. Black women in New York, like Sojourner Truth, confronted a mix of racism and sexism that limited their political power. More recently, in 1913, Harriet Tubman, who spent the latter years of her life in Auburn, New York, acted as a bridge between the suffrage struggle of the nineteenth and twentieth centuries. She stumped for women's right to vote in New York just prior to her death.[11]

The days they spent in Saratoga exposed differences among New York's Black suffragists, although press coverage depicted them as a "fine group." Upon their return to the city, a special meeting was called. The women needed to work through a stinging accusation: Mary Sharperson Young charged some among Saratoga's white delegates of having snubbed Black attendees. Back in the city, Annie Lewis called upon Young to speak publicly about her experience. When she declined, the meeting went on without her. Lewis primed her membership by refuting Young's claim: "The colored delegates received the same treatment as the white delegates, having been given delegate badges, were seated on the floor of the convention with the New York City representation, had been allowed a vote on all questions that came up, and were cordially treated in private conversations." Helen Christian echoed Lewis; she "had not seen the slightest indication on the part of anyone to snub the colored women."[12]

Young's accusation went beyond her reception at the Saratoga meeting—it raised an important question, one that went to the heart of Black women's power within the suffrage movement. White women were attempting to set the terms by which Black women organized themselves. Once the meeting dispensed with Young's accusation, a Mrs. Goode took the floor to complain "about the colored suffragists of Harlem and their affiliations, advancing the idea that colored women ought to form an independent organization." Black suffragists disagreed over how closely they should work with their white counterparts. They were uncertain about whether their distinct interests could be served in an umbrella organization that reduced their power to a minority vote. Some Black suffragists wondered what would become of their special concerns about what it meant to vote at the crossroads of racism and sexism.[13]

Anne Wright Watkins, the Manhattan chair of the Woman Suffrage Party, arrived at the Harlem meeting expecting to quell Black women's concerns, but her remarks only reinforced the fears expressed by women like Young and Goode. Watkins offered a thorny olive branch to Black suffragists. They were welcome in the movement, but only if they conformed "to the rules and regulations of the party." She chastised Lewis and her members: "You would have been given some such representation [in the Woman Suffrage Party] long ago had you not kept to the club idea." It was a rough bargain: Watkins and her party demanded that Black women abandon the National Association of Colored Women's club approach to political organizing in favor of a structure "organized along the lines of the political parties." In Watkins's view, "the system we used to have of being a union of clubs has gone out," and with this Watkins urged the Black women seated before her, "in the same cordial spirit we feel for you," to reorganize their work to fit a new model that rested upon assembly district leaders and election district captains. Clubs might persist for "sociability and convenience," Watkins explained, but within the Woman Suffrage Party they had no standing and would exert no influence. It was a steep price for Black women to pay.[14]

WHEN THE NINETEENTH Amendment was added to the Constitution, Black and white women stood alongside one another more equal than ever before. But what equality meant depended upon where you were in a nation divided by Jim Crow. Strife led to new battles as women attempted to register to vote in the fall of 1920. Officials in Southern states confronted Black women with unevenness, hostility, and downright refusal. And without the opportunity to register, many Black women never made it to the polls. In the North and to the west, Black women successfully cast ballots in 1920, voting for the very first time alongside their husbands, fathers, and sons.

Given all this, Black women in Savannah were not surprised when their state earned a curious distinction. On July 24, 1919, Georgia had been the first state to refuse ratification of the Nineteenth Amendment. The women knew that the matter would not be settled in Georgia, and still they prepared for approval of the Nineteenth Amendment. There was much for the members of the Woman's Suffrage Club of Chatham County to do. Voter education went on in the club's night schools. They staged a "mock registration" to which "men who thoroughly understand the preparation for elections will be asked to manage the affair." Club members visited "churches and societies," where they recruited new members. They were part of a grassroots uprising of Black women's suffrage clubs in the South.[15]

By April 1920, the prospect of the women's suffrage amendment was enough to fill Savannah's Asbury Methodist Church to the rafters. Three issues brought the city's Black women out in such large numbers. First, the promise that Lucy Craft Laney was making the trek from her home in Augusta, where in 1883 she had founded the Haines Normal and Industrial Institute. A senior stateswoman born before the Civil War, Laney might help steer local suffrage efforts. She was, as NAACP founder Mary White Ovington later put it, a pioneer who deserved to be recognized along with figures such as Lucretia Mott, Frances Williams, and Lillie Devereux Blake. Laney was "ahead of her time." As an educator, club movement organizer, and NAACP and YWCA activist, she provided much needed encouragement. For her, the vote was essential, the "only guarantee of fair dealing and justice for the Negro." Black communities relied upon political power as a collective working toward "the wholesome development of the whole community."[16]

Among those filling the church sanctuary that evening were Black men. Women's suffrage debates in Savannah also reinvigorated efforts to enable Black men to vote, and some of the men who packed the church shared women's concerns about access to the ballot. Reporting on a November 1919 voters' rally, during which speeches encouraged women's votes, the editors of the *Savannah Tribune* reminded men that coming up was "registration Sunday" and asked ministers to "urge the men to pay their poll tax and register now." Disfranchisement was not only a women's concern in Savannah.[17]

More so than headline speakers and registering Black men, it's likely that what brought so many Savannah residents out in April was the trouble brewing among Black suffragists. That evening it boiled over. Two factions faced off. The older was the city's Woman's Suffrage Club, which was led by Mamie George Williams and advocated preparing Black women for the moment when they would be eligible to register. The second, newer faction was led by Pearl Smith, and it wanted the group's suffrage work to be organized under the umbrella of the recently founded League of Women Voters, the successor to the National Woman's Party and the National American Woman Suffrage Association. Raised voices dominated the meeting; at least one speaker refused to cede the floor. The factions ultimately reconciled, and both Williams and Smith would go on to lead Black women's voting in Savannah after the Nineteenth Amendment's ratification. But before constitutional change even happened, Black women in Savannah came to near blows over voting rights.[18]

EQUALITY AFTER THE Nineteenth Amendment also meant that Black women and men were equally disadvantaged by state laws designed to keep African Americans from the polls. States in the South, along with some in the West, had years before set in place high hurdles. These laws did not ban African American voters expressly. Instead, they schemed to disproportionately disenfranchise Black men and women. For example, Louisiana, Mississippi, Missouri, North Carolina, Oklahoma, Virginia, and

Washington imposed grandfather clauses that ensured that the descendants of disenfranchised slaves, though now free people, could not vote.[19]

Beyond the grandfather clauses, other laws permitted election officials to let racism determine who registered. Administrators subjected voters to literacy tests in Alabama, Arizona, California, Colorado, Connecticut, Delaware, Georgia, South Carolina, and Virginia. Many Black Americans had been deprived of schooling, and exams disproportionately barred them from voting. Local election officials administered literacy tests differently to Black versus white voters: African Americans had to pass more difficult exams, and this all but ensured that they would fail. So-called understanding clauses demanded that potential voters read and then explain a text, often a portion of a state or the federal constitution—another requirement that disproportionately disenfranchised Black Americans. As with literacy tests, officials administered understanding clauses differently depending upon the race of the voter. Black voters were often asked to interpret the most complex or obscure parts of the Constitution.[20]

Dollars and cents also arbitrated who could vote. State officials imposed polls taxes more widely than any other restriction, requiring voters to pay up months prior to Election Day. Poor voters faced an especially difficult choice: spend their scarce cash to meet daily needs, or invest in the possibility that they *might* be permitted to vote. African Americans confronted this dilemma in sixteen states—Alabama, Arizona, Arkansas, Delaware, Florida, Georgia, Kentucky, Louisiana, Maryland, Mississippi, Nevada, North Carolina, South Carolina, Tennessee, Texas, and Virginia. When Black voters did overcome the hurdles of grandfather clauses and literacy and understanding tests, they often learned that they had accumulated years of unpaid poll taxes, all of which had to be paid before they could cast a ballot: A tax of one to five dollars per year for the chance to vote was a hefty sum.[21]

Registration numbers reflected the effects of discriminatory laws. When it came time, in fall 1920, for American women to register, Black women did present themselves to officials, but many found the doors closed. "During the supplemental registration, 2,200 were women. All the women were white except about 100." Their numbers in Kent County, Delaware, were "unusually large," but officials refused Black women who "failed to comply with the constitutional tests." In Alabama local officials refused Black women when they appeared to register, leading them to organize through the AME Zion Church and appeal to the United States attorney. In Jefferson County, Alabama, laws stymied Black women when they set out to register, and some blamed Black leaders, who themselves could not navigate the maze of requirements. In Huntsville, Alabama, "only a half dozen Black women" were among the 1,445 who registered, and the explanation was clear: officials applied "practically the same rules of qualification to [women] as are applied to colored men." "Attempts are being made by the republican leaders of the Seventh District to register negro women....Repeated requests to register negro women as voters are reported to have been made yesterday and today. What is the position of board of registrars on the question of negro registration? was the question put up to Chairman Harris of the board today. The decision of the board is: We are registering white ladies."[22]

Worried that Black women might manage to register, state lawmakers went so far as to change laws to keep the doors locked shut. In Mississippi, rule makers changed poll taxes to "require the same poll tax of $2.00 of women, as now required of men." It was no secret that this change was important, vital even, to those who feared that the old law "would permit negro women to register without being required to pay a poll tax." In Savannah, officials imposed the letter of the law, concluding that although "many negro women have registered here since the suffrage amendment became effective...the election judges ruled that they were not entitled to vote because of a state law which requires registration six months before an election." This ruling meant that no woman in the state of Georgia could vote—too little time had passed between the ratification of the Nineteenth

Amendment and Election Day. But this was a reading of the law meant to suppress Black women's votes because "no white women presented themselves at the polls."[23]

In North Carolina, Charlotte Hawkins Brown got caught in the crosshairs of voting rights strife in fall 1920. It was no accident that she landed there. Brown had long been a public figure in her native state, a woman who made herself visible in the years of Jim Crow. The granddaughter of enslaved people, she had studied in New England with the support of educator and philanthropist Alice Freeman Palmer. Brown was not yet twenty years old when she returned to North Carolina to found a combined day and boarding school for Black students, naming it the Palmer Memorial Institute in honor of her benefactor. By 1902, she was a teacher and institution builder, raising funds, building a staff, overseeing construction, and serving as the face of African American education in the state.[24]

As she worked to educate fellow Black Americans, Brown also set her sights on politics. She organized women to do their part during the First World War and support Black soldiers. Audiences eagerly attended her public talks, which included speeches such as "The Negro Woman in the Program of Reconstruction." Brown was a clubwoman, leading North Carolina's State Federation of Colored Women's Clubs, where she promoted vocational education. Local newspapers touted her as a woman who "has the confidence of both races," giving her work on behalf of Palmer Memorial Institute and Black women's clubs a veneer of interracial cooperation that permitted Brown to work across the color line. In 1919, she addressed the white-led North Carolina Federation of Women's Clubs, the first Black woman to do so. The next year, delegates to the National Federation of Colored Women's Clubs meeting at Tuskegee Institute voted Brown corresponding secretary.[25]

None of this spared her from the indignities of the polling place. In fall 1920, Brown was a lightning rod for Democratic Party anxiety about how Black women might gain political power in North Carolina. In early October, reports surfaced about a letter that was appearing in mailboxes across the South. The letter was addressed to Black women and explained the terms of the Nineteenth Amendment, which gave "all women the right of the ballot regardless of color." It went on to "beg all the colored women of North Carolina to register and vote on November 2nd, 1920." It was a call to action: "The time for negroes has come. Now is our chance to redeem our liberty." If refused at the polls, the notice instructed Black women to "go at once to a Republican lawyer and start proceedings in the United States courts—don't waste time with State courts... the State courts are Controlled by Democrats." The tone was militant and it emphasized that Black voters might overtake the system: "white women of North Carolina will not vote and while they sleep let the negro be up and doing. When we get our party in power we can demand what we wish and get it." It was postmarked Greensboro, North Carolina, and signed "Yours for negro liberty. COLORED WOMEN'S RIGHTS ASSOCIATION, FOR COLORED WOMEN."[26]

Who, newspaper editors and Democratic Party leaders asked, was responsible for this incendiary manifesto, one that was branded a conspiracy influenced by Republican Party promoters "from the North"? Charlotte Hawkins Brown's name very quickly surfaced; Democrats charged her with conspiring to oppose them and of using the new political power of Black women to do so. Her defenders stepped in, calling the circular and the charges against Brown "the lowest, dirtiest piece of political trickery that has ever been practiced by any political party." These were awkward defenses, ones that labeled a circular that stridently promoted Black women's power at the polls and in party politics "Bosh!" It must be a Democratic Party ploy that aimed to undercut Brown and that state's clubwomen. It was unthinkable (or, at least, unspeakable) that they would be so out front in anticipation of Election Day 1920.[27]

Brown's record of political activism, including the leadership of women's clubs, drew the most fire. The storm was rough enough that Brown publicly issued a rebuttal, one in which she invoked the name of every white philanthropist who had supported her school and emphasized her commitment to education, not politics. Brown denied how Black women were intently interested in the potential of 1920 and what it could mean to vote. Once, twice, and then a third time on the pages of the *Stanly Albemarle News-Herald*, where the controversy had begun, Brown denied the circular and its views: "I do not hold, or endorse, the views which [the circular] expresses." Between the lines, Brown expressed her indignation but also her fear of retribution. An association with voting rights could have cost her school its supporters, land, buildings, and students—her reputation and her power.[28]

Though it was risky, in many places Black women organized and prepared one another. They understood how barriers to the franchise worked and had witnessed how local officials imposed rules at their discretion to keep Black men from the polls. Now women faced the same challenges. In some places, they hoped, women who had mastered basic literacy and civics could overcome literacy tests and understanding clauses, at least. They trained for such challenges: In St. Louis, Black women organized in a "Citizenship League" and ran suffrage schools, where women and men readied themselves to face the scrutiny of local officials. In New Albany, Indiana, Black women met in local churches where Republican Party officials made a "great effort" to have them register and vote. In Akron, Ohio, they met under the auspices of the Colored Women's Republican Club and canvassed, going house to house to encourage women to register. In Chattanooga, Tennessee, Black women coached one another in how to register and vote. In Baltimore, from the pulpit a local minister urged that women's votes were part of God's vision and the ballot was a "weapon of protection to self and home." In Tulsa, Oklahoma, Black women heard how when "negroes unite at the polls [it] strikes at the very heart of white supremacy." In that city, "seven hundred Negro women registered."[29]

It some places, Black women triumphed, registering to vote in important numbers. In Frederick, Maryland, 75 percent of

Black women planned to register. In September, the first two Black women in Leon County, Florida, registered. In Staunton, Virginia, the local newspaper noted those Black women who registered by name and, at least on one day, they outnumbered white women eighteen to one. In Wilmington, Delaware, Black women were early to the registrar's office. In Chatham County, Georgia, the courthouse was "stormed by Negro women who wanted to put their names on the registration books." In Asheville, North Carolina, women participated in a mass meeting and then "appeared at the various polling places in the city and nearly 100 were registered." Their presence, it was reported, "came as a surprise to Democrats."[30]

Black women's rush to register alarmed some. They put their names on the books and then went to the polls with power on their minds. Those who aimed to suppress Black political power had good reason to fear the women's enthusiasm. In Richmond, Virginia, a fracas followed when Black women outnumbered white, three to one, at a registrar's office. The official in charge underscored the sense that Black women were unwelcome when, in response to the demand, he called upon police to "keep the applicants in line" according to Jim Crow rules: white and Black women were separated.[31]

In the days leading up to this confrontation, Maggie Lena Walker recorded how she and other Black women in Richmond prepared to meet the voting registrar. One week before, a Saturday, she paid her "first poll tax, $1.50." On Sunday she was part of a meeting at the Elks Home Conference of Women and then met with a local attorney to strategize about the women's plans. And then on Monday there was a "grand meeting" at St. Luke's Hall for women. "Good results," she remarked, noting the women were prepared to register. It is difficult to imagine Walker doing anything but organizing to win Black women's voting rights in 1920. She was a towering figure in her hometown, whose career had included time as a teacher, insurance agent, and finally head of the Independent Order of St. Luke, a fraternal business organization where she also edited the *St. Luke Herald*. Walker later founded the St. Luke Penny Savings Bank, making her the first Black woman to head a bank—another "first" foremother. She had always blazed the path toward women's power. And tensions between white and Black Republicans in Richmond made it a likely space for such a confrontation. Walker was part of a faction dubbed the "Lily-Blacks" that opposed the "Lily-White" party leaders who planned to jettison the votes of African American Virginians.[32]

At the registrar's office, Walker and the other Black women present were segregated and then directed to the building's basement. Walker charged that "partiality" was being shown to white women, going from the registrar to a judge, then to the secretary of the electoral board to complain, without satisfaction. The women waited. When the registrar moved to close up for the day, with Black women still waiting to sign up, Walker again raised her voice, pointing out that a hundred women remained in line. The registrar directed them to return in two weeks, the "general" registration day. Walker countered, urging the women to "come again tomorrow," and offered that she would serve as a deputy registrar. Black women, like white ones, should be permitted to fulfill such duties, she asserted.

African Americans in Richmond linked the histories of the Fifteenth and Nineteenth Amendments on their own terms. They saw, in the long lines of women waiting to register, shadows of the Black men who had in "years gone by," during Reconstruction, "vainly attempted to vote." For white Virginians and Lily-Whites, Maggie Lena Walker and Richmond's Black women voters generated anxiety. The scrutiny did not discourage those who kept on after organizing hundreds of Black women to vote. Power was in hand, and Black women were determined to do something with it. In 1921, they found a cause. The state's Republican Party flatly excluded Black delegates, as did the Democrats. Black leaders convened their own convention and nominated an independent ticket. John Mitchell Jr. was put up as head of the Lily-Black Republican slate as candidate for governor. "Women were recognized with the nomination of Maggie

Lena Walker for Superintendent of Public Instruction." As one editor put it: "The war is on and we are compelled to fight with fire." Walker, who aimed to hold office as well as to vote, and the hundreds of women whom she represented, were now part of that battle.[33]

AS RATIFICATION OF the Nineteenth Amendment grew distant, Black women confronted new political terrain. On the one hand, some of them now held political power. With the vote came electing representatives, office holding, and the inner negotiations of political parties. On the other hand, Jim Crow remained, leaving Black women and men in too many places with their power suppressed. When in 1920 the National Association of Colored Women convened in Tuskegee, Alabama, the delegates hoped to chart a way forward. Charlotte Hawkins Brown made the trip from North Carolina, heading a delegation of thirteen women. Maggie Lena Walker traveled south and west from Richmond, in the company of fifteen members of her Virginia federation. Both women championed Black women's interests and their distinct way of understanding politics and power.[34]

During that same meeting, Ohio's Hallie Quinn Brown was elected president of the clubwomen's organization. She brought with her deep experience. As early as 1889, before clubwomen had united in a national organization, she had a vision for its purpose: "I believe there are as great possibilities in women as there are in men." Women had built momentum: "We are marching onward grandly." Women's votes were for the good of family and community: "We love to think of the great women of our race—the mothers who have struggled through poverty to educate their children....There are many wives who are now helping to educate their husbands at school, by taking in sewing and washing." Brown demanded equity: "I believe in equalizing the matter. Instead of going to school a whole year, he ought to stay at home one half, and send his wife the other six months." Black women would vote and they would lead: "I repeat, we want a grand and noble womanhood, scattered all over the land. There is a great vanguard of scholars and teachers of our sex who are at the head of institutions of learning all over the country. We need teachers, lecturers of force and character to help to teach this great nation of women." These remarks, delivered before a conference of the African Methodist Episcopal Church, anticipated how Brown would emerge as an important advocate of women's rights, including the right to vote.[35]

For Brown, education was the foundation of women's political power. Though she was free born in 1849 in Pittsburgh, Brown's parents had been enslaved. To better educate their children, the household migrated to Chatham in Canada when Brown was a teenager. There, the family lived alongside fugitive slaves and dissident Black emigrants who had abandoned the United States. By 1870, in the wake of the Civil War and early

Hallie Quinn
Brown
(1849–1949)
GETTY IMAGES

Reconstruction, Brown returned to the United States, where she enrolled at the AME Church's Wilberforce University, in Ohio. After graduation, her career as an educator took her to public schools, North and South, and to Allen University in South Carolina and Alabama's Tuskegee Institute. Along the way, she studied elocution, and in 1893 Brown settled in as a professor at her alma mater, Wilberforce. It would be her institutional home for the next decade.[36]

"Give her your votes," insisted Gertrude Bustill Mossell, referring to Brown in 1892. Mossell admonished those men who saw Brown's womanhood as a bar to her holding the office of Secretary of Education in the AME Church: "Let the sex have its representation for we all know they willingly accept more than their share of the taxation." With that—a run for office—Brown was baptized into women's politics, part of a maelstrom in which, alongside her, other churchwomen claimed the right to hold office as ordained ministers. The resulting debates rocked the AME Church and Brown learned how to work through alliances with women like Mossell.[37]

In the decades leading to ratification of the Nineteenth Amendment, Brown avoided any sustained association with NAWSA or the National Women's Party (NWP). The anti-Black racism that ran through such organizations likely kept her at a distance. Brown did not, however, avoid suffrage politics, and along the way she met white women. Temperance took her to London, where she spoke at the 1895 convention of the World's Woman's Christian Temperance Union, one of only three Black American women to do so.[38] In the summer of 1900, Brown was in London to attend the International Congress of Women, where she heard women's suffrage debated and reported favorably on an exchange in which anti–women's suffrage ideas were "torn to shreds."[39]

Black women's clubs became the heart of Brown's public work. There, by 1899, leaders heralded the movement for women's suffrage as "the pioneer force for woman's emancipation and progress." By 1901, NACW president Mary Church Terrell won an "ovation" for her remarks titled "The Justice of Women Suffrage": "Woman's rights were not protected as they should be. Not until woman…had the ballot to be used for her protection and self-defence can she hope to secure the rights and privileges to which she is entitled." Brown, in 1904, helped write a resolution that suggested "that the women of our Association prepare themselves by the study of civic government and kindred subjects for the problems of city, State, and National life that they may be able to perform, intelligently, the duties that have come to some and will come to others in the natural progress of the Woman Suffrage movement." In 1911 and 1912, she headed the NACW's "Suffrage" department and, in 1920, Brown assumed the association's presidency.[40]

Serving as head of the NACW propelled Brown onto the national stage, where she discovered that there was no straight path to voting rights. Indignities knew few limits. In 1922, the United Daughters of the Confederacy (UDC) proposed to dedicate a monument to the mythical "Black Mammy of the South"—a figure in servant's garb cradling a white infant. Her words cut: rather than loyal supplicants, "slave women were brutalized, the victims of white man's caprice and lust. Often the babe torn from her arms was the child of her oppressor." As president of the National Association of Colored Women, Brown voiced the views of many thousands of enslaved women's descendants, who derided the hypocrisy of white Southerners who in "one generation held the Black mammy in abject slavery [and in] the next would erect a monument to her fidelity." She doubted that the monument emanated from a "deep reverence and gratitude" as the UDC professed. White Southern women would better "make restitution," Brown advised, by interceding with their husbands and fathers to "with one hand upraised… stop mob rule and lynching."[41]

The "mammy" figure was one feature of a Lost Cause myth, which relied on the fiction that enslaved people had been docile, content, and loyal to slaveholders. But by 1922, the notion of a "Monument to the Faithful Colored Mammies of the South" had attracted the interest of Congress. A bill followed, authorizing the Washington, DC, chapter of the UDC to install such a figure on public grounds "as a gift to the people of the United States." Black Americans saw through to the irony of such a framing and cried foul. The monument was mere propaganda aimed to distract the nation from real, twentieth-century needs: adequate homes, schools, and health care. Brown joined others—from grassroots activists to luminaries like W. E. B. DuBois—in opposition. The bill died of inaction.[42]

The "mammy" monument controversy erupted at a historical crossroads. It was one part a story about how the UDC promoted the Lost Cause through sponsorship of monuments and memorials. It was also a story about the emerging power of the NAACP. The young civil rights organization worked on multiple fronts, from litigation and lobbying to research and publishing. Hallie Quinn Brown's role points to yet one more story. Black women knew how to organize their political power, including the vote, and then wield it. As leader of the NACW, Brown condemned the monument for its degrading caricature of an African American woman.[43]

Brown and women like her came to the cause of women's suffrage by paths that ran through African American–led institutions: antislavery societies, churches, and women's clubs. Committed to winning political rights in the early twentieth century, most Black women remained just where they had begun, in Black-led institutions, testing ideas and building political savvy. Those that could—mostly women in northern and western states where Jim Crow did not exclude them from politics— signed on as supporters of the Republican Party. Their purpose was often distinct. Black women sought the vote to further what they termed the interests of humanity, meaning the rights of women and men alike. Their concerns were not single issue, and they battled for political rights while also advocating for temperance, education, prison reform, and the labor rights of working people. They especially attended to troubles that arose at the crossroads of race and gender. When Brown railed against the prospect of a "mammy" monument in the nation's capital, she did so knowing that the promotion of such a false and degrading image undercut Black women's political aspirations. She was part of a "great vanguard" prepared to fight back and further empower a "great nation of women."[44]

Looking ahead from 1920, Brown committed to leading the NACW forward from where the Nineteenth Amendment had left off. The enfranchisement of many thousands of Black women, the majority in the American South, was not yet complete. Brown's aim was to harness Black women's votes and win them influence in the Republican Party and in Washington. She urged that the ratification of the Nineteenth Amendment was an opening for Black women's power: "Let us remember that we are making our own history. That we are character builders; building for all eternity. Woman's horizon has widened. Her sphere of usefulness is greatly enlarged. Her capabilities are acknowledged....Let us not ask: what shall we do with our newly acquired power? Rather, what manner of women are we going to be?" She framed women's votes as a next chapter in the long struggle for Black political rights: "We stand at the open door of a new era. For the first time in the history of this country, women have exercised the right of franchise. The right for which the pioneers of our race fought, but died without the sight."[45]

Brown went on the offensive in the years that followed. Her book, *Homespun Heroines and Other Women of Distinction*, published in 1926, leveled one of Brown's best shots at those who doubted Black women's suitability as voters. She collaborated with more than twenty-five other women to produce—across 250 pages and sixty biographical sketches, essays, and poems—an argument about the past, present, and future of Black women. The book demolished myths and brought to light the lives of real women—their ideas and their activism. As Brown put it in her introduction, *Homespun Heroines* aimed to inspire young people to "cleave more tenaciously to the truth and to battle more heroically for the right." On the horizon, Brown suggested, was a time when universal womanhood suffrage would be realized.[46]

Homespun Heroines exposed the falsehoods of the "mammy" image of enslaved women as having been subservient, content, and enduringly loyal. In its place, Brown introduced readers to enslaved women who recognized their exploitation, resisted at great personal risk, and were committed to their own families rather than to those of slaveholders, even when subjected to forced, prolonged separation. Dinah Cox, for example, battled in court for more than fourteen years when her late owner's family refused to free her as provided for by his will. Upon her manumission, Charlotta Gordon MacHenry Pyles and her family risked a treacherous journey from Kentucky through Missouri to finally arrive in the Free State of Iowa. Once settled, Pyles set out to purchase family members who remained enslaved and reunited loved ones separated by sale. Harriet Tubman freed herself, returned at great risk to liberate her family and neighbors on Maryland's Eastern Shore, and then aided Union Army officials, "outwitting the Confederates." Lucretia Harper Simpson had been separated from her family while enslaved in Kentucky and, when the war came, she and three other young women took their chance and crossed the river into Ohio. *Homespun Heroines* made clear that enslaved women had been neither docile nor content. Nor had they been loyal, at least not to those who had held them in bondage.[47]

Citizenship was a birthright for which Black women were prepared. The women of *Homespun Heroines* were paradigmatic voters, women of independence and integrity. For many, formal education had bestowed the insight, reason, and discernment that suited them for citizenship. Others, especially those born enslaved, still made manifest qualities—piousness, fidelity, benevolence, selflessness, and compassion—all of which evidenced their suitability as voters. Elizabeth Smith had won her education despite violent opposition to the presence of young Black women at Prudence Crandall's school in Canterbury, Connecticut. Caroline Sherman Andrews-Hill, though enslaved, stole learning during lessons for her household's white children, and when discovered was banned from working nearby. Anne Baltimore, Mary Burnett

Talbert, and Mary J. Patterson attended Oberlin College. So did Fannie Jackson Coppin, who took the "gentleman's course," despite advice that she do otherwise.[48]

Black women had earned the vote, *Homespun Heroines* argued. As suffragists, they had worked to secure for all American women a constitutional amendment. Sojourner Truth had been a "zealous advocate for the enfranchisement of women" who "saved the day and won the victory for women," at an 1851 suffrage convention. Harriet Tubman had embraced the cause of women's suffrage and allied with the Empire State Federation of Colored Women's Clubs, to whom she sent a last message before her death: "Tell the women to stick together. God is fighting for them and all will be well." Journalist Mary Ann Shadd Cary toured alongside white antislavery lecturers who also spoke on women's rights, including Abby Kelley, Lucretia Mott, and Lucy Stone. In the 1880s, Cary joined the National Woman's Suffrage Association. Sarah J. S. Garnet was the woman behind the Brooklyn, New York, Equal Suffrage Club and superintendent of the NACW's suffrage department. Eliza Ann Gardner helped found Boston's Woman's Era Club and championed women's rights in the AME Zion Church. Amanda Berry Smith preached in pulpits around the globe and "wherever she went there always sprang up an eager discussion on the subject of women's right to preach." Laura A. Brown was, during the administration of President Warren Harding, appointed a member of the Executive Board of the Republican Women's Committee of Allegheny (PA) County, and in 1922 she ran for the state legislature, perhaps, Brown suggested, the first Black woman in the United States to do so.[49]

Brown was a suffragist and she was a writer. *Homespun Heroines* may have been shorter than the six-volume *History of Woman Suffrage*, begun by Elizabeth Cady Stanton, Susan Anthony, and Matilda Joslyn Gage in the 1880s. But it was no less a chronicle of the history of women's activism. As the celebration in 1920 of the Nineteenth Amendment faded, Brown and the women of the NACW were left with serious work ahead of them. Jim Crow still kept too many of their sisters away from the polls, and untruths wrought from racism and sexism sustained their disenfranchisement. The way forward was fraught—the NACW faced competition from the increasingly influential NAACP, and suffered from the indifference of women's suffrage organizations like the National Women's Party. The elite politics of respectability kept the NACW at a distance from Black women of the working class. It lost members who rejected the vote and party politics in favor of radical, internationalist, and pan-African approaches to power. Still, Brown's book endured, aiding those activists who followed her to better understand and build upon that "great nation of women" of which she was a part.[50]

NOT ALL BLACK women pursued the vote after 1920. Some had been discouraged by the racism they had confronted in the campaign for the Nineteenth Amendment. Even after that seeming victory was secured, Black women faced opposition, legal and extralegal, to their participation in politics. Many of them still could not cast ballots and very few stood a chance to hold office. Before 1920, Mary Sharperson Young had been an active suffragist. In 1917, she had charged white suffragists with prejudice, only to have her word doubted. So, she turned away from electoral politics and voted with her feet.

Those new steps took Young to the United Negro Improvement Association (UNIA), a pan-African movement that stressed the economic independence and political unity of people of African descent. Launched in 1918 to unite people of Africa and its diaspora around the globe, the movement quickly grew into a multifaceted organization, with a newspaper, Harlem meeting hall, and plans for an international shipping line. In 1920, the first UNIA convention attracted twenty thousand delegates to New York's Madison Square Garden, but they represented only a small fraction of the members spread across nineteen hundred divisions in forty countries. Founded by a Jamaican immigrant to New York, Marcus Garvey, the UNIA offered an alternative to women frustrated by the troubles that animated domestic politics. Mary Sharperson Young had relocated to New York City from Orangeburg, South Carolina, as a young woman just after the turn of the century and she settled in Harlem. If women's suffrage had held her attention for a time, by 1920 she was ready to shift alliances to the Garvey movement.[51]

In the United States, the UNIA was a compelling alternative to political parties and state legislatures, where too often racism distorted the proceedings. It signaled an important internationalist turn by which visions for Black liberation took shape across lines of nation, region, and continent. In this movement, antiracism and anticolonialism were twin critiques. Garvey's special emphasis was on economic independence and prosperity for African peoples. For many women, his movement became an important alternative to the troubled interracial politics of women's suffrage.[52]

Joining the UNIA liberated Young from the crude barbs of racism, but it did not excuse her from the troubles of gender politics. The Garvey movement operated by a structure that was in some ways gender neutral, women and men shared titles and status. Young made her mark and founded the Royal Court of Ethiopia, a UNIA women's auxiliary. She was among the women who, in 1926, raised funds to save the property of the UNIA's New York branch. In 1927, when Garvey was deported by US officials, women's authority expanded. Loss of the movement's charismatic head left a void that UNIA women filled, using an approach to leadership that blended their nationalism with their womanhood. They became practitioners of "efficient womanhood," a leadership style that mixed negotiation with public confrontations and permitted women to direct the UNIA's future.[53]

Young shifted her loyalties from the women's suffrage movement to the UNIA. But neither movement wholly contained her ambitions, and her leadership style was typical of how many Black suffragists worked. There were times when securing the ballot occupied center stage in her work. But Young's attention shifted, sometimes in response to racism within the suffrage movement and at other times in line with new political views or orientations. Over the course of her life, Young variously committed herself to postwar relief work, child welfare services, and the "Circle for Negro Relief." Suffrage, for her, was only one route to Black women's overall liberation.[54]

FOR BLACK WOMEN, ratification of the Nineteenth Amendment was not a guarantee of the vote, but it was a clarifying moment. Like the Fifteenth Amendment before it, so much about voting rights depended upon state law and the discretion of local officials that the Nineteenth Amendment was little more than a broad umbrella under which a wide range of women's experiences unfolded. More than anything, it marked a turn: Black women were the new keepers of voting rights in the United States. They were at the fore of a new movement—one that linked women's rights and civil rights in one great push for dignity and power. There were casualties along the way, women who turned to new movements that looked beyond the bounds of the vote or party politics and that adopted an internationalist vision for their futures. Still, as the club movement mixed with civil rights organizations in the next years, Black women discovered that their voting rights, though partial and oftentimes denied, gave them a new platform upon which to build influence, especially in the nation's capital.

Chapter 8

HER WEAPON OF MORAL DEFENSE

No single issue had ever driven Black women's politics. Nor had Black women invested in a single tactic. As the Depression wracked the nation in 1929, they brought their skills to problems of politics and policy in Washington. Black Americans needed powerbrokers—advocates, lobbyists, and public administrators—who could steer federal resources toward those hardest hit by joblessness and price inflation. Church activist, educator, and journalist Nannie Helen Burroughs explained: "The economic plight of the Negro woman is tragic. During this depression she is bearing the economic burden of the race almost alone. She has the longest hours and she gets the lowest pay. Her home is either neglected because of her enforced absence or it is crowded with relatives and roomers because of financial conditions." The net result, for Burroughs, was the dire fate of children for whom it was "impossible for them to have a ghost of a chance to grow up decently." A lifelong Washingtonian, Burroughs knew that for Black women, influence there was a matter of life and death.[1]

THE DEPRESSION, SET off by sharply declining stock prices in the United States, was a global catastrophe. At home, Americans felt its reverberations on a scale deeply personal, as incomes dropped and unemployment rose. Workers in construction, farming, mining, and logging were especially hard hit. President Herbert Hoover's initial recovery strategy, which asked businesses to voluntarily keep workers on and pay wages, failed. Then, the administration's half-hearted efforts to restart the economy had little effect. Banks continued to go under. The election of 1932 was a referendum on Hoover's leadership and voters showed him the door, electing Democrat Franklin Delano Roosevelt, who promised that nothing short of a wholesale remaking of the economy would follow his election.[2]

Roosevelt's New Deal was the most important reordering of federal power since Reconstruction. The administration set in place a new, far-reaching administrative state that changed forever how governance and authority would be allocated in Washington. In a first wave, the administration reformed banking, securities, and agriculture while the National Recovery Act regulated prices, wages, labor, and competition. Roosevelt met stiff resistance when the Supreme Court ruled this last measure unconstitutional. A second wave of legislation set in place an income safety net termed Social Security, provided jobs through the Works Progress Administration, and encouraged union organizing through a new National Labor Relations Board. Federal spending skyrocketed and by 1936, the economy showed important signs of recovery.[3]

Roosevelt's reelection in 1936 marked a turning point in African American politics. Historically, most Black Americans had been allied with the Republican Party, for its associations with Abraham Lincoln, emancipation, and radical Reconstruction. By voting for Roosevelt, African Americans endorsed the modest recovery his programs provided and marked the start of their turn toward the Democrats. Only 28 percent of Black voters nationally voted for the Republican nominee that year. The Democratic Party was not yet the party of civil rights, and Roosevelt himself was uneasy with trading racial justice for the support of a Black constituency. Roosevelt resisted, aiming to sustain his power through an alliance with white Southern voters.[4]

New Deal programs reflected an indifference to the needs of Black Americans in the wake of the Depression. The posture was not the president's alone. Congress crafted New Deal legislation that favored white Americans and left Black communities further behind. The National Recovery Act, for example, provided white workers with first dibs when it came to jobs, and then authorized only separate, low-wage positions for African Americans. Forty percent of all Black workers were sharecroppers or tenant farmers, and still the Agricultural Adjustment Administration encouraged landowners to leave fields fallow and left African Americans, who relied upon the same land for income, without wages and without recourse. The Social Security Act generally excluded agricultural and domestic laborers, ensuring that too many Black Americans would subsist without the safety net that would benefit white workers.

Up and running by the mid-1930s, the New Deal agencies required a new workforce. Among the thousands who flocked to Washington—trained in law, business, and social work—were men and women for whom federal service secured them middle-class status. They came to establish systems, ply expertise, and construct a new politics that turned not on law but on regulation. Jobs in the federal government, which had numbered half a million at the start of the Roosevelt years, reached 3.5 million by 1945. The new administrative state relied not upon elections but upon appointments. It would soon outpace the effect of Congress and the judiciary, touching the lives of more Americans than any other branch.[5]

If the president failed to give serious thought to civil rights, the NAACP and its offshoot, the Legal Defense Fund, made sure that the demands of Black Americans were a sharp thorn in the nation's side. The US Supreme Court was the forum of choice and the Constitution a preferred weapon. A legal team led by Charles Hamilton Houston and later Thurgood Marshall hammered away at Jim Crow, winning victories against segregated professional schools in *Murray v. Pearson*, against all-white primaries in *Smith v. Alright*, and separate cars on interstate travel in *Morgan v. Virginia*. Voting rights, however, eluded them for the moment. In 1940, for example, only 3 percent of Black Southerners were registered to vote.[6]

World War II and the economic stimulus generated by federal spending and war industries are credited with ending the Depression. But the war was far more. The service demands it made upon all Americans, especially men, fueled rethinking of the social contract. The GI Bill that followed would be the single most important factor in the construction of an American middle class. But the change went farther. A war against racism in Europe held a mirror up to a nation that had, since Reconstruction, relied upon its own brand of racism as it allocated power and resources. After the war, the United States led on a global stage and some in the federal government recognized the new costs associated with denying Black Americans full civil and political rights. Roosevelt understood that asking Black Americans to serve, abroad or at home, set the stage for a new bargain and he began to reverse the segregation that Woodrow Wilson had imposed a generation earlier.[7]

Black Americans had more than Roosevelt's desegregation of federal agencies in mind as they took up the work of war in 1941. The Black-owned *Pittsburgh Courier* coined the slogan "Democracy—Double Victory, At Home—Abroad." This "Double V" resonated and, whether on the home front in defense industries or on foreign soil in Europe, Asia, or North Africa, Black Americans came to think of wartime service as a complement to the NAACP Legal Defense Fund's litigation. A bargain was being struck even if one party, the federal government, was not yet wholly at the table.[8]

It was in these years that Black women became politicians, drawn to places of consequence and sites of power by a compelling mix of opportunity and necessity. They began to staff federal New Deal agencies. Some held places high enough that they shaped policy. Quite a few found a partner in the First Lady, Eleanor Roosevelt, a figure with whom Black women built political power in Washington. There were important firsts. Jane Bolin became the first Black woman judge in the nation, appointed to New York City's Domestic Relations Court. Crystal Bird Fauset became the first Black woman elected to a state legislature in Pennsylvania. One measure of Black women's political ambition came in 1935 when Mary McLeod Bethune founded the National Council of Negro Women. It was a rival to the older National Association of Colored Women's Clubs, but the two organizations shared a similar outlook, one that understood the drive for Black women's power as a route to economic justice and human rights.[9]

THERE WAS NOTHING easy about being a Black woman in Washington during the 1920s. Even in the most scripted settings, Black women unsettled the assumption that only white women had been empowered by the Nineteenth Amendment. In 1929, an afternoon tea at the White House generated a firestorm when Mrs. Jessie DePriest was among the guests. DePriest was married to the only African American member of Congress, her husband Oscar. The new First Lady, Lou Hoover, planned to host lawmakers' wives at afternoon tea. Everyone around her knew that DePriest's entry into a circle of women that had been all white since Reconstruction would require careful planning. The implications were far-reaching. Hoover's administration was at work on a Southern strategy that would capitalize on the president's 1928 victory in key Southern states. Having DePriest to the White House might trouble political alliances among white leaders unless it was framed just right.[10]

DePriest was no stranger to politics. Her husband had long been a public figure and his position in Washington was due, in no small part, to Chicago's Black women, who organized, turned out at the polls, and propelled him to a historic victory. Once she arrived in Washington, it was no surprise when

DePriest received a quiet invitation from Mrs. Hoover. The First Lady made the gesture reluctantly. She fretted over guest lists. Her office vetted the dozen or so carefully chosen white women for their willingness to share the afternoon with DePriest and to take no offense. Timing mattered and the "DePriest" tea was the last of five such gatherings. Hoover was hoping to avoid a Southern boycott of her hospitality. The planning paid off and the occasion was uneventful. Trouble erupted only later as word got out that Hoover had hosted the Black congressmember's wife.[11]

From all quarters, commentary swirled around the fact that a Black woman was politely received at the White House. It was more than a matter of women's sociability—this highly visible breach of the color line had the power to disrupt politics, including party cohesion and alignments. Southerners decried a defiance of racial etiquette. Northerners worried that the occasion compromised their political alliances with men to the south. The Hoover administration maintained its initial position and minimized DePriest's visit to the White House. The occasion had been unremarkable because men of color, including foreign diplomats, already regularly visited there. The official view was that having DePriest at tea was not a "social" occasion, it was just politics.[12]

When next back home in Chicago, DePriest spoke for herself. She took the podium before the three hundred women who filled the Pilgrim Baptist Church, and everyone hoped to hear her impressions of the much-talked-about afternoon. Editor of the *California Eagle*, Charlotta Bass, reported that DePriest's remarks lasted only three minutes. She praised Mrs. Hoover as "a most charming woman cosmopolite [and] a wonderful hostess." She confirmed there had been "no excitement" when she entered the White House. It was instead an unremarkable affair: "The other ladies at the party discussed problems as you and I might discuss." DePriest visited the White House as a peer and an equal rather than an interloper. Any controversy had been manufactured by Southerners: "All the storm of criticism has been stirred up…outside the capital, mostly below the Mason and

Dixon line." Her words were a reassurance. DePriest had entered the White House and endured the political fray uninjured, and she planned to rejoin the white women who ran Washington unbowed.[13]

When DePriest took the public stage in Washington, she did so with the support of a community of Black women who had been casting ballots since 1913. That year, Illinois had enfranchised women, the first state east of the Mississippi to guarantee to its women the vote. But not all contests took place at the ballot box, and the vote was neither the start nor the finish of DePriest's politics. In Washington, as the wife of a member of Congress, DePriest had the power to unsettle matters far beyond guest lists and seating plans. Black women went to Washington and expected to stand shoulder to shoulder with their white counterparts. On a June afternoon in 1929, in an awkward and unspoken alliance, Mrs. Hoover and Mrs. DePriest set the stage for just that.[14]

Jessie DePriest was a newcomer to Washington, but Nannie Helen Burroughs called the city home. There, she had built a career that followed on the work of her mother's generation, the women who built a club movement. But Burroughs was no acolyte; she was going to make her own way, building on what had come before. Burroughs also took a firm stand in solidarity with poor and working women, whose voices were not always heard at deliberations in the National Association of Colored Women. When Burroughs advocated for women's votes, whether before or after the Nineteenth Amendment, she foregrounded one matter above all: Black women must be free from sexual abuse. This call gave Burroughs and her work an unparalleled moral power. Only Black women, Burroughs suggested, could redeem the nation.[15]

Burroughs distanced herself from the past when she adopted interracial cooperation as her approach to white women activists. A leader in the Baptist Church, Burroughs never lost sight of

Nannie Helen Burroughs (1879–1961), with members of the Woman's National Baptist Convention, ca. 1910
LIBRARY OF CONGRESS

how her power could be enhanced through alliances with white Baptist women. In politics, she frequented circles that included many women who shared the view that the lives of many millions of Black Americans would only be changed through political partnerships across the color line. Burroughs collaborated on issues from antilynching to suffrage rights. Interracial cooperation was neither capitulation nor deference. Instead, it was a framework through which Black women like Burroughs came together with their white counterparts as political equals.[16]

Burroughs was just a girl when she migrated with her mother from Orange, Virginia, nearly a hundred miles northeast to the nation's capital in 1883. Burroughs studied at the city's fabled M Street High School, where she was a standout student. Her teachers imparted more than book lessons. They broke new ground in Black women's politics while also training young women like Burroughs to be leaders. Burroughs's teacher Anna

Julia Cooper published her treatise on Black women's political theory, *A Voice from the South*. The year that Burroughs graduated with honors, 1896, her teacher Mary Church Terrell took the helm of the newly founded National Association of Colored Women. The M Street School was a training ground for a next, rising generation of Black women leaders, and Burroughs was among its brightest stars.[17]

After graduation, work took Burroughs west to Louisville, Kentucky, where she signed on to support the National Baptist Convention's Foreign Mission Board. There, Burroughs practiced an old brand of Black women's politics. She asked questions about women's power in church and began to organize, speaking at the founding of the Woman's Convention of the Black-led National Baptist Convention. Burroughs would spend the next half century as an advocate for churchwomen, leading the largest Black women's organization in the country. She was an institution builder. In 1909 she returned to Washington and founded the National Training School for Women and Girls, the first vocational school for Black women and girls to be headed by a Black woman. Burroughs remained at its helm until her death in 1961.[18]

In the summer of 1915, Burroughs joined the ranks of the nation's leading thinkers when W. E. B. DuBois included her essay in a special "Votes for Women" issue of the NAACP's magazine, *The Crisis*. Burroughs was featured alongside her former teacher Mary Church Terrell; that year's NACW president Mary Talbert; Carrie Clifford, head of the Federation of Colored Women's Clubs of Ohio; and others. Burroughs advised that Black women's capacities had been underestimated. Their votes would affirm the "correct estimate" of the Black woman as a "tower of strength." They would remedy how men had misused the ballot. Their leadership would prove to be "aggressive, progressive and dependable." Most importantly, the nation's moral destiny rested with Black women. They had been "prey for the men of every race" but had "held the enemies of Negro female chastity at bay." Why support women's votes? Burroughs explained that the ballot would bring Black women "respect and protection" and serve as "her weapon of moral defence." With the vote, Black women would further shape their destinies, including the enactment of law and policy "in favor of her own protection."[19]

With ratification of the Nineteenth Amendment, Burroughs moved immediately into Republican Party politics. By 1925, she was president of the National League of Republican Colored Women, a post that brought a community of women voters under her leadership. Burroughs presided when Black women from twenty-three states convened at Washington's Phillis Wheatley YWCA. Over three days of deliberations, the party's Black women leaders drafted a "statement for the enlightenment of the administration" that included pointed questions about the future of voting rights, such as "What are the Amendments to the Constitution Good for?" They chose as their slogan for the coming year "Oppose in State and National Campaigns any Candidate who will not Commit Him or Herself on the Enforcement of the 13th, 14th and 15th Amendments." Burroughs was now working inside the party to elevate her vision.[20]

Burroughs's leadership in the Republican Party opened a new frontier of Black women's power. During the 1927 convention, she led activist women who themselves had been pathbreakers, including the NACW's Mary Church Terrell and the AME Zion Church's Rev. Mary J. Small. But the moment represented more than a generational shift. Burroughs led an interracial gathering during which white Republican Party members participated under her direction. Burroughs invited several Coolidge administration cabinet members along with women leaders of the Republican National Committee to address the Black women delegates. Before the meeting ended, Burroughs escorted her delegation to meet with President Coolidge himself.[21]

When it came to women's votes, the ground had shifted. White women thought themselves now entitled to cast ballots. Too many Black women did not. When Burroughs commented on the future of women's voting rights, she spoke in an ominous tone. She warned white women against being naive as they played the game of politics. If they thought their futures lay with political parties, organizations that would buy and sell them, they were mistaken. If they passed on the chance to partner with African American women, they invited "political menace." Black women were the "safest and most valuable ally."[22] Black women were not above reproach in Burroughs's view, however. She warned against those who were handpicked by men—"Tom, Dick or Harry"—and "clamoring for leadership" and "without followers in their own race." Burroughs instead celebrated those Black leaders selected by the people they represented. Black Americans were capable of selecting their own leaders: "Leave them to it!"[23]

Burroughs did not intend to repel or crush white women. To the contrary, she sought to work in cooperation with them. She moved past the marginalization and denigration that had run through the suffrage movement. Burroughs never occupied an ancillary or subordinate position. She entered into interracial cooperation secure in her strength, including the thousands of Black Baptist and Republican Party women who were her base.

Burroughs returned from a 1934 meeting of the Atlanta-based Commission on Interracial Cooperation, the head of a network of liberal white Southerners who worked with Black activists against lynching, mob violence, and peonage. She was "inspired" by what she'd seen. Members of the commission were neither Republicans nor Democrats; they were the "Abolitionist Party of the New South." They worked face-to-face: "white and colored, men and women," and acknowledged the enormity of the work ahead. No one expected to be "performing miracles." Still, Burroughs found commitment and courage that matched her own: "These people are dead in earnest. They are unafraid." Most compelling was the commission's sweeping agenda, which included economic justice—improving "conditions for domestics"—and winning political rights, "full citizenship rights to vote and to serve on juries." In a cross-racial alliance Burroughs found a movement that might sustain her.[24]

The interracial cooperation approach carried over into Burroughs's church work, and by 1940 she was bringing Black and white women together in the Baptist Church through a "Christian cooperative venture" between the Women's Convention Auxiliary of the National Baptist Convention, the organization she had long led, and the Women's Missionary Union (WMU) of the white-led Southern Baptist Convention. Burroughs blazed a way forward through interracial cooperation, authoring a pamphlet that revised the terms of the collaboration originally authored by the WMU. Her words were a corrective, but not a rebuke. Optimistic, Burroughs aimed to build upon the "many changes taking place in the social and economic life of the nation." She explained: "A new social order is in the making," one in which "lynchings cannot happen, children will have a chance to learn…justice will be dealt to all, the poor will be cared for, the sick nursed, and the unfortunate protected." She stood up as a leader of a new community of women, "active Christian women of both races."[25]

The balance of power between Black and white women had shifted across Burroughs's most active years, and she had come to many tables with a commitment to interracial cooperation that did not subordinate or diminish her. First was the Baptist Church, where Burroughs led hundreds of thousands in the nation's largest organization of Black women. Burroughs held her place in the Republican Party with her rootedness in a Black women's caucus that was allied with influential men, Black and white. She joined with fellow travelers in the Commission on Interracial Cooperation. This was, however, no repeat of the tensions that characterized the women's suffrage movement. Burroughs was an equal and even a leader in work that privileged her vision of what women's power must accomplish.

WHEN FRANCES WILLIAMS delivered her speech "Power of the Ballot" to an audience in Louisville, Kentucky, it was a homecoming of sorts. Williams's father had been enslaved in that city as a boy before the Civil War. She traveled to Louisville from Washington, DC, in 1940 to join a crowd gathered in the AME Church's Quinn Chapel, speaking as a member of the NAACP's board of directors. She aimed to guide the work of Black activists in her native state, and her topic was no accident. Despite barriers like poll taxes, Williams had come to encourage local activists to build the same political power she knew was on the rise in Washington. In the years since the ratification of the Nineteenth Amendment, Williams had built her power through education, organizing, activism, and public administration. Still, she never gave up on the import of voting rights.[26]

Williams came of age under the guidance of two formidable women. The first was her mother, Fannie Williams, born enslaved in Danville, Kentucky, educated at Berea College, and a lifelong club activist and national YWCA leader in St. Louis, Missouri. Fannie was ambitious for her youngest daughter and, despite the doubts of administrators, enrolled Frances at Mount Holyoke College, where the young woman joined the class of 1919. There, Frances fell under the spell of President Mary Emma Woolley. Before becoming one of the nation's youngest college presidents in 1901, Woolley had been among the first women students at Brown University and a member of the faculty at Wellesley College. Williams wrote to her mother that Woolley's approach—training women as intellectuals while also attending to their personal lives—ensured that she was happy at Mount Holyoke.[27]

Williams then readied herself for a life in politics, part of a generation of Black women who began to build their power with professional degrees. First, she attended the New York School of Social Work, where she earned a master's in social work. At the University of Chicago, she continued her studies, working with Harold Gosnell on his book *Negro Politicians: Rise of Negro Politics in Chicago*, and guided by sociologist Robert Park, earning a master's in political science in 1931: "The Role of the Negroes in Chicago in the Senatorial Election, 1930." Working for the YWCA as a student secretary—a field organizer among girls and young women—pulled Williams toward her vocation. She was soon crisscrossing the nation, often through Southern cities, mixing young women's political education with lessons on interracial cooperation.[28]

Williams promoted her early ideas about interracial cooperation in a series of pamphlets authored in the 1930s. She prepared young Black and white women to build a world that defied the color line. She judged that white Americans really knew too little about Black Americans. Her writings were not encyclopedic, but they presented a slice of Black politics and culture that Williams curated. In her stories, Black women remained undefeated. She took up civil rights, asking why the nation deprived Black Americans of the vote, access to public accommodations, employment, public welfare, and education. She used the 1936 case of *Harvey's, Inc. v. Sissle* to teach how Black women had no legal recourse when denied service in retail stores, even in Ohio. Black women were workers across a stunning array of occupations, but their numbers were concentrated in agricultural and domestic work. Williams did not avoid the strife that resulted when Black and white women confronted one another. Racism inevitably marred these moments, but Williams depicted Black women characters who thought themselves equals, challenged the "storms" to which they were subjected, pressed for their rights, and won victories that affirmed their power in relationships with white women.[29]

Williams also met Black men as equals. From her platform at the YWCA, she forged close alliances with men who held the reins of the early civil rights movement. In 1933, she was among the women invited to the NAACP's second Armenia conference, an effort to bring in a new generation of thinkers and activists. Afterward, Williams regularly corresponded with the NAACP's Walter White and Charles Hamilton Houston and the Associated Negro Press's Claude Barnett, and built her influence behind the scenes in Washington and beyond, as a counselor, ally, and advocate for organizations that steered the African American political future. She joined the NAACP board, where her interests stretched from lynching to maternal and child health. Williams made certain that women's issues were also civil rights issues, documenting the disproportionate death rates for Black mothers and infants in states where they did not get their share of public resources.[30]

Williams was among the nearly 450 delegates who gathered in 1940 when the National Council of Negro Women convened in Washington, DC, for its sixth annual conference. That show of strength must have been impressive enough—hundreds of Black women moving about the city's sidewalks, streetcars, hotels, and restaurants to determine their political agenda. The women gathered on the steps of Constitution Avenue's neoclassical Mellon Auditorium for a group photo, a wide-angle shot that took in dozens. Williams was there that October afternoon, standing to the far left in a plain cloth coat and with a bare head—in stark contrast to the fur stoles and fashionable hats worn by many others, including Mary McLeod Bethune and Mary Church Terrell, who stood front and center.

Bethune, as the council president, had big plans for the delegates, and Williams figured prominently. The meeting's theme was "Negro Women Face New Frontiers." Yes, there was business to be conducted, with addresses titled "The Negro Woman in Public Affairs," "The Problem of Citizenship," "Consumer

Annual conference of the National Council of Negro Women, October 24–26, 1940, Washington, DC. Scurlock Studios
NATIONAL PARKS SERVICE, NATIONAL ARCHIVES FOR BLACK WOMEN'S HISTORY

Education," "The International Program," and "The Negro in National Defense." But the conference was also an opportunity to forge a tighter relationship between the council and the White House. Bethune worked with First Lady Eleanor Roosevelt to arrange a public affair during which many of the nation's leading Black women could introduce their issues and themselves. It was an arresting sight, dozens of Black women, many in their finest, making their way to the White House.[31]

Bethune began with introductions and presented gifts to Roosevelt. Then she turned the podium over to Williams. Williams's remarks to the First Lady set out the organization's "aims and efforts." Her precise words have not survived, but her letters from the same period give some sense of how Williams approached her assignment. Her ideas were always partly explication, the thoughts of a social scientist intent upon ensuring that the White House understood the broad facts of Black life. Williams was also a keen tactician who knew how to build an alliance by finding common ground. Though she never led her own classroom, Williams was oftentimes a teacher, offering references to history and literature as an essential part of ethical and political reflection. And she was also a politician, one who charted the way forward, pressing others to join her. She was there that afternoon to lobby Roosevelt on the economic interests of Black women and their families, and then for enhanced access to federal power for herself and the women of the NCNW.[32]

Williams got her own opportunity to directly shape federal policy and the complexion of the workforce when she joined the staff of President Franklin Roosevelt's Office of Price Administration. There, she not only aided Black women and their families in their ongoing recovery from the Depression but also hired Black staff in unprecedented numbers. In subsequent years, she would be appointed to President Truman's Committee on Civil Rights and work as a research assistant to New York senator Herbert Lehman. Winning power in Washington made Williams an object of admiration mixed with derision, such as when a *Chicago Defender* columnist paid her a twisted compliment.

She was an administrator of "tact, efficiency, drive and effectiveness," but something about her leadership style set Williams against the Black men in her midst. The cut that she "shows up most male Negro government executives" was a reminder that Black women still worked at their own vexed crossroads.[33]

THE ARC OF Mary McLeod Bethune's life linked two moments of optimism for Black Americans. She was born in 1875, making her a child of Reconstruction, the nation's first experiment in interracial democracy. Born Mary McLeod, she lived until 1955, long enough to see the dawn of the modern civil rights era. She might have preferred a different framing of her life's work. It stretched from the nineteenth century's woman's era to the eve of the modern women's movement. Throughout these years, Bethune was nothing if not a race woman. Her power was rooted in her leadership of Black women from across the nation through the National Council of Negro Women, in the school she built—Bethune-Cookman University—and in her capacity to broker relationships across the color line with some of the nation's most influential white women.

Bethune understood that she was an individual working at a political crossroads. She learned this approach from her mother and grandmother, women who were born enslaved and who had endured the exploitation of their production and their reproduction and had then survived to ensure their children thrived. The fifteenth of seventeen children, Mary was special in the McLeod household. She was plucked out to attend school while her siblings continued to labor around the family's Sumter County, South Carolina, farm. She also understood her purpose. Beyond self-fulfillment and even after addressing the pressing needs of Black Americans, Mary was destined to shape the future for all humankind.[34]

By 1922, Mary had completed her education at Scotia Seminary and then Moody's Bible Institute. She taught school and married Albertus Bethune, and they had a son. She acquired a keen capacity for institution building and launched her own school for girls and young women, known as the Daytona Educational and Industrial Training School for Negro Girls, later becoming the Bethune-Cookman University. With the ratification of the Nineteenth Amendment, in 1920, Bethune leapt to register Black women on her campus and in the surrounding community.[35]

In 1922, Bethune faced off against the Ku Klux Klan in defense of Black voting rights in Daytona, Florida. There are two versions of this story. Both begin with Daytona's 1922 mayoral election. The candidates were at odds over whether to establish a local high school for Black students. Bethune openly organized Black voter turnout, urging support for the new school. Klan members aimed to stop her, threatening to destroy her school. One version of the story goes that on election eve, hooded Klansmen marched onto campus while Bethune stood out in the open alone, arms folded in defiance. She had sequestered students in their dormitories, while faculty stood like sentries across the grounds. The mob briefly trespassed but then departed without leaving a mark on the campus or its leadership. The following morning, Bethune rose to get hundreds of Black Daytonaites out to vote, and she remained a watchful presence there throughout the day.[36]

Bethune herself told a slightly different version of the story, one in which she confronted the Klan flanked by students. The young people faced the trespassing terrorists and filled the air with the sound of their voices. They sang a hymn. In the aftermath, Bethune described "a band of women as far back as you could look" that accompanied her to the polls and "stood for hours and hours until we got our chance to cast our votes." Both versions of this story reach the same conclusion. Black voters cast their ballots and ensured that Daytona's first Black high school finally came into being.[37]

In the 1930s, Bethune took what she'd learned in Florida to Washington and the White House. There, she advised President Franklin Roosevelt on forming his "Black cabinet," a testament to Bethune's ambition and savvy. The moment signaled that Black women could become highly valued advisors to the Democratic

Party, federal administrators, and the president himself. Bethune had emerged from her experience building Bethune-Cookman and the NCNW as just that. Though mindful of its limitations, Bethune rejected the view that the New Deal was a "raw deal" for Black Americans, as some put it. She came to the administration's attention when she won the NAACP's 1935 Spingarn Medal for her "outstanding achievement," only the second woman to be so honored. Roosevelt appointed Bethune first to the National Youth Administration's National Advisory Committee, one of two Black members, and then as head of a new division, the Office of Minority Affairs, making her the most highly placed Black woman in the Roosevelt years.[38]

Bethune dominated Black politics in Washington, but the wrangling there did not consume her. By 1943, her burgeoning internationalist vision built upon struggles against racism and sexism at home to embrace similar fights across the globe. Bethune linked the fight against anti-Black racism in the United States with anticolonial movements around the globe. She marched the National Council of Negro Women deep into wartime organizing and sat at the table when questions about the contours of postwar politics were debated. Bethune's NCNW was among the groups that pressured the Allied powers to open the deliberations that led to the 1945 United Nations Conference on International Organization. Her message to US, British, and Soviet diplomats, as well as to her fellow activists, was singular: women of color must be at the center of any analysis of international human rights. But making this so was a struggle. When the State Department appointed more than four dozen organizations as consultants to the US delegation, only men affiliated with the NAACP—Walter White and W. E. B. DuBois—represented the interests of Black Americans. Bethune and the women of the NCNW protested, and after the intervention of Eleanor Roosevelt, the NAACP delegation was expanded to three representatives. Bethune became part of the team.[39]

The planning of the United Nations meeting did not follow a regular path. The two men with whom Bethune served—White and DuBois—generally marginalized her. Their differences were rooted in contrasting leadership styles. The men worked by way of a brokerage model, whereas Bethune adopted a broad-based approach that was rooted in community. Bethune looked elsewhere for allies, eventually finding common ground with other women, including Vijaya Lakshmi Pandit of India and Eslanda Robeson, an unofficial observer for the Council on African Affairs, who proved to be one of Bethune's steadfast collaborators. A contingent of NCNW women always accompanied Bethune. They never received formal credentials, and still Bethune's council members remained ever-present observers.[40]

Bethune's thinking deepened through the new associations she built in a community of international activists. She continued to draw upon her long-standing ideas about the close relationship between women's rights and human rights. Her vision also expanded to far beyond the United States, and old ideas took on new meaning as she stepped onto a global stage. The distinctiveness of Bethune's leadership stood out when she worked alongside men like White and DuBois. All three spoke up for human rights and against colonialism during the 1945 conference. But Bethune alone spoke expressly in support of the rights of women. Her rising awareness paralleled what she explained was a worldwide awakening about how the circumstances of women of color around the globe must be a key measure of the United Nations' success.[41]

BETHUNE NEVER GAVE up her platform at the National Council of Negro Women: a place from which Black women could work toward their visions of the political future. In 1946, with the first United Nations conference fresh in her mind, she planned for the NCNW's annual meeting. The postwar era had arrived, and the lessons of the world war would exert tremendous force on domestic affairs. The defeat of the Nazi regime, and the racism at its core, bequeathed to Americans a new, deeply critical perspective on the perniciousness of pseudoscientific thinking about human difference. The term *racism* entered the nation's vocabulary, now to condemn the injustice of Jim Crow. The Double V campaign meant military service abroad—including combat valor—was the currency by which Black Americans had paid the price for equality at home. The opportunity was not lost on Bethune.[42]

In Washington, hundreds of delegates convened at the NCNW's headquarters for their annual meeting. Even ahead of the opening benediction, Bethune made sure that Black Americans knew the women's purpose. The NCNW would talk about organization and policy. Members would confer on issues and share resources. But in 1946, the NCNW would host its own awards ceremony and lift up a pantheon of women. Bethune proposed to honor twelve distinguished women for their leadership, vision, and creativity. They were, Bethune urged, multifaceted, interlocking, and transformational. Her words contained

Mary McLeod Bethune (1875–1955) and Eleanor Roosevelt (1884–1962) in 1937
GETTY IMAGES

both a summing up of their contributions since the Great War and a statement about what the world could expect from women going forward after the Second World War. The honorees were both a boast and an inspiration.[43]

The NCNW award ceremony was Bethune's chance to put on display the vast reach of Black women's political leadership. She honored the interests of working women by singling out labor activist Maida Stewart Springer, who, since the 1920s, had been an organizer for the International Ladies' Garment Workers' Union in New York. In the 1940s, Springer's political work blossomed when she ran for the state assembly and President Roosevelt appointed her to the Office of Price Administration in Washington. By 1946, Springer had just returned from representing the United States abroad as part of the Office of War Information delegation to England—a first for a Black woman. Radical intellectual and thought leader Eslanda Goode Robeson was also honored, a choice that signaled how Black women's politics were not limited by respectability. Robeson was married to the activist and performer Paul Robeson and was an anthropologist whose work on Africa linked her to Communist Party critiques of racism, colonialism, and imperialism. It was risky for the NCNW to ally with Robeson, but she was someone Bethune had come to know and respect precisely for her internationalist perspective.[44]

Arenia Mallory was a more conventional choice for recognition by the NCNW; she had been with Bethune a founder of the organization. But Mallory was also a church activist affiliated with the Church of God in Christ and an educator, having founded a school in Lexington, Mississippi. Although her education and public life took Mallory to Jackson State University and the University of Illinois and then to Washington and even the White House, her concerns never traveled far from those of her home state's working poor. In addition to this trio, Bethune recognized four additional Black women: sculptor Lois Mailou Jones, youth organizer Pauli Murray, New York State judge Jane Bolin, and Lieutenant Colonel Charity Adams Earley, the first African American woman officer in the Women's Army Auxiliary Corps. Bethune's argument was clear. By 1946, Black women leaders had arrived. Americans felt their authority in diverse quarters, and the NCNW was the big-tent organization that recognized their past, present, and future.[45]

Bethune also honored the role that interracial cooperation played in charting American women's futures. White women were among the NCNW honorees in 1946, a gesture that evidenced how Black and white women worked together across the color line on terms of equality. The selection of Agnes Meyer signaled that women in the arts, journalism, and philanthropy were partners with Black women because they all worked toward human rights. Even in the suffrage movement of the past, Bethune found peers. The NCNW recognized Florence Jaffray Harriman, a suffragist who was not a household name but who was distinguished for her support for women's votes, of the League of Nations, and of the Democratic Party. As US minister to Norway in the 1930s, Harriman had aided refugees and eventually secured the safety of Americans and the Norwegian royal family after the German invasion.

No awardee more embodied the interracial cooperation philosophy than did Virginia Foster Durr. An Alabama native, Durr had been a founding member of the Southern Conference for Human Welfare. Like Bethune, Durr had worked closely with Eleanor Roosevelt. She especially championed voting rights and had taken on outlawing the poll tax in an effort to extend the ballot to all Southerners. Bethune also honored her colleague from the National Youth Administration and Congress member from California, Helen Gahagan Douglas.[46]

Ebony magazine published what Bethune called her "Last Will and Testament" shortly after her death in 1955. She anticipated the end of her life and shared her legacy: a commitment to "faith, courage, brotherhood, dignity, ambition and responsibility." She pointed to those among her contemporaries who led with courage, moral stature, and ability. Among them was Mary Church Terrell, who had died just one year earlier. Then Bethune reached back to hold up the "great men and women in the past: Frederick Douglass, Booker T. Washington, Harriet Tubman and Sojourner Truth." Though Bethune had very much lived in the present, in her final words to Black Americans she revealed how she had always been bound up with a grand past of women who had waged the same struggles more than a century before.[47]

Above all, ambition defined Bethune's life. She promoted Black women as national leaders, both by way of their accomplishments and by their authority to judge the work of white women. Her theory about political power stretched from early suffrage struggles through to diplomacy and office holding in the World War II era, leadership that stretched from the Northeast to the South and West. She refused to be limited by any orthodoxy, finding allies in both political parties and even those branded outsider dissidents. Drawing this kaleidoscopic picture of American women's politics, Bethune also positioned Black women for modern civil rights struggles. Their experience, their skills, and their networks would all prove essential as Black women looked to dismantle those barriers that still kept them from full citizenship.

Chapter 9

A WAY TO EXPRESS THEMSELVES...
AND MAKE CHANGE

Struggles for political power had always put Black women's bodies on the front lines. The post–World War II civil rights movement called upon them to do more. They wrote and spoke in public. They organized, taught, strategized, marched, and sat-in. Black women also met the wrath of local officials, mobs, and party bosses. They clocked many more firsts along the way. Journalist Alice Allison Dunnigan became the first Black woman member of the congressional Press Galleries in 1947 and then the first to cover a president, Harry Truman, during his run for office. Constance Baker Motley was the first woman to join the NAACP Legal Defense Fund litigation team and, in 1965, she became Manhattan Borough president, the first woman to hold that office. The following year, President Lyndon Johnson appointed Motley as the first Black woman federal judge in US history. State legislatures seated Black women for the first time in West Virginia, Michigan, New York, Maryland, New Jersey, Illinois, and Indiana. In 1952, newspaper owner and editor Charlotta Bass became the first Black woman nominated for national office, the vice presidency. With the 1965 Voting Rights Act in hand, Black women showed once again that they were the vanguard, blazing a trail to the ballot box and bringing the nation closer than ever to its ideals.[1]

THE 1965 VOTING Rights Act topped a series of victories for the modern civil rights movement won following World War II. The nation lurched toward the ideal of an interracial democracy by giant steps that put Jim Crow's principle of separate but equal in the past. President Truman desegregated the military. The US Supreme Court declared segregated public schools unconstitutional in _Brown v. Board of Education_ in 1954. A decade later, with passage of the Civil Rights Act in 1964, Congress outlawed discrimination based in race, color, religion, sex, or national origin in schools, employment, and places of public accommodation. Political rights came in 1965, with adoption of the Voting Rights Act, which promised to Black women and men power at the polls as voters and in legislatures as office holders. It set in place the rights that African Americans had been struggling toward since the years of Reconstruction, nearly a century before.[2]

Black Americans brought the nation to these changes. They litigated, making the courts a forum for resetting power. They lobbied in state legislatures and in Congress, making the argument that affirming the rights of Black Americans would benefit the whole nation. They organized at the grass roots when officials shut them out of the halls of power. Black activists did this work in the face of great personal risk. The story of the modern civil rights movement is draped in mourning cloth, set there in honor of those who fought and died for justice.[3]

The movement had its architects. Many of them stood before the cameras, while others labored behind the scenes, taking on racism through varied strategies and tactics: nonviolence, direct action, and by any means necessary. The movement was never the sum of its high-level strategists alone. Millions of Black Americans—many of their names known only in families or local lore—picked up the burden that the generations before had borne. They marched. They sat-in. They picketed. They sang and provided the response to a speaker's call. They filled jails and they crowded public offices. They provided a safe haven and they practiced self-defense. They submitted to photographers' lenses and television's cameras, which broadcast their images to the nation and the world from Selma and Greensboro, Birmingham and Topeka, Little Rock and Memphis.[4]

When the interests of Black Americans matched the interests of public officials, civil rights victories were nearly guaranteed. The stage for this meeting of the minds was set when the close of World War II brought on a new conflict, the Cold War. The Marshall Plan remade a world destroyed by fascism and bombs, and the United States became a global powerbroker as wartime allies divided Europe into spheres of interest. A battle for global influence began, and the United States vied with another emerging power, the Soviet Union, for alliance with and even dominion over the peoples of Eastern Europe, the Americas, and Africa. The Soviets did not waste any ammunition when it came to the war of propaganda. They saw in Jim Crow—and the deeply rooted racism that it grew out of—a potent repellant, one that might keep people of color around the globe from siding easily with the United States.[5]

Federal officials felt the sting of this Soviet offensive and began to rethink the terms of American inequality. The Soviet propaganda embarrassed them. News reports amplified instances in which diplomats and foreign service officials of color were discriminated against when they went to dine out in Washington, DC, restaurants. How, the argument went, could the United States be a good ally to Black and brown people around the world when it did not honor the human rights of its own citizens? Nonallied nations should expect that if they signed on to a US-led coalition, racism would follow along with military and economic aid. Members of the Eisenhower administration recalibrated their interests, and civil rights activists exploited the opening. At the US Supreme Court, the US Department of

Justice filed a brief in support of Black schoolchildren in the *Brown* case. A consensus for dismantling Jim Crow emerged.[6]

Even with federal allies, every victory was hard won. Jim Crow's advocates waged their own fight. Among white Southerners were those committed to resisting the full citizenship of Black Americans. In the wake of *Brown*, Southern states defunded public education and countenanced the establishment of private all-white segregated academies. Getting to integration required the direct intervention of federal officials and the National Guard, along with the courage of Black families that risked their children's bodily well-being to defeat separate but equal in some districts. The Freedom Rides of 1961 put teams of Black and white activists on interstate buses, breathing life into court decisions that condemned segregated transportation. Still, as mobs attacked, police and public officials looked away, and in Washington the Justice Department intervened only reluctantly and with too little effect. In the US Senate, some lawmakers vowed to block the Civil Rights Act in 1964. When they failed, the opposition moved closer to the ground. In 1968, South Carolina highway patrol officers in Orangeburg opened fire on two hundred local college students as they attempted to desegregate a bowling alley. It was a brutal example of how painful and costly civil rights victories continued to be.[7]

When it resurfaced in the 1960s, the struggle for voting rights was as old as any cause. It was the latest chapter in the two-hundred-year-long story of how Black Americans had fought against laws and customs that kept them from the ballot box. History revealed the power of the vote—Black men had steered politics after Reconstruction and in some places Black women had influenced elections after 1920. Big changes fueled the quest for voting rights. In 1964, the Twenty-Fourth Amendment to the Constitution made it illegal to demand poll tax payments as a condition for voting in federal elections. Still, getting to the passage of a federal Voting Rights Act would require all the vision, organizing, and risk-taking that Black Americans could muster. Black women were on the front lines, as they always had been.[8]

BY THE LATE 1940s, Black women knew their way around politics. Whether casting ballots at the polls, knocking on officeholders' doors, trading horses in party caucuses, or making grassroots efforts in clubs, they knew how it felt to hold the rough reins of power. Their lives were embattled by the snail's-pace recovery from the Depression in Black communities. They watched as fascism took hold in Europe, and then they volunteered for military service out of a deep commitment to securing human rights, abroad and at home. They helped a new, modern civil rights movement gain a toehold—in courts, Congress, and the local meeting halls and churches that dotted the nation's landscape. From the cosmopolitan salons of the nation's capital to the cramped quarters of Southern sharecroppers' homes, Black women showed what it meant to be full members of political culture.

Winning voting rights became a steady aim. Too many African Americans—women and men—were being kept from the polls by law, custom, and the specter of violence. But women's activism still always mixed the fight for political rights with other long-standing concerns, including freedom from sexual violence, equality in the church, and the liberty to set the terms of work, wages, and family life. Black women were knit together by their critique of how racism and sexism truncated their access to political power. This was an old insight, one that had inspired Black women since Maria Stewart's Boston speeches of the 1830s. But something was new by the 1940s. Black women aimed to secure their political power, and the impediments to that, they insisted, must be a central concern of any movement with which they were affiliated. They offered their allies a new lens through which to view injustice and to define human rights.

A century earlier, *Harper's Weekly* had published another image of African Americans and "The First Vote" in 1867. It depicts African American men only, though a varied trio. The three are lining up before a solitary poll official, himself a plainly dressed, mature man with a generous gray beard. He stands over two jars, his gaze fixed upon the ballots being cast. The first, a working man, a patch on one knee of his loose-fitting pants and the tools of his trade—a mallet and a ruler—tucked in a jacket pocket, places his slip of paper in a jar. He appears modest but dignified, with a tie around his neck and hat in hand. The artist hints that he is a former slave by giving him white hair, a sign that he was born many decades before this post Civil War

A. R. Waud,
"The First Vote."
Harper's Weekly,
November 16, 1867
GETTY IMAGES

moment. Behind him is a gentleman of means, sporting a finely tailored ensemble: jacket, slacks, and wide-brimmed white hat. In his pocket is a book, suggesting he is formally educated. His mustache is carefully groomed, and his stance is one of easy confidence. Perhaps he has been free a long time. Third in line is a soldier—still decked in his Union Army attire. Three stripes are visible on his left sleeve, marking him an officer. The medal on his left breast is a sign of his valor. Together—casting their first ballots—these figures explain that Black men were entitled to voting rights after the Civil War in recognition of their labor, education, and military service.[9]

The editors at *Harper's* encouraged support for Black men's voting rights. "Good sense and discretion, and above all modesty" characterized the Black men who, for the first time in the 1860s, exercised the "vast power that accompanies the privilege" of the vote. Artist Alfred Waud left Black women out of the scene, when in reality they had been very much present. Not only were Black women participants in the Reconstruction-era political conventions. They deliberated with men about politics. They stood guard at polling places while men voted. There is no echo of Elizabeth Cady Stanton, who insisted that white women's votes should come before those of Black men. There is also no sign of Frances Ellen Watkins Harper, who might have critiqued the scene for leaving Black women to be represented by their fathers, husbands, and sons. This veneration of Black voting rights left a great deal unsaid when it came to women.[10]

Fascination with first votes persisted long after 1867. More so than with other political rights, such as jury service or office holding, voting resides at the core of a democracy. Legitimate governance rests upon a mythical people who nominate, deliberate, and finally elect those who carry a sacred trust and bear a collective responsibility for the well-being of all. And so, images of individuals casting their inaugural ballots occupies an iconic place in the American political imagination. The first vote marks a crossing over into political adulthood and entrée into the political culture. Each is an affirmation and recommitment to the ideals of a representative government. Each time a first vote is cast, it is a new expression of faith in the nation. Black Americans have enacted this act of political faith—they have cast first votes—for generations.[11]

Still, many Black women waited longer than most Americans to cast their first votes. In 1965, Joe Ella Moore was nearly seventy years old when a federal official finally administered an oath that made her a registered voter in Prentiss, Mississippi. Federal officials took over twenty-four rooms in a local motel and, according to one report, they "cut connecting doors in the walls, moved out furniture and moved in registration desks." When things there got too cramped, they took over the town post office. Black registration in Prentiss jumped from 5 to 19 percent in just one week.[12]

A local news photographer captured the sight of Joe Ella Moore just as she was being sworn in as a first-time voter. The image went viral, at least in 1965 terms, when the Associated Press distributed the photo to its network of regional newspapers. Bespectacled, with pen in one hand and the text of the oath in another, registrar Crawford A. Phillips of the federal Civil Service Commission welcomes Moore to the state's roster of voters. Moore is dressed for a hot day, wearing a broad, low-brimmed straw hat that shields her face from the sun. A loose, sleeveless blouse is tied modestly, with a white ribbon, just below her chin. Her slender arm is uplifted, her right hand raised, signaling that she swears to the truth of those facts that made her eligible to vote.[13]

Moore had witnessed struggles for dignity and voting rights in Prentiss over many decades. Lynching persisted there until at least 1947, when Versie Johnson was killed by three white police officers who were charged and then found not guilty of manslaughter. In 1956, local officials purged minister Henderson Darby from the voters' rolls in a sweep that cut the number of Black voters in Prentiss from 1,221 to just 60. Along with his wife, Darby attempted to reregister four times in 1957 before finally suing the officials who used an understanding clause to keep him off the

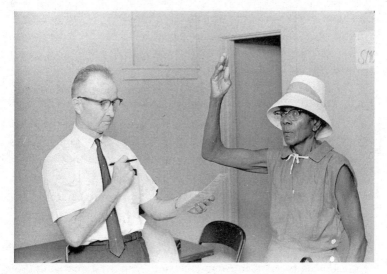

Winfred Moncrief, "Joe Ella Moore" (Prentiss, Mississippi, August 25, 1965)
MISSISSIPPI DEPARTMENT OF ARCHIVES AND HISTORY

rolls. He filed suit on behalf of himself and all those in Prentiss who were being kept from the polls, aided by the state NAACP head, Medgar Evers. Defending the state against Darby, Governor James Plemon "J. P." Coleman remarked that he did not "believe Mississippi Negroes are ready to vote." A three-judge federal court agreed, and Black voters in Prentiss would vote only after passage of the Voting Rights Act. In the interim, Evers was assassinated in front of his home in the early hours of June 12, 1963. He survived if only in memory as a martyr to the cause of voting rights in Mississippi. Joe Ella Moore kept the struggle alive.[14]

That 1965 day in the Magnolia Motel was the first time Moore had *successfully* registered to vote. But she had spent years fighting for this. Like Darby she had already tried on seven occasions to get her name onto Mississippi's voter rolls, only to be rejected at each turn. It was a dangerous and discouraging undertaking. Still, Moore took a final shot at registering, this time at the beckoning of federal officials: "She had heard the president say on the radio this morning that she could register." And so, she appeared at a makeshift office before the federal registrars, one team among the many who arrived in Mississippi to enforce the Voting Rights Act.[15]

The dry language of the radio announcement masked its radical significance. Voting rights had arrived: "The U.S. Civil Service Commission at the request of the attorney general of the United States, acting under the Voting Rights Act of 1965, today started its program to list eligible voters in Prentiss and Jeff Davis County, Miss., without regard to race or color." The political consequences would be wide-reaching, almost immediately. The Mississippi Freedom Democratic Party leader Fannie Lou Hamer had charged and Congressman William Ryan of New York had agreed that there was nothing legitimate about Mississippi's last election because African Americans had been "systematically excluded." Ryan called for the wholesale recall of the state's delegation if things did not change. The entire nation watched as Black Mississippians like Moore breathed life into the Voting Rights Act. Each one understood the import of her raised hand.[16]

In the months that followed, scenes of first votes were enacted again and again. They may have become a regular sight, but they never became ordinary. It would always be extraordinary: thousands of Black Americans joining political culture. The mood was both jubilant and somber. A steep price had been paid for voting rights. In Mississippi, blood stained the fields, the roadways, and the hands of local officials and the ordinary men and women for whom white supremacy had been a cause worth killing for. Still, in the month after the act's passage, Black enrollment increased by 120 percent and five years later, by 1970, 71 percent of eligible Black voters in Mississippi were registered. By 1971, Mississippi had elected a total of fifty Black officials, outranking Black office holding among the Southern states.[17]

DIANE NASH DID not come to the civil rights movement seeking to be a leader, though she certainly was one as a student at Nashville's Fisk University. She had begun her journey many miles to the north, in Chicago, a city free from many of Jim Crow's overt restrictions. Nash had been raised in the hometown of Ida B. Wells's Alpha Suffrage Club, where Black women voters had helped elect an African American, Oscar DePriest, to Congress as far back as 1928. Nash knew that she had been sent to college for good reasons, perhaps to find a vocation. She had not been sent South to get involved with the "wrong bunch" and foment unrest, but with them she found her purpose. During an afternoon at the Tennessee State Fair, Nash was required to use a restroom marked for "colored women." She realized how much work was yet to be done to undo segregation, and she never looked back.[18]

She took leadership seriously. Nash began to guide Nashville's students in a series of sit-ins that intended to desegregate downtown eateries. She was already an organizer and a strategist at heart, more often found in meeting rooms than at the podium. She was not someone who led in front of the camera, in the spotlight, or through generating the adulation of crowds that charismatic leaders thrived upon. Her quiet, steely presence was often most effective just behind the scenes, where young Black Americans learned how to confront oppression together with the violence their protests unleashed.

Nash worked small and she aimed big. Service to others—fellow Fisk students, Black Tennesseans, and African Americans across the South—guided her efforts. In her, the philosophy of nonviolence and its deep and abiding belief in the power of peaceful direct action ran deep. But it was not a selfless approach to leadership. Nash's own interests in dignity, rights, and power were bound up with those whom she served. Many of the images that survive from these early years capture her as part of a crowd, giving directions, and on the move—a blur of action. The best place to find Diane Nash is in the faces of the countless troops for justice that she mobilized.[19]

Nash was a true student of her vocation. She trained in nonviolent civil disobedience under Methodist minister and teacher of Ghandian nonviolence James Lawson, gaining the discipline needed to confront those who would taunt, and then assault, demonstrators who broke with law and custom in the effort to end segregation. Nash was among the students who defeated Nashville's notorious Post House Restaurant—a major victory. She continued the sit-ins and then escalated the protests by being among those who, upon being arrested, refused bail. Nash spent time in solitary confinement and emerged more resolute. She would be arrested over and over, ensuring her place among the movement's leaders for her willingness to put her body on the front lines of change.[20]

Segregation preoccupied Nash's attention. In 1961, when Freedom Riders began to challenge segregation in public transportation she refocused. The Congress of Racial Equality (CORE) arranged for groups of travelers—Black and white, men and women—to ride interstate buses south from Washington, DC, to New Orleans. Mobs, encouraged by local officials, brutally attacked the riders, fire-bombing buses and savagely beating the CORE riders. Despite the intervention of federal officials, the assaults continued. When the riders were forced to abandon their route in Birmingham, Alabama, Nash leapt to action. She could not, Nash explained, permit civil rights to be stopped by violence, and she sent off young people from Tennessee to Alabama to continue the rides. Nash acknowledged that her young activists were putting their lives on the line and she was right. Violence continued in Montgomery even after Nash arrived there with Martin Luther King Jr. They were among those who passed a harrowing night in the city's First Baptist Church, beset by a mob throwing tear gas. As a coordinator of the Nashville Freedom Riders, Nash broke down every night under the burden of having to put the lives of so many others in grave danger.[21]

When she is asked to explain how she came to the fight for voting rights in Selma, Alabama, Nash has always said it started with the girls. The news from Birmingham came from a familiar place, the city's 16th Street Baptist Church, the headquarters for the city's 1963 Children's Crusade. In that moment, hundreds of young people had boycotted schools, marched on downtown streets, and demanded the integration of public buildings, businesses, and classrooms. Scores of arrestees filled the city's jails, successfully pressuring local officials to negotiate with Martin Luther King Jr.'s Southern Christian Leadership Conference (SCLC). A site of triumph soon became one of tragedy: Not so many months later, in September, four members of the United Klans of America planted dynamite at the church. When it exploded on a Sunday morning at nine a.m., four girls lay dead and twenty other worshipers were injured. News about the murders of Addie Mae Collins, Cynthia Wesley, Carole Robertson, and Carol Denise McNair reached Nash and her husband, activist James Bevel, in Edenton, North Carolina, where they were taking part in a SCLC voter registration project.[22]

Nash and Bevel grieved, but their organizer's instincts quickly kicked in. That same afternoon, the two drafted what became the Selma plan. Nash presented the strategy to King, but took many months to persuade the SCLC leadership to target Alabama. Nash began by writing pamphlets and collecting statistics. Soon she was on the ground in Selma, where she organized "people who needed and wanted a way to express themselves and wanted a way that they could make change." Nash negotiated the tense relationship between the Student Nonviolent Coordinating Committee (SNCC) and SCLC. She spoke decisively to demonstrators at Brown Chapel African Methodist Episcopal Church, the Selma campaign's headquarters. When it came time for the fateful marches out of Selma, Nash mapped out where protesters would go and when, and ran the logistics. When state officials unleashed police billy clubs, fists, and hard-toed boots on marchers as they paused on the far side of the Edmund Pettus Bridge, it was Nash who made sure that medics were soon on the scene. Later, as marchers finally reached Montgomery, Nash completed the last few blocks alongside King.

At Selma, Nash harnessed all of the principles that had brought her to that moment. She understood the bargain that would bring federal officials to the table when it came to voting rights. "The principles of nonviolence had left marchers especially vulnerable to violence. But it also won them supporters from those across the country, including in Washington, D.C." There was a terrible price to be paid by those who put their bodies on the front lines and met brutality with nonviolence. She was emboldened by what transpired at Selma when a "peaceful demonstration" exposed "the brutal intransigence of anti-voting rights state officials." Within just a few months of the Selma demonstrations, President Johnson signed the Voting Rights Act into law. But it was Nash who brought about voting rights in Alabama on the ground.[23]

In August 1965, the SCLC held its annual meeting in Birmingham. The theme was "Human Rights, Basic Issues, the Grand Alliance." It was, for Nash, a return to the city where murderous violence had sharpened her commitment to winning voting rights. She may have paid respect to the four girls killed at the 16th Street Baptist Church that day; no doubt they were on her mind. Nash surfaced only amid the crowd of four thousand that had gathered in the city's Municipal Center. Many had come to hear Martin Luther King Jr., who had won the Nobel Peace Prize the previous year. King's subject that night was the war in Vietnam, and he urged the nation to end its cycle of "mistrust, violence, and war" in Southeast Asia.[24]

The program at Birmingham also honored Black women's leadership. The banquet speaker was former NAACP Legal Defense Fund attorney Constance Baker Motley, who had since been elected to the New York State Senate and the "first" Manhattan Borough president. Rosa Parks was also honored, "for her most historical role in the civil rights movement," in a ceremony presided over by Septima Clark, director of the SCLC's Citizenship Schools. Women struggled within the SCLC to win authority and independence, but the force of their leadership was nearly irresistible.[25]

The conference "highlight" arrived when King presented the organization's highest honor, the Rosa Parks Award, to James Bevel and Diane Nash, "SCLC workers in Alabama." The two were lauded for being "at the forefront of almost every major civil rights campaign" and "long-time, front line 'freedom fighters.'" There was a panel discussion during which Bevel pressed his commitment to nonviolence into the realm of international affairs, calling for the formation of a "peace team" comprising King, the pope, and Mrs. Nikita Khrushchev that would personally urge President Johnson to end the war. If Nash spoke even a word during the conference, it went unrecorded. Her force, however, lay only partly in words. Nash's political leadership was most powerful behind the scenes, where she planned, maneuvered, conspired, and built cooperation among activists, all keys to the success of the Selma movement.[26]

DIANE NASH, AS a strategist and an organizer, avoided the limelight. Not all women were so retiring. Pauli Murray knew she wanted to be seen and recognized in the battle against what she came to call "Jane Crow," that particular brand of racism that was cut through with sexism. Murray made plain how, even when men and women worked alongside one another, their challenges were not the same. Murray's maneuverings through circles of law, politics, and religion illustrate how Black women, even as they were on the precipice of gaining political rights, continued to develop a kind of power that kept them nimble. It made them effective. Murray was an ally to those women who, like Nash, took up the quest for voting rights, but she charted her own path.[27]

As a young woman, Murray doubted the value politics of parties and candidates, and her first appearances at the polls were uneasy. She voted in her first presidential contest in 1932, an election that ended with Democrat Franklin Roosevelt resoundingly defeating the Republican Herbert Hoover. Murray cast her ballot in New York City, where she had recently graduated from Hunter College for Women. Hers was, as she later put it, "a vote of protest." She could not bring herself to support either major party, and so she cast her ballot for the Socialist

Norman Thomas. The next election cycle was no less fraught. In 1936, Murray was just ending her affiliation with the Communist Party Opposition, and she bridled against pressure to vote for the Communist candidate, Earl Browder. By the 1950s, her views had shifted and, in the wake of the 1965 Voting Rights Act, Murray, by then a civil rights attorney, joined a team that defeated the exclusion of Black women from juries in the Lowndes County, Mississippi, case of *White v. Crook*. Murray came to see Black women's power at the polls as critical. But that was only later.[28]

Murray's real entrée into politics came in March 1940, when she joined the annals of women traveling while Black. It was the eve of an Easter Sunday visit with her Durham, North Carolina, family. Riding by bus from New York City, Murray and her friend, Adeline McBean, were required to change buses in a Virginia depot. The company relegated the two women to a vastly inferior bus, one brought out to accommodate heavier-than-usual holiday traffic demand; they found the seats for Black riders uncomfortable and in disrepair. The women asked the driver to rearrange a few white passengers to make room for them closer to the front. He refused "curtly," and with his arm pushed Murray backward into the bus. After a heated back-and-forth with the driver, Murray and McBean were arrested pursuant to charges that shifted in the coming hours and days. This was not part of any plan or test case. With the support of civil rights attorneys, the women were found guilty of only a minor, disturbing-the-peace charge.[29]

Interstate buses did not set aside seats for "ladies." Nor did Murray and McBean fit easily into how Black women were expected to appear in public. Murray did not carry herself as a woman, and initially other passengers, and perhaps the driver himself, believed her—slim, dressed in slacks and a shirt, and with her hair combed back—to be a man. This was, it is important to note, her aim. But in what followed, gender, as in womanhood, still mattered. McBean was the more compelling and sympathetic of the two, at least in the eyes of one observer.

McBean's unambiguous womanhood—along with an infirmity that had overtaken her aboard the second bus—gave her pleas for just treatment a persuasive quality that Murray's words—practiced, professional, and appearing to emanate from a young man—did not.[30]

The confrontation on that Virginia bus activated Murray, ushering her into civil rights politics and law. The women's legal wrangling brought them to Washington, where they met Thurgood Marshall and Link Johnson. They also met Judge William Hastie and Dr. Leon Ransom, members of the Howard University Law faculty. These were fateful encounters. The following fall, with the support of Ransom, Murray began her studies at Howard Law School. In that legendary setting—the crucible for the development of the NAACP's civil rights litigation strategy—Murray's expectations were high. Still, it took some happenstance, including a chance encounter with Ransom, who encouraged her application, to get her to Washington to enroll for the fall 1941 semester.[31]

At Howard, Murray's education went far beyond any course or curriculum. She learned lessons about the double bind of racism and sexism. Murray was not wholly certain she belonged. Howard Law was already a fabled place by 1940, with a reputation that was well earned. There, Houston had trained young Black men—including the civil rights warrior Thurgood Marshall. Murray was as ambitious as any young man. She quickly demonstrated her intellectual prowess and ranked first in the class. As a woman in a law school populated almost entirely by men, she was tested as never before. Sexism at Howard Law sometimes came in the form of demeaning remarks or outright disregard. More often, it was more insidious: indifference and a failure to wholly see the young woman student and her capacities for lawyering and leadership.[32]

Murray's refuge came about solely out of necessity. Her scholarship money did not add up, even when supplemented by the gift of a generous benefactor. To make ends meet, she accepted the offer from a cousin and Howard's Dean of Women, Susie

Elliott, of a space in the university's dormitory for undergraduate women, Sojourner Truth Hall. For some students, a tiny room at the end of a first-floor corridor might have been a depressing if not demeaning circumstance. For Murray, it was the place that gave her purpose. In a small "powder room," there in a hall named for a pioneer of Black women's rights, Murray set up a study hall and meeting space. After hours, Howard's young women students sought out Murray for her growing legal expertise and her willingness to share it. Sitting cross-legged, leaning against a nearby wall, or perhaps perched on the edge of a bed, Howard's young women students gathered as Murray held court, serving as counselor, teacher, and organizer at the dawn of the modern civil rights era.[33]

It was a woman's time at Howard. Of course, men still attended, and they dominated the faculty. But those who were draft-eligible, along with some who voluntarily heeded the call to enlist, were absent. Sixty percent of the university's students were women, but for Murray, any number of men was new. Howard's atmosphere was distinct from the women-only undergraduate scene at Hunter. Sexism was, for the first time in her formal education, a regular part of her daily strife, even as racism receded there on a predominantly Black campus. Murray may have felt disoriented and disappointed, but she pushed back. When a call to join the Phi Alpha Delta law fraternity invited only men students, Murray confronted her beloved professor and mentor, Leon Ransom, only to be dismissed. He told her that if she desired such a professional opportunity, she was welcome to begin a parallel sorority. Ransom's words stung, but they also contributed to Murray's self-awareness of how gender worked, and how it could work against her. Murray's excellence would ultimately be recognized when the Law Students Guild elected her Chief Justice of the Court of Peers. Still, her thinking was forever changed.[34]

At Howard, a community of women surrounded Murray, and she grew to depend upon them for emotional, intellectual, and political sustenance. Caroline Ware, a history professor, became a friend and guide through a world of new ideas, especially those about inequality and the law. National Woman's Party member and sculptor Betsy Graves Reyneau arrived at Howard to produce a portrait of the school's first African American president, Mordecai Johnson. Reyneau introduced Murray to the long history of women's rights and their entanglement with slavery and racism. Ruth Powell, an undergraduate from Massachusetts, headed Howard's NAACP Direct Action Committee and befriended Murray. Nearby, Pauline Redmond, who had joined the staff of the National Youth Administration, was a confidante who encouraged Murray to take her concerns to Washington's highest officials. The two shared an afternoon at the White House with First Lady Eleanor Roosevelt that led to enduring alliances. Murray's political identity coalesced as she adopted a more conventional vantage point—that of a woman—even as internally she wrestled with being a man in a woman's body and experiencing desires for which she did not yet have words.[35]

In collaboration with Howard's young women students, Murray was about to receive an education outside the classroom. She had been a student of nonviolent direct action through the pacifist Fellowship of Reconciliation, and she had even developed her own version of the approach, one that combined nonviolence with what she called "American techniques of showmanship." An opportunity to test her theory arrived in winter of 1943, when three sophomore women insisted on being served at a Pennsylvania Avenue food counter. It took a police officer's directive to finally get them their cups of hot chocolate—the young women were breaking no local law by demanding service. But when the bill arrived, the students were overcharged. Upon exiting, they paid only the regular price, giving police a reason to arrest and jail them.[36]

Murray soon learned that among the three protesters was her friend Ruth Powell, who had been quietly waging her own sit-in campaign for nearly a year. From Massachusetts, Powell was a newcomer to the capital's Jim Crow routines and later explained that she believed "all these little bits of agitation would go toward that vital...awakening process" that would enlighten white Americans. Powell's strategy became the core of Murray's plan, and her tiny quarters in Truth Hall buzzed as the young women prepared for direct action. They surveyed campus attitudes about segregation. They researched and publicized pending civil rights legislation. Pep rallies and town hall meetings built support. In-class discussions led to deeper insights. Among the lessons were those derived from Black women's respectability politics: dress, decorum, and dignity, at all times. Powell headed the committee that sponsored weekly actions at local restaurants "sitting quietly, requesting service." They rebuffed Howard's president, Mordecai Johnson, who feared for the school's future funding should students upset the admittedly unjust racial etiquette of the District of Columbia.[37]

The full weight of their planning was brought to bear on a rainy Saturday afternoon in April. A dozen or so students sat down at tables in the Little Palace Cafeteria. They waited to be served. A second group assembled outside and formed a picket line: "Our Boys, our Bonds, our Brothers Are Fighting for YOU! Why Can't We Eat Here?" It was a long forty-eight hours before the restaurant capitulated and agreed to serve Black customers.[38]

Murray later considered these moments as critical to sharpening her analysis of Black women's political power. Most of those who emerged victorious after the Little Palace Cafeteria action were women. Still, it was the strategic linking of two strains of African American contributions to the war—young men's service abroad and young women's action at home—that was fundamental to their success. In this, they borrowed from the logic of the Double V campaign: "Democracy—Double Victory, at Home—Abroad." The long-term effects were real. The student actions were not mere outbursts, nor were they episodes of youthful exuberance. Murray later looked back to appreciate how the young women she came to know so well in the early months of 1943 went on to lead in social service, education, government administration, and civil rights politics. It was a signature feature of Murray's work—she was often both protégée and mentor, blurring generational lines to broaden the movement's aims.[39]

At Howard, Murray's most influential idea was born: Jane Crow. *Jim Crow* had long before entered everyday parlance as a phrase that captured the elements of American disenfranchisement, segregation, and violence. Murray was searching for a similar kind of phrase, one that would offer a framework that recognized the burdens borne by women. How could the civil rights movement better speak to contests over the ladies' car or the ubiquity of sexual assault? How could activists better account for the subordination of women in their own circles and for the disabilities women faced in courthouses? It would be two decades more before Murray would publish her defining article: "Jane Crow and the Law: Sex Discrimination and Title VII." But it was at Howard, in Sojourner Truth Hall, that Murray came to understand how her analysis needed to meet the challenges that she and other Black women were living.[40]

Murray's life was nothing short of extraordinary in the decades that followed her years at Howard Law. Her work singularly shaped the rights of American women. Still, none of her many accomplishments resonated more with the long history of Black women's politics than her ordination to the priesthood in 1977. Had she read the memoirs of nineteenth-century women like Jarena Lee and Julia Foote, Murray would have recognized how the same thinking that had kept Lee and Foote from the pulpit still animated church debates more than a century later. Murray battled over the rights of women in the place that had been her spiritual home nearly her entire life. She agitated on the issue first in her local parish—St. Mark's-on-the-Bowery on New York City's Lower East Side—and continued through her time, starting at age sixty-two, as a student at the General Theological Seminary.[41]

The Episcopalian hierarchy was debating the future of women in the church, and Murray was not shy about calling for change. In a final year spent at the Virginia Theological Seminary, where overall thinking was more compatible with hers,

Murray confronted women's ordination head-on. The debate grew heated as women were ordained by progressive bishops, and then denied licenses by conservative others. In September 1976, the church-wide General Convention finally concluded that "no one shall be denied access" to ordination on the basis of sex, effective January 1, 1977. Murray became the first Black woman elevated to full privileges in the Episcopal Church. Preceding her investiture at Washington's National Cathedral, Murray understood the historic nature of her ordination: "It appears I am the first Negro (my preference) woman to be approved for admission to the priesthood in the Anglican communion in the USA, some 172 years after Absalom Jones, the *first* Afro-American to be ordained a priest—in 1804 at the age of 58."[42]

On the day of her ordination, Murray ensured that she would be seen, in every sense of the word. She dressed herself that morning in a simple white smock with a priest's collar around her neck, its distinctive tab covered by a collaret of black that left just a small square of white visible at the front of her throat. The ceremony itself was held in the nation's most prominent house of worship, the Episcopal Church at the Washington National Cathedral. Murray was among six candidates, or ordinates, affirmed by the bishop for the Diocese of Washington, the Right Reverend William F. Creighton. News outlets gave Murray's latest distinction broad coverage. She might have especially appreciated the irony in the *Washington Post*'s wording, which noted that she was the only "regular" woman candidate; the two others were "irregularly ordained" women who were finally being recognized. The *Chicago Tribune* noted that among the thirty Episcopal women slated for ordination that same month, one was "an acknowledged lesbian in New York City," though the article referred to someone other than Murray.[43]

Perhaps most striking of all was how Murray came to see herself. Through faith, she discovered another view that transcended the man-made differences that too often troubled the lives of Black women: "All the strands of my life had come together. Descendant of slave and of slave owner, I had already been called poet, lawyer, teacher, and friend." In faith and her identity as a priest, Murray looked past how others saw her: "Now I was empowered to minster the sacrament of One in whom there is no north or south, no Black or white, no male or female—only the spirit of love and reconciliation drawing us all toward the goal of human wholeness." It was a concern for all of humanity that ensured that Black women would continue to claim Murray as their sister. Her concerns were theirs, too.[44]

Murray did not take singular credit for her ordination. Instead, she encouraged others to regard her achievement as reflecting women's broader struggles for power. She was, for example, a founder of the National Organization for Women (NOW), a manifestation of her commitment to winning women's equality that fit with her church activism. Murray's ordination bookended a tale that began with the first Black men who had been made ministers in the same church at the start of the nineteenth century: "One-hundred and seventy-two years after ordaining the first Black man into the priesthood, the Episcopal Church admitted its first Black woman, the Reverend Pauli Murray." Murray characteristically offered her own reinterpretation, clarifying that she was not a "first": "I supported the women who went ahead of me (in the church ministry) and it was their agony which made my own ordination possible." She was part of a collective and a longer effort, a story of which she was but one part. And although she knew she was a first at many things, being ordained "is the end of a long series of firsts for me," she explained. But that alone wasn't enough to humble Murray in light of her lifetime of accomplishments. Being a woman, she believed, was not her defining qualifier in all things: "It isn't being the first Negro woman (priest), it is being a priest that frightens me." Perhaps she had transcended.[45]

Even in the heyday of voting rights activism, Pauli Murray was singular. She lived by a brand of nimbleness and versatility, and no movement defined or contained her. Instead, Murray, the intellectual, crystallized Black women's thinking in the civil rights era when she proposed Jane Crow as its own brand of discrimination, one that required distinct thinking and tactics. At each phase of her life, she self-consciously aimed for the cutting edge and intersected with other Black women at many junctures, from segregated buses and lunch counters to courthouses and churches. Her distance from the center of voting rights activism, through this lens, demonstrates how old frameworks for Black women's politics, alongside new ones, persisted.

IF PAULI MURRAY believed she saw the civil rights revolution coming, nobody told Rosa McCauley Parks, growing up in Montgomery, Alabama, that she was destined for a life in politics. Parks came of age in the grass roots of Black America, where the challenges faced by her family and friends determined her concerns. Parks shared with Pauli Murray a keen sense of how women fit within the broader Black freedom struggle, and she would develop a similarly deft approach, one that let her move easily between issues and tactics on the road to human rights. Parks is best known for refusing to give up her bus seat and launching a game-changing boycott in Montgomery, Alabama. But it was her early training in the politics of sexual violence and voting rights that meant Parks never separated the rights of women from those of Black Americans. When invoked as a symbol of women's modest, commonsense contributions to the civil rights movement, what is left unacknowledged is Parks's identity as a sophisticated activist and tactician, for whom women's rights and civil rights were one and the same struggle.[46]

Born in 1913 in south-central Alabama, Rosa's education came about through a patchwork of experiences. Her mother, a teacher, wove learning into her everyday life. Her grandfather taught Rosa lessons about self-defense, self-determination, and the pan-African philosophy of the Garvey movement. Nothing about her elders' aspirations shielded Rosa from hard work, and her fingers knew the sharp edges of the cotton boll that inflicted cuts and slices during hours spent picking. At the white-run Miss White's Industrial School for Girls, among the African American students, Rosa prepared for a life of domestic labor. She did not earn a diploma, but she did make lifelong friends.[47]

Life soon taught Rosa the purpose of Black women's rights when an encounter in an employer's kitchen drove home the threat of sexual violence. It was 1931, the midst of the Depression, and Rosa, still a teen, thought herself lucky to have a position as a maid and babysitter, even if it required she work seven days and many nights. An otherwise ordinary day ended with Rosa alone in the house. She settled into the living room, where her habit was to read the newspaper, listen to the radio, or hear records on the phonograph. It was the time of day she most looked forward to. A knock on the back door brought Rosa face-to-face with the household's maintenance man, who uttered a pretense about having left behind his coat. Rosa did not find a coat, but she did recognize that over his shoulder stood a white man—someone she identified with the generic "Mr. Charlie"— who then entered the kitchen. Her coworker disappeared and the intruder poured himself a whiskey while Rosa began washing dishes. She offered him a seat in the living room, where he might wait for the homeowners, but the visitor continued to hover. It was only another moment before the man's intent became plain. He had come to see Parks, not her employers. Finding his hand on her waist, Rosa was "just plain scared nearly to death."[48]

She knew she was in danger as a thin ritual of seduction unfolded: he offered her a drink, reassured her that she would not be "hurt," professed affection, promised to cure her loneliness, pled for sweetness, and offered money. Emotions—from hurt and helplessness to anger and disgust—coursed through Rosa: "I felt filthy and stripped naked of every shred of decency." Assessing that her "puny" body was no physical match for the "tall, heavy set man," Rosa also judged that white supremacy framed the confrontation: "The white man's dominance over the Negro's submissive subjection through the history of chattel slavery—semi-freedom to this moment." Her thoughts turned to God, and then Rosa reached for history as a weapon. She "talked and talked of everything [she] knew about the white man's inhuman treatment of the Negro." By law and custom, Black women and white men were intended to be separate in all things intimate, Rosa reminded her assailant. She intended to honor the color line drawn by antimiscegenation laws and he should do the same.[49]

Rosa revealed her careful thinking about how Black women figured in a world fractured by lines of race and sex. For example, when her assailant asserted that her coworker had said it was "alright for him to be there with her," Rosa was indignant and shot back a proclamation of her autonomy as a woman. Her coworker, she said, "had nothing to do with me of what I chose to do or not do. He did not own me and could not offer me for sale." She intended to set the terms of her intimate life by the principles of choice and consent. Rosa continued: "I hoped to marry and live a decent respectable life rather than be a white man's tramp." She was unafraid, Rosa explained, "ready and willing to die, but give any consent, never. Never. Never. It was absolutely unthinkable." In those fraught moments, Rosa chose dignity over life: "If he wanted to kill me and rape a dead body, he was welcome....While I lived, I would stand alone in my belief, no matter who was against me." Rosa once again insisted that her assailant leave the house, emphasizing that the encounter was over by sitting herself in an armchair, opening a newspaper, and beginning to read. The experience haunted her.[50]

By 1932, Rosa had met and married barber Raymond Parks, the husband with whom she enjoyed a partnership that stretched from family life to politics. She quickly became his ally in the defense of nine young men accused of rape in Scottsboro, Alabama. The Black defendants were charged with sexually assaulting two white women aboard a freight train traveling between Chattanooga and Memphis, Tennessee. In rushed trials and without adequate counsel, all but one of the young men were convicted and sentenced to death. Harassed and coerced, their records included confessions of wrongdoing, but ultimately, they asserted their innocence. Their story revealed how white supremacy victimized the South's Black working poor, and both the legal arm of the Communist Party USA (CPUSA) and the NAACP stepped in to defend the accused.[51]

Black Southerners risked being branded dissidents when they supported the Scottsboro defendants, especially after the CPUSA International Labor Defense took over the case. Public support could lead to the loss of employment, harassment, and worse. Still, there is no sign that Parks hesitated when she joined her husband as he organized support for a lengthy series of appeals and retrials. The case spoke to her own experience, another example of how sexual violence threatened Black Americans. In the Scottsboro case, the direct victims were not Black women, though the young men's mothers would go public to encourage support for their sons' freedom. In Scottsboro, the victims were young men for whom a false charge of committing sexual assault against white women promised death, be it by a lynch mob, a hangman's noose, or the electric chair. In Parks's world, the issue of sexual assault cut two ways for Black Americans. Encounters with predatory white men placed women's dignity at risk, while false accusations threatened the well-being of Black men.[52]

As she made sense of the twisted logics of sexual violence, Parks charted her own course through politics. She drew upon examples of those who came before her, many of them women. There were those in her own family, including Parks's great-grandmother: "In slavery days [she] could not do more or know more than to be used and abused by the slave owner. She was bred, born and reared to serve no other purpose than that which resulted in the bastard issue to be trampled, mistreated and abused by both Negro slave and white master." Parks read the histories of influential Black activists from Crispus Attucks, the first man to fall during the American Revolution, to the African Methodist Episcopal Church's founding bishop, Richard Allen. She admired her Baptist Church contemporaries, pastor Adam Clayton Powell Sr. and his son, the minister and member of Congress, Adam Clayton Powell Jr. Her models among Black women stretched across nearly two hundred years, from the eighteenth-century enslaved woman and poet Phillis Wheatley, to the nineteenth-century advocates of abolition and women's rights, Sojourner Truth and Harriet Tubman. Among her twentieth-century contemporaries, Parks singled out Mary McLeod Bethune as among the women whose work informed Parks's activism.[53]

Parks might have chosen to settle into an ordinary life in Montgomery. But even the ordinary was anything but that in Alabama. Parks's schoolmate Johnnie Carr described the city as the state capital and "the Cradle of the Confederacy and the Heart of Dixie." Discontent simmered in Montgomery, "a place where Negroes seemed very polite to the other group. Always giving up their rights for peace. But this kind of peace was only on the surface; way deep down inside they were sick at heart of the many humiliating experiences which led to deep resentment." Parks's own grievances led her to make a fateful decision. In 1943, she spotted a photo of Carr in attendance at a local NAACP meeting, a branch of the venerable civil rights organization. When the next meeting was called, Parks headed to the hall. With a quick scan of the room, she confirmed that she was the only woman present and set about to make herself useful. Before the proceedings concluded, she was selected branch secretary and took a seat among the leadership.[54]

That same night, she met E. D. Nixon, a Montgomery-based Pullman porter and union activist who was spearheading a voter registration campaign. Nixon's Montgomery Voters League aimed to grow the woefully small number of Black voters in the city: just thirty-one Black residents, out of thousands, were on the rolls. The state of Alabama's application demanded that prospective voters disclose their employer, business, education, and history of drug or alcohol use and declare their loyalty to the government. All registrants were asked if they had previously attempted registration. Officials demanded that those who did not own property pass additional tests. When successful, the names of registrants were published in the local newspaper, inviting retribution. And, even after all that, registrants were required to pay retrospective poll taxes, placing voting nearly always out of reach.[55]

Parks tried more than once to register and when, in 1944, Nixon assembled 750 people to add their names to the rolls, Parks and her mother joined the group. They succeeded, though she was required to pass the state tests and then pay back poll taxes. In 1945, she voted for gubernatorial candidate James Folsom, an integration moderate and modest advocate of Black civil rights. Her work continued with the local Youth Council through which she encouraged voter education and the registration of young people. It had all been an ordeal, and Parks described the "trying...hazardous conditions, such as being denied a number of times, and feeling that there was a threat just to become a registered voter and cast my ballot to elect offices." Voting rights were the foundation of Parks's political training.[56]

Through the lens of her early experiences, it is apparent how Parks continued to blend the concerns of women with those of Black men to arrive at an enduring commitment to collective human rights. The Montgomery challenge to segregated transportation began when city officials arrested Parks for failing to heed a bus driver's order to move from her seat and culminated in a victory for all Black Americans: the US Supreme Court, in *Browder v. Gayle*, ruled that segregated transportation was unconstitutional in Alabama and across the nation. Women were the heart of the Montgomery movement, starting with the domestic workers who walked, carpooled, took taxis, or rode with employers and risked themselves on the streets of a city rife with tension. Members of the city's Women's Political Council roused support for Parks by framing the indignities of segregated buses as especially offensive when imposed upon women: "If we do not do something to stop these arrests, they will continue. The next time it may be you, or your daughter, or mother."[57]

Parks took her seat as President Lyndon Johnson's staff attended to the final details of the 1965 Voting Rights Act signing ceremony. She had arrived there by Johnson's special invitation, and a casual observer might have mistaken Parks for a seamstress whose tired feet had sparked a critical episode on the road to African American political rights. Parks came to Washington to celebrate expanding access to the polls, but those who knew Parks well were aware that she stood not only for Black women's voting rights but also for their liberation from some of Jim Crow's worst horrors. She was also there as a survivor of white men's harassment and as an advocate for women who had not escaped the sexual violence that pervaded their work and their lives. She was an icon from the past, but Parks was also a harbinger of Black women's futures.

FANNIE LOU HAMER had been rebuffed, harassed, beaten, and sexually assaulted at the hands of local officials. Her experiences as an activist in the early 1960s was a testament to why Black women needed the vote and needed it immediately. Without political power, they could not expect the state to address their concerns or take up their interests in fair wages and equitable work conditions, along with decent housing, public schools, and municipal services. Hamer's approach to power rejected benevolence and meager accommodations that white Mississippians might dole out. If sociologists or demographers might cast Hamer as a lesser, she held herself out as an equal. Her work was to awaken her home state and the nation to those places in American politics that Black Americans intended to inhabit. She began at the polls, but traveled all the way to the heart of the Democratic Party. And she brought with her thousands of Black women who would never again retreat.[58]

When Hamer spoke of voting rights, history ran through her thinking. Early in her days as a field secretary for the Student Nonviolent Coordinating Committee, she testified about registering as a Black woman in rural Mississippi. Violence, intimidation, and retaliation were ever present—running through many of Hamer's days and rendering most of her nights harrowing. Important to Hamer's thinking was a historical perspective: she and others labored for African American freedom during one of western Mississippi's most haunted chapters, and they were making history. When she told her story, as she often did with eloquence, Hamer explained her voting rights activism of the 1960s and 1970s as one chapter in the same African American freedom struggle that had touched the generations that preceded her.[59]

The youngest of twenty children, Hamer was born in Montgomery County, Mississippi, in 1917 and spent the first part of her life raising a family and picking cotton as a sharecropper. She began to talk of rights in 1962, when local officials prevented her and a group of neighbors, all rural Mississippians, from registering to vote. Racial discrimination was an offense, as Hamer put it to a Harlem audience, "based upon the violation of the Thirteenth, Fourteenth, and Fifteenth Amendments to the United States Constitution, which hadn't done anything for us yet." As Hamer analyzed inequality in Mississippi and across the nation, the US Constitution was important. She believed that its principles guaranteed Black Americans voting rights, and her aim as an organizer was to compel the nation to make good on that promise.[60]

Hamer spoke on behalf of the hundreds of thousands of Black Americans who, like her, were denied voting rights, even one hundred years after Reconstruction's constitutional revolution. She noted how denial of the ballot persisted, particularly in the Deep South, because Mississippi's election authorities were using literacy and understanding tests to disqualify Black men and women. Hamer was quick to explain that the imposition of such qualifications and the related terror were violations of their rights as citizens and of equal protection before the law. Law mattered. But Hamer never spoke of the Nineteenth Amendment the way she did of the Fourteenth and Fifteenth Amendments. Yes, she was a woman. But she did not see the terms of the Nineteenth Amendment—the one that constitutionalized women's voting rights—as protecting her.

If the ballot box was a battleground, so too was Hamer's body. Even before she became an activist, racism exacted a brutal price when, without her knowledge, doctors performed a hysterectomy on her. That started a long-standing confrontation between Hamer, her body, and the state. Another encounter with racist brutality in 1963 left her permanently damaged. Traveling home by bus from an SNCC conference, Hamer and colleagues stopped in Winona, Mississippi, for a bite to eat and to use the restroom. Local police confronted the group and, rankled by their refusal to defer to the white men's authority, arrested them all. Harrowing days followed, nearly costing Hamer and others their lives.[61]

Hamer described what happened when it was her turn to be interrogated in jail. She was alone with one highway patrol officer and two Black prisoners:

> The state highway patrolmen ordered the first Negro to take the Blackjack. The first Negro prisoner ordered me, by orders from the state highway patrol man, for me to lay down on a bunk bed on my face. And I laid on my face and the first Negro began to beat me. And I was beat by the first Negro until he was exhausted....After the first Negro had beat until he was exhausted, the state highway patrolman ordered the second Negro to take the Blackjack. The second Negro began to beat me to sit on my feet to keep me from working my feet. I began to scream and one white man got up and began to beat me in my head and tell me to hush. One white man—my dress had worked up high—he walked over and pulled my dress, I pulled my dress down and he pulled my dress back up.[62]

Hamer later disclosed that a sexual assault followed.

She sustained "devastating and permanent injuries" and was forever changed. Hamer lost sight in her left eye and suffered permanent kidney damage. The limp she had long lived with, one she believed was the result of a childhood bout with polio, worsened. In this way, Hamer wore the struggle for voting rights for all to see. The injuries she sustained were one price

Hamer paid for her insistence on her rights. As her public reputation grew over the years, when Hamer took the podium across the nation, the injuries inflicted at Winona were her first form of testimony about the price that Black women paid for the vote.[63]

In 1964, Hamer's image was broadcast into thousands upon thousands of American homes, live from that summer's Democratic National Committee (DNC) convention in Atlantic City, New Jersey. Hamer arrived there as a member of the Mississippi Freedom Democratic Party (MFDP) delegation, a dissenting body that sought to displace the state's party representatives, all of whom had been designated without the input of Black citizens who had been denied the ballot during the state's primary election in 1963. The MFDP's unwavering insistence upon being seated inaugurated a series of complicated negotiations. Behind the scenes, Hamer went back and forth between party officials, agents of the Johnson administration, and civil rights leaders, including Martin Luther King Jr. At some moments she was nearly cut out from the wrangling. But she managed to steer her party throughout.[64]

Hamer prepared herself to stand and speak before an audience that extended far beyond the DNC's 110-member credentials committee. Television viewers watched as NBC broadcast Hamer's civil rights initiative into living rooms across the nation. By the 1960s, live television news ensured that images circulated with unprecedented speed, and women in the Black freedom struggle understood that viewers would assess them in part through their comportment and their dress. This was not the era of respectability politics. Instead, Black women had a broadening repertoire upon which to draw as they dressed to buttress their political authority. The backdrop for Hamer's appearance was a new "soul style" of dress that signaled, even before they spoke a word, how women who donned it were practicing the politics of liberation.[65]

Hamer made no secret of her origins. She said that she began life as a working person and that her body bore the signs of countless hours spent picking cotton—the ache of a back too long bent over in the fields and the rough skin of hands too often cut by the sharp pod that held cotton bolls. But in Atlantic City, Hamer did not don a sharecropper's signature denim coveralls— even as many of her young women allies in SNCC did so as a gesture of solidarity with women like her. Nor did Hamer don a scarf or head wrap, which would have suggested how she had been impoverished as local white people retaliated against her family for her political activism.

News cameras panned to capture Hamer as she stepped to the DNC credentials committee witness table, self-styled as a middle-class woman, finely dressed for the occasion. Most prominent was Hamer's light-colored handbag, hooked over her forearm, prominently carried, a sign of her membership in a class of women for whom a purse signaled the possession of accouterments, from a pack of mints and a cosmetic case to a wallet with cash and perhaps a credit card. Hamer's short-sleeved dress was belted at the waist, complementing her full figure. Its elaborate pattern, light flowers set along dark, scalloped, horizontal borders, suggested that it was deliberately chosen—a dress for a special occasion—making Hamer stand out amid a sea of men's dark suits and light shirt sleeves. Hamer's head was bare, her hair in a natural bob, neatly tucked behind her ears, and earrings dangled from her lobes. She might have been headed to a lunch or on a shopping excursion, though the badge that identified her as a MFDP delegate marked her plainly as on political business rather than an afternoon's leisure.[66]

Hamer recited her often-told story of losing her job and her home after first attempting to register as a voter in Mississippi. Then, abruptly, the television broadcast cut over to remarks by Lyndon Johnson. The president's timing was intended to draw attention away from the MFDP testimony. But the full committee remained in their seats, rapt, during the eight or so minutes when Hamer recounted the terror of her time held and then brutally assaulted by officials in Winona. Later that day, Hamer's full remarks were broadcast for the world to watch. She was briefly lifted by an outpouring of support—both from the committee and from across the nation.

Compromise proposals deeply undercut the goals of the MFDP—which included winning real influence for its members—and would leave them with little more than symbolic inclusion. Negotiations soured in the hours that followed, and Hamer and the MFDP walked away, refusing to settle. They returned to Mississippi to continue the struggle for voting rights. Still, Hamer had managed the unthinkable. She had elevated her person, her story, and the politics she embodied—that of a Black woman sharecropper turned handbag-toting political operative—to national consequence. Americans were tuned in to the struggle for voting rights as never before, and had Hamer to thank for it.

THREE BLACK WOMEN stepped forward, illuminated by the flash of camera bulbs, during the signing ceremony for the 1965 Voting Rights Act. Photographers swarmed and jockeyed to capture just the right pantheon of faces from among those gathered to mark the moment when federal law committed the nation to protecting Black Americans' access to the ballot. Not since the adoption of the Fifteenth Amendment in 1870 had the United States so boldly affirmed that racism must not compromise membership in political culture. These were images that not only would circulate on the pages of the nation's newspapers but also would be preserved in archives as a patrimony, evidence of how a new political order had been forged out of an old struggle.

While the women's names were nearly lost by those who otherwise preserved the moment, the men in the scene are well remembered for their roles in the quest for voting rights. There was President Lyndon Johnson, signing the act into law, handing out ceremonial pens, and shaking hands. For Johnson, this event punctuated his victory over Southern Democrats, who had long aimed to block civil rights legislation. Standing to Johnson's left were a trio of Black leaders, men who stood at the helm of the movement's establishment. Martin Luther King Jr. and Ralph

Signing of the Voting Rights Act, August 6, 1965, featuring Patricia Roberts Harris, Vivian Malone, and Zephyr Wright (l. to r.)
LYNDON BAINES JOHNSON PHOTO ARCHIVES, LYNDON BAINES JOHNSON ARCHIVES

Abernathy represented the Southern Christian Leadership Conference and were credited with sponsoring Selma's decisive voting rights campaign. Clarence Mitchell was the chief lobbyist for the NAACP and was responsible for behind-the-scenes work in Washington, DC, that transformed an ideal into the text of a congressional act.[67]

The three women standing just to the left of Clarence Mitchell had their own stories to tell about voting rights. First, their names: Patricia Roberts Harris was a law professor at Howard University and a party ally to Lyndon Johnson, having seconded his nomination for president at the 1964 Democratic National Convention. Harris's political education began under the mentorship of Pauli Murray—the two had collaborated on the sit-ins led by Howard University students in 1943. Standing to Harris's far left was Vivian Malone, who staffed the Voter Education Project at the US Department of Justice. She had recently migrated from Montgomery, Alabama, to Washington, DC, one of two Black students who defied Governor George Wallace and integrated the University of Alabama. Two years later, in 1965, Malone became the school's first Black graduate. And the third woman: Zephyr Wright was the Johnson family's cook, having long traveled between their homes in Texas and Washington, DC. When Wright sat with the Johnson family during the president's first address to Congress, just weeks after the assassination of President John F. Kennedy, it signaled that her advice extended beyond culinary preparations to issues of race and justice. Commentators tried to characterize Wright as a servant in an effort to illustrate the Johnson family's home life. But Wright, a graduate of Wiley College, had long advised the president about the discrimination she endured when traveling and in Washington's restaurants. Her story was part of Johnson's own and a foundation for his commitment to civil rights. These three women were a tableau all their own, drawing together diverse strands of Black women's history and activism.[68]

Zephyr Wright's story reflected how so much of Black women's political activism had its origins in the educations they earned as domestic workers. From Jarena Lee and Maria Stewart, who began their lives as indentured servants, to the trials of Harriet Jacobs and Sojourner Truth as enslaved women, to Nannie Helen Burroughs as an organizer and advocate through her training school and the National Baptist Women's Convention, and Rosa Parks in a Montgomery, Alabama, kitchen, Black women defined their political goals through the gritty and often troubled realm of work. Their concerns about wages and working conditions coupled with their vulnerability to sexual harassment and assault defined a key facet of what the right to vote meant and why it was worth fighting for. Wright's relationship to the Johnsons and her capacity to influence their thinking on civil rights signaled how working women also maneuvered along their own routes to power. A kitchen was a place to prepare meals and a place from which to plot the future.

Vivian Malone, the youngest among the three, underscored how Black women's struggle for voting rights stretched across generations. As teachers, women like Maria Stewart, Susan Paul, Frances Ellen Watkins Harper, Hallie Quinn Brown, Mary Church Terrell, and Fannie Williams had invested in their daughters and granddaughters as new agents of change. As institution builders, Charlotte Hawkins Brown, Nannie Helen Burroughs, and Mary McLeod Bethune built schools in which younger women studied and thrived. Black women's classrooms were safe spaces and training grounds where the lessons might begin with textbooks. But the learning always included teachers who were role models that showed young women like Malone that they were entitled to a place in political culture. Malone, when she presented herself in the dormitories, cafeterias, and classrooms of the University of Alabama, took part in a longstanding necessity. Black women put their bodies on the front lines and in the line of fire, finding a capacity to confront those who overlooked or otherwise outright denied them.

Patricia Roberts Harris was linked to a story about Black women "firsts," especially those who broke into circles that had long been closed to them. This took education and—like Mary Church Terrell's years at Oberlin or Frances Williams's studies at Mount Holyoke or Pauli Murray's legal training at Howard Law School—Harris came to voting rights with credentials and networks that furthered her cause. It also took the building of alliances, oftentimes across difference. Harris in her relationship to Lyndon Johnson was not unlike Mary McLeod Bethune's collaboration with Eleanor Roosevelt.

Shortly after signing the Voting Rights Act into law, Johnson appointed Harris US Ambassador to Luxembourg. She became the first Black woman to hold that high foreign service post. Secretary of State Dean Rusk presided over Harris's swearing in. Newspapers nearly reduced Harris to her attire: "An ensemble in blue, consisting of a raw silk dress and jacket, and matching straw hat." But at the podium, she made a short speech that reset the terms of her appearance: "She was delighted on the basis of race and sex to have the opportunity, but...considered both sex and race irrelevant to the job." Harris credited her mother, a federal worker in Chicago, with instilling in her confidence and a philosophy of women's rights, and she disarmed the small crowd with feigned naivete. "The question of the role of women in the world," she chided, "is one that is relatively new to her." It was to her self-evident how she had come to be appointed a United States representative to the world. Generational wisdom had been passed down: "Her very competent mother had never told her that women weren't supposed to be confident." Whether fact or mere prophesy, Harris planted a flag for Black women and their futures. Her mother, who rose from her nearby seat to place a kiss on her daughter's cheek, endorsed her vision.[69]

The sight of Patricia Harris, outfitted in fine fabric in a flattering shade of blue, might have misled those present. Her body, the center of much pomp in a State Department reception room, remained in the crosshairs of a world in which political power required Black women to take risks. Harris knew that her position was vexed, and she confessed that there was a "sad side" to being a "first." She lamented that her distinction rested upon a history that had kept Black women from many quarters of political influence: either they lacked the formal training or "extrinsic factors" kept Black women at a distance from leadership. There was, indeed, something akin to hazing in the press's preoccupation with her wardrobe. Would Harris dress the part of US Ambassador, was the question. Could she? She repeatedly resorted to gentle humor mixed with studied modesty. Harris explained she had but a single formal dress, the one she had worn to President Johnson's inaugural ball. She then confessed to being frugal, but also discerning: "I buy my clothes to wear forever." She deflected, observing that foreign service appointments should be made on the basis of "qualifications" rather than an appointee's "estate." She had broken down yet another barrier. Still, no post was so high that a Black woman would not be exactingly read as she came to occupy it.

Conclusion

CANDIDATES OF THE PEOPLE

Moving forward from the Voting Rights Act, Black women carried their history into a new present, looking back while they moved forward. Some explained their entry into politics through stories of the parents and grandparents who raised them to embrace leadership. Others emerged when they became "firsts," breaking through new ceilings. Everyone told a story of the women who came before them: role models, cautionary tales, and lots of inspiration. It helped to consult the road maps that legendary woman left behind. There is Mary Church Terrell's 1940 memoir, *A Colored Woman in a White World*, and Pauli Murray's family history, *Proud Shoes*, published in 1956. The daughter of Ida B. Wells, Alfreda Duster, released her mother's autobiography, *Crusade for Justice*, in 1970. That same year, Hallie Quinn Brown's *Homespun Heroines and Other Women of Distinction*, long out of print, was republished for the very first time.[1]

Collectives kept Black women's politics innovative and ambitious. In 1973, the National Black Feminist Organization brought together veterans of civil rights, Black power, and women's rights movements. The Combahee River Collective issued a guiding manifesto that called for a Black women's politics that critiqued racism, sexism, class prejudice, and homophobia. Black women's labor organizations—the National Domestic Workers Union, the Domestic Workers of America, and the Household Workers Organization—gave voice to the demands of working women. The National Welfare Rights Organization made public benefits a women's issue, and Black women led there. In 1991, when the testimony of Professor Anita Hill charged US Supreme Court nominee Clarence Thomas with sexual harassment, more than sixteen hundred African American women organized to place a full-page advertisement in the *New York Times* titled "African American Women in Defense of Ourselves."[2]

New histories recovered stories of Black women in politics that had been nearly lost or forgotten. Between 1968 and 1969, Arno Press reissued the narrative of Sojourner Truth, the Civil War–era memoirs of Susie King Taylor and Mary Peake, and the White House reminiscences of Elizabeth Keckley. A trio of anthologies published from 1970 to 1972 serve as near-bibles that explained Black women's quest in their own words: Toni Cade's *The Black Woman*, Gerda Lerner's *Black Women in White America: A Documentary History*, and Dorothy Wesley Porter's *Early Negro Writing, 1760–1837*. In 1978, Sharon Harley and Rosalyn Terborg-Penn published an anthology of essays that ranged from labor and politics to biographies of Anna Julia Cooper and Nannie Helen Burroughs, titled *The Afro-American Woman: Struggles and Images*. Black women's histories became squarely the subject of scholarly study. On Black women and the vote, it was in this volume that Terborg-Penn published some of her early and pathbreaking findings in the essay "Discrimination Against Afro-American Women in the Woman's Movement, 1830–1920." From there on out, when Black women made history they could count on historians to take notice and make note.[3]

THE STORY OF the Vanguard is still being written. Black women continue to innovate, challenge, and lead American politics to its best ideals in our own moment. Today's political culture reflects the wave, the surge, the storm of Black women who claimed their places in American politics after enactment of the Voting Rights Act in 1965. Nothing short of an encyclopedia could account for the hundreds and then thousands of women who have kept burning the fires lit two centuries ago by women like Jarena Lee, Maria Stewart, and Sarah Mapps Douglass. Standing among such women in the late twentieth century and then in the twenty-first is to be part of a grand chorus of thinkers and doers. They are Black women who speak from an experience shaped by racism and sexism, and then call out injustice in the interest of all humanity. Even if America is still learning the history of Black women's politics, the women of the Vanguard know where they come from and how they got to be who they are.

Shirley Chisholm explained that she came of age in Brooklyn College's Harriet Tubman Society, where she heard "talk about white oppression, Black racial consciousness, and Black pride" and studied figures such as Tubman, Frederick Douglass, W. E. B. DuBois, and George W. Carver. In 1965, Chisholm entered politics with the slogan "Unbought and Unbossed," and by 1968, she was on her way to Washington, the first Black woman elected to Congress. There, she championed the Equal Rights Amendment, "one of the most clear-cut opportunities we are likely to have to declare our faith in the principles that shaped our Constitution, making the 5th and the 14th Amendments unequivocally applicable to 'sex distinctions.' "[4]

Chisholm tested the Democratic Party in 1972 with a run for president. It was yet another "first." Chisholm knew the significance of her candidacy and made plain her sweeping aims: "I am not the candidate of Black America, although I am Black and proud. I am not the candidate of the women's movement of this country, although I am a woman and equally proud of that. I am the candidate of the people and my presence before you symbolizes a new era in American political history." Chisholm knew that thousands upon thousands of Black Americans possessed the right to vote for the first time, and she inspired them to use it.[5]

Shirley Chisholm (1924–2005) speaking in Detroit, Michigan, May 17, 1972
GETTY IMAGES

Listen to Barbara Jordan and you'll learn that she was raised in Houston, Texas, the child of Baptist Church leaders, knowing that history mattered, even before she was poised to make it. Jordan graduated from Phillis Wheatley High School, then enrolled at Texas Southern University when the University of Texas refused to admit Black students. She went on to law school in Boston, but then returned to Texas and, in 1972, Houstonians elected her to Congress, making her the first woman from Texas, Black or white, to represent the state in her own right. Jordan opened the impeachment proceedings against President Richard Nixon in a speech to the House Judiciary Committee. She recalled the Preamble to the Constitution of the United States and its opening words, "We, the people." Times had changed, Jordan explained, "It's a very eloquent beginning. But when that document was completed on the seventeenth of September in 1787, I was not included in that 'We, the people.'…But through the process of amendment, interpretation, and court decision, I have finally been included in 'We, the people.' " Nixon would soon be out, but Jordan was in.[6]

Lottie Shackleford called Little Rock, Arkansas, home, a city destined to make civil rights history. Shackelford entered politics almost by accident, as a PTA mother who learned the ins and outs of the state house and city hall. Shackelford was elected her hometown's mayor in 1987, even before Sharon Pratt Kelley became the first Black woman to lead a major city, Washington, DC, in 1991. Shackleford may not be the best-remembered politician to come out of Little Rock—that honor goes to the forty-second president, Bill Clinton. Still, the two are part of one story. Shackelford served as Clinton's deputy campaign manager during his 1992 run for the White House. Shackelford stepped up as cochair of the Democratic National Convention. She'd always been a proponent of voting rights and in 2019 commented on the Nineteenth Amendment's anniversary: "It's great that we're celebrating," she began, and then her tone shifted: "I have some ambivalent feelings at this point.…I'm also a little depressed that we're still fighting so many of the battles over and over again. So it's a sort of mixed bag for me." Yes, women are at the polls, she conceded, but "not in the numbers we need to be."[7]

Lani Guinier was born into politics but took a different path from that of her activist mother, who raised her daughter in Queens, New York. Her direction was clear after, as a girl, Guinier saw NAACP Legal Defense Fund attorney Constance Baker Motley challenge the color line that kept James Meredith from enrolling at the University of Mississippi. Motley inspired Guinier to become a civil rights lawyer. She followed in Motley's footsteps, working at the Civil Rights Division of the US Justice Department during the Carter administration and then joining the fabled NAACP Legal Defense Fund, where she headed the voting rights project. Though the nominee for Assistant Attorney General for Civil Rights in 1993, Guinier never saw the inside of the Senate chamber. After weeks of political wrangling, President Bill Clinton withdrew her nomination. Guinier's views on voting rights, especially her departure from the principle one person, one vote, were too radical, and she was "vilified as a mad woman with strange hair…a strange name and strange ideas." The opposition branded Guinier a "quota queen," a caricature that denigrated her as a supporter of affirmative action, hence the quota reference. At the same time, she was said to be like the "welfare queen," a parody that maligned Black women for choosing self-imposed poverty and then living high on public dollars.[8]

The civil rights movement was baked into the city streets of Greensboro, North Carolina, where Loretta Lynch was born. Even after she was elevated to US Attorney General, Lynch regarded history as her foundation. Black women, like their white counterparts, were daughters of "the organizers of the Seneca Falls Convention in 1848," a gathering that "galvanized and empowered women to this day." Black women in the twenty-first century were also the descendants of the students "who sat at a Greensboro lunch counter." Lynch's father had welcomed them to the basement of his church, where they planned their next moves. When she spoke to the young Black women graduates of Atlanta's Spelman College, Lynch reminded them that "eleven women, some of them former slaves," had 135 years earlier "sought an education in the dim basement of an Atlanta church." Lynch urged them, as she did, to "draw strength from that inheritance, to lean on that example and never doubt the smallest step can create the most sweeping change." By knowing their history, Black women were positioned to aid "our comrades in humanity on whose behalf we are called to work."[9]

Lynch rooted her journey in lessons from African American history, then reached further: "We are a country that shares a bond of common humanity, all of us together." The human family was, she believed, "stronger than anything that can divide us, it's stronger than race, it's stronger than ethnicity; stronger than nationality, gender and gender identity or sexual orientation." Among her most demanding legal cases was the deadly shooting massacre at Pulse, the Orlando, Florida, nightclub, in 2016.

As attorney general, Lynch was charged with investigating the atrocity as a crime. She went further and embraced the victims, their families, and their community as one part of the great bundle of humanity, as her Black foremothers had taught her.[10]

For those Americans who might think that Stacey Abrams came out of nowhere, she is usually the first to set them straight. Abrams knows the political tradition out of which she comes, and she stands on the shoulders of generations of Black women. Her run for the governorship of Georgia in 2018 brought Abrams unprecedented attention and she explained her bid to become the nation's first Black woman governor as growing out of a long track record in politics. Her path began in Abrams's college years, when, as a student at Spelman College, she earned her way onto Mayor Maynard Jackson's staff after challenging the mayor in a public forum. Her graduate studies propelled her forward. After acquiring her master's in public administration and then her law degree, Abrams returned to Georgia, where she was elected City Attorney for Atlanta and then a member of

Stacey Abrams (b. 1973), election watch party, November 6, 2018
GETTY IMAGES

the Georgia State Assembly. Her professional bona fides were in order.[11]

Abrams's roots go deeper still. Her understanding of how to make a life in politics over the long haul derives from the Black women who came before her: "I know that Sojourner Truth, and Harriet Tubman, and Carolyn Abrams, my mother, that they have each faced difficult, heart-wrenching challenges, and that my obligation is to remain viable for the fight." Her first lessons in voting rights grew out of her study of Fannie Lou Hamer, from whom she learned to stand her ground, use the podium and the press, and play the long game: "In 1964, Fannie Lou Hamer defied President Lyndon B. Johnson and threatened his election, going on national television to excoriate the Democratic Party's insensitivity to the plight of Blacks seeking a vote in the South....The Mississippi Freedom Democratic Party lost its bid to be seated in 1964, but the delegation gained full recognition in 1968, a delayed victory but a win nonetheless."[12]

Abrams is of course a woman of her own time and she learned one of her first lessons about voting rights from an intimate family story. Her own grandmother had won access to the polls with passage of the Voting Rights Act. Still, Abrams explained how her grandmother "almost didn't vote the first time she was allowed to in 1968." Her grandmother was battle weary: "The other times she had tried to register and tried to vote they sicced dogs on her...they sprayed her with fire hoses." Voter suppression persisted in the form of fear long after formal barriers had been lifted. "By the time the right to vote became real in Mississippi she was just terrified and so she had decided not to vote." But recalling the price that others had paid for her changed the older woman's mind. Abrams explains: "My grandfather took her to task and said your sons and daughters went to jail for this, your children have fought for this right they're too young to enjoy. You owe this to them."[13]

Abrams has moved between office holding and advocacy with equal parts skill and persistence. When her bid for Georgia's governorship ended, a race that Abrams maintains was denied her through the suppression of Black votes, she shifted gears to put her energy into Fair Fight, a political action organization where she champions the voting rights of all Georgians. That same grandmother who soothed her own fears about voting supported Abrams in her bid for high office. Poetic justice runs through their intergenerational story: "She was so grateful that she had a granddaughter who had a chance to actually possibly become the first Black woman to be a governor in the history of the United States. Being from the South she understood how important governors are, that it was the governors of the southern states that created and implemented and maintained Jim Crow, it was the governors who authorized the treatment of Black people as less than human."[14]

Today, the fate of Abrams's political career is ahead of her. Wherever she may land, to hear her tell it, Abrams knows few limits: "I'm a Black woman who's in a conversation about possibly being second in command to the leader of the free world and I will not diminish my ambition or the ambition of any other women of color by saying that's not something I'd be willing to do." If a question should arise about how Abrams grew to be so bold, so assured, and so certain about the future of Black women in American politics, listen in as she narrates the tradition out of which she has emerged.

Harriet Tubman imparted insight into how leaders must awaken the consciousness of their people. Abrams often quotes Tubman: "I freed a whole lot of slaves. I could have freed a whole lot more, if they'd only known that they were slaves." Ida B. Wells mastered "the power of her words," making "real the sin of lynching" and helping "to launch a civil rights movement with the founding of the NAACP." Abrams claims white and Latinx women as among her foremothers: Bella Abzug "defied her party bosses to advocate for women, the poor, and the oppressed in New York, in Congress and beyond," and Linda Alvarado "created one of the top ranked construction firms in the nation and then bought herself a baseball team."[15]

The metaphor of standing on the shoulders of others is apt in Abrams's case. Seeing Black women as mayors had at one time set her high bar: "My highest ambition when I was in college thinking about politics was to become mayor of Atlanta because that was the highest job I'd ever seen a Black woman have." Studying the history of Black women in politics shifted her ambition: "I knew enough about Shirley Chisholm and about Barbara Jordan to know that you could go to Congress, maybe, but that was unlikely because there had never been a Black congresswoman." The lesson? "Don't be bound by what you've seen." Whether calling for the full and unfettered voting rights of Black Americans in Georgia or contemplating who is likely to run the nation's executive branch in 2020, Abrams is bold and emboldened by a past that, for all its ambition, could not have wholly seen her coming. When voter suppression meets Stacey Abrams, an old fight meets a new challenger, and Abrams, in the spirit of the two centuries of Black women before her, is in it for the long haul.

ACKNOWLEDGMENTS

Recently, someone asked me to name my "favorite" Black suffragist. Now, choosing favorites is not exactly a historian's endeavor, so I dodged the question. But I can admit here that I did know the answer. For me, no figure looms larger than Ida B. Wells. For two decades I have taught her epic life story, with its beginnings in the burdens borne by an orphaned oldest sibling and then as a young teacher in a clash with a railroad conductor. The lawsuit that followed foretold how Wells would go on to insist upon recognition of her humanity and the dignity of all Black Americans. Her lessons often grew out of brutality. Wells became a fierce opponent of lynching after confronting the murder of friends in Memphis, Tennessee. Her journalist's pen was ignited in that moment, and even today Wells's fiery condemnation of lynching's brutal reign of terror are words to live by.

Vanguard is deeply indebted to Wells. She lived the theory of intersectionality long before we came to explain Black women's lives by that term. All she knew emerged from her simultaneous encounters with racism and sexism. Her 1883 battle over a seat in the whites-only car on the Chesapeake, Ohio, Southwestern Railroad seared that dilemma into her consciousness, and ours. When the conductor directed her to move, Wells shot back that "if he wished to treat me like a lady, he would leave me alone." In the struggle that followed, Wells recounted: "My dress was torn...one sleeve was almost torn off." Wells mixed respectability with bold resistance on that rail car headed to Memphis and then she sued. She is a model of how Black women came to political personhood and then used it.[1]

When it came to injustice and her commitment to undoing it, Wells never confined concerns to her own circumstances. She worked broadly against lynching and school segregation, and for worker's rights and civil rights. Wells was also a staunch suffragist, and her founding of Chicago's Alpha Suffrage Club not only impelled Black women to the polls but also shaped outcomes, such as the election of Oscar DePriest to Congress in 1928 as the first Black man to be seated in Washington since Reconstruction. Still, Wells always defied boundaries between political movements. This was the style that so many Black women have adopted. Winning the vote was one facet of a vision that aimed to win dignity for all humanity.[2]

Wells exemplified the spirit that runs through all the women in *Vanguard*. It is a spirit that also runs through the community of Black women historians of which I am a part. The members of the Association of Black Women Historians (ABWH)—their work and their life examples—have inspired and emboldened my thinking. *Vanguard* is especially indebted to the work of the late Dr. Rosalyn Terborg-Penn, an ABWH founder and author of the field-defining book *African American Women in the Struggle for the Vote, 1850–1920*. Our mission as historians includes excavating the past to promote well-being in our own time. *Vanguard* joins the collective work of ABWH historians, one part of a mighty whole.

I woke up on an August morning sure that I needed to write *Vanguard*. The nation was awakening to the upcoming anniversary of the Nineteenth Amendment, but it was at risk for forgetting Black women's side of that story. I am grateful to Roz Foster, who took my call and then worked with me to transform a late-summer urge into a book worthy of the women whose lives it chronicles. At Basic Books, Brian Distelberg has been a frank, demanding, and committed editor whose team has made *Vanguard* the best book it could be. Johns Hopkins University has supported my commitment to these stories by providing time and research support. Special thanks go to the Hopkins students in my courses on the history of women and the vote. *Vanguard* has benefited from their careful criticism of early drafts.[3]

It is my great fortune to be surrounded by people who believe in my work and guide my ambitions. I must single out two of them here. First is my friend, historian Erica Armstrong Dunbar. When I first whispered to her my desire to tell the story of two hundred years of Black women's politics, Erica told me I could and that I must. In the months since, she has shown me how to do just that, even while juggling the demands of her own important work. My advice to students: pay attention to that interesting classmate seated next to you in the lecture hall, because she might just be the lifelong friend who shares your values and commitments. Second is my agent, Tanya McKinnon. Our partnership emerged out of one part happenstance—a shared taxi ride—and another part of deep connection that feels timeless. Tanya and her team generously came on board to support *Vanguard* and help me project its stories out into a world that badly needs them.

My families, Jones and Hébrard, are my foundation. Thank you to my brother, Paul, and his wife, Heidi, for their unflagging support for my work and for permitting me to tell a bit of our own family story here. Much of this book was written in La Grande-Motte, France, in the seaside home of my mother-in-law, Blanche "Mimi" Hébrard, who has mostly forgiven me for the hours stolen from family time to write. My husband, historian Jean Hébrard, has been *Vanguard*'s biggest champion. He has carved time out of his own work to support the book, from the afternoon I interrupted our summer vacation to hatch an idea, through the days and nights spent turning that idea into prose. Jean's steady love for me and for the women from whom I come lifts us all up.

This book is dedicated to my great-great-great-grandmother Nancy Belle Graves. She was born enslaved in 1808, lived to see emancipation, and then remade her family in partnership with her husband, Edmund Graves, after the Civil War and in freedom. Understanding Nancy's life story and how a women's movement grew up out of her experiences and her concerns has forever changed my perception of what voting rights can and should mean. *Vanguard* is also dedicated to Nancy's daughters, and I count myself among them. But when I speak of Nancy's daughters, I am referring to women far beyond those in my particular family. I have written *Vanguard* for all the daughters of Black women like Nancy Graves, who persisted in the face of some of the most brutal, degrading, and undignified circumstances this nation has ever known. Out of their lives—a mix of grief, despair, joy, and hope—we produce our own beautiful truths.

NOTES

Preface to the Paperback Edition

1. The Democrats, "Democratic National Convention, Day 3, https://youtu.be
/CY7C4zkMjkM; on Harris's political rise see Dan Morain, *Kamala's Way: An American Life* (New York: Simon & Schuster, 2021).

2. Martha S. Jones, "Histories, Fictions, and Black Womanhood Bodies: Rethinking Race, Gender, and Politics in the Twenty-First Century," in *Toward an Intellectual History of Black Women*, eds. Mia Bay, Farah Griffin, Martha S. Jones, and Barbara D. Savage (University of North Carolina Press, 2015).

3. Jessica Bennett, "Overlooked No More: Before Kamala Harris, There Was Charlotta Bass," *New York Times*, September 4, 2020. In her 2018 memoir, *The Truths We Hold*, Harris briefly describes Chisholm's 1971 visit to Berkeley, California's The Rainbow Sign, a Black cultural center that was a second home to Harris and her family. Kamala Harris, *The Turths We Hold: An American Journey* (New York: Penguin, 2019): 18.

4. The Democrats, "Democratic National Convention, Day 3; on Harris's political rise see Dan Morain, *Kamala's Way: An American Life.*

5. The Democrats, "Democratic National Convention, Day 3; on Harris's political rise see Dan Morain, *Kamala's Way: An American Life.* In her 2018 memoir, *The Truths We Hold*, Harris briefly describes Fannie Lou Hamer's visit to her parents civil rights-era study group in Berkeley, California. Harris, *The Truths We Hold*, 9.

6. Martha S. Jones, "Black Women Led Us Through the Most Consequential Political Contest of Our Lifetimes. It's High Time We Thank Them," *Talking Points Memo*, November 6, 2020; Martha S. Jones, "Black Women Voters Changed the Shape of the U.S. Election. It's Time to Thank Them," *Thompson Reuters Foundation News*, November 12, 2020.

7. Armstead W. Herndon, "Georgia Was a Big Win for Democrats. Black Women Did the Ground Work," *New York Times*, December 3, 2020; Andre M. Perry,

David Harshbarger, and Anthony Piano, "Last Night in Georgia, Black Americans Saved Democracy," *Brookings*, January 6, 2021, www.brookings.edu/blog/the-avenue/2021/01/06/last-night-in-georgia-black-americans-saved-democracy/.

8. Martha S. Jones, "Black Women in Politics are no Longer a 'first.' They are a Force," *Washington Post*, August 13, 2020; Rutgers University Center for American Women and Politics, "Women of Color in Elective Office 2021," https://cawp.rutgers.edu/women-color-elective-office-2021; Kelly Dittmar, "The 2020 Primaries Are Over. Here's What You need to Know About the Record Number of Women Nominees," https://cawp.rutgers.edu/election-analysis/post-primary-analysis-women-2020.

9. "National Exit Polls: How Different Groups Voted," *New York Times*, www.nytimes.com/interactive/2020/11/03/us/elections/exit-polls-president.html.

10. Jones, "Black Women Led Us";. Jones, "Black Women Voters."

11. Senator Brian Benjamin (@NYSenBenjamin), "I want to thank Black women for saving the Democratic Party once again," Twitter, November 7, 2020, 1:00 p.m. https://twitter.com/NYSenBenjamin/status/1325166230303629313?s=20; NAACP LDF, "Thank Black Women: Saving Democracy," www.bonfire.com/store/thank-black-women-saving-democracy-naacp-ep/.

12. CNN, "Transcripts, December 17, 2020," http://transcripts.cnn.com/TRANSCRIPTS/2012/17/cnr.07.html; Shawn Hubler, "Alex Padilla Will Replace Kamala Harris in the Senate," *New York Times*, December 22, 2020.

13. PBS New Hour, "Watch: Amanda Gorman Reads Inauguration Poem, 'The Hill We Climb,'" www.youtube.com/watch?v=LZ055ilIiN4; Amanda Gorman, *The Hill We Climb: An Inaugural Poem for the Country* (New York: Viking Books, 2021).

14. Carol Jago, "Lesson of the Day: Amanda Gorman and 'The Hill We Climb,'" *New York Times*, January 20, 2021.

15. Maya Angelou, *On the Pulse of Morning: The Inaugural Poem* (New York: Random House, 1993); Clinton Library, "Maya Angelou's Poem 'On the Pulse of Morning,'" www.youtube.com/watch?v=59xGmHzxtZ4. Elizabeth Alexander, *Praise Song for the Day: A Poem for Barack Obama's Presidential Inauguration* (New York: Greywolf Press, 2009); Obama White House, "Inaugural Poem: 'Praise Song for the Day,'" www.youtube.com/watch?v=_vLBnFk-OFc.

16. Gretchen Holbrook Gerzina, *Mr. and Mrs. Prince: How an Extraordinary Eighteenth-Century Family Moved Out of Slavery and into Legend* (New York: Amistad, 2009); Phillis Wheatley, *Poems on Various Subjects, Religious and Moral* (London and Boston, 1771); Vincent Carretta, *Phillis Wheatley: Biography of a Genius in Bondage* (Athens: University of Georgia Press, 2011); Frances Smith Foster, *A Brighter Coming Day: A Frances Ellen Watkins Harper Reader* (New York: Feminist Press, 1990); Melba Joyce Boyd, *Discarded Legacy: Politics and Poetics in the Life of Frances E. W. Harper, 1825–1911* (Detroit: Wayne State University Press, 1994).

Introduction: Our Mothers' Gardens

1. George C. Wright, *Life Behind a Veil: Blacks in Louisville, Kentucky, 1865–1930* (Baton Rouge: Louisiana State University Press, 2004); Marion B. Lucas, *A History of Blacks in Kentucky, Volume 1: From Slavery to Segregation, 1760–1891* (Lexington: University of Kentucky Press, 2003); George C. Wright, *A History of Blacks in Kentucky, Volume 2: In Pursuit of Equality, 1890–1980* (Frankfort: Kentucky Historical

Society, 1992); Hambleton Tapp and James C. Klotter, *Kentucky: Decades of Discord, 1865–1900* (Frankfort: Kentucky Historical Society, 1977); "Susan Davis, Pensioner, Widow of Samuel Kincade aka Samuel Davis," Records of the Department of Veterans Affairs, 1773–2007, Record Group 15, US Civil War Pension Index: General Index to Pension Files, 1861–1934, Series Number T288, National Archives Research Center, Washington, DC.

2. "Colored Notes," *Advocate-Messenger* (Danville, KY), May 26, 1948; "Instruct Negro Women to Vote," *Advocate-Messenger* (Danville, KY), September 30, 1920; "Democrats Gain: In the City Registration in Danville Yesterday of Sixty-Three Votes over Last Year," *Kentucky Advocate* (Danville), October 6, 1920; "Wrangle: Republican Leader Insisted the Colored Woman Be Put In as Election Officer," *Kentucky Advocate* (Danville), October 5, 1920; "Registration in Danville Is Heavy: Officers Have Been Busy All Day Writing Out the Certificates. Negroes Coming Out," *Advocate-Messenger* (Danville, KY), October 5, 1920; "The Women's Vote," *Kentucky Advocate* (Danville), September 13, 1920.

3. "Berea College Commencement," *Richmond (KY) Climax*, June 27, 1888; Frank Williams would go on to earn his AM degree (Master of Arts) from Berea College in 1904. "Berea College Commencement," *The Citizen* (Berea, KY), June 16, 1904; "The Colored Teachers," *Interior Journal* (Stanford, KY), August 4, 1885; "Handsomely Engraved Invitations," *Kentucky Advocate* (Danville), February 10, 1891; "An American Family," *Headlines and Pictures: A Monthly Negro News Review* (New York), August 1946.

4. "500 NAACP Delegates in Session. 15 States Represented," *Afro-American* (Baltimore), July 11, 1936.

5. "Wards Soon to Hold Meetings to Plan Citizenship League," *St. Louis Globe-Democrat*, June 29, 1919; "Colored Women Register," *Macon (MO) Chronicle-Herald*, September 18, 1920; "Men to Attend Suffrage Schools," *St. Louis Star and Times*, June 4, 1919.

6. "Campaign to Line Up Women Votes Lively in South…Activity Spurred by Fear of Negro Vote," *St. Louis Post-Dispatch*, October 10, 1920; "Women Can Help Save Missouri…by Outnumbering the Colored Women Vote," *St. Joseph (MO) Observer*, September 25, 1920; "The College Club of St. Louis," *St. Louis Post-Dispatch*, May 1, 1927.

7. "Aunt Susan Davis," *Advocate-Messenger* (Danville, KY), March 4, 1925; "500 NAACP Delegates in Session. 15 States Represented," *Afro-American* (Baltimore), July 11, 1936; "Council on Colored Work," *Southern Workman* (Hampton, VA), January 1922; "Baltimore Conference Resolutions," *The Crisis*, September 1936; Judith Weisenfeld, *African American Women and Christian Activism: New York's Black YWCA, 1905–1945* (Cambridge, MA: Harvard University Press, 1998); Nancy Marie Robertson, *Christian Sisterhood, Race Relations, and the YWCA, 1906–1946* (Urbana: University of Illinois Press, 2007).

8. I. N. Fact, "A Few Plain Truths for the Colored People and Others," *Greensboro (NC) Patriot*, September 15, 1880; "To the Colored People of Guilford," *Greensboro (NC) North State*, September 16, 1880; "Guilford County Republican Convention," *Greensboro (NC) North State*, October 5, 1882; "Republican County Convention," *Greensboro (NC) Patriot*, October 6, 1882; "Dallas Jones Succeeds Mr. Hanner," *Greensboro (NC) North State*, August 1, 1889; "Township Meetings," *Greensboro (NC) North State*, August 12, 1880.

9. J. Stephen Catlett, "A Recently Acquired Disfranchisement Document, Greensboro, circa 1890," October 2011, Greensboro Historical Museum.

10. "Oral History Interview with Susie Jones by William Chafe, 1978," William Henry Chafe Oral History Collection, Rare Book, Manuscript, and Special Collections Library, Duke University, Durham, NC; Pauli Murray, *States' Laws on Race and Color* (Cincinnati: Woman's Division of Christian Service, Board of Missions and Church Extension, Methodist Church, 1951). Pauli Murray, *Pauli Murray: The Autobiography of a Black Activist, Feminist, Lawyer, Priest, and Poet* (Knoxville: University of Tennessee Press, 1989), 283–289; Rosalind Rosenberg, *Jane Crow: The Life of Pauli Murray* (New York: Oxford University Press, 2017); Linda Beatrice Brown, *Belles of Liberty: Gender, Bennett College and The Civil Rights Movement* (Greensboro, NC: Women and Wisdom Press, 2013); William H. Chafe, *Civilities and Civil Rights: Greensboro, North Carolina, and the Black Struggle for Freedom* (New York: Oxford University Press, 1981); Jennifer Ash, "The Power of Black Women's Political Labor Remembered: Bennett College and the Civil Rights Movement," *Public Seminar*, March 9, 2018.

11. Alice Walker, *In Search of Our Mothers' Gardens* (New York: Harcourt, 1983).

12. The history of Black women's politics is the subject of a vast literature. *Vanguard* is especially indebted to Rosalyn Terborg-Penn, *African American Women in the Struggle for the Vote, 1850–1920* (Bloomington: Indiana University Press, 1998); Deborah Gray White, *Too Heavy a Load: Black Women in Defense of Themselves, 1894–1994* (New York: W. W. Norton, 1999); Ann D. Gordon, with Bettye Collier-Thomas, John H. Bracey, Arlene Voski Avakian, and Joyce Avrech Berkman, eds., *African American Women and the Vote, 1837–1965* (Amherst: University of Massachusetts Press, 1997); Darlene Clark Hine and Kathleen Thompson, *A Shining Thread of Hope: The History of Black Women in America* (New York: Broadway Books, 1998); Evelyn Brooks Higginbotham, *Righteous Discontent: The Women's Movement in the Black Baptist Church, 1880–1920* (Cambridge, MA: Harvard University Press, 1994); Paula Giddings, *When and Where I Enter: The Impact of Black Women on Race and Sex in America* (New York: W. Morrow, 1984).

13. On the history of voter suppression in the United States, see Carol Anderson, *One Person, One Vote: How Voter Suppression Is Destroying Our Democracy* (New York: Bloomsbury, 2018).

14. Keisha N. Blain, *Set the World on Fire: Black Nationalist Women and the Global Struggle for Freedom* (Philadelphia: University of Pennsylvania Press, 2018); Keisha N. Blain and Tiffany M. Gill, eds., *To Turn the Whole World Over: Black Women and Internationalism* (Urbana: Indiana University Press, 2019).

15. Kimberle Crenshaw, "Demarginalizing the Intersection of Race and Sex: A Black Feminist Critique of Antidiscrimination Doctrine, Feminist Theory and Antiracist Politics," *University of Chicago Legal Forum* 1 (1989): 139–167; Patricia Hill Collins, *Black Feminist Thought: Knowledge, Consciousness and the Politics of Empowerment* (New York: Routledge,1990).

16. On the myths and fictions of women's history, see Lisa Tetraut, *The Myth of Seneca Falls: Memory and the Women's Suffrage Movement, 1848–1898* (Chapel Hill: University of North Carolina Press, 2014); Lori D. Ginzberg, *Elizabeth Cady Stanton: An American Life* (New York: Hill and Wang, 2010).

17. On Black women's voices and the archive, see Shirley Wilson Logan, *"We Are Coming": The Persuasive Discourse of Nineteenth-Century Black Women* (Carbondale:

Southern Illinois University Press, 1999); Carla L. Peterson, *"Doers of the Word": African American Women Speakers in the North, 1830–1880* (New Brunswick, NJ: Rutgers University Press, 1995); William L. Andrews, ed., *Sisters of the Spirit: Three Black Women's Autobiographies of the Nineteenth Century* (Bloomington: University of Indiana Press, 1986); Beverly Guy-Sheftall, ed., *Words of Fire: An Anthology of African-American Feminist Thought* (New York: The New Press, 1995); Dorothy Sterling, ed., *We Are Your Sisters: Black Women in the Nineteenth Century* (New York: W. W. Norton, 1985); Marilyn Richardson, ed., *Maria W. Stewart: America's First Black Woman Political Writer, Essays and Speeches* (Bloomington: Indiana University Press, 1987); Gerda Lerner, *Black Women in White America: A Documentary History* (New York: Vintage Books, 1992).

18. "Oral History Interview with Susie Williams Jones by Merze Tate, 1977," Black Women Oral History Project Interviews, 1976–1981, Schlesinger Library, Radcliffe Institute for Advanced Study, Harvard University, Cambridge, MA; "Oral History Interview with Frances Harriet Williams by Merze Tate, 1977," Black Women Oral History Project Interviews, 1976–1981, Schlesinger Library, Radcliffe Institute for Advanced Study, Harvard University, Cambridge, MA.

19. "Pulaski," *Kentucky Advocate* (Danville), February 5, 1889.

20. "Pulaski," *Kentucky Advocate* (Danville), February 5, 1889.

21. "Pulaski," *Kentucky Advocate* (Danville), February 5, 1889.

Chapter 1: Daughters of Africa, Awake!

1. *Freedom's Journal*, April 20, 1827.

2. Benjamin Quarles, *The Negro in the American Revolution* (Chapel Hill: University of North Carolina Press, 1996); Christopher L. Brown, "Empire Without Slaves: British Concepts of Emancipation in the Age of the American Revolution," *William and Mary Quarterly* 56, no. 2 (April 1999): 273–306; Gary B. Nash, *The Forgotten Fifth: African Americans in the Age of Revolution* (Cambridge, MA: Harvard University Press, 2006); Robert C. Parkinson, *The Common Cause: Creating Race and Nation in the American Revolution* (Chapel Hill: University of North Carolina Press, 2016); Judith L. Van Buskirk, *Standing in Their Own Light: African American Patriots in the American Revolution* (Norman: University of Oklahoma Press, 2017).

3. Emily Blanck, "Seventeen Eighty-Three: The Turning Point in the Law of Slavery and Freedom in Massachusetts," *New England Quarterly* 75, no. 1 (March 2002): 24–51; Arthur Zilversmit, "Quok Walker, Mumbet, and the Abolition of Slavery in Massachusetts," *William and Mary Quarterly* 25, no. 4 (October 1968): 614–624; David N. Gellman, *Emancipating New York: The Politics of Slavery and Freedom, 1777–1827* (Baton Rouge: Louisiana State University Press, 2006); Richard S. Newman, *The Transformation of American Abolitionism: Fighting Slavery in the Early Republic* (Chapel Hill: University of North Carolina Press, 2002); Erica Armstrong Dunbar, *A Fragile Freedom: African American Women and Emancipation in the Antebellum City* (New Haven, CT: Yale University Press, 2008).

4. Arthur Zilversmit, *The First Emancipation: The Abolition of Slavery in the North* (Chicago: University of Chicago Press, 1967); Emily Blanck, *Tyrannicide: Forging an American Law of Slavery in Revolutionary South Carolina and Massachusetts* (Athens: University of Georgia Press, 2014); James J. Gigantino II, *The Ragged Road to Abolition: Slavery and Freedom in New Jersey, 1775–1865* (Philadelphia: University of

Pennsylvania Press, 2014); Manisha Sinha, *The Slave's Cause: A History of Abolition* (New Haven, CT: Yale University Press, 2016).

5. Leon F. Litwack, *North of Slavery: The Negro in the Free States* (Chicago: University of Chicago Press, 1961); Ira Berlin, *Slaves Without Masters: The Free Negro in the Antebellum South* (New York: Pantheon Books, 1964); Leonard P. Curry, *The Free Black in Urban America, 1800–1850: The Shadow of the Dream* (Chicago: University of Chicago Press, 1981).

6. Leslie M. Harris, *In the Shadow of Slavery: African Americans in New York City, 1626–1863* (Chicago: University of Chicago Press, 2003); Julie Winch, *A Gentleman of Color: The Life of James Forten* (New York: Oxford University Press, 2003); Martha S. Jones, *All Bound Up Together: The Woman Question in Antebellum Public Culture, 1830–1900* (Chapel Hill: University of North Carolina Press, 2007); Dunbar, *A Fragile Freedom*; Stephen David Kantrowitz, *More Than Freedom: Fighting for Black Citizenship in a White Republic, 1829–1889* (New York: Penguin, 2012).

7. Eric Burin, *Slavery and the Peculiar Solution: A History of the American Colonization Society* (Gainesville, FL: University of Florida Press, 2008); Beverly C. Tomek, *Colonization and Its Discontents: Emancipation, Emigration, and Antislavery in Antebellum Pennsylvania* (New York: New York University Press, 2011); Ousamane K. Power-Greene, *Against the Wind and Tide: The African American Struggle against the Colonization Movement* (New York: New York University Press, 2014); Martha S. Jones, *Birthright Citizens: A History of Race and Rights in Antebellum America* (New York: Cambridge University Press, 2018).

8. James Oliver Horton, *Free People of Color: Inside the African American Community* (Washington, DC: Smithsonian Institution Press, 1993); Patrick Rael, *Black Identity and Black Protest in the Antebellum North* (Chapel Hill: University of North Carolina Press, 2002); Christopher Bonner, *A New Republic: Black Protest and the Creation of American Citizenship* (Philadelphia: University of Pennsylvania Press, 2020).

9. Alexander Keyssar, *The Right to Vote: The Contested History of Democracy in the United States* (New York: Basic Books, 2009).

10. Rael, *Black Identity and Black Protest*; Richard Newman, *Freedom's Prophet: Bishop Richard Allen, the AME Church, and the Black Founding Fathers* (New York: New York University Press, 2008); Christopher Cameron, *To Plead Our Own Cause: African Americans in Massachusetts and the Making of the Antislavery Movement* (Kent, OH: Kent State University Press, 2014); Bonner, *A New Republic*.

11. Carla L. Peterson, *"Doers of the Word": African-American Women Speakers and Writers in the North (1830–1880)* (New York: Oxford University Press, 1995); Gayle T. Tate, *Unknown Tongues: Black Women's Political Activism in the Antebellum Era, 1830–1860* (East Lansing: Michigan State University Press, 2003); Jones, *All Bound Up Together*; Dunbar, *A Fragile Freedom*.

12. Jones, *All Bound Up Together*.

13. Samuel Cornish and John Russwurm edited *Freedom's Journal*, first published in March 1827. The paper ceased publication in March 1829, but Cornish had resigned after just six months to begin publication of *The Rights of All*. Jacqueline Bacon, *Freedom's Journal: The First African American Newspaper* (Lanham, MD: Lexington Books, 2007).

14. "Managers; African Dorcas Association; Christie Street," *Freedom's Journal*, February 1, 1828; "Manumission Society; Rev. Peter Williams; Jno. B. Russwurm,"

Freedom's Journal, February 1, 1828; "New-York African Free School," *Freedom's Journal*, March 7, 1828; "Female Dorcas Society," *Freedom's Journal*, September 25, 1828; Leslie M. Alexander, *African or American? Black Identity and Political Activism in New York City, 1784–1861* (Urbana: University of Illinois Press, 2011), 67–68.

15. "To the Senior Editor—No. III," *Freedom's Journal*, August 17, 1827.

16. "Miss Frances Wright," *Freedom's Journal*, January 16, 1829; "Summary," *Freedom's Journal*, June 1, 1827; "Summary," *Freedom's Journal*, January 25, 1828; "Summary," *Freedom's Journal*, September 14, 1827. Kim Klein, "A 'Petticoat Polity'? Women Voters in New Brunswick Before Confederation," *Acadiensis* 26, no. 1 (Fall 1996): 71–75.

17. Jones, *All Bound Up Together*, 25–40.

18. Matilda, "[Letter to the Editor]," *Freedom's Journal*, August 10, 1827.

19. Jarena Lee, *Religious Experience and Journal of Mrs. Jarena Lee, Giving an Account of Her Call to Preach the Gospel, Revised and Corrected from the Original Manuscript Written by Herself* (Philadelphia: For the Author, 1849); William L. Andrews, "Introduction," in *Sisters of the Spirit: Three Black Women's Autobiographies of the Nineteenth Century* (Bloomington: Indiana University Press, 1986), 1–22; Willi Coleman, "Architects of a Vision: Black Women and Their Antebellum Quest for Political and Social Equality," in *African American Women and the Vote, 1837–1965*, ed. Ann D. Gordon, with Bettye Collier-Thomas, John H. Bracey, Arlene Voski Avakian, and Joyce Avrech Berkman (Amherst: University of Massachusetts Press, 1997), 24–40.

20. Lee, *Religious Experience and Journal of Mrs. Jarena Lee*.

21. Lee, *Religious Experience and Journal of Mrs. Jarena Lee*.

22. Lee, *Religious Experience and Journal of Mrs. Jarena Lee*; Newman, *Freedom's Prophet*, 230–234.

23. Lee, *Religious Experience and Journal of Mrs. Jarena Lee*; Newman, *Freedom's Prophet*, 230–234.

24. Lee, *Religious Experience and Journal of Mrs. Jarena Lee*.

25. Lee, *Religious Experience and Journal of Mrs. Jarena Lee*; Newman, *Freedom's Prophet*, 230–234.

26. Lee, *Religious Experience and Journal of Mrs. Jarena Lee*; Chanta M. Haywood, "Prophetic Journeying: The Trope of Travel in Black Women Preachers' Narratives," in *Prophesying Daughters: Black Women Preachers and the Word, 1823–1913* (Columbia: University of Missouri Press, 2003), 51–71; Susan L. Roberson, "'A Higher Call': Mobility, Spirituality and Social Uplift in the Narratives of Maria Stewart and Jarena Lee," in *Antebellum American Women Writers and the Road: American Mobilities* (New York: Routledge, 2010); Newman, *Freedom's Prophet*, 230–234.

27. Lee, *Religious Experience and Journal of Mrs. Jarena Lee*.

28. Lee, *Religious Experience and Journal of Mrs. Jarena Lee*.

29. Jarena Lee, *Life and Religious Experience of Jarena Lee* (n.p., 1836); Lee, *Religious Experience and Journal of Mrs. Jarena Lee*.

30. Lee, *Religious Experience and Journal of Mrs. Jarena Lee*.

31. William Lloyd Garrison to Maria W. Stewart, April 4, 1879, in Maria W. Stewart, *Meditations From the Pen of Mrs. Maria W. Stewart*, ed. Marilyn Richardson (Washington, DC: Enterprise Publishing, 1879), 89–90; Maria W. Steward [*sic*], *Religion and the Pure Principles of Morality, the Sure Foundation on Which We Must Build*

(Boston, 1831). On Stewart's life, Marilyn Richardson, "Introduction," in *Maria W. Stewart: America's First Black Woman Political Writer, Essays and Speeches* (Bloomington: Indiana University Press, 1987), 3–27; Coleman, "Architects of a Vision," 24–40.

32. Stewart, *Meditations From the Pen of Mrs. Maria W. Stewart.*

33. Stewart, *Meditations From the Pen of Mrs. Maria W. Stewart*; Peter P. Hinks, "Frequently Plunged into Slavery: Free Blacks and Kidnapping in Antebellum Boston," *Historical Journal of Massachusetts* 20, no. 1 (April 1992): 16–31; Peter P. Hinks, *To Awaken My Afflicted Brethren: David Walker and the Problem of Antebellum Slave Resistance* (University Park: Penn State University Press, 1997).

34. Wilma King, *Stolen Childhood: Slave Youth in Nineteenth-Century America* (Bloomington: Indiana University Press, 1995); Wilma King, *African American Childhoods: Historical Perspectives from Slavery to Civil Rights* (New York: Palgrave Macmillan, 2005); Nazera Sadiq Wright, *Black Girlhood in the Nineteenth Century* (Urbana: University of Illinois Press, 2016).

35. Stewart, *Meditations From the Pen of Mrs. Maria W. Stewart.* James Oliver Horton, "Generations of Protest: Black Families and Social Reform in Ante-Bellum Boston," *New England Quarterly* 49, no. 2 (January 1976): 242–256; David B. Landon and Teresa D. Bulger, "Constructing Community: Experiences of Identity, Economic Opportunity, and Institution Building at Boston's African Meeting House," *International Journal of Historical Archaeology* 17, no. 1 (March 2013): 119–142.

36. Hinks, *To Awaken My Afflicted Brethren*; David Walker, *David Walker's Appeal to the Coloured Citizens of the World*, ed. Peter P. Hinks (University Park: Penn State University Press, 2000).

37. Stewart, *Meditations From the Pen of Mrs. Maria W. Stewart.*

38. Stewart, *Meditations From the Pen of Mrs. Maria W. Stewart.*

39. Stewart, *Meditations From the Pen of Mrs. Maria W. Stewart.*

40. Marilyn Richardson, ed., *Maria W. Stewart: America's First Black Woman Political Writer: Essays and Speeches* (Bloomington: Indiana University Press, 1987), 30, 37.

41. Richardson, "Introduction," 3–27; Shirley Wilson Logan, "African Origins/ American Appropriations: Maria Stewart and 'Ethiopia Rising,'" in *We Are Coming: The Persuasive Discourse of Nineteenth-Century Black Women* (Carbondale: Southern Illinois University Press, 1999), 23–43.

42. Richardson, *Maria W. Stewart*, 65–74.

43. Richardson, "Introduction," *Maria W. Stewart*, 3–27.

44. "Female Celebration of the First of August," *The Liberator* (Boston), September 17, 1836; Marie Lindhorst, "Politics in a Box: Sarah Mapps Douglass and the Female Literary Association, 1831–1833," *Pennsylvania History: A Journal of Mid-Atlantic Studies* 65, no. 3 (1998): 263–278.

45. "Female Celebration of the First of August," *The Liberator* (Boston), September 17, 1836; Lindhorst, "Politics in a Box," 263–278; Elizabeth McHenry, *Forgotten Readers: Recovering the Lost History of African American Literary Societies* (Durham, NC: Duke University Press, 2002); Dunbar, *A Fragile Freedom.*

46. Gerda Lerner, "Sarah Mapps Douglass," in *Notable American Women, 1607–1950, Volume I: A–F*, ed. Janet Wilson James, Paul Samuel Boyer, and Edward T. James (Cambridge, MA: Harvard University Press, 1971), 557–558; Margaret Hope Beacon, "New Light on Sarah Mapps Douglass and Her Reconciliation with Friends," *Quaker*

History 90, no. 1 (April 2001): 28–49; Jones, *All Bound Up Together*, 38–49; Coleman, "Architects of a Vision," 24–40.

47. "Sarah Mapps Douglass," *Women & Social Movements in the United States, 1600–2000* 18, no. 1 (2014): 116; Lindhorst, "Politics in a Box."

48. McHenry, *Forgotten Readers*; Mary Kelley, "'A More Glorious Revolution': Women's Antebellum Reading Circles and the Pursuit of Public Influence," *New England Quarterly* 76, no. 2 (June 2003): 163–196.

49. "Miscellaneous. From the West Chester Register," *The Liberator* (Boston), December 3, 1831.

50. "Miscellaneous. From the West Chester Register," *The Liberator* (Boston), December 3, 1831; Ada, "Ladies' Department," *The Liberator* (Boston), June 30, 1832.

51. "Ladies' Department. To Zillah," *The Liberator* (Boston), August 18, 1832; "Ladies' Department. Reply to Woodby," *The Liberator* (Boston), August 18, 1832.

52. Martha S. Jones, "Edward Clay's Life in Philadelphia," in *An Americana Sampler: Essays on Selections from the William L. Clements Library*, ed. Brian Leigh Dunnigan and J. Kevin Graffagnino (Ann Arbor: University of Michigan Press, 2011); Nancy Reynolds Davison, "E.W. Clay: American Political Caricaturist of the Jacksonian Era, Volumes I and II" (PhD diss., University of Michigan, 1980); Jasmine Nichole Cobb, *Picture Freedom: Remaking Black Visuality in the Early Nineteenth Century* (New York: New York University Press, 2015).

53. "Reframing the Color Line: Race and the Visual Culture of the Atlantic World" [exhibit], presented by the William L. Clements Library and the Center for Afroamerican and African Studies at the University of Michigan, cocurated by Martha S. Jones, William L. Clements Library, October 2009, https://clements.umich.edu/exhibit/reframing-the-color-line/.

54. Lee, *Religious Experience and Journal of Mrs. Jarena Lee.*

Chapter 2: The Cause of the Slave, as Well as of Women

1. Elizabeth Wicks, *Address Delivered Before the African Female Benevolent Society of Troy on Wednesday, February 12, 1834. To Which is Annexed an Eulogy on the Death of Mrs. Jane Lansing. With an Address by Eliza A.T. Dungy* (Troy, NY: R. Buckley, 1834).

2. Richard S. Newman, *The Transformation of American Abolitionism: Fighting Slavery in the Early Republic* (Chapel Hill: University of North Carolina Press, 2002); David N. Gellman, *Emancipating New York: The Politics of Slavery and Freedom, 1777–1827* (Baton Rouge: Louisiana State University Press, 2006); Manisha Sinha, *The Slave's Cause: A History of Abolition* (New Haven, CT: Yale University Press, 2017).

3. Henry Mayer, *All on Fire: William Lloyd Garrison and the Abolition of Slavery* (New York: St. Martin's Press, 1998); Caleb W. McDaniel, *The Problem of Democracy in the Age of Slavery: Garrisonian Abolitionists and Transatlantic Reform* (Baton Rouge: Louisiana State University Press, 2015); Sinha, *The Slave's Cause.*

4. Phillip Lapsansky, "Graphic Discord: Abolitionist and Antiabolitionist Images," in *The Abolitionist Sisterhood: Women's Political Culture in Antebellum America*, ed. Jean Fagan Yellin and John C. Van Horne (Ithaca, NY: Cornell University Press, 1994),

201–230; Jeannine Marie DeLombard, *Slavery on Trial: Law, Abolitionism, and Print Culture* (Chapel Hill: University of North Carolina Press, 2007).

5. David W. Blight, "The Martyrdom of Elijah P. Lovejoy," *American History Illustrated* 12, no. 7 (November 1977): 20–27; Richard B. Kielbowicz, "The Law and Mob Law in Attacks on Antislavery Newspapers, 1833–1860," *Law & History Review* 24, no. 3 (Fall 2006): 559–600.

6. Benjamin Quarles, *Black Abolitionists* (New York: Da Capo Press, 1991); Shirley J. Yee, *Black Women Abolitionists: Study in Activism, 1828–1860* (Knoxville: University of Tennessee Press, 1992); Jean Fagan Yellin and John C. Van Horne, eds., *The Abolitionist Sisterhood: Women's Political Culture in Antebellum America* (Ithaca, NY: Cornell University Press, 1994); Christopher Cameron, *To Plead Our Own Cause: African Americans in Massachusetts and the Making of the Antislavery Movement* (Kent, OH: Kent State University Press, 2014); *Writing History from the Margins: African Americans and the Quest for Freedom*, ed. Claire Parfait, Hélène Le Dantic-Lowry, and Claire Bourhis-Mariotti (New York: Routledge, 2017); Eric Foner, *Gateway to Freedom: The Hidden History of the Underground Railroad* (New York: W. W. Norton, 2015); Richard Bell, *Stolen: Five Free Boys Kidnapped into Slavery and Their Astonishing Odyssey Home* (New York: 37 Ink, 2019).

7. Blanche Gassman Hersh, *The Slavery of Sex: Feminist-Abolitionists in America* (Urbana: University of Illinois Press, 1978); Yellin and Van Horne, *The Abolitionist Sisterhood*; Gerda Lerner, *The Grimké Sisters from South Carolina: Pioneers for Women's Rights and Abolition* (Boston: Houghton Mifflin, 1967).

8. Yee, *Black Women Abolitionists*, 2–39; Martha S. Jones, *All Bound Up Together: The Woman Question in African American Public Culture, 1830–1900* (Chapel Hill: University of North Carolina Press, 2007).

9. Willi Coleman, "Architects of a Vision: Black Women and Their Antebellum Quest for Political and Social Equality," in *African American Women and the Vote, 1837–1965*, ed. Ann D. Gordon, with Bettye Collier-Thomas, John H. Bracey, Arlene Voski Avakian, and Joyce Avrech Berkman (Amherst: University of Massachusetts Press, 1997), 24–40.

10. Lois Brown, "Out of the Mouths of Babes: The Abolitionist Campaign of Susan Paul and the Juvenile Choir of Boston," *New England Quarterly* 75, no. 1 (March 2002): 52–80.

11. Susan Paul, *Memoir of James Jackson: the attentive and obedient scholar, who died in Boston, October 31, 1833, aged six years and eleven months*, ed. Lois Brown (Cambridge, MA: Harvard University Press, 2000); Julie Winch, "Review of Lois Brown, ed., *Memoir of James Jackson, the Attentive and Obedient Scholar, Who Died in Boston, October 31, 1833, Aged Six Years and Eleven Months*, By His Teacher, Miss Susan Paul," H-SHEAR, March 1, 2002.

12. Brown, "Out of the Mouths of Babes," 52–80.

13. Mary A. Battys, et al., "To the Editor," *The Liberator* (Boston), November 17, 1832; Mayer, *All on Fire*; "Susan Paul," *Notable Black American Women*, Gale in Context: Biography series, 2002, www.gale.com/c/in-context-biography; Brown, "Out of the Mouths of Babes," 52–80; Ira V. Brown, "Am I Not a Woman and a Sister? The Anti-Slavery Convention of American Women, 1837–1839," *Pennsylvania History* 50, no. 1 (Winter 1983): 1–19.

14. *Proceedings of the Anti-Slavery Convention of American Women, held in Philadelphia, May 15th, 16th, 17th and 18th, 1838* (Philadelphia: Merrihew and Gunn, 1838); Brown, "Am I Not a Woman and a Sister?," 1–19; Debra Gold Hansen, "The Boston Female Anti-Slavery Society," in Yellin and Van Horne, *The Abolitionist Sisterhood*, 45–66.

15. *Proceedings of the Anti-Slavery Convention of American Women*; Brown, "Am I Not a Woman and a Sister?," 1–19.

16. *History of Pennsylvania Hall, Which Was Destroyed by a Mob, on the 17th of May, 1838* (Philadelphia: Merrihew and Gunn, 1838); *William Lloyd Garrison, 1805–1879: The Story of His Life Told by His Children, Volume II, 1835–1840* (New York: The Century, 1885). Beverly C. Tomek, *Pennsylvania Hall: A "Legal Lynching" in the Shadow of the Liberty Bell* (New York: Oxford University Press, 2014).

17. *History of Pennsylvania Hall*; Tomek, *Pennsylvania Hall: A "Legal Lynching."*

18. *History of Pennsylvania Hall*; Tomek, *Pennsylvania Hall: A "Legal Lynching."*

19. *History of Pennsylvania Hall*; Tomek, *Pennsylvania Hall: A "Legal Lynching."*

20. The 1828 city directory for Manhattan notes Lane as a "Whitewasher on Sullivan Street." E. S. Abdy, *Residence and Tour of the United States of North America* (London: John Murray, 1835), 32–33; *Proceedings of the General Anti-Slavery Convention, Called by the Committee of the British and Foreign Anti-Slavery Society, and Held in London from Tuesday June 13th to Tuesday June 20th, 1843* (London: John Snow, 1843), 213.

21. J. F. Johnson, *Proceedings of the General Anti-Slavery Convention, called by the Committee of the British and Foreign Anti-Slavery Society, Held in London* (London: John Snow, 1843), 213.

22. Graham Russell Gao Hodges, *David Ruggles: A Radical Abolitionist and the Underground Railroad in New York City* (Chapel Hill: University of North Carolina Press, 2010); Eric Foner, *Gateway to Freedom: The Hidden History of the Underground Railroad* (New York: Norton, 2015).

23. D.R., "Woman's Rights," *Mirror of Liberty*, July 1, 1838.

24. *The First Annual Report of the New York Committee of Vigilance for the Year 1837* (New York: Piercy & Reed, 1837), 84; "Kidnapping in New York," *The Liberator* (Boston), April 21, 1937. Carla L. Peterson, *Black Gotham: A Family History of African Americans in Nineteenth-Century New York City* (New Haven, CT: Yale University Press, 2012), 136; Kellie Carter-Jackson, *Force and Freedom: Black Abolitionists and the Politics of Violence* (Philadelphia: University of Pennsylvania Press, 2019).

25. "Slander," *Colored American* (New York City), February 10, 1838; "At one of the African Churches up town, a Trial," *Colored American* (New York City), February 10, 1838; "Mrs. Hester Lane," *Colored American* (New York City), February 10, 1838.

26. *The Antislavery Record. Vol. II, for 1836* (New York: R. G. Williams, 1836), 120; Charles H. Wesley, *Journal of Negro History* 24, no. 1 (January 1939): 65–103.

27. *Sixth Annual Report of the American Anti-Slavery Society: With the Speeches Delivered at the Anniversary Meeting, held in the city of New York, on the 7th May, 1839* (New York: William S. Dorr, 1839).

28. *Sixth Annual Report of the American Anti-Slavery Society.*

29. *Sixth Annual Report of the American Anti-Slavery Society.*

30. "Proceedings of the Annual Meeting of the A.A.S. Society. Resolutions on Political Action," *Colored American* (New York City), May 30, 1840.

31. "Proceedings of the Annual Meeting of the A.A.S. Society. Resolutions on Political Action," *Colored American* (New York City), May 30, 1840.

32. "Proceedings of the Annual Meeting of the A.A.S. Society. Resolutions on Political Action," *Colored American* (New York City), May 30, 1840.

33. *Proceedings of the General Anti-Slavery Convention*, 213; "Died," *National Anti-Slavery Standard* (New York City and Philadelphia), July 12, 1849.

34. Lisa Tetrault, *The Myth of Seneca Falls: Memory and the Women's Suffrage Movement, 1848–1898* (Chapel Hill: University of North Carolina Press, 2014).

35. Jones, *All Bound Up Together*, 23–57, 87–117; Bettye Collier-Thomas, *Jesus, Jobs, and Justice: African American Women and Religion* (New York: Alfred A. Knopf, 2010); Jualynne E. Dodson, *Engendering Church: Women, Power, and the A.M.E. Church* (Lanham, MD: Rowman & Littlefield, 2002).

36. Jones, *All Bound Up Together*, 59–85; Collier-Thomas, *Jesus, Jobs, and Justice*; Dodson, *Engendering Church*.

37. B. T. Tanner, *An Outline of Our History and Government for African Methodist Churchmen. Ministerial and Lay. In Catechetical Form. Two Parts with Appendix* (Philadelphia: Grant, Faires, & Rodgers, Printers, 1844), 185–186; C. S. Smith, *a History of the African Methodist Episcopal Church: Being a Volume Supplemental to A History of the African Methodist Episcopal Church, by Daniel Alexander Payne, D.D., LL.D., Late One of Its Bishops: Chronicling the Principal Events in the Advance of the African Methodist Episcopal Church from 1856 to 1922* (Philadelphia: Book Concern of the AME Church, 1922), 415. Jones, *All Bound Up Together*, 59–85; Collier-Thomas, *Jesus, Jobs, and Justice*; Dodson, *Engendering Church*.

38. Tanner, *An Outline of Our History and Government for African Methodist Churchmen*, 185–186; Smith, *A History of the African Methodist Episcopal Church*, 415; Jones, *All Bound Up Together*, 59–85.

39. Tanner, *An Outline of Our History and Government for African Methodist Churchmen*, 185–186; Smith, *A History of the African Methodist Episcopal Church*, 415; Jones, *All Bound Up Together*, 59–85; Collier-Thomas, *Jesus, Jobs, and Justice*.

40. Tanner, *An Outline of Our History and Government for African Methodist Churchmen*, 185–186; Jones, *All Bound Up Together*, 59–85; Collier-Thomas, *Jesus, Jobs, and Justice*.

41. Tanner, *An Outline of Our History and Government for African Methodist Churchmen*, 185–186; "Proceedings of the Third Annual Meeting of the American Moral Reform Society," *National Reformer*, September 1839; Jones, *All Bound Up Together*, 59–85; Collier-Thomas, *Jesus, Jobs, and Justice*; Eric Rose, "American Moral Reform Society," in *Encyclopedia of African American History*, Vol. 2, ed. Leslie M. Alexander and Walter C. Rucker (Santa Barbara, CA: ABC-CLIO, 2010), 309–310.

42. Tanner, *An Outline of Our History and Government for African Methodist Churchmen*, 185–186.

43. "Women's Rights: Seneca Falls Declaration of Sentiments," *Gale Encyclopedia of American Law*, Vol. 13, 3rd ed., ed. Donna Bratten (Farmington Hills, MI: Gale, 2011), 436–437. Ellen Carol DuBois, *Suffrage: Women's Long Battle for the Vote* (New York: Simon & Schuster, 2020), 7–15; Lisa Tetrault, *The Myth of Seneca Falls:*

Memory and the Women's Suffrage Movement, 1848–1898 (Chapel Hill: University of North Carolina Press, 2014).

44. Walter Gable, Judith Wellman, with Tanya Warren, *Discovering the Underground Railroad, Abolitionism, and African American Life, in Seneca County, New York, 1820–1880* (Fulton, NY: County of Seneca, March 2006); Walter J. Gable, *Thomas James, Freedom Seeker* (Fulton, NY: County of Seneca, February 2007); Judith Wellman, *The Road to Seneca Falls: Elizabeth Cady Stanton and the First Women's Rights Convention* (Urbana: University of Illinois Press, 2010).

45. Elizabeth Cady Stanton, *Address in Favor of Universal Suffrage for the Election of Delegates to the Constitutional Convention* (Albany, NY: Weed, Parsons, 1867), 9; *History of Woman Suffrage, Volume II, 1861–1876*, ed. Elizabeth Cady Stanton, Susan B. Anthony, and Matilda Joslyn Gage (1881) [referred to by Stanton as "Abby Gomore"]; Walter Gable, Judith Wellman, with Tanya Warren, *Discovering the Underground Railroad, Abolitionism and African American Life*.

46. *Report of the Proceedings of the Colored National Convention, Held at Cleveland, Ohio, on Wednesday, September 6, 1848* (Rochester, NY: John Dick, 1848).

47. *Report of the Proceedings of the Colored National Convention, 1848*; Sydna E. R. Francis, "To a Charitable Public," *Frederick Douglass' Paper* (Rochester, NY), February 22, 1850. Heather Sinkinson, "Black Wealth and the 1843 National Colored Convention: Sydna E. R. Francis," Colored Conventions Project, https://coloredconventions.org/black-wealth/biographies/sydna-e-r-francis/.

48. *Report of the Proceedings of the Colored National Convention, 1848*.

49. *Report of the Proceedings of the Colored National Convention, 1848*; Coleman, "Architects of a Vision," 24–40.

50. *Report of the Proceedings of the Colored National Convention, 1848*.

51. *Report of the Proceedings of the Colored National Convention, 1848*.

52. *Report of the Proceedings of the Colored National Convention, 1848*.

Chapter 3: To Be Black and Female

1. Quintard Taylor and Shirley Ann Wilson Moore, eds., *African American Women Confront the West, 1600–2000* (Norman: University of Oklahoma Press, 2003); Patrick Rael, *Black Identity and Black Protest in the Antebellum North* (Chapel Hill: University of North Carolina Press, 2002); Quintard Taylor, *In Search of the Racial Frontier: African Americans in the American West, 1528–1990* (New York: W. W. Norton, 1998); James Oliver Horton and Lois E. Horton, *In Hope of Liberty: Culture, Community, and Protest among Northern Free Blacks, 1700–1860* (New York: Oxford University Press, 1997); James Oliver Horton, *Free People of Color: Inside the African American Community* (Washington, DC: Smithsonian Institution Press, 1993); Elizabeth Rauh Bethel, *The Roots of African-American Identity: Memory and History in Antebellum Free Communities* (New York: St. Martin's Press, 1997).

2. Kellie Carter-Jackson, *Force and Freedom: Black Abolitionists and the Politics of Violence* (Philadelphia: University of Pennsylvania Press, 2019); Manish Sinha, *The Slave's Cause: A History of Abolition* (New Haven, CT: Yale University Press, 2016); Ira Berlin, *The Long Emancipation: The Demise of Slavery in the United States* (Cambridge, MA: Harvard University Press, 2015).

3. Jermain Wesley Loguen, *The Rev. J.W. Loguen, as a Slave and as a Freeman: A Narrative of Real Life* (Syracuse, NY: J. G. K. Truair, 1859); William Wells Brown, *Narrative of William W. Brown, a Fugitive Slave. Written by Himself* (Boston: Anti-Slavery Office, 1847); Solomon Northup, *Twelve Years a Slave: Narrative of Solomon Northup, a Citizen of New-York, Kidnapped in Washington City in 1841, and Rescued in 1853* (Auburn, NY: Derby and Miller, 1853); Sojourner Truth, *Narrative of Sojourner Truth, a Northern Slave, Emancipated from Bodily Servitude by the State of New York, in 1828* (Boston: The Author, 1850); Frances Smith Foster, *Witnessing Slavery: The Development of Ante-bellum Slave Narratives* (Madison: University of Wisconsin Press, 1994).

4. R. J. M. Blackett, *The Captive's Quest for Freedom: Fugitive Slaves, the 1850 Fugitive Slave Law, and the Politics of Slavery* (New York: Cambridge University Press, 2018).

5. Ousamane K. Power-Greene, *Against the Wind and Tide: The African American Struggle against the Colonization Movement* (New York: New York University Press, 2014).

6. Ellen Carol DuBois, *Suffrage: Women's Long Battle for the Vote* (New York: Simon & Schuster, 2020), 27–43.

7. Mary Ann Shadd, *A Plea for Emigration; or Notes of Canada West* (Peterborough, Canada: Broadview Press, 2016); Jane Rhodes, *Mary Ann Shadd Cary: The Black Press and Protest in the Nineteenth Century* (Bloomington: Indiana University Press, 1999); Willi Coleman, "Architects of a Vision: Black Women and Their Antebellum Quest for Political and Social Equality," in *African American Women and the Vote, 1837–1965,* ed. Ann D. Gordon, with Bettye Collier-Thomas, John H. Bracey, Arlene Voski Avakian, and Joyce Avrech Berkman (Amherst: University of Massachusetts Press, 1997), 24–40.

8. J.B.Y. "Miss Shadd's Pamphlet," *The North Star,* June 8, 1849; Rhodes, *Mary Ann Shadd Cary,* 20–23, citing Martin R. Delany, *The Condition, Elevation, Emigration, and Destiny of the Colored People of the United States* (New York: Arno Press, 1968), 131.

9. Rhodes, *Mary Ann Shadd Cary,* 70–99.

10. "The Provincial Freeman," *Provincial Freeman* (Windsor, Ontario), March 24, 1854 ("Committees of Publication" includes only men, while "letters must be addressed" to "Mary A. Shadd."); "Prospectus of the *Provincial Freeman,*" *Provincial Freeman* (Windsor, Ontario), March 25, 1854 (signed by Rev. S. R. Ward, Editor, and Rev. Alex. McArthur, Cor. Editor); "Mr. M.A. Shadd," *Provincial Freeman* (Windsor, Ontario), August 26, 1854 (Correspondent to "Mr. M.A. Shadd" writes "may the Lord bless you, brother, Shadd," and she replies, "We would simply correct, for the future, our error, by giving, here, the name in full [Mary A. Shadd] as we do not like the Mr. and Esq., by which we are so often addressed."); "Prospectus of the *Provincial Freeman,*" *Provincial Freeman* (Windsor, Ontario), January 20, 1855 ("M.A. Shadd" noted as "publishing agent" and the person to whom "all letters...must be addressed); "At the Close of the Recent Session," *Provincial Freeman* (Windsor, Ontario), November 3, 1855 (Note that "Miss M.A. Shadd" had "filled the editorial of the Provincial Freedom for the past year."); "Prospectus of the *Provincial Freeman,*" *Provincial Freeman* (Windsor, Ontario), May 10, 1856 (H. Ford Douglass, Isaac D. Shadd, Mary A. Shadd, Editors); Rhodes, *Mary Ann Shadd Cary,* 100–134.

11. Rhodes, *Mary Ann Shadd Cary*, 100–134.

12. Rhodes, *Mary Ann Shadd Cary*, 100–134.

13. Henrietta W., [Letter to the Editor], *Provincial Freeman* (Windsor, Ontario), April 22, 1854; Dolly Bangs, [Letter to the Editor], *Provincial Freeman* (Windsor, Ontario), April 29, 1854.

14. Henrietta W., [Letter to the Editor], *Provincial Freeman* (Windsor, Ontario), April 22, 1854; Dolly Bangs, [Letter to the Editor], *Provincial Freeman* (Windsor, Ontario), April 29, 1854.

15. "To the Editor," *Provincial Freeman* (Windsor, Ontario), September 2, 1854; "From the Portland Advertiser," *Provincial Freeman* (Windsor, Ontario), March 15, 1856.

16. "Letter from our Esteemed Philadelphia Correspondent," *Provincial Freeman* (Windsor, Ontario), March 7, 1857; Bettye Collier-Thomas, "Frances Ellen Watkins Harper: Abolitionist and Feminist Reformer, 1825–1911," in Gordon et al., *African American Women and the Vote*, 41–65.

17. "The Humbug of Reform," *Provincial Freeman* (Windsor, Ontario), May 27, 1854.

18. Nell Irvin Painter, *Sojourner Truth: A Life, a Symbol* (New York: W. W. Norton, 1997). Historian Susan Ware situates Truth in the long history of women's fight for the vote. Susan Ware, *Why They Marched: Untold Stories of the Women Who Fought for the Right to Vote* (Cambridge, MA: Belknap Press, 2019), 29–39.

19. Painter, *Sojourner Truth*.

20. Painter, *Sojourner Truth*, 111–131.

21. Painter, *Sojourner Truth*, 113–116; J. G. Forman, "Women's Rights Convention at Worcester, Mass.," *New York Daily Tribune*, October 26, 1850; *Proceedings of the Woman's Rights Convention, held at Worcester, October 23 & 24, 1850* (Boston: Prentiss & Sawyer, 1851), 9.

22. Painter, *Sojourner Truth*, 113–116; *Proceedings of the Woman's Rights Convention, held at Worcester, October 23 & 24, 1850* (Boston: Prentiss & Sawyer, 1851), 4, 20, 53.

23. Martha S. Jones, *All Bound Up Together: The Woman Question in African American Public Culture, 1830–1900* (Chapel Hill: University of North Carolina Press, 2007).

24. "Women's Rights Convention. Sojourner Truth," *Anti-Slavery Bugle* (New Lisbon, OH), June 21, 1851.

25. "Women's Rights Convention. Sojourner Truth," *Anti-Slavery Bugle* (New Lisbon, OH), June 21, 1851.

26. Painter, *Sojourner Truth*, 138–142.

27. *Proceedings of the Colored National Convention, Held in Franklin Hall, Sixth Street, Below Arch, Philadelphia, October 16th, 17th and 18th* (Salem, NJ: National Standard Office, 1856).

28. Austin Steward, *Twenty-Two Years a Slave and Forty Years a Freeman Embracing a Correspondence of Several Years While President of Wilberforce Colony, Liberia, London, Canada West* (Rochester, NY: W. Alling, 1857); "Meeting of Colored Citizens in Rochester," *Frederick Douglass' Paper* (Rochester, NY), September 21, 1855; Coleman, "Architects of a Vision," 24–40.

29. "Meeting of Colored Citizens in Rochester," *Frederick Douglass' Paper* (Rochester, NY), September 21, 1855; Coleman, "Architects of a Vision," 24–40.

30. Jones, *All Bound Up Together*, 104, 135.

31. "Convention at Geneva," *Frederick Douglass' Paper* (Rochester, NY), December 16, 1853; "Selected Matter. Anti-Slavery Lectures," *Frederick Douglass' Paper* (Rochester, NY), November 9, 1855.

32. "Meeting of Colored Citizens in Rochester," *Frederick Douglass' Paper* (Rochester, NY), September 21, 1855; "Colored Men's State Convention of New York, Troy, September 4, 1855," *Proceedings of the Black State Conventions, 1840–1965*, Vol. I, ed. Philip S. Foner and George E. Walker (Philadelphia: Temple University Press, 1979), 88–97; Yee, *Black Women Abolitionists*, 146.

33. *State v. Mann*, 13 N.C. 263 (N.C. 1830); Sally Greene, "State v. Mann Exumed," *North Carolina Law Review* 87, no. 3 (March 2009): 701–756.

34. "A Woman Hanged," *Provincial Freeman* (Windsor, Ontario), February 2, 1856; *State of Missouri v. Celia; Records of the Callaway County Circuit Court, File no. 4496, 1855–1856*, Famous Trials, www.famous-trials.com; Melton A. McLaurin, *Celia, a Slave: A True Story* (New York: Avon, 1991).

35. *State of Missouri v. Celia; Records of the Callaway County Circuit Court*, Famous Trials.

36. *State of Missouri v. Celia; Records of the Callaway County Circuit Court*, Famous Trials.

37. *State of Missouri v. Celia; Records of the Callaway County Circuit*, Famous Trials.

38. *State of Missouri v. Celia; Records of the Callaway County Circuit Court*, Famous Trials.

39. Harriet A. Jacobs, *Incidents in the Life of a Slave Girl, Written by Herself*, ed. L. Maria Child (1861; reprint, Cambridge, MA: Harvard University Press, 1987), 5–113; Jean Yellin Fagan, *Harriet Jacobs: A Life* (New York: Civitas Books, 2005), 3–62.

40. Jacobs, *Incidents in the Life of a Slave Girl*, 114–163; Fagan, *Harriet Jacobs*, 83–136

41. Harriet Jacobs, "Letter to Amy Post, October 9, [1853]," in *Incidents in the Life of a Slave Girl: A Norton Critical Edition*, ed. Nellie Y. McKay and Frances Smith Foster (New York: W. W. Norton, 2001), 172–173; Fagan, *Harriet Jacobs*, 117–153.

42. "Lecture by Miss F.E. Watkins," *The Liberator* (Boston), September 8, 1854; "A Colored Lady Lecturer and Poet," *Anti-Slavery Bugle* (Lisbon, OH), July 14, 1855 (reprint from the Philadelphia *Woman's Advocate*).

43. Francis Ellen Watkins, "Letter from Miss Watkins," *Anti-Slavery Bugle* (Lisbon, OH), April 23, 1859.

44. "Anti-Slavery Lecture—Miss Watkins," *Cleveland Daily Leader*, February 25, 1860; "Letter from William C. Nell," *The Liberator* (Boston), September 17, 1858; "Miss Frances Ellen Watkins," *The Liberator* (Boston), December 5, 1856; "Miss Watkins' Lecture," *Findlay (OH) Jeffersonian*, May 25, 1860; "A Colored Lady Lecturer and Poet," *Anti-Slavery Bugle* (Lisbon, OH), July 14, 1855 (reprint from the Philadelphia *Woman's Advocate*); "Lights and Shadows of American Institutions," *Cleveland Daily Leader*, February 17, 1859.

45. *Proceedings of a Convention of the Colored Men of Ohio, Held in the City of Cincinnati, on the 23d, 24th, 25th and 26th Days of November, 1858* (Cincinnati, OH: Moore, Wilstach, Keys, 1858); William C. Nell, "Sketch of a Tour to the West," *The Liberator* (Boston), November 12, 1858; J. Greenly Ampey, "First of August Celebration," *Anti-Slavery Bugle* (Lisbon, OH), August 27, 1859; "Great Anti-Colonization Meeting in Philadelphia, August 30," *The Liberator* (Boston), October 7, 1853; "Convention of Colored Citizens of Ohio," *Cleveland Daily Leader*, November 27, 1858; W.L.G., "From the Liberator. Syracuse, October 25, 1858," *Anti-Slavery Bugle* (Lisbon, OH), November 6, 1858.

46. Subrosa, "Our Rural Correspondence," *Randolph Journal* (Winchester, IN), July 14, 1859; Subrosa, "To the Editor," *Randolph Journal* (Winchester, IN), July 28, 1959; "Grand Abolition Pow-wow," *New Orleans Crescent*, May 21, 1857; "The Anniversaries," *Brooklyn Daily Eagle*, May 14, 1857; "Negro Lecturing," *Charlotte (NC) Democrat*, April 29, 1856; "Miss Ellen Watkins," *Daily Memphis Whig*, April 18, 1856.

47. "Extracts from a Letter of Frances Ellen Watkins to a Friend," *The Liberator* (Boston), April 23, 1858.

48. "Extracts from a Letter of Frances Ellen Watkins to a Friend," *The Liberator* (Boston), April 23, 1858; Frances Ellen Watkins, "Letters. Green Plain, O. Sept 21, 1860," *Anti-Slavery Bugle* (Lisbon, OH), September 29, 1860; "Meeting a Cool Spring," *Anti-Slavery Bugle* (Lisbon, OH), January 1, 1859; "A New Champion for the Church," *Anti-Slavery Bugle* (Lisbon, OH), November 20, 1858.

49. "Extracts from a Letter of Frances Ellen Watkins to a Friend," *The Liberator* (Boston), April 23, 1858; Frances Ellen Watkins, "Letters. Green Plain, O. Sept 21, 1860," *Anti-Slavery Bugle* (Lisbon, OH), September 29, 1860; "Meeting a Cool Spring," *Anti-Slavery Bugle* (Lisbon, OH), January 1, 1859; "A New Champion for the Church," *Anti-Slavery Bugle* (Lisbon, OH), November 20, 1858.

Chapter 4: One Great Bundle of Humanity

1. *Proceedings of the Eleventh National Woman's Rights Convention, Held at the Church of the Puritans, New York, May 10, 1866* (New York: Robert J. Johnston, 1866).

2. Elizabeth R. Varon, *Armies of Deliverance: A New History of the Civil War* (New York: Oxford University Press, 2019); Eric Foner, *Reconstruction: America's Unfinished Revolution, 1863–1877, Updated Edition* (New York: Harper, 2014).

3. Foner, *Reconstruction*.

4. Foner, *Reconstruction*.

5. Ira Berlin, Barbara J. Fields, Steven F. Miller, Joseph P. Reidy, and Leslie S. Rowland, *Slaves No More: Three Essays on Emancipation and the Civil War* (New York: Cambridge University Press, 1992); Steven Hahn, *A Nation under Our Feet: Black Political Struggles in the Rural South from Slavery to the Great Migration* (Cambridge, MA: Belknap Press of Harvard University Press, 2005); Foner, *Reconstruction*.

6. Thavolia Glymph, *The Women's Fight: The Civil War's Battles for Home, Freedom, and Nation* (Chapel Hill: University of North Carolina Press, 2020); Stephanie McCurry, *Women's War: Fighting and Surviving the American Civil War* (Cambridge,

MA: Belknap Press of Harvard University Press, 2019); Judith Giesberg and Randall M. Miller, eds., *Women and the American Civil War: North–South Counterpoints* (Kent, OH: Kent State University Press, 2018).

7. Glymph, *The Women's Fight*; McCurry, *Women's War*; Giesberg and Miller, *Women and the American Civil War*.

8. Glymph, *The Women's Fight*; McCurry, *Women's War*; Giesberg and Miller, *Women and the American Civil War*; Martha S. Jones, *All Bound Up Together: The Woman Question in African American Public Culture, 1830–1900* (Chapel Hill: University of North Carolina Press, 2007).

9. Foner, *Reconstruction*.

10. Foner, *Reconstruction*.

11. Foner, *Reconstruction*.

12. Foner, *Reconstruction*; Eric Foner, *The Second Founding: How the Civil War and Reconstruction Remade the Constitution* (New York: W. W. Norton, 2019).

13. Thomas L. Altherr, "'A Convention of Moral Lunatics': The Rutland, Vermont, Free Convention of 1858," *Rutland Historical Quarterly* 39, no. 3 (1999): 91–103; Carol Faulkner, *Unfaithful: Love, Adultery, and Marriage Reform in Nineteenth-Century America* (Philadelphia: University of Pennsylvania Press, 2019).

14. "Equal Rights," *Rutland (VT) Weekly Herald*, June 22, 1865.

15. "Equal Rights," *Rutland (VT) Weekly Herald*, June 22, 1865.

16. "Equal Rights," *Rutland (VT) Weekly Herald*, June 22, 1865.

17. "Equal Rights," *Rutland (VT) Weekly Herald*, June 22, 1865.

18. "Equal Rights," *Rutland (VT) Weekly Herald*, June 22, 1865.

19. Jane Rhodes, *Mary Ann Shadd Cary: The Black Press and Protest in the Nineteenth Century* (Bloomington: Indiana University Press, 1998), 135–162.

20. Rhodes, *Mary Ann Shadd Cary*, 135–162.

21. Rhodes, *Mary Ann Shadd Cary*, 135–162.

22. Glymph, *The Women's Fight*; Ira Berlin, Steven Hahn, Thavolia Glymph, Joseph P. Reidy, René Hayden, Steven F. Miller, Leslie S. Rowland, and Julie Saville, eds., *Freedom: Volume 2, Series 1: The Wartime Genesis of Free Labor: The Upper South: A Documentary History of Emancipation, 1861–1867* (New York: Cambridge University Press, 1993); Thavolia Glymph, "'Invisible Disabilities': Black Women in War and Freedom," *Proceedings of the American Philosophical Society* 160, no. 3 (September 2016): 237–246; Chandra Manning, *Troubled Refuge: Struggling for Freedom in the Civil War* (New York: Alfred A. Knopf, 2016).

23. Harriet Jacobs, "Life Among the Contrabands," *The Liberator* (Boston), September 5, 1862; Jean Fagan Yellin, *Harriet Jacobs: A Life* (New York: Basic Civitas Books, 2004), 175–209.

24. Yellin, *Harriet Jacobs*, 175–209.

25. Josephine S. Griffing, "Treason in Disguise," *The Liberator* (Boston), June 21, 1861; Nell Irvin Painter, *Sojourner Truth: A Life, a Symbol* (New York: W. W. Norton, 1996), 179–182.

26. Painter, *Sojourner Truth*, 209–219.

27. "Sojourner Truth: Sharp as Ever," *Cleveland Daily Leader*, April 7, 1866; Painter, *Sojourner Truth*, 209–212.

28. Sojourner Truth to Amy Post, October 1, 1865, cited in Painter, *Sojourner Truth*, 209–211; "Alleged Assault upon Sojourner Truth," *Daily National Republican*, September 22, 1865; Painter, *Sojourner Truth*, 209–212.

29. "Alleged Assault upon Sojourner Truth," *Daily National Republican* (Washington, DC), September 22, 1865; Painter, *Sojourner Truth*, 209–212.

30. Sojourner Truth to Amy Post, October 1, 1865, cited in Painter, *Sojourner Truth*, 209–211; "Alleged Assault upon Sojourner Truth," *Daily National Republican* (Washington, DC), September 22, 1865; Painter, *Sojourner Truth*, 209–212; Carleton Mabee and Susan Mabee Newhouse, *Sojourner Truth: Slave, Prophet, Legend* (New York: New York University Press, 1995).

31. Willie Lee Rose, *Rehearsal for Reconstruction: The Port Royal Experiment* (New York: Oxford University Press, 1964); Jean M. Humez, *Harriet Tubman: The Life and Life Stories* (Madison: University of Wisconsin Press, 2003), 45–68; Catherine Clinton, *Harriet Tubman: The Road to Freedom* (Boston: Little, Brown, 2004); Kate Clifford Larson, *Bound for the Promised Land: Harriet Tubman, Portrait of an American Hero* (New York: Ballantine, 2004).

32. Susie King Taylor, *Reminiscences of My Life in Camp with the 33rd United States Colored Troops Late 1st S.C. Volunteers* (Boston: The Author, 1902). Catherine Clinton, "Susie King Taylor (1848–1912): 'I Give My Services Willingly,'" in *Georgia Women: Their Lives and Times*, Vol. I, ed. Ann Short Chirhart and Betty Wood (Athens: University of Georgia Press, 2009), 130–146.

33. Charlotte L. Forten Grimké, *The Journals of Charlotte Forten Grimké* (New York: Oxford University Press, 1988). Emma Jones Lapsansky, "Feminism, Freedom, and Community: Charlotte Forten and Women Activists in Nineteenth-Century Philadelphia," *Pennsylvania Magazine of History & Biography* 113, no. 1 (January 1989): 3–19; Carla Peterson, "Reconstructing the Nation: Francis Harper, Charlotte Forten, and the Racial Politics of Periodical Publication," *Proceedings of the American Antiquarian Society* 107 (October 1997): 301–334; Brenda Stevenson, "Introduction," in *The Journals of Charlotte Forten Grimké* (New York: Oxford University Press, 1988), 3–55.

34. "Friday, March 6 [1857]," in Grimké, *The Journals of Charlotte Forten Grimké*, 200; Lapsansky, "Feminism, Freedom, and Community," 3–19; Jean R. Soderlund, "Priorities and Power: The Philadelphia Female Anti-Slavery Society," *The Abolitionist Sisterhood: Women's Political Culture in Antebellum America*, ed. Jean Fagan Yellin and John C. Van Horne (Ithaca, NY: Cornell University Press, 1994), 67–99; Peterson, "Reconstructing the Nation," 301–334.

35. "Thursday, November 27 [1862]," in Grimké, *The Journals of Charlotte Forten Grimké*, 405–406; Lapsansky, "Feminism, Freedom, and Community," 3–19; Winch, *A Gentleman of Color*; Peterson, "Reconstructing the Nation," 301–334.

36. F. E. W. Harper, "Mrs. Frances E. Watkins Harper on the War and the President's Colonization Scheme," *Christian Recorder*, September 27, 1862; Eric Gardner, "Frances Ellen Watkins Harper's Civil War and Militant Intersectionality," *Mississippi Quarterly* 70–71, no. 4 (Fall 2017/2018): 505–518.

37. "Mrs. Watkins Harper," *Age* (Philadelphia), May 19, 1864; "Mrs. Watkins Harper," *Boston Post*, May 19, 1964; "A Colored Poetess," *Providence Evening Press*,

November 1, 1864; "Colored Jubilee in New York. The Maryland 'Big Thing' Celebrated," *Age* (Philadelphia), November 30, 1864; "Free Maryland," *Massachusetts Spy* (Worcester), November 2, 1864; "Celebration of the Adoption of a Free Constitution by Maryland," *Daily Constitution* (Augusta, GA), December 10, 1864.

38. *Proceedings of the National Convention of Colored Men, Held in the City of Syracuse, N.Y., October 4, 5, 6, and 7, 1864* (Boston: J. S. Rock and Geo. L. Ruffin, 1864); "National Convention of Colored Men," *New Orleans Tribune*, October 26, 1864; Shirley Wilson Logan, *We Are Coming: The Persuasive Discourse of Nineteenth-Century Black Women* (Carbondale: Southern Illinois University Press, 1999), 19–20.

39. Melba Joyce Boyd, *Discarded Legacy: Politics and Poetics in the Life of Frances E. W. Harper, 1825–1911* (Detroit: Wayne State University, 1994), 411, 62–65, 133–135.

40. "The Martyrdom of Crispus Attucks," *Boston Evening Transcript*, March 8, 1865; "Celebration of Emancipation Day in Boston," *Manufacturers' and Farmers' Journal* (Providence, RI), January 4, 1869. Privately, Cary admitted that she not only admired Watkins but also saw her as a rival. Jane Rhodes, *Mary Ann Shadd Cary: The Black Press and Protest in the Nineteenth Century* (Bloomington: Indiana University Press, 1998), 131; Field, *The Struggle for Equal Adulthood*; Logan, *We Are Coming*, 44–69.

41. "[Miss Anna E. Dickinson; Mrs. F.E. Watkins Harper]," *Alexandria (VA) Gazette*, March 4, 1865; "[Mrs. F.E. Watkins; Colored]," *Daily Ohio Statesman* (Columbus), March 16, 1865; "News Paragraphs. Personal, Political, and Miscellaneous," *Plain Dealer* (Cleveland, OH), July 29, 1867.

42. *Proceedings of the Eleventh National Woman's Rights Convention, Held at the Church of the Puritans, New York, May 10, 1866* (New York: Robert J. Johnston, 1866); Field, *The Struggle for Equal Adulthood*, 118–149; Corinne T. Field, "Frances E.W. Harper and the Politics of Maturity," in *Toward an Intellectual History of Black Women*, ed. Mia Bay, Farah J. Griffin, Martha S. Jones, and Barbara D. Savage (Chapel Hill: University of North Carolina Press, 2015), 110–126. On the founding of the American Equal Rights Association, see Ellen Carol DuBois, *Suffrage: Women's Long Battle for the Vote* (New York: Simon & Schuster, 2020), 58–61.

43. *Proceedings of the Eleventh National Woman's Rights Convention, 1866*; Blair L. M. Kelley, "New York: The Antebellum Roots of Segregation and Discrimination," *Right to Ride: Streetcar Boycotts and African American Citizenship in the Era of* Plessy v. Ferguson (Chapel Hill: University of North Carolina Press, 2010), 15–32; Barbara Young Welke, *Recasting American Liberty: Race, Gender, Law, and the Railroad Revolution, 1865–1920* (New York: Cambridge University Press, 2001), 43–80, 171–202, 280–322.

44. *Proceedings of the Eleventh National Woman's Rights Convention, 1866.*

45. *Proceedings of the Eleventh National Woman's Rights Convention, 1866.*

46. *Proceedings of the Eleventh National Woman's Rights Convention, 1866.*

47. *Proceedings of the Eleventh National Woman's Rights Convention, 1866*; "Debates at the American Equal Rights Association Meeting, New York City, May 12,14, 1869," in *The Concise History of Woman Suffrage: Selections from History of Woman Suffrage, Edited by Elizabeth Cady Stanton, Susan B. Anthony, Matilda Joslyn Gage, and the National American Woman Suffrage Association*, ed. Mari Jo Buhle and Paul Buhle (Urbana: University of Illinois Press, 2005), 257–274; "The May Anniversaries

in New York and Brooklyn," *History of Woman Suffrage*, Vol. II, ed. Elizabeth Cady Stanton, Susan B. Anthony, and Matilda Joslyn Gage (Rochester, NY: Susan B. Anthony, 1881), 378–402; Jones, *All Bound Up Together*, 119–149; Field, *The Struggle for Equal Adulthood*, 118–149; Field, "Frances E.W. Harper and the Politics of Maturity." On the founding of the American Equal Rights Association, see DuBois, *Suffrage*, 58–61, 79–88.

48. Historians have variously dated these remarks as from 1872 and 1874. All agree that Cary drafted them for delivery before a congressional judiciary committee. Mary Ann Shadd Cary, "Speech to Judiciary Committee re: The Rights of Women to Vote," Mary Ann Shadd Cary Papers, Moorland-Spingarn Research Center, Howard University, Washington, DC.

49. Rhodes, *Mary Ann Shadd Cary*,167–171, 185–191.

50. Mary Shadd Cary, "Communications from the State and Territories. From District of Columbia," *New National Era* (Washington, DC), February 5, 1874.

51. *Spencer v. Board of Registration* (Supreme Court of the District of Columbia), *American Law Times* 4 (November 1871): 199; "A New Phase of the Woman Question," *Evening Star* (Washington, DC), April 14, 1871; "Justice for Women. A Large Number of Ladies Ask to Be Registered," *New National Era* (Washington, DC), April 20, 1871; "Want to Vote," *Evening Star* (Washington, DC), April 14, 1871; Rhodes, *Mary Ann Shadd Cary*, 163–211; Carla Peterson, *"Doers of the Word": African-American Women Speakers and Writers in the North (1830–1880)* (New York: Oxford University Press, 1995), 224–225.

52. Cary, "Speech to Judiciary Committee re: The Rights of Women to Vote, January 1872." On early women's suffrage efforts in the District of Columbia generally, see Kate Masur, *An Example for All the Land: Emancipation and the Struggle over Equality in Washington, DC* (Chapel Hill: University of North Carolina Press, 2010).

53. Rhodes, *Mary Ann Shadd Cary*,167–211.

Chapter 5: Make Us a Power

1. Anna Julia Cooper, *A Voice from the South* (Xenia, OH: Aldine Printing House, 1892), 31.

2. Eric Foner, *Freedom's Lawmakers: A Directory of Black Officeholders during Reconstruction* (New York: Oxford University Press, 1993); Eric Foner, *Reconstruction: America's Unfinished Revolution, 1863–1877, Updated Edition* (New York: Harper, 2014).

3. Elsa Barkley Brown, "Negotiating and Transforming the Public Sphere: African American Political Life in the Transition from Slavery to Freedom," *Public Culture* 7 (1994): 107–146; Elsa Barkley Brown, "To Catch the Vision of Freedom: Reconstructing Southern Black Women's Political History, 1865–1880," in *African American Women and the Vote, 1837–1965*, ed. Ann D. Gordon, with Bettye Collier-Thomas, John H. Bracey, Arlene Voski Avakian, and Joyce Avrech Berkman (Amherst: University of Massachusetts Press, 1997), 66–99.

4. Ellen Carol DuBois, *Feminism and Suffrage: The Emergence of an Independent Women's Movement in America, 1848–1869* (Ithaca, NY: Cornell University Press, 1978), 189–202; Ellen Carol DuBois, *Suffrage: Women's Long Battle for the Vote* (New York: Simon & Schuster, 2020), 79–83; Rosalyn Terborg-Penn, *African American*

Women in the Struggle for the Vote, 1850–1920 (Bloomington: Indiana University Press, 1998).

5. *Hall v. DeCuir*, 95 U.S. 485 (1877); *Transcript of Record. Supreme Court of the United States*, No. 294, John G. Benson, Plaintiff in Error vs. Josephine DeCuir, In Error to the Supreme Court of the State of Louisiana, Field, October 6, 1875; Barbara Young Welke, *Recasting American Liberty: Gender, Race, Law, and the Railroad Revolution, 1865–1920* (New York: Cambridge University Press, 2001), 302–303, 329–339.

6. *Hall v. DeCuir*, 95 US 485 (1877); *Transcript of Record. Supreme Court of the United States*, No. 294, John G. Benson, Plaintiff in Error vs. Josephine DeCuir, In Error to the Supreme Court of the State of Louisiana, Field, October 6, 1875; Welke, *Recasting American Liberty*, 302–303, 329–339.

7. Evelyn Brooks Higginbotham, *Righteous Discontent: The Women's Movement in the Black Baptist Church, 1880–1920* (Cambridge, MA: Harvard University Press, 1993); Martha S. Jones, *All Bound Up Together: The Woman Question in African American Public Culture, 1830–1900* (Chapel Hill: University of North Carolina Press, 2007).

8. Amanda Smith, *An Autobiography: The Story of the Lord's Dealings with Mrs. Amanda Smith, the Colored Evangelist* (Chicago: Meyer & Brother, 1893).

9. Smith, *An Autobiography*.

10. Smith, *An Autobiography*, 193–198.

11. Smith, *An Autobiography*, 260–264.

12. Phebe A. Hanaford, *Women of the Century* (Boston: B. B. Russell, 1877).

13. Hanaford, *Women of the Century*, 35, 168, 291, 568, 574, 264–265.

14. Hanaford, *Women of the Century*, 363–437, 529–545; Martha S. Jones, "'Make Us a Power': African-American Methodists Debate the Rights of Women, 1870–1900," *Women and Religion in the African Diaspora*, ed. R. Marie Griffith and Barbara D. Savage (Baltimore: Johns Hopkins University Press, 2006), 128–154.

15. Smith, *An Autobiography*.

16. Jones, "'Make Us a Power,'" 128–154.

17. James O. Horton and Lois E. Horton, *In Hope of Liberty: Culture, Community and Protest Among Northern Free Blacks, 1700–1860* (New York: Oxford University Press), 110.

18. Hallie Quinn Brown, *Homespun Heroines, and Other Women of Distinction* (Xenia, OH: Aldine Publishing, 1926), 117; Horton and Horton, *In Hope of Liberty*, 111.

19. Rev. B. W. Swain, "Miss Eliza Gardner, Saintly Mother in Zion, Devoted Friend and Counselor Is No More. Her Funeral Services from the Columbus Avenue A.M.E. Zion Church of Boston, Mass.," *Star of Zion*, January 19, 1922.

20. Swain, "Miss Eliza Gardner, Saintly Mother in Zion, Devoted Friend and Counselor Is No More. Her Funeral Services from the Columbus Avenue A.M.E. Zion Church of Boston, Mass.," *Star of Zion*, January 19, 1922; "The Ladies of the Zion's Chapel," *Boston Evening Transcript*, December 9, 1858.

21. Stephen Kantrowitz, *More Than Freedom: Fighting for Black Citizenship in a White Republic, 1829–1889* (New York: Penguin, 2012), 361; Dale Baum, "Woman Suffrage and the 'Chinese Question': The Limits of Radical Republicanism in Massachusetts, 1865–1876," *New England Quarterly* 56, no. 1 (1983): 60–77.

22. Ladies' Excelsior Charitable Association (Boston), *From the Slavery of 1776 to the Freedom of 1876: An Account of the Labors and of the Ladies' Charitable Association of Boston, in Recognition of, and Homage to, the Declaration of Independence* (Boston: Wright & Potter, 1876).

23. *Daily Journal of the Sixteenth Quadrennial Session of the General Conference of the A.M.E. Zion Church, of America, Held at Montgomery, Alabama, May, A.D., 1880* (New York: Book Concern of the AME Zion Church, 1880), 71.

24. Jones, *All Bound Up Together*, 151–171.

25. William J. Walls, *The A.M.E. Zion Church: Reality of the Black Church* (Charlotte, NC: AME Zion Publishing House, 1974), 392.

26. Miss Emily V. Bird-Walters, "Woman's Place in Church and State," *A.M.E. Zion Quarterly Review*, April 1900, 56–65.

27. Julia A. J. Foote, *A Brand Plucked from the Fire. An Autobiographical Sketch* (Cleveland, OH: W. F. Schneider, 1879).

28. "Independence, 2d Ch.," *Kansas Methodist* (Topeka), September 19, 1883.

29. 1880 US Census, Bridgeport, CT; "Silver Wedding Celebration," *York (PA) Daily*, October 27, 1898; "A Lady Will Fill the Pulpit," *York (PA) Daily*, November 26, 1892; "A Woman Revivalist. Mrs. Small's Good Work at a Rochester Church" [on the back of a news clipping from the *New York Age*, February 13, 1896]; "Baltimore Conference. Sixty-Eighth Session of the Zion A.M.E. Church," *Evening Star* (Washington, DC), June 17, 1896; Walls, *The A.M.E. Zion Church*, 111–112.

30. Jones, *All Bound Up Together*, 151–204; Bettye Collier-Thomas, *Jesus, Jobs, and Justice: African American Women and Religion* (New York: Alfred A. Knopf, 2010).

31. "A Bishops Wife an Elder. Mrs. Mary J. Small, Colored Elected by the Conference of the A.M.E. Zion Church," *Baltimore Sun*, May 24, 1898; "Female Preachers," *Star of Zion*, June 30, 1898 (reprint from the *Charlotte (NC) Independent*); "A Female Elder," *Star of Zion*, July 21, 1898.

32. Jones, "Make Us a Power," 128–154.

33. Rev. S. A. Chambers, "Redhot Cannon Ball: No Authority in Scripture for the Ordination of Women," *Star of Zion*, June 16, 1898; Rev. Josie C. Mayes, "Our Women Preachers and Their Influence," *A.M.E. Zion Quarterly Review* 9, no. 4 (October 1899–January 1900).

34. Rev. S. A. Chambers, "Cannon Balls: Reply to Rev. J. H. Gilmer, Jr.," *Star of Zion*, July 21, 1898; "Physically Unfit," *Star of Zion*, August 18, 1898.

35. Bishop C. R. Harris, "Episcopal Dots: Women Elders—Railroad Discrimination—Coleman Factory," *Star of Zion*, August 4, 1898; Bishop J. W. Hood, "The Woman Question: Woman Originally Was Man's Equal and Will Be Again," *Star of Zion*, January 12, 1898; Miss Maggie L. Hood, "Woman in the Literary Field," *A.M.E. Zion Quarterly Review* 9, no. 4 (October 1899–January 1900).

36. Hood, "The Woman Question: Woman Originally Was Man's Equal and Will Be Again," *Star of Zion*, January 12, 1898; Gardner, "Welcome Address," 54–55.

37. "Physically Unfit," *Star of Zion*, August 18, 1898; Mrs. Rev. W. L. Moore, "Eyes of Jealousy," *Star of Zion*, July 28, 1898; Bishop J. B. Small, "Woman Ordination: An Onward Movement Always Meets with Fierce Attacks," *Star of Zion*, August 18, 1898.

38. Mrs. F. A. Clinton, "Take My Advice," *Star of Zion*, August 10, 1898.

39. "Female Preachers," *Star of Zion*, June 30, 1898 (reprint from the *Charlotte (NC) Independent)*; Mrs. Clarissa Betties, "Let Rev. Mrs. Small Alone," *Star of Zion*, December 22, 1898; "Cannot Frighten Her," *Star of Zion*, November 23, 1899.

40. Rev. J. H. Gilmer Jr., "Women Preachers: Reply to Rev. S. A. Chambers," *Star of Zion*, June 30, 1898; Harris, "Episcopal Dots: Women Elders—Railroad Discrimination—Coleman Factory," *Star of Zion*, August 4, 1898.

41. Eliza A. Gardner, "From Boston, Mass.," *Star of Zion*, February 16, 1899; Gardner, "Welcome Address," *A.M.E. Zion Quarterly Review* (April 1899).

42. Small, "Woman Ordination: An Onward Movement Always Meets with Fierce Attacks," *Star of Zion*, August 11, 1898; John D. Dancy, "Frederick Douglass: Address of John D. Dancy, Delivered at Rochester, N.Y., September 14th, 1898," *A.M.E. Zion Quarterly Review*, January–February 1899.

43. Mrs. Holden "Noble Woman: How Far Can She Be Trusted?," *Star of Zion*, October 6, 1898; Elizabeth Margaret Chandler, *The Poetical Works of Elizabeth Margaret Chandler* (Philadelphia: Lemuel Howell, 1836), 23; on Chandler, and the ideas of early white feminist abolitionists, see Blanche Glassman Hersh, *The Slavery of Sex: Feminist Abolitionists in America* (Urbana: University of Illinois Press, 1978).

44. "The Missionary Department: Shall the Women or Men Control It," *Star of Zion*, April 19, 1900.

45. "The Missionary Department: Shall the Women or Men Control It," *Star of Zion*, April 19, 1900.

46. "The Color Line and the Ladies' Car: Segregation on Southern Rails before *Plessy*," in Blair L. M. Kelley, *Right to Ride: Streetcar Boycotts and African American Citizenship in the Era of Plessy v. Ferguson* (Chapel Hill: University of North Carolina Press, 2010), 32–49; Barbara Young Welke, *Recasting American Liberty: Gender, Race, Law, and the Railroad Revolution, 1865–1920* (New York: Cambridge University Press, 2001), 43–80, 171–202, 280–322.

47. *Gray v. Cincinnati Southern Railroad Company*, 11 F 683 (1882); "William Gray and Wife Selena Gray Sue the Cincinnati Railroad Company 1881," *Athens Post* (AL), September 14, 1881.

48. "The Color Line and the Ladies' Car," in Kelley, *Right to Ride*, 32–49; Welke, *Recasting American Liberty*, 28–29.

49. On the ideas of Anna Julia Cooper, see Brittney C. Cooper, *Beyond Respectability: The Intellectual Thought of Race Women* (Urbana: University of Illinois Press, 2017).

50. Anna Julia Cooper, *A Voice from the South: By a Black Woman of the South* (Xenia, OH: Aldine Printing House, 1892), 37–47.

51. Cooper, *A Voice from the South*; Janice Sumler-Edmond, "The Quest for Justice: African American Women Litigants, 1867–1890," in *African American Women and the Vote, 1837–1965*, ed. Ann D. Gordon, with Bettye Collier-Thomas, John H. Bracey, Arlene Voski Avakian, and Joyce Avrech Berkman (Amherst: University of Massachusetts Press, 1997), 100–119.

52. Cooper, *A Voice from the South*, 94–95.

53. Cooper, *A Voice from the South*, 91–93.

54. Cooper, *A Voice from the South*, 89–90.

55. Cooper, *A Voice from the South*, iii, 11, 135.

56. Cooper, *A Voice from the South*, 98, 117–118.

57. Deborah Gray White, *Too Heavy a Load: Black Women in Defense of Themselves, 1894–1994* (New York: W. W. Norton, 1998), 56–86; Evelyn Brooks Higginbotham, "Clubwomen and Electoral Politics in the 1920s," in Gordon et al., *African American Women and the Vote*.

58. E[liza] A[nn] Gardner, "From Boston Mass.," *Star of Zion*, February 16, 1899.

Chapter 6: Lifting as We Climb

1. "Address of Josephine St. P. Ruffin," *Woman's Era*, August 1895, 14–15.

2. *Plessy v. Ferguson*, 163 US 537 (1896); *Minor v. Happersett*, 88 US (21 Wall) 163 (1875).

3. Rayford Whittingham Logan, *The Negro in American Life and Thought: The Nadir, 1877–1901* (New York: Dial Press, 1954; reissued 1997); David W. Blight, *Race and Reunion: The Civil War in American Memory* (Cambridge, MA: Harvard University Press, 2001); Heather Cox Richardson, *The Death of Reconstruction: Race, Labor, and Politics in the Post–Civil War North, 1865–1901* (Cambridge, MA: Harvard University Press, 2004).

4. Amy Louise Wood, *Lynching and Spectacle: Witnessing Racial Violence in America, 1890–1949* (Chapel Hill: University of North Carolina Press, 2011); Crystal N. Feimster, *Southern Horrors: Women and the Politics of Rape and Lynching* (Cambridge, MA: Harvard University Press, 2011).

5. J. Volney Riser, *Defying Disfranchisement: Black Voting Rights Activism in the Jim Crow South, 1890–1908* (Baton Rouge: Louisiana State University Press, 2010).

6. David Levering Lewis, *W.E.B. DuBois, 1868–1919: Biography of a Race* (New York: Henry Holt, 1993); Shawn Leigh Alexander, *An Army of Lions: The Civil Rights Struggle Before the NAACP* (Philadelphia: University of Pennsylvania Press, 2011).

7. Ellen Carol DuBois, *Suffrage: Women's Long Battle for the Vote* (New York: Simon & Schuster, 2020), 130–165.

8. Stephanie J. Shaw, "Black Club Women and the Creation of the National Association of Colored Women," *Journal of Women's History* 3, no. 2 (1991): 11–25; Brittney C. Cooper, *Beyond Respectability: The Intellectual Thought of Race Women* (Urbana: University of Illinois Press, 2017), 33–55; Cynthia Neverdon-Morton, "Advancement of the Race through African American Women's Organizations in the South, 1895–1925," in *African American Women and the Vote, 1837–1965*, ed. Ann D. Gordon, with Bettye Collier-Thomas, John H. Bracey, Arlene Voski Avakian, and Joyce Avrech Berkman (Amherst: University of Massachusetts Press, 1997), 120–133.

9. Shaw, "Black Club Women," 11–25.

10. Shaw, "Black Club Women," 11–25; Cooper, *Beyond Respectability*.

11. Shaw, "Black Club Women," 11–25.

12. Ann Massa, "Black Women in the 'White City,'" *Journal of American Studies* (Great Britain), 8 (1974): 319–337; Kathryn Kish Sklar and Erin Shaughnessy, "Introduction," in *How Did African-American Women Define Their Citizenship at the Chicago World's Fair in 1893?* (Binghamton: State University of New York at Binghamton, 1997); Shaw, "Black Club Women," 10–25; Davis, *Lifting as They Climb*, 15; Mary

Church Terrell, *The Progress of Colored Women* (Washington, DC: Smith Brothers, 1898); Paula Giddings, *Ida, a Sword among Lions: Ida B. Wells and the Campaign Against Lynching* (New York: Amistad, 2008), 342–368.

13. On industrious partnership, see Glenda Elizabeth Gilmore, *Gender and Jim Crow: Women and the Politics of White Supremacy in North Carolina, 1896–1920* (Chapel Hill: University of North Carolina Press, 1996), 18; Claudia Tate, *Domestic Allegories of Political Desire: The Black Heroine's Text at the Turn of the Century* (New York: Oxford University Press, 1996), 127. On the ideas of Mary Church Terrell, see Cooper, *Beyond Respectability*.

14. Mary Church Terrell, "President's First Address to the National Association of Colored Women, September 15, 1897," Speeches and Writings, 1866–1953, Mary Church Terrell Papers, Library of Congress.

15. "National Capital Topics," *New York Age*, January 16, 1892; "Famous Bethel Literary Society," *Cleveland Gazette*, January 23, 1892.

16. "Race Gleanings," *Indianapolis Freeman*, February 25, 1893; "Doings of the Race," *Cleveland Gazette*, March 11, 1893; "A Valuable Man to the Race," *Colored American* (New York City), March 26, 1898 (on Wells and Terrell together before the House); Paula Giddings, *Ida, a Sword among Lions*, 247–248.

17. Mary Church Terrell, *A Colored Woman in a White World* (Washington, DC: Randsell, 1940), 127–129; "District Afro-American Council," *Colored American* (New York City), June 17, 1899; "'The Bright Side': Mrs. Mary Church Terrell . . . at the Commencement of the A. and M. College for the Colored Race," *Colored American*, June 9, 1900; "Woman's World," *Indianapolis Freeman*, June 17, 1905; "At the Nation's Capital," *Indianapolis Freeman*, May 25, 1907; "College Closing," *Savannah Tribune*, June 5, 1909; "Washington Under the Calcium," *Colored American* (New York City), September 13, 1902; "Legislative Acts/Legal Proceedings," *Indianapolis Freeman*, June 19, 1909; "Covington, Ky.," *Indianapolis Freeman*, June 26, 1909; "Eighth Atlanta Negro Conference. Atlanta, Ga. May 26," *Washington Bee*, May 30, 1903; "President William H. Taft Will Not Recommend to Congress," *Broad Ax* (Chicago), June 10, 1911; "At the National Capital," *Indianapolis Freeman*, June 10, 1911; "President and Mrs. Taft Invite Four Thousand," *Appeal*, June 17, 1911; "New York Letter," *Washington Bee*, February 14, 1914; "The Women to Honor Mrs. Mary Church Terrell," *Indianapolis Freeman*, March 30, 1912.

18. "The Justice of Woman Suffrage. Mrs. Mary Church Terrell Appears before the Second Baptist Lyceum," *Colored American* (New York City), January 26, 1901; "Mrs. Terrell on Woman Suffrage, the Distinguished President of the National Association of Colored Women Urges the Ballot," *Indianapolis Freeman*, February 2, 1901.

19. "Desirable Presents for Well-Known People," *Indianapolis Freeman*, December 25, 1909; "Short Flights," *Indianapolis Freeman*, August 24, 1912.

20. "Our Women. Meeting of the American Women Suffrage Association—Mrs. Terrell's Address" (the *Broad Ax* republished the *Colored American*'s coverage, "Progress of Colored Women. Mrs. Mary Church Terrell's Eloquent Plen [*sic*] Before the Woman Suffragist Convention," March 12, 1898); "Honoring Mrs. Mary Church Terrell," *Colored American* (Washington, DC), March 22, 1902.

21. "For Colored Women. Meeting of the National League to Be Held Here," *Evening Star* (Washington, DC), July 4, 1896.

22. Mrs. Rosetta E. Lawson, in "Colored Women in the Reform Movement," *National Association Notes*, January 1899; "Women's Improvement Club," *National Association Notes*, March 1899.

23. "Mrs. Mary Church Terrell Spoke at Oberlin and to Speak at Berlin, Germany," *Colored American* (New York City), May 14, 1904; "Mrs. M.C. Terrell Honored Colored Citizens of the District of Columbia," *Colored American* (New York City), August 13, 1904; "Mrs. Terrell's Triumph," *Washington Bee*, July 25, 1896; Mrs. Rosetta E. Lawson, in "Colored Women in the Reform Movement," *National Association Notes*, January 1899; "Women's Improvement Club," *National Association Notes*, March 1899; Adella Hunt Logan, "Why the National Association of Colored Women Should Become Part of the National Council of Women of the United States," *National Association Notes*, December 1899 and January 1900. On Logan, Adele Logan Alexander, "Adella Hunt Logan, the Tuskegee Woman's Club, and African Americans in the Suffrage Movement," in *Votes for Women! The Woman Suffrage Movement in Tennessee, the South, and the Nation*, ed. Marjorie Spruill Wheeler (Knoxville: University of Tennessee Press, 1995), 71–104; Adele Logan Alexander, *Princess of the Hither Isles: A Black Suffragist's Story from the Jim Crow South* (New Haven, CT: Yale University Press, 2019).

24. Mrs. Booker T. Washington, "Club Work as a Factor in the Advance of Colored Women," *National Association Notes*, August 1906.

25. "Women Gather. The National Federation Meeting a Great Success. Ohioans and Others in Attendance," *Cleveland Gazette*, July 21, 1906; "Thompson's Weekly Review," *Indianapolis Freeman*, July 28, 1906.

26. "The Man on the Corner," *Colored American* (New York City), March 22, 1902; "To Commemorate First Woman's Rights Conventions," *Buffalo Commercial* (New York), May 27, 1908; "Tell of Pioneers in Fight to Gain Liberty for Women," *Rochester Democrat and Chronicle* (New York), May 28, 1908.

27. Mary Church Terrell, "The Justice of Woman Suffrage," *The Crisis*, September 1912.

28. "The Southern Negress Discussed by Lecturer," *Brooklyn Citizen*, February 28, 1913; "The North Eastern Federation of Women's Cubs," *New York Age*, February 13, 1913; "Terrell to Lecture in Brooklyn," *Evening Star* (Washington, DC), February 25, 1913.

29. George C. Osborn, "Woodrow Wilson Appoints a Negro Judge," *Journal of Southern History* 24, no. 4 (November 1958): 481–493.

30. Brian D. Page, "Stand By the Flag: Nationalism and African-American Celebrations of the Fourth of July in Memphis, 1866–1887," *Tennessee Historical Quarterly* 58, no. 4 (December 1999): 284–301.

31. Shane White, "'It Was a Proud Day': African Americans, Festivals, and Parades in the North, 1741–1834," *Journal of American History* 81, no. 1 (June 1994): 13–50; Martha S. Jones, "Forgetting the Abolition of the Slave Trade in the United States: How History Troubled Memory in 2008," in *Distant Ripples of the British Abolitionist Wave: Africa, Asia, and the Americas*, ed. Myriam Cottias and Marie Jeanne Rossignol (Trenton, NJ: Africa World Press Tubman Institute Series, 2018).

32. J. D. Zahniser and Amelia R. Fry, "Conversations with Alice Paul: Woman Suffrage and the Equal Rights Amendment," in *Alice Paul: Claiming Power* (New York: Oxford University Press, 2014), 137–141; "Suffrage Paraders," *The Crisis*, April 1913;

"The Equal Suffrage Parade Was Viewed by Many Thousand People from All Parts," *Broad Ax* (Chicago), March 8, 1913.

33. "The Equal Suffrage Parade," *Broad Ax* (Chicago), March 8, 1913; Giddings, *Ida, a Sword among Lions*, 515–518. For an insightful reading of the 1913 parade and how Black women in Washington, DC, navigated it, see Treva B. Lindsey, *Colored No More: Reinventing Black Womanhood in Washington, DC* (Urbana: Indiana University Press, 2017), 86–110. Mia Bay, *To Tell the Truth Freely: The Life of Ida B. Wells* (New York: Hill and Wang, 2010), 274–313; Patricia A. Schecter, *Ida B. Wells-Barnett & American Reform, 1880–1930* (Chapel Hill: University of North Carolina Press, 2001), 198–207.

34. "The Equal Suffrage Parade Was Viewed by Many Thousand People from All Parts," *Broad Ax* (Chicago), March 8, 1913.

35. "Testimony of Mrs. Elizabeth A. Balloch, Washington, DC," *Suffrage Parade. Hearing before a Subcommittee of the Committee on the District of Columbia* (Washington, DC: Government Printing Office, 1913), 271; Mary-Elizabeth Murphy, "Make Washington Safe for Negro Womanhood: The Politics of Police Brutality," in *Jim Crow Capital: Women and Black Freedom Struggles in Washington, D.C., 1920–1945* (Chapel Hill: University of North Carolina Press, 2018), 76–109.

36. "What Does It Mean?," *Washington Bee*, May 28, 1910; "What We Could Afford," *Washington Bee*, October 1, 1910; "A Colored Sergeant," *Washington Bee*, April 8, 1911; "Ex-Commissioner West," *Washington Bee*, August 24, 1912; "Insulting Colored Women," *Washington Bee*, April 15, 1911.

37. "Senator James K. Vardaman," *Cleveland Gazette*, November 23, 1912.

38. "The News in a Nut-Shell," *Indianapolis Freeman*, April 26, 1913.

39. "United States Senator James K. Vardaman of Mississippi Starts on the War Path to Disfranchise," *Broad Ax* (Chicago), May 10, 1913; "The News in a Nut-Shell," *Indianapolis Freeman*, April 26, 1913; "Vardaman," *Washington Bee*, April 12, 1913; "Vardaman to Propose Disfranchisement Law," *Washington Bee*, May 3, 1913; "A New Senatorial Punching Bag," *Washington Bee*, August 19, 1911. *The Appeal* also condemned his election: "Vardaman," September 9, 1911; and *Indianapolis Freeman*, "Editorial Comments on Vardanmanism," November 4, 1911.

40. "Logical and Eloquent Address Delivered by Attorney Walter M. Farmer," *Broad Ax* (Chicago), January 18, 1913.

41. "Negro Issue vs. Suffrage. Vardaman Injects Question into Senate Debate," *Los Angeles Times*, March 5, 1914. Liette Gidlow, "The Sequel: the Fifteenth Amendment, the Nineteenth Amendment, and Southern Black Women's Struggle to Vote," *Journal of the Gilded Age and Progressive Era* 17, no. 3 (July 2018): 433–449.

42. *Congressional Record*, March 5, 1914, 4338.

43. "Doom of Suffrage," *Washington Bee*, March 21, 1914.

44. "Suffrage," *Indianapolis Freeman*, March 28, 1914; "Senators' Records," *The Crisis*, June 1914; *Congressional Record*, March 19, 1914, 5088–5108; "Colored Americans Meet," *Washington Bee*, April 11, 1914.

45. [Maggie Lena Walker], *St. Luke Herald*, April 4, 1914. On Walker and her vision for economic independence, see Shennette Garrett-Scott, *Banking on Freedom: Black Women in U.S. Finance Before the New Deal* (New York: Columbia University Press, 2019).

46. S. Cecilia De Nellottz, "Our Women's Attitude. Toward the Movement for the Emancipation of Women," *Washington Bee*, June 27, 1914; "A Great Woman [Mrs. De Nellottz]," *Washington Bee*, May 2, 1914. De Nellottz letter mixed her own thoughts with quotes from Rheta Childe Dorr's 1910 book, *What Eight Million Women Want*, and Alfred, Lord Tennyson's poem *The Princess*, not attributed here. Thank you to Jay Winston Driskell for his close reading of De Nellottz's letter.

47. "The Patterson Appointment," *Cleveland Gazette*, August 2, 1913; "U.G. Napier Resigns…Lawyer Patterson to Succeed Him," *Indianapolis Freeman*, August 2, 1913; "Today," *Savannah Tribune*, August 16, 1913; "Washington," *Indianapolis Freeman*, November 16, 1912; Eric S. Yellin, *Racism in the Nation's Service: Government Workers and the Color Line in Woodrow Wilson's America* (Chapel Hill: University of North Carolina Press, 2013), 108–109.

48. "Turning the Negro Back," *Savannah Tribune*, November 8, 1913; "Let Colored Judge Stay," *The Appeal* (St. Paul, MN), February 7, 1914; *Broad Ax* (Chicago), February 28, 1914; "Judge Terrell Reappointed," *Cleveland Gazette*, February 28, 1914; George C. Osborn, "Woodrow Wilson Appoints Robert H. Terrell Judge of Municipal Court, District of Columbia," *Negro History Bulletin* 22, no. 5 (February 1959): 111–115, 118; George C. Osborn, "Woodrow Wilson Appoints a Negro Judge," *Journal of Southern History* 24, no. 4 (November 1959): 481–493.

49. Terrell, *A Colored Woman in a White World*, 260–267.

50. Terrell, *A Colored Woman in a White World*, 260–267; "Mary Church Terrell to Senator Burton, dated March 19, 1914," Mary Church Terrell Papers: Correspondence, 1886–1954, 1914, Library of Congress.

51. "Vardaman Gets a Very Rude Jolt," *New York Age*, March 26, 1914; "Judge Terrell Reappointed," *Cleveland Gazette*, February 28, 1914; "Favorable to Terrell," *The Appeal* (St. Paul, MN), March 28, 1914.

52. "Lecture and Reception," *Savannah Tribune*, February 25, 1905.

Chapter 7: Amendment

1. Kathryn Kish Sklar and Jill Dias, *How Did the National Woman's Party Address the Issue of the Enfranchisement of Black Women, 1919–1924?*, Women and Social Movements series (Binghamton: State University of New York, 1997); Letter from Hallie Quinn Brown to Alice Paul, Wilberforce, Ohio, January 22, 1921, National Woman's Party Papers, 1913–1974, Library of Congress; Ella Rush Murray, "The Woman's Party and the Violation of the 19th Amendment," *The Crisis*, April 1921; Sandra Weber, *The Woman Suffrage Statue: A History of Adelaide Johnson's Portrait Monument to Lucretia Mott, Elizabeth Cady Stanton and Susan B. Anthony at the United States Capitol* (Jefferson, NC: McFarland, 2016).

2. Paul Frymer, *Building an American Empire: The Era of Territorial and Political Expansion* (Princeton, NJ: Princeton University Press, 2017).

3. Eric S. Yellin, *Racism in the Nation's Service: Government Workers and the Color Line in Woodrow Wilson's America* (Chapel Hill: University of North Carolina Press, 2013).

4. Melvyn Stokes, *D.W. Griffith's "The Birth of a Nation": A History of "The Most Controversial Motion Picture of All Time"* (New York: Oxford University Press, 2007).

5. Christopher Capozzola, *Uncle Sam Wants You: World War I and the Making of the Modern American Citizen* (New York: Oxford University Press, 2008).

6. Charles L. Lumpkins, *American Pogrom: The East St. Louis Race Riot and Black Politics* (Athens: Ohio University Press, 2008).

7. Ellen Carol DuBois, *Suffrage: Women's Long Battle for the Vote* (New York: Simon & Schuster, 2020), 130–165.

8. DuBois, *Suffrage*, 130–165.

9. DuBois, *Suffrage*, 130–165.

10. Ethel E. Dreier, "Impressions of Suffrage Conference at Saratoga," *Brooklyn Daily Eagle*, September 2, 1917; "Colored Women Attend Suffragette Meeting," *New York Age*, September 6, 1917.

11. Hallie Quinn Brown, *Homespun Heroines, and Other Women of Distinction* (Xenia, OH: Aldine Publishing, 1926), 64–65.

12. Dreier, "Impressions of Suffrage Conference at Saratoga," *Brooklyn Daily Eagle*, September 2, 1917; "Suffragists Drew No Line: Decision Reached at Meeting of Colored Woman's Suffrage Club," *New York Age*, September 20, 1917.

13. "Suffragists Drew No Line: Decision Reached at Meeting of Colored Woman's Suffrage Club," *New York Age*, September 20, 1917.

14. For another view of this scene, see Dubois, *Suffrage*, 236–237.

15. "Mock Registration and Election," *Savannah Tribune*, April 3, 1920; "Suffrage Club Closes Year Report Shows Much Work Accomplished," *Savannah Tribune*, July 10, 1920. Nikki Brown, *Private Politics and Public Voices: Black Women's Activism from World War I to the New Deal* (Bloomington: Indiana University Press, 2006), 147.

16. Mary White Ovington, "Lucy Laney," in *Portraits in Color* (New York: Viking Press, 1927), 53–63. Laney joined Mary McLeod Bethune, Margaret Murray Washington, Charlotte Hawkins Brown, Lugenia Burns Hope, and others as members of the Southeastern Federation of Colored Women's Clubs to issue a manifesto titled *Southern Negro Women and Race Cooperation* (Atlanta: Southeastern Federation of Colored Women's Clubs, 1921).

17. "Suffrage Rally," *Savannah Tribune*, November 29, 1919.

18. "Suffrage Club Closes Year," *Savannah Tribune*, July 10, 1920; "Women's Meeting Strikes a Snag," *Tribune*, April 17, 1920.

19. *Guinn v. Oklahoma*, 238 US 347 (1915); Alexander Keyssar, *The Right to Vote: The Contested History of Democracy in the United States* (New York: Basic Books, 2009), 305–368.

20. Keyssar, *The Right to Vote*, 305–368.

21. Keyssar, *The Right to Vote*, 305–368; Harvey Walker, "The Poll Tax in the United States," *Bulletin of the National Tax Association* 9, no. 2 (November 1923): 46–50.

22. "Few Negro Women Register at Knoxville," *Tennessean* (Nashville), October 15, 1920; "Many Women Are Qualifying Today for the Election," *News Journal* (Wilmington, DE), September 18, 1920; "Kent Women Interested. They Turned Out in Large Numbers at Saturday's Registration," *News Journal* (Wilmington, DE), September 20, 1920; "The Colored Female Voter," *Voice of the People* (Birmingham, AL), October 23, 1920; "1,445 Women Register," *Tennessean* (Nashville), October 28, 1920; "Herzberg

Says Women Needed to Defeat G.O.P. Registrars Answer Request of Negro Women's Representatives," *Gadsden Times* (Gadsden, AL), October 21, 1920.

23. "Explanation Pending Amendments to Mississippi Constitution," *Vicksburg (MS) Herald*, October 20, 1920; "Negro Women Turned Down," *Hamilton (OH) Evening Journal*, November 2, 1920.

24. Charles W. Wadelington and Richard F. Knapp, *Charlotte Hawkins Brown and Palmer Memorial Institute: What One Young African American Woman Could Do* (Chapel Hill: University of North Carolina Press, 1999).

25. "Negro Women Urged to Help in War Campaign: Charlotte Hawkins, Noted Educator, Calls on Members of Race to Rally to Cause," *Greensboro (NC) Daily News*, November 11, 1918; "Don't Fail to Hear Mrs. Charlotte Hawkins Brown," *Bystander* (Des Moines, IA), February 7, 1919; "An Effort to Help and Save Negro Youth," *Salisbury (NC) Evening Post*, November 3, 1919; "Convention This Year of State Federation Is Most Progressive…a Negro Woman for First Time Addresses Carolina Federation Members," *Greensboro (NC) Daily News*, April 29, 1920; "Report of National Federation C.W.C. Which Met at Tuskegee Inst. Last Week," *Bystander* (Des Moines, IA), July 23, 1920; Glenda Elizabeth Gilmore, *Gender and Jim Crow: Women and the Politics of White Supremacy in North Carolina, 1896–1920* (Chapel Hill: University of North Carolina Press, 1996).

26. "A Mischievous Letter," *Charlotte Observer*, September 25, 1920; "Fight Stand of Alabama on Colored Women's Vote," *Washington Herald*, October 6, 1920.

27. "The Effort to Get Negro Women to Register," *Concord (NC) Daily Tribune*, October 21, 1920; "Old Case," *Daily Free Press* (Kinston, NC), October 21, 1920; "A Voice from Surry County," *Union Republican* (Winston-Salem, NC), October 28, 1920; "A Voice from Beaufort County," *Union Republican* (Winston-Salem, NC), October 28, 1920.

28. "Charlotte Hawkins Brown Makes Statement," *Stanly News-Herald* (Albemarle, NC), October 19, 1920.

29. "Wards Soon to Hold Meetings to Plan Citizenship League," *St. Louis Globe-Democrat*, June 29, 1919; "Colored Women Register," *Macon (MO) Chronicle-Herald*, September 18, 1920; "Men to Attend Suffrage Schools," *St. Louis Star and Times*, June 4, 1919; "New Albany Republicans Register Negro Women," *Herald* (Jasper, IN), September 10, 1920; "Start Campaign to Have Colored Women Register," *Akron (OH) Beacon Journal*, September 24, 1920; "Women Must Register If Democracy Wins," *Chattanooga (TN) News*, October 4, 1920; "Negro Women Get Call to Register and Vote," *Baltimore Sun*, September 7, 1920.

30. "Party Organizations Formed at Frederick. Both Sides Open Their Campaigns with Meetings of Committees for County. Negresses' Plans Related," *Baltimore Sun*, August 29, 1920; "Lavinia Wilson and Emily Smith," *Tallahassee Democrat*, September 9, 1920; "Last Day for Registration Has Arrived," *News Leader* (Staunton, VA), October 2, 1920; "Negro Women Register. Many Follow Appeal of Preachers in Savannah," *Dallas Express*, October 2, 1920; "Many Negro Women Register in Asheville," *Lenoir (NC) News-Topic*, October 22, 1920.

31. "Colored Women Register Strong in Virginia," *Tulsa Star*, October 2, 1920; Kimberly S. Johnson, "From Politics to Protest: African American Voting in Virginia in the Pre–Civil Rights Movement Era, 1940–1954," *Studies in American Political*

Development 31, no. 2 (October 2017): 218–237; Liette Gidlow, "Resistance After Ratification: The Nineteenth Amendment, African American Women, and the Problem of Female Disfranchisement after 1920," *Women and Social Movements in the U.S., 1600–2000* 20, no. 2 (March 2017); Liette Gidlow, "The Sequel: The Fifteenth Amendment, the Nineteenth Amendment, and Southern Black Women's Struggle to Vote, 1890s–1920s," *Journal of the Gilded Age and Progressive Era* 17, no. 3 (July 2019); Cynthia Neverdon-Morton, "Advancement of the Race through African American Women's Organizations in the South, 1895–1925," in *African American Women and the Vote, 1837–1965*, ed. Ann D. Gordon, with Bettye Collier-Thomas, John H. Bracey, Arlene Voski Avakian, and Joyce Avrech Berkman (Amherst: University of Massachusetts Press, 1997).

32. Maggie Lena Walker, "Excerpts, Maggie Lena Walker Diary, September 11–23, 1920," in Maggie L. Walker Family Papers, United States National Park Service, Museum Resource Center, Women and Social Movements. Shennette Garrett-Scott, *Banking on Freedom: Black Women in U.S. Finance Before the New Deal* (New York. Columbia University Press, 2019), Elsa Barkley Brown, "Womanist Consciousness: Maggie Lena Walker and the Independent Order of Saint Luke," *Signs* 14, no. 3 (Spring 1989): 610–633; Elsa Barkley Brown, "Constructing a Life and a Community: A Partial Story of Maggie Lena Walker," *OAH Magazine of History* 7, no. 4 (January 1993): 28–31; "Richmond Women Register at Rate of 578 in One Day," *Richmond (VA) Times Dispatch*, September 21, 1920.

33. "The Political Situation," *Richmond (VA) Planet*, October 2, 1920; "Lily Blacks Find Picking City Treasurer Hard Job," *Times Dispatch* (Richmond, VA), September 23, 1920; "Slemp and the Negroes," *Bristol (TN) Herald Courier*, October 29, 1920; "Afro-Americans of Virginia Accept the Lily White Challenge," *Richmond (VA) Planet*, August 20, 1921; Garrett-Scott, *Banking on Freedom*; Brown, "Womanist Consciousness," 610–633; Brown, "Constructing a Life and a Community," 28–31.

34. "The National Convention Held at Tuskegee," *Competitor*, August–September 1920; Evelyn Brooks Higginbotham, "Clubwomen and Electoral Politics in the 1920s," in Gordon et al., *African American Women and the Vote, 1837–1965*, 134–155.

35. Hallie Quinn Brown, "Woman, Her Influence," *Proceedings of the Quarto-Centennial Conference of the African M.E. Church of South Carolina, at Charleston, S.C., May 15, 16 and 17, 1889*, ed. Bishop Benjamin W. Arnett (Xenia, OH: Aldine Printing House, 1890).

36. Martha S. Jones, "Black Suffragists: Hallie Quinn Brown and Other Homespun Heroines," *Humanities* 40, no. 3 (Summer 2019): 20–23, 46–47.

37. Gertrude E. H. Bustill Mossell, "Our Woman's Department," *Indianapolis World*, June 11, 1892; Martha S. Jones, *All Bound Up Together: The Woman Question in African American Public Culture, 1830–1900* (Chapel Hill: University of North Carolina Press, 2007), 151–171.

38. Adrienne M. Israel, *Amanda Berry Smith: From Washerwoman to Evangelist* (Lanham, MD: Scarecrow Press, 1998), 105.

39. Hallie Quinn Brown, "Echoes from the International Congress of Women, London, England, June, July 1900," in *Sowing for Others to Reap; a Collection of Papers of the Ohio Federation of Colored Women's Clubs*, ed. Carrie Williams Clifford (Boston: C. Alexander, 1900), 11–18.

40. Rosetta E. Lawson, "Colored Woman in the Reform Movement," *National Association Notes*, January 1899; "Lecture on Women Suffrage. Mrs. Terrell Addresses a Meeting of Colored People," *Washington Times*, January 21, 1901; "N.A.C.W. Convention in St. Louis," *National Association Notes*, October 1904, 1; "Roster of State Officers. Departments of N.A.C.W. Heads of Departments," *National Association Notes*, December 1911, 6; "Roster of State Officers. Departments of N.A.C.W. Heads of Departments," *National Association Notes*, January 1912, 15.

41. Hallie Quinn Brown, "The Black Mammy Statue," *National Association Notes* 25, no. 7 (April 1923): 3–4.

42. Lopez D. Matthews, "Celebrating the Faithful Colored Mammies of the South," National Archives: Rediscovering Black History, April 4, 2013, https://rediscovering -Black-history.blogs.archives.gov/2013/04/04/celebrating-the-faithful-mammies-of-the -south/. On the emergence of the mythical "mammy" figure, see Kimberly Wallace-Sanders, *Mammy: A Century of Race, Gender, and Southern Memory* (Ann Arbor: University of Michigan Press, 2008) and Micki McElya, *Clinging to Mammy: The Faithful Slave in Twentieth-Century America* (Cambridge, MA: Harvard University Press, 2009).

43. Jones, "Black Suffragists," 20–23, 46–47.

44. Jones, "Black Suffragists," 20–23, 46–47.

45. Brown, *Private Politics and Public Voices*, 117, et seq.; Hallie Quinn Brown, "Blanket-Making Time," *The Competitor* 1, no. 3 (March 1920): 58–59; Hallie Quinn Brown, "Dear Co-Workers," *National Association Notes* 23, nos. 1–3 (October–December 1920): 4–5. On Brown's politics in this period, I am especially indebted to Nikki Brown, *Private Politics and Public Voices: Black Women's Activism from World War I to the New Deal* (Bloomington: Indiana University Press, 2006); and Evelyn Brooks Higginbotham, "Club Women and Electoral Politics in the 1920s," in Gordon et al., *Black Women and the Vote*, 134–155.

46. Brown, *Homespun Heroines*, vii. On Brown's life, including *Homespun Heroines*, see Daleah B. Goodwin, "'A Torch in the Valley': The Life and Work of Miss Hallie Quinn Brown" (PhD diss., University of Georgia, 2014). Brown was not the first to adopt this form, but the timing of her book and its details made it an especially important tool for post–Nineteenth Amendment Black women's politics. For example, Lawson Andrew Scruggs had published *Women of Distinction: Remarkable in Works and Invincible in Character* (Raleigh, NC, 1893). Monroe Majors had published *Noted Negro Women: Their Triumphs and Activities* (Chicago: Donohue & Henneberry, 1893). Both volumes included Brown among the many women featured. For more on the genre of "listings," see Brittney C. Cooper, *Beyond Respectability: The Intellectual Thought of Race Women* (Urbana: University of Illinois Press, 2017), 137.

47. Brown, *Homespun Heroines*, 30, 36–46, 55–58, 84–85.

48. Brown, *Homespun Heroines*, 19, 104, 121.

49. Brown, *Homespun Heroines*, 16, 64–65, 93, 95, 110–116, 117–118, 131, 237.

50. On Black women's internationalism, see Keisha Blain, *Set the World on Fire: Black Nationalist Women and the Global Struggle for Freedom* (Philadelphia: University of Pennsylvania Press, 2018) and Keisha Blain and Tiffany Gill, eds., *To Turn the Whole World Over: Black Women and Internationalism* (Urbana: University of Illinois Press, 2019).

51. Thank you to Anna Sargeantson for her research on Mary Sharperson Young conducted at Johns Hopkins University in fall 2019.

52. Blain, *Set the World on Fire*, 11–46.

53. "Women Working to Save U.N.I.A. Property," *New York Age*, May 1, 1926; Barbara Blair, "'Ethiopia Shall Stretch Forth Her Hands Unto God': Laura Korea and the Vision of Redemption," in *A Mighty Baptism: Race, Gender, and the Creation of American Protestantism*, ed. Susan Juster and Lisa MacFarlane (Ithaca, NY: Cornell University Press, 1996); Natanya Duncan, "'If Our Men Hesitate Then the Women of the Race Must Come Forward': Henrietta Vinton Davis and the UNIA in New York," *New York History 95*, no. 4 (Fall 2014): 558–583; Natanya Keisha Duncan, "Princess Laura Kofey and the Reverse Atlantic Experience," in *The American South and the Atlantic World*, ed. Brian Ward (Gainesville: University of Florida Press, 2013).

54. "Doings of the Circle," *New York Age*, April 26, 1919; "Child Welfare Committee," *New York Age*, March 26, 1921; "Circle for Negro Relief Dance to Secure Funds for Its Health Relief Activity," *New York Age*, December 19, 1923; "Chicago Women's Minstrels in Brooklyn Performance," *New York Age*, April 29, 1922.

Chapter 8: Her Weapon of Moral Defense

1. Nannie Helen Burroughs, "Miss Burroughs Plans a 'New Deal' to Conserve Girlhood of the Race," *Pittsburgh (PA) Courier*, April 26, 1933, 7, cited in *Nannie Helen Burroughs: A Documentary Portrait of an Early Civil Rights Pioneer, 1900–1959*, ed. Keisha D. Graves (South Bend, IN: University of Notre Dame Press, 2019), 37–38; Treva B. Lindsey, *Colored No More: Reinventing Black Womanhood in Washington, DC* (Urbana: University of Illinois Press, 2017); Nikki Brown, *Private Politics and Public Voices: Black Women's Activism from World War I to the New Deal* (Bloomington: Indiana University Press, 2006); Brittney C. Cooper, *Beyond Respectability: The Intellectual Thought of Race Women* (Urbana: University of Illinois Press, 2017); Mary-Elizabeth B. Murphy, *Jim Crow Capital: Women and Black Freedom Struggles in Washington, D.C., 1920–1945* (Chapel Hill: University of North Carolina Press, 2018).

2. R. Morris Charles, *A Rabble of Dead Money: The Great Crash and the Global Depression: 1929–1939* (New York: PublicAffairs, 2017); Kenneth J. Bindas, *Modernity and the Great Depression: The Transformation of American Society, 1930–1941* (Lawrence: University of Kansas Press, 2017); Cheryl Lynn Greenberg, *To Ask for an Equal Chance: African Americans in the Great Depression* (New York: Rowman & Littlefield, 2009); Robin D. G. Kelley, *Hammer and Hoe: Alabama Communists During the Great Depression* (Chapel Hill: University of North Carolina Press, 1990).

3. Henry B. Sirgo, "Women, Blacks and the New Deal," *Women & Politics 14*, no. 3 (1994): 357–376; Elliot A. Rosen, *The Republican Party in the Age of Roosevelt: Sources of Anti-Government Conservatism in the United States* (Charlottesville: University of Virginia Press, 2014); John Thomas McGuire, "Working within the Labyrinth of Race: Crystal Bird Fauset, Urban African American Women, and the National Democratic Party, 1934–1944," *Journal of Urban History 39*, no. 2 (March 2013): 172–192.

4. Sirgo, "Women, Blacks and the New Deal," 357–376; Rosen, *The Republican Party in the Age of Roosevelt*; McGuire, "Working within the Labyrinth of Race," 172–192.

5. Cohen, *Making a New Deal*.

6. Patricia Sullivan, *Lift Every Voice: The NAACP and the Making of the Civil Rights Movement* (New York: New Press, 2009); Leah Wright Rigueur, *The Loneliness of the Black Republican: Pragmatic Politics and the Pursuit of Power* (Princeton, NJ: Princeton University Press, 2015), 318n21.

7. Sullivan, *Lift Every Voice*.

8. Kimberley L. Phillips, *War! What Is It Good For?: Black Freedom Struggles and the U.S. Military from World War II to Iraq* (Chapel Hill: University of North Carolina Press, 2012).

9. McGuire, "Working within the Labyrinth of Race," 172–192; Eric Ledell Smith, "Crystal Bird Fauset Raises Her Voice for Human Rights," *Pennsylvania Heritage* 23, no. 1 (March 1997): 34–39; Jacqueline A. McLeod, *Daughter of the Empire State: The Life of Judge Jane Bolin* (Urbana: University of Illinois Press, 2011); Rebecca Tuuri, *Strategic Sisterhood: The National Council of Negro Women in the Black Freedom Struggle* (Chapel Hill: University of North Carolina Press, 2018).

10. Annette B. Dunlap, "Tea & Equality: The Hoover Administration and the De Priest Incident," *Prologue* (Summer 2015): 16–22; David S. Day, "A New Perspective on the 'De Priest Tea' Historiographic Controversy," *Journal of Negro History* 75, nos. 3–4 (Summer–Autumn, 1990): 120–124; David S. Day, "Herbert Hoover and Racial Politics: The De Priest Incident," *Journal of Negro History* 65, no. 1 (Winter, 1980): 6–17.

11. Wanda A. Hendricks, " 'Vote for the Advantage of Ourselves and Our Race': The Election of the First Black Alderman in Chicago," *Illinois Historical Journal* 87, no. 3 (1994): 171–184; Lisa G. Materson, *For the Freedom of Her Race: Black Women and Electoral Politics in Illinois, 1877–1932* (Chapel Hill: University of North Carolina Press, 2009); Annette B. Dunlap, "Tea & Equality: The Hoover Administration and the De Priest Incident," *Prologue* (Summer 2015): 16–22; Day, "A New Perspective on the 'De Priest Tea," 120–124; Day, "Herbert Hoover and Racial Politics," 6–17.

12. Dunlap, "Tea & Equality," 16–22; Day, "A New Perspective on the 'De Priest Tea,' " 120–124; Day, "Herbert Hoover and Racial Politics," 6–17.

13. "White House Lady Is Most Charming Says Mrs. De Priest," *Chicago Tribune*, July 17, 1929.

14. Day, "A New Perspective on the 'DePriest Tea,' " 120–124; Day, "Herbert Hoover and Racial Politics," 6–17

15. Evelyn Brooks Higginbotham, *Righteous Discontent: The Women's Movement in the Black Baptist Church, 1880–1920* (Cambridge, MA: Harvard University Press, 1993), 150–180; Audrey McCluskey, *A Forgotten Sisterhood: Pioneering Black Women Educators and Activists in the Jim Crow South* (Lanham, MD: Rowman & Littlefield, 2014).

16. Higginbotham, *Righteous Discontent*, 88–119; McCluskey, *A Forgotten Sisterhood*; Glenda Elizabeth Gilmore, *Gender and Jim Crow: Women and the Politics of White Supremacy in North Carolina, 1896–1920* (Chapel Hill: University of North Carolina Press, 1996), 178; Cynthia Neverdon-Morton, "Advancement of the Race through African American Women's Organizations in the South, 1895–1925," in *African American Women and the Vote, 1837–1965*, ed. Ann D. Gordon, with Bettye

Collier-Thomas, John H. Bracey, Arlene Voski Avakian, and Joyce Avrech Berkman (Amherst: University of Massachusetts Press, 1997), 120–133.

17. Rosalyn Terborg-Penn, *African American Women in the Struggle for the Vote, 1850–1920* (Bloomington: University of Indiana Press, 1998), 64–65.

18. Terborg-Penn, *African American Women in the Struggle for the Vote*, 96–97; Higginbotham, *Righteous Discontent*, 211–229.

19. Nannie Helen Burroughs, "Black Women and Reform," in *Nannie Helen Burroughs: A Documentary Portrait of an Early Civil Rights Pioneer, 1900–1959*, ed. Keisha D. Graves (South Bend, IN: University of Notre Dame Press, 2019), 35–36; Higginbotham, *Righteous Discontent*, 211–229; Terborg-Penn, *African American Women in the Struggle for the Vote*, 68.

20. "Republican Colored Women Meet and Plan," *Pittsburgh (PA) Courier*, May 21, 1927.

21. "Republican Colored Women Meet and Plan," *Pittsburgh (PA) Courier*, May 21, 1927; "Miss Burroughs Coming," *Pittsburgh (PA) Courier*, June 6, 1925.

22. Nannie Helen Burroughs, "The Negro Woman and Suffrage," *West Virginia Woman's Voice*, June 15, 1923, cited in Audrey McCluskey, *A Forgotten Sisterhood: Pioneering Black Women Educators and Activists in the Jim Crow South* (Lanham, MD: Rowman & Littlefield, 2014).

23. Burroughs, "The Negro Woman and Suffrage."

24. *Annual Report of Miss Nannie H. Burroughs, Corresponding Secretary of the Woman's Convention, Auxiliary to the National Baptist Convention, Made at Oklahoma City, September 5–9, 1934* (Oklahoma City, OK: National Baptist Convention, 1934), 10.

25. Nannie Helen Burroughs, *New and Old Paths to Fertile Fields* (Washington, DC: Woman's Convention Auxiliary to the National Baptist Convention, 1940).

26. "Effective Use of Votes Urged by NAACP Speaker," *Negro Star* (Wichita, KS), June 7, 1940; "Effective Use of Votes Urged by NAACP Speaker," *Pittsburgh (PA) Courier*, June 8, 1940.

27. Jeanette Marks, *Life and Letters of Mary Emma Woolley* (Washington, DC: PublicAffairs, 1955), 66.

28. "Interview with Frances Williams," Oral History 31, Black Women's Oral History Project, Schlesinger Library, Radcliffe Institute, Harvard University; Frances Williams McLemore, "The Role of the Negroes in Chicago in the Senatorial Election, 1930" (master's thesis, University of Chicago, 1931); "An American Family," *Headlines and Pictures: A Monthly Negro News Review* (New York), August 1946.

29. Frances Harriet Williams, *The Business Girl Looks at the Negro World* (New York: Woman's Press, 1937); *Harvey's, Inc. v. Sissle*, 53 Ohio App. 405 (Ohio Ct. App. 1936); Rosanna D. Charlton, "Book Review. Pudge Grows Up," *Pittsburgh Courier*, April 11, 1936; Williams authored the first in the series Pudge and Her Friends in the late 1930s (published in New York by Women's Press); *Pudge Grows Up*, coauthored with Wenonah Bond Logan, was published in 1936 (New York: Women's Press). Judith Weisenfeld explains the context for Pudge and Her Friends in *African American Women and Christian Activism: New York's Black YWCA, 1905–1945* (Cambridge, MA: Harvard University Press, 1997), 97–98.

30. "Second Armenia Conference," Papers of the NAACP, Part 11: Special Subject Files, 1912–1939, Series A: Africa through Garvey, Marcus; Jean Grigsby Paxton to

Claude Barnett, March 28, 1935, Claude A. Barnett Papers: The Associated Negro Press, 1918–1967, Part 3: Subject Files on Black Americans, 1918–1967, Series G: Philanthropic and Social Organizations, 1925–1966; "Says Nat'l Health Act Is Unfair. NAACP Wages Fight for Race Group," *Atlanta Daily World*, December 21, 1939; "Three Named for Board of NAACP," *New York Amsterdam News*, December 21, 1940; Eben Miller, *Born along the Color Line: The 1933 Armenia Conference and the Rise of a National Civil Rights Movement* (New York: Oxford University Press, 2012).

31. "National Council of Negro Women to Discuss National Defense Consumer Education International Relations Citizenship," *Negro Star* (Wichita, KS), October 18, 1940.

32. Elizabeth Galbreath recounted the day for the *Chicago Defender:* "Typovision," November 2, 1940.

33. Charley Cherokee [Lou Downings], *National Grapevine*, September 12, 1942; "OPA Integrates 13% Negroes in Wash'ton," *Atlanta Daily World*, November 11, 1945.

34. Joyce A. Hanson, *Mary McLeod Bethune & Black Women's Political Activism* (Columbia: University of Missouri Press, 2003), 11–55.

35. Hanson, *Mary McLeod Bethune*, 51, 56–90.

36. Hanson, *Mary McLeod Bethune*, 78–79.

37. Hanson, *Mary McLeod Bethune*, 78–79.

38. Hanson, *Mary McLeod Bethune*, 137. For an example of Bethune's approach to advising President Roosevelt, see Mary McLeod Bethune, "Letter to Franklin D. Roosevelt [draft] (1939)," in *Mary McLeod Bethune: Building a Better World. Essays and Selected Documents*, ed. Audrey Thomas McCluskey and Elaine Smith (Bloomington: Indiana University Press, 1999), 236–240.

39. Grace V. Leslie, "'United, We Build a Free World': The Internationalism of Mary McLeod Bethune and the National Council of Negro Women," in *To Turn the World Over*, ed. Keisha Blain and Tiffany Gill (Urbana: University of Illinois Press), 192–218.

40. Brenda Gayle Plummer, *Rising Wind: Black Americans and U.S. Foreign Affairs, 1935–1960* (Chapel Hill: University of North Carolina Press, 1996), 135–143.

41. Mary McLeod Bethune, "San Francisco Conference [1945]," in McCluskey and Smith, *Mary McLeod Bethune*, 248–253; Plummer, *Rising Wind*, 135–143.

42. Plummer, *Rising Wind*, 135–143.

43. "Bethune Group Announces Vote for Twelve Women of the Year," *Chicago Defender*, March 9, 1946; "Natl Council of Women Name Outstanding Women," *Kansas City (KS) Plain Dealer*, March 22, 1946.

44. Yevette Richards, "Race, Gender, and Anticommunism in the International Labor Movement: The Pan-African Connections of Maida Springer," *Journal of Women's History* 11, no. 2 (1999): 35–59; Barbara Ransby, *Eslanda: The Large and Unconventional Life of Mrs. Paul Robeson* (New Haven, CT: Yale University Press, 2013).

45. "Arenia C. Mallory," *Notable Black American Women*, Gale in Context: Biography series, 1992, www.gale.com/c/in-context-biography; David C. Driskell, "Lois Mailou Jones," *American Art* 12, no. 3 (January 10, 1998): 86–88; Rosalind Rosenberg, *Jane Crow: The Life of Pauli Murray* (New York: Oxford University Press, 2017); Charity Adams Earley, *One Woman's Army: A Black Officer Remembers the WAC* (College Station: Texas A&M University, 1989).

46. "Natl Council of Women Name Outstanding Women," *Kansas City (KS) Plain Dealer*, March 22, 1946.

47. Mary McLeod Bethune, "My Last Will and Testament," *Ebony*, August 1955; Elaine M. Smith, "Mary McLeod Bethune's 'Last Will and Testament': A Legacy for Race Vindication," *Journal of Negro History* 81, no. 1/4 (Winter–Autumn, 1996): 105–122.

Chapter 9: A Way to Express Themselves... and Make Change

1. Janet Dewart Bell, *Lighting the Fires of Freedom: African American Women in the Civil Rights Movement* (New York: New Press, 2018); Bettye Collier-Thomas and V. P. Franklin, eds., *Sisters in the Struggle: African American Women in the Civil Rights–Black Power Movement* (New York: New York University Press, 2001); Davis W. Houck and David E. Dixon, eds., *Women and the Civil Rights Movement, 1954–1965* (Jackson: University of Mississippi Press, 2009); Shannon King, "'In the Fabled Land of Make-Believe': Charlotta Bass and Jim Crow Los Angeles," in *The Strange Careers of the Jim Crow North*, ed. Brian Purcell and Jeanne Theoharis, with Komozi Woodard (New York: New York University Press, 2019); Regina Freer, "L.A. Race Woman: Charlotta Bass and the Complexities of Black Political Development in Los Angeles," *American Quarterly* 53, no. 3 (2004): 607–632; "Charlotta Bass," in Houck and Dixon, *Women and the Civil Rights Movement*, 148–153; Gerald R. Gill, "From Progressive Republican to Independent Progressive: The Political Career of Charlotta A. Bass," in *African American Women and the Vote, 1837–1965*, ed. Ann D. Gordon, with Bettye Collier-Thomas, John H. Bracey, Arlene Voski Avakian, and Joyce Avrech Berkman (Amherst: University of Massachusetts Press, 1997), 156–171.

2. Robert Shogan, *Harry Truman and the Struggle for Racial Justice* (Lawrence: University Press of Kansas, 2013); Richard Kluger, *Simple Justice: The History of Brown v. Board of Education and Black America's Struggle for Equality* (New York: Vintage Books, 1977); Clifford M. Lytle, "The History of the Civil Rights Bill of 1964," *Journal of Negro History* 51, no. 4 (October, 1966): 275–296; Clay Risen, *The Bill of the Century: The Epic Battle for the Civil Rights Act* (New York: Bloomsbury, 2014); Robert D. Lovey, *To End All Segregation: The Politics of the Passage of the Civil Rights Act of 1964* (Lanham, MD: University Press of America, 1990).

3. Jason Morgan Ward, *Hanging Bridge: Racial Violence and America's Civil Rights Century* (New York: Oxford University Press, 2016); Christopher Waldrep, *African Americans Confront Lynching: Strategies of Resistance from the Civil War to the Civil Rights Era* (New York: Rowman & Littlefield, 2008); Danielle L. McGuire, *At the Dark End of the Street: Black Women, Rape, and Resistance, a New History of the Civil Rights Movement from Rosa Parks to the Rise of Black Power* (New York: Alfred A. Knopf, 2010).

4. Clayborne Carson, "Martin Luther King, Jr.: Charismatic Leadership in a Mass Struggle," *Journal of American History* 74, no. 2 (September 1987): 448–454; Nathan Irvin Huggins, "Martin Luther King, Jr.: Charisma and Leadership," *Journal of American History* 74, no. 2 (September 1987): 477–481; Kenneth W. Mack, *Representing the Race: The Creation of the Civil Rights Lawyer* (Cambridge, MA: Harvard

University Press, 2012); Carol Giardina, "The Making of a Modern Feminist Vanguard, 1964–1973: Southern Women Whose Leadership Shaped the Movement and the Nation—a Synthetic Analysis," *Journal of Southern History* 85, no. 3 (August 2019): 611–652.

5. Derrick A. Bell Jr., "Brown v. Board of Education and the Interest-Convergence Dilemma," *Harvard Law Review* 93, no. 3 (January 1980): 518–533; Mary L. Dudziak, *Cold War Civil Rights: Race and the Image of American Democracy* (Princeton, NJ: Princeton University Press, 2001).

6. Bell, "Brown v. Board of Education and the Interest-Convergence Dilemma," 518–533; Dudziak, *Cold War Civil Rights*; Yashuhiro Katagiri, *Black Freedom, White Resistance, and Red Menace: Civil Rights and Anticommunism in the Jim Crow South* (Baton Rouge: Louisiana State University Press, 2014).

7. John Kyle Day, *The Southern Manifesto: Massive Resistance and the Fight to Preserve Segregation* (Jackson: University Press of Mississippi, 2014); Mark Golub, "Remembering Massive Resistance to School Desegregation," *Law & History Review* 31, no. 3 (August 2013): 491–530; Jason Morgan Ward, *Defending White Democracy: The Making of a Segregationist Movement & the Remaking of Racial Politics, 1936–1965* (Chapel Hill: University of North Carolina Press, 2011); Jack Shuler, *Blood and Bone: Truth and Reconciliation in a Southern Town* (Columbia: University of South Carolina Press, 2012).

8. Liette Gidlow, "The Sequel: The Fifteenth Amendment, the Nineteenth Amendment, and Southern Black Women's Struggle to Vote," *Journal of the Gilded Age & Progressive Era* 17, no. 3 (July 2018): 433–449; Gloria J. Browne-Marshall, *The Voting Rights War: The N.A.A.C.P. and the On-Going Struggle for Justice* (Lanham, MD: Rowman & Littlefield, 2016); R. Volley Riser, *Defying Disfranchisement: Black Voting Rights Activism in the Jim Crow South, 1890–1980* (Baton Rouge: Louisiana State University Press, 2010); Carol Anderson, *One Person, No Vote: How Voter Suppression Is Destroying Our Democracy* (New York: Bloomsbury, 2018).

9. Alfred Rudolph Waud, "The First Vote," *Harper's Weekly*, November 16, 1867.

10. Waud, "The First Vote."

11. The Brennan Center for Justice at New York University Law School has published *My First Vote*, a collection of first-person stories of Americans who voted for the first time in 2008. Susan Jayne Hadden, "Great-Great Grandmother's First Vote," *Illinois Heritage* 20, no. 1 (January/February 2017): 16–17; Sean Yoes, "My First Vote," *Baltimore Afro-American*, November 8, 2008; Robert M. Press, "Black Alabama Woman Recalls Her First Vote," *Christian Science Monitor*, February 21, 1984.

12. Robert E. Baker, "Negro Progress Report: Revolution in South: 1 Million New Voters," *Washington Post*, September 6, 1965.

13. "Federal Registrars at Work in Prentiss Motel. Begin Listing Voters as Owner of Place Confers with Attorney on Legal Action," *Hattiesburg (MS) American*, August 25, 1965; "Registered at Last," *Pittsburgh (PA) Courier*, September 11, 1965; "Finally Succeeded," *Clarion-Ledger* (Jackson, MS), August 26, 1965; "Registered at Last," *The Record* (Hackensack, NJ), August 26, 1965; "Rights: At the Time, Little Was Said About Women or Project," *Star Tribune* (Minneapolis, MN), July 1, 2001; Neil R. McMillen, "Black Enfranchisement in Mississippi: Federal Enforcement and Black Protest in the 1960's," *Journal of Southern History* 43, no. 3 (August 1977): 351–372.

14. William L. Patterson, ed., *We Charge Genocide: The Historical Petition to the United Nations for Relief from a Crime of the United States Government against the Negro People* (New York: International Publishers, 1951), 10, 68; "Negro Sues on Vote: Asserts He Was Barred from Registering in Mississippi," *New York Times*, March 18, 1958; "U.S. Court Backs Mississippi in Barring Negro from Voting," *New York Times*, November 7, 1958; *Darby v. Daniel*, 168 F. Supp. 170 (S.D. Miss. 1958); Thomas Armstrong and Natalie Bell, *Autobiography of a Freedom Rider: My Life as a Foot Soldier for Civil Rights* (New York: Simon & Schuster, 2011); Michael Vinson Williams, "With Determination and Fortitude We Come to Vote: Black Organization and Resistance to Voter Suppression in Mississippi," *Journal of Mississippi History* 74, no. 3 (Fall 2012): 195–238.

15. "Federal Registrars at Work in Prentiss Motel," *Hattiesburg (MS) American*, August 25, 1965.

16. "Plans to Seek Vote on Unseating Bared," *Hattiesburg (MS) American*, August 25, 1965.

17. Paul E. Joubert and Ben M. Crouch, "Mississippi Blacks and the Voting Rights Act of 1965," *Journal of Negro Education* 46 no. 2 (Spring 1977): 157–167; Richard J. Timpone, "The Voting Rights Act and Electoral Empowerment: The Case of Mississippi," *Social Science Quarterly* 78, no. 1 (March 1997): 177–185.

18. Diane Nash, interview by Trey Ellis, *King in the Wilderness*, Kunhardt Film Foundation, July 14, 2017, kunhardtfilmfoundation.org/featured-interviews/diane-nash; Janet Dewart Bell, *Lighting the Fires of Freedom: African American Women in the Civil Rights Movement* (New York: New Press, 2018); Houck and Dixon, *Women and the Civil Rights Movement*, 154–168.

19. Diane Nash, interview by Trey Ellis, *King in the Wilderness*; Bell, *Lighting the Fires of Freedom*; Houck and Dixon, *Women and the Civil Rights Movement*, 154–168.

20. Diane Nash, interview by Trey Ellis, *King in the Wilderness*; Bell, *Lighting the Fires of Freedom*; Houck and Dixon, *Women and the Civil Rights Movement*, 154–168.

21. Diane Nash, interview by Trey Ellis, *King in the Wilderness*; Bell, *Lighting the Fires of Freedom*; Houck and Dixon, *Women and the Civil Rights Movement*, 154–168; Raymond Arsenault, *Freedom Riders: 1961 and the Struggle for Racial Justice* (New York: Oxford University Press, 2006); Benjamin Houston, *The Nashville Way: Racial Etiquette and the Struggle for Social Justice in a Southern City* (Athens: University of Georgia Press, 2012).

22. Diane Nash, interview by Trey Ellis, *King in the Wilderness*.

23. Diane Nash, interview by Trey Ellis, *King in the Wilderness*; Robert A. Pratt, *Selma's Bloody Sunday: Protest, Voting Rights, and the Struggle for Racial Equality* (Baltimore: Johns Hopkins University Press, 2017); David J. Barrow, *Protest at Selma: Martin Luther King, Jr., and the Voting Rights Act of 1965* (New Haven, CT: Yale University Press, 1978); J. Mills Thornton III, *Dividing Lines: Municipal Politics and the Struggle for Civil Rights in Montgomery, Birmingham, and Selma* (Tuscaloosa: University of Alabama Press, 2002).

24. "Dr. King May Appeal to Both Sides to Negotiate in Vietnam War," *Evening Sun* (Baltimore), August 13, 1965; "SCLC's Highest Award: Civil Rights Team Honored," *Chicago Defender*, August 7, 1965; "1,000 Delegates Expected at SCLC Convention in Birmingham, Aug. 9–13" (press release), Southern Christian Leadership Conference, July

26, 1965, Folder 130.25, Press Releases, 1965, Part 3: Records of the Public Relations Department, Series XIII, Records of Conventions and Meetings, 1959–1969, Records of the Southern Christian Leadership Conference, 1954–1970; "James & Diane Bevel to Get SCLC's Highest Award at B'ham Convention" (press release), Southern Christian Leadership Conference, July 26, 1965, Folder 130.25, Press Releases, 1965, Part 3: Records of the Public Relations Department, Series XIII, Records of Conventions and Meetings, 1959–1969, Records of the Southern Christian Leadership Conference, 1954–1970.

25. Giardina, "The Making of a Modern Feminist Vanguard," 611–652; Bell, *Lighting the Fires of Freedom*; Jacqueline A. Rouse, "'We Seek to Know…in Order to Speak the Truth': Nurturing the Seeds of Discontent—Septima P. Clark and Participatory Leadership," in Collier-Thomas and Franklin, *Sisters in the Struggle*, 95–120; Houck and Dixon, *Women and the Civil Rights Movement*, 307–314; Grace Jordan McFadden, "Septima P. Clark and the Struggle for Human Rights," in *Women in the Civil Rights Movement: Trailblazers and Torchbearers, 1941–1965*, ed. Vicki L. Crawford, Jacqueline Anne Rouse, and Barbara Woods (Bloomington: Indiana University Press, 1990), 85–98.

26. "Dr. King May Appeal to Both Sides to Negotiate in Vietnam War," *Evening Sun* (Baltimore), August 13, 1965.

27. Patricia Bell-Scott, *The Firebrand and the First Lady: Portrait of a Friendship; Pauli Murray, Eleanor Roosevelt, and the Struggle for Social Justice* (New York: Alfred A. Knopf, 2016); Rosalind Rosenberg, *Jane Crow: The Life of Pauli Murray* (New York: Oxford University Press, 2017); Brittney C. Cooper, *Beyond Respectability: The Intellectual Thought of Race Women* (Urbana: University of Illinois Press, 2017).

28. Rosenberg, *Jane Crow*, 55, 295.

29. Rosenberg, *Jane Crow*.

30. Pauli Murray, *Song in a Weary Throat: An American Pilgrimage* (New York: Harper & Row, 1987).

31. Pauli Murray, *Pauli Murray: The Autobiography of a Black Activist, Feminist, Lawyer, Priest, and Poet* (Knoxville: University of Tennessee Press, 1989), 177–188.

32. Murray, *Pauli Murray: The Autobiography*, 177–188; Rosenberg, *Jane Crow*, 90. Treva B. Lindsey explains how in the 1920s and 1930s, Lucy Diggs Slowe, the school's dean of women, had waged her own campaign for women's dignity and power at Howard University. Treva B. Lindsey, "Climbing the Hilltop: New Negro Womanhood at Howard University," in *Colored No More: Reinventing Black Womanhood in Washington, D.C.* (Urbana: University of Illinois Press, 2017), 25–51.

33. Murray, *Pauli Murray: The Autobiography*, 189–209; Rosenberg, *Jane Crow*; Cooper, *Beyond Respectability*.

34. Murray, *Pauli Murray: The Autobiography*, 217–219; Cooper, *Beyond Respectability*; Rosenberg, *Jane Crow*, 117–118.

35. Pauli Murray, *Pauli Murray: The Autobiography*, 189–206, 215–217; Rosenberg, *Jane Crow*; Cooper, *Beyond Respectability*.

36. Murray, *Pauli Murray: The Autobiography*. On Howard students and civil rights battles, see "Jim Crow Must Go: Civil Rights Struggles during World War II," in Mary-Elizabeth B. Murphy, *Jim Crow Capital: Women and Black Freedom Struggles in Washington, D.C., 1920–1945* (Chapel Hill: University of North Carolina Press, 2018), 173–200.

37. Murray, *Song in a Weary Throat*, 201–205.

38. Murray, *Song in a Weary Throat*, 203–220.

39. Carol Anderson, *Eyes off the Prize: African Americans, the United Nations, and the Struggle for Human Rights, 1944–1955* (New York: Cambridge University Press, 2003), 1–15; Brenda Gayle Plummer, *Rising Wind: Black Americans and U.S. Foreign Affairs, 1935–1960* (Chapel Hill: University of North Carolina Press, 1996).

40. Pauli Murray, "Jane Crow and the Law: Sex Discrimination and Title VII," *George Washington Law Review* 34, no. 2 (December 1965): 232–256.

41. Murray, *Pauli Murray: The Autobiography*, 426–435.

42. Murray, *Pauli Murray: The Autobiography*, 426–435; "Pauli Murray Letter and Photo of Her Ordination, 1977," 75 Stories, 75 Years: Documenting the Lives of American Women at the Schlesinger Library, https://schlesinger75radcliffe.org/objects/pauli-murray-letter-and-photo-of-her-ordination-1977; Rosenberg, *Jane Crow*; Cooper, *Beyond Respectability*.

43. Marjorie Hyer, "First Black Woman to Be Ordained by Episcopal Bishop," *Washington Post*, January 7, 1977; James Robison, "Religion: Church Ordains First Black Women," *Chicago Tribune*, January 8, 1977.

44. Murray, *Song in a Weary Throat*, 435; Sonja Hillgren, "Black Woman Episcopalian Is Ordained," *Baltimore Afro-American*, January 15, 1977.

45. Ruth Jenkins, "Pioneer Priest Eyed the Ministry for Years," *Baltimore Afro-American*, January 15, 1977; Renee Moseley, "First Woman Ordained," *New York Amsterdam News*, January 29, 1977.

46. Jeanne Theoharis, *The Rebellious Life of Mrs. Rosa Parks* (Boston: Beacon Press, 2013); Rosa Parks, with Jim Haskins, *Rosa Parks: My Story* (New York: Dial Books, 1992); Douglas Brinkley, *Rosa Parks: A Life* (New York: Viking, 2000); Rosa Parks, with Gregory J. Reed, *Reflections by Rosa Parks: The Quiet Strength and Faith of a Woman Who Changed a Nation* (Grand Rapids, MI: Zondervan, 2017).

47. "Rosa Parks and Myles Horton with Studs Terkel, June 8, 1973," Studs Terkel Radio Archive, Chicago History Museum. This chapter is indebted to the biography of Parks's life by Jeanne Theoharis, *The Rebellious Life of Mrs. Rosa Parks* (Boston: Beacon Press, 2013).

48. See Library of Congress, Image 13 of Rosa Parks Papers: Writings, Notes, and Statements, 1956–1998, Drafts of early writings, Autobiographical, circa 1956, undated.

49. See Library of Congress, Rosa Parks Papers: Writings, Notes, and Statements, 1956–1998, Drafts of early writings, Autobiographical, circa 1956, undated.

50. See Library of Congress, Rosa Parks Papers: Writings, Notes, and Statements, 1956–1998, Drafts of early writings, Autobiographical, circa 1956, undated.

51. Theoharis, *The Rebellious Life of Mrs. Rosa Parks*, 14–37. On the Scottsboro case, see Dan T. Carter, *Scottsboro: A Tragedy of the American South* (Baton Rouge: Louisiana State University Press, 1979) and James Goodman, *Stories of Scottsboro* (New York: Vintage, 1994).

52. Theoharis, *The Rebellious Life of Mrs. Rosa Parks*, 14–37.

53. See Library of Congress, Rosa Parks Papers: Writings, Notes, and Statements, 1956–1998, Drafts of early writings, Autobiographical, circa 1956, undated; Image 9 of Rosa Parks Papers: Writings, Notes, and Statements, 1956–1998, Drafts of early writings; accounts of her arrest and the subsequent boycott, as well as general reflections on race relations in the South, 1956–circa 1958, undated, Folder 1, Library of Congress, Rosa Parks Papers.

54. Houck and Dixon, "Johnnie Carr. June 1957, Women's Auxiliary Baptist State Convention of Illinois, Chicago, Illinois," in *Women and the Civil Rights Movement*, 82–87. Parks explained to Studs Terkel: "For a long time, I had been very much against, as far back as I can remember myself, I had been very much against being treated a certain way because of race and for a reason that over which I had no control, had always been taught that this was America, the land of the free and home of the brave, and we were free people. And I felt that it should be actual in action rather than just something that we hear and talk about. And as my reason is a little hard to explain to most people, but I just feel that I was being mistreated as a human being and I wanted to in this way make known that I felt that I should have the same rights and privileges." "Rosa Parks and Myles Horton with Studs Terkel, June 8, 1973," Studs Terkel Radio Archive, Chicago History Museum.

55. Theoharis, *The Rebellious Life of Mrs. Rosa Parks*, 17–45.

56. "Rosa Parks and Myles Horton with Studs Terkel, June 8, 1973," Studs Terkel Radio Archive, Chicago History Museum.

57. Burt M. Rieff, "*Browder v. Gayle*: The Legal Vehicle of the Montgomery Bus Boycott," *Alabama Review* 41, no. 3 (July 1988): 193–208; Jo Ann Gibson Robinson, *The Montgomery Bus Boycott and the Women Who Started It: The Memoir of Jo Ann Gibson Robinson*, ed. David J. Garrow (Knoxville: University of Tennessee Press, 1987).

58. Chana Kai Lee, *For Freedom's Sake: The Life of Fannie Lou Hamer* (Urbana: University of Illinois Press, 1999); Martha Prescod Norman, "Shining in the Dark: Black Women and the Struggle for the Vote, 1955–1965," in *African American Women and the Vote, 1837–1965*, ed. Ann D. Gordon, with Bettye Collier-Thomas, John H. Bracey, Arlene Voski Avakian, and Joyce Avrech Berkman (Amherst: University of Massachusetts Press, 1997).

59. Fannie Lou Hamer, "Testimony before the Credentials Committee at the Democratic National Convention, Atlantic City, New Jersey, August 22, 1964," in Hamer, *The Speeches of Fannie Lou Hamer: To Tell It Like It Is*, ed. Maegan Parker Brooks and Davis W. Houck (Jackson: University of Mississippi Press, 2010), 63–66. On Hamer's life generally, see Chana Kai Lee, *For Freedom's Sake*, 23–44.

60. Fannie Lou Hamer, "'I'm Sick and Tired of Being Sick and Tired': Speech Delivered with Malcolm X at the Williams Institutional CME Church, Harlem, New York, December 20, 1964," in Hamer, *Speeches of Fannie Lou Hamer*, 75–81; Lee, *For Freedom's Sake*, 4–22.

61. Lee, *For Freedom's Sake*, 45–60.

62. Fannie Lou Hamer, "Testimony Before the Credentials Committee at the Democratic National Convention, Atlantic City, New Jersey, August 22, 1964."

63. Lee, *For Freedom's Sake*, 49–53.

64. Lee, *For Freedom's Sake*, 85–102; Alan Draper, "Class and Politics in the Mississippi Movement: An Analysis of the Mississippi Freedom Democratic Delegation," *Journal of Southern History* 82, no. 2 (May 2018): 269–304.

65. Lee, *For Freedom's Sake*, 85–102; Draper, "Class and Politics in the Mississippi Movement," 269–304; Tanisha Ford, *Liberated Threads: Black Women, Style, and the Global Politics of Soul* (Chapel Hill: University of North Carolina Press, 2017).

66. Lee, *For Freedom's Sake*, 85–102; Draper, "Class and Politics in the Mississippi Movement," 269–304.

67. Also present, though not pictured, were Roy Wilkins, head of the NAACP; James Farmer of the Congress of Racial Equality (CORE); and John Lewis of the Student Nonviolent Coordinating Committee (SNCC), who had been gravely injured during the first march across the Edmund Pettus Bridge in Selma. E. W. Kenworthy, "Johnson Signs Voting Rights Bill, Orders Immediate Enforcement," *New York Times*, August 7, 1965.

68. Newspapers reported that Rosa Parks was also in attendance, though she was not photographed here. Patricia Roberts Harris, "Law and Moral Issues," *Journal of Religious Thought* 21, no. 1 (1964–1965): 65–71; "Only Whites Can Erase Image," *Washington Post*, September 19, 1963; Bruce Kauffman, "The Inspiration Behind the Civil Rights Act of 1964," *New York Times*, June 16, 2019; Gail K. Bell, "Four Marshallites' Roles in the Passage of the Civil Rights Act of 1964," *Southwestern Historical Quarterly* 106, no. 1 (July 2002): 1–29; E. Culpepper Clark, *The Schoolhouse Door: Segregation's Last Stand at the University of Alabama* (New York: Oxford University Press, 1995).

69. "Race and Sex Irrelevant Says Mrs. Harris at Swearing In," *Afro-American*, July 17, 1965.

Conclusion: Candidates of the People

1. Mary Church Terrell, *A Colored Woman in a White World* (Washington, DC: Ransdell, 1940); Ida B. Wells-Barnett, *Crusade for Justice: The Autobiography of Ida B. Wells*, ed. Alfreda M. Duster (Chicago: University of Chicago Press, 1970); Hallie Q. Brown, *Homespun Heroines and Other Women of Distinction* (Freeport, NY: Books for Libraries, 1971); Pauli Murray, *Proud Shoes: The Story of an American Family* (New York: Harper, 1956).

2. Combahee River Collective, "A Black Feminist Statement," *Off Our Backs* 9, no. 6 (June 1979): 6–8; Keeanga-Yamahtta Taylor, *How We Get Free: Black Feminism and the Combahee River Collective* (Chicago: Haymarket Books, 2017); Premilla Nadasen, *Household Workers United: The Untold Story of African American Women Who Built a Movement* (Boston: Beacon Press, 2015); Premilla Nadasen, *Welfare Warriors: The Welfare Rights Movement in the United States* (New York: Routledge, 2005); Kimberly Springer, *Living for the Revolution: Black Feminist Organizations, 1968–1980* (Durham, NC: Duke University Press, 2005); Rhonda Y. Williams, *The Politics of Public Housing: Black Women's Struggles Against Urban Inequality* (New York: Oxford University Press, 2005); Toni Morrison, ed., *Race-ing Justice, En-Gendering Power: Essays on Anita Hill, Clarence Thomas, and the Construction of Social Reality* (New York: Pantheon, 1992); Anita Hill, *Speaking Truth to Power* (New York: Doubleday, 1997); "African American Women in Defense of Ourselves," *New York Times*, November 17, 1991.

3. Charlotte L. Forten and Lewis C. Lockwood, *Two Black Teachers During the Civil War: Mary S. Peake, the Colored Teacher at Fortress Monroe* (New York: Arno Press, 1969); Elizabeth Keckley, *Behind the Scenes: Thirty Years a Slave and Four Years in the White House* (New York: Arno Press, 1968); Susie King Taylor, *Reminiscences of My Life in Camp* (New York: Arno Press, 1968); Sojourner Truth, with Olive Gilbert, *Narrative of Sojourner Truth* (New York: Arno Press, 1968); Toni Cade, ed., *The Black Woman: An Anthology* (New York: New American Library, 1970); Gerda Lerner,

ed., *Black Women in White America: A Documentary History* (New York: Pantheon, 1972); Dorothy Porter Wesley, ed., *Early Negro Writing, 1760–1837* (Boston: Beacon Press, 1971); Sharon Harley and Rosalyn Terborg-Penn, eds., *The Afro-American Woman: Struggles and Images* (Port Washington: National University Publications, 1978). On the "problems and possibilities" of Black women, see Brittney Cooper, *Beyond Respectability: The Intellectual Thought of Race Women* (Urbana: University of Illinois Press, 2017), 115–139.

4. Chisholm recounted her political career in two memoirs. Shirley Chisholm, *The Good Fight* (New York: Harper & Row, 1973); Shirley Chisholm, *Unbought and Unbossed* (Boston: Houghton Mifflin, 1970).

5. Barbara Winslow, *Shirley Chisholm* (New York: Routledge, 2013); Chisholm, *Unbought and Unbossed*.

6. Barbara Jordan, "The Constitutional Basis for Impeachment, U.S. House Judiciary Committee Impeachment Hearings, Washington, D.C., July 25, 1974," in *Barbara Jordan: Speaking Truth with Eloquent Thunder*, ed. Max Sherman (Austin: University of Texas Press, 2007); Mary Ellen Curtin, "Barbara Jordan: The Paradox of Black Female Abolition," in *Texas Women: Their Histories, Their Lives*, ed. Elizabeth Hayes Turner, Stephanie Cole, and Rebecca Sharpless (Athens: University of Georgia Press, 2015); Mary Ellen Curtin, "Women in Politics from the 1920s to Today," Organization of American Historians Annual Meeting, Philadelphia, April 5, 2019, CSPAN, www.c-span.org/video/?459603-3/women-politics-1920s-today; Mary Ellen Curtin, "Barbara Jordan and the Politics of Insertion and Accommodation," *Critical Review of International Social and Political Philosophy (CRISPP)* 7, no. 4 (Winter 2004): 279–303; Mary Ellen Curtin, "Reaching for Power: Barbara Jordan and Texas Liberals, 1966–1972," *Southwestern Historical Quarterly* 108, no. 1 (October 2004): 211–231; Paula Giddings, "Will the Real Barbara Jordan Please Stand?," *Encore American and Worldwide News*, May 9, 1977; Barbara C. Jordan, *Selected Speeches*, ed. Sandra Parham (Washington, DC: Howard University Press, 1999); Barbara A. Holmes, *A Private Woman in Public Spaces: Barbara Jordan's Speeches on Ethics, Public Religion, and Law* (Harrisburg, PA: Trinity Press, 2000); Barbara Jordan and Shelby Hearon, *Barbara Jordan: A Self-Portrait* (Garden City, NY: Doubleday, 1979).

7. "Little Rock's First Female Mayor: Lottie Shackleford," Voices of the Civil Rights Movement, https://voicesofthecivilrightsmovement.com/Video-Collection/2015/12/04/little-rocks-female-mayor; "The Nation's First Elected Black Female Mayor: 'I Believed in God, and I Believed in Myself,'" *Washington Post*, April 2, 2019.

8. Lani Guinier, *Lift Every Voice: Turning a Civil Rights Setback into a New Vision of Social Justice* (New York: Simon & Schuster, 1998), 23–131; Lani Guinier, "Who's Afraid of Lani Guinier," *New York Times*, February 27, 1994.

9. Loretta Lynch, "Commencement Address at Spelman College, May 15, 2016," Archives of Women's Political Communication, Iowa State University, https://awpc.cattcenter.iastate.edu/2017/03/09/commencement-address-at-spelman-college-may-15-2016/.

10. Loretta Lynch, "Remarks at United State of Women Summit, June 15, 2016," CSPAN, www.c-span.org/video/?411151-1/attorney-general-loretta-lynch-speaks-mass-shooting-orlando-florida.

11. Stacey Abrams, *Lead from the Outside: How to Build Your Future and Make Real Change* (New York: Henry Holt, 2018), 19–21.

12. Stacey Abrams, *Lead from the Outside*, 156.

13. Abigail Pesta, "Stacey Abrams on 2020: Don't Focus on Beating Trump— Focus on Winning America," Women in the World, April 11, 2019, https://women intheworld.com/2019/04/11/stacey-abrams-on-2020-dont-focus-on-beating-trump -focus-on-winning-america/; Stacey Abrams, with Tina Brown, Women in the World Summit (video), April 11, 2019, www.facebook.com/NowThisNews/videos/20103308 89065006/?v=2010330889065006.

14. Abigail Pesta, "Stacey Abrams on 2020: Don't Focus on Beating Trump— Focus on Winning America," Women in the World, April 11, 2019, https://women intheworld.com/2019/04/11/stacey-abrams-on-2020-dont-focus-on-beating-trump -focus-on-winning-america/; Stacey Abrams, with Tina Brown, Women in the World Summit (video), April 11, 2019, www.facebook.com/NowThisNews/videos/20103308 89065006/?v=2010330889065006.

15. Stacey Abrams, *Lead from the Outside*, 38, 58, 136.

Acknowledgments

1. "Plaintiff's Brief," *Chesapeake, Ohio & Southwestern Railroad Company v Ida B. Wells*, Tennessee Supreme Court, 1885. Tennessee Supreme Court, RG 170. Tennessee State Library & Archives.

2. Paula J. Giddings, *Ida, a Sword among Lions: Ida B. Wells and the Campaign Against Lynching* (New York: Amistad, 2008), 514–547; Susan Ware, "Ida Wells-Barnett and the Alpha Suffrage Club," in *Why They Marched: Untold Stories of the Women Who Fought for the Right to Vote* (Cambridge, MA: Belknap Press, 2019), 99–109; Lisa G. Materson, *For the Freedom of Her Race: Black Women and Electoral Politics in Illinois, 1877–1932* (Chapel Hill: University of North Carolina Press, 2009), 60–107, 185–227; Mia Bay, *To Tell the Truth Freely: The Life of Ida B. Wells* (New York: Hill and Wang, 2010), 274–313.

3. Martha S. Jones, "How New York's New Monument Whitewashes the Women's Rights Movement," *Washington Post*, March 22, 2019.

INDEX

condemning, 11–14, 20
coping with, 1–11
inequality and, 29, 44, 68, 102, 115,
    152–153, 229, 257
oppression and, 38, 46, 91,
    138–141, 160, 195, 237, 269,
    275
political power and, 181–182
promoting, 17–19
sexism and, 1–11, 75–81, 94,
    111, 138–141, 153, 156–157,
    181–182, 200, 221, 231,
    241–244, 269
violence and, 2, 4, 9, 17, 45–47,
    92–93, 100–108, 123, 134–135,
    145–146, 150–157, 198,
    213–214, 230, 237–256
women's rights and, 245
Ransom, Leon, 243, 244
Ray, Charles, 58
Ray, Charlotte, 127
Ray, Henrietta, 58
Reconstruction, 99–113, 121–124,
    134, 150, 177, 187, 191, 194,
    204–207, 219, 228–233, 257
Recovery Act, 204–205
Redmond, Pauline, 245
re-enslavement, 101. *See also* slavery
*Religion and the Pure Principles of
    Morality* (book), 29
*Religious Experience and Journal of
    Mrs. Jarena Lee* (book), 27, 41
    (fig.), 41–42
*Reminiscences of My Life in Camp
    with the 33rd United States
    Colored Troops, Late 1st S.C.
    Volunteers* (book), 109
Remond, Charles, 83, 92, 110
Remond, Sarah, 83, 110
Republican National Committee, 212
Republican Party, 3–4, 131, 168–169,
    188–191, 196–199, 204,
    212–214, 241
Republican Women's Committee of
    Allegheny (PA) County, 199
Reyneau, Betsy Graves, 245
Ridley, Florida R., 129
Robertson, Carole, 239

Robeson, Eslanda, 222, 224
Robeson, Paul, 224
Robinson, Emily, 81
Robinson, Marius, 81
Roosevelt, Eleanor, 207, 218, 223
    (fig.), 225, 245, 264
Roosevelt, Franklin Delano, 204–205,
    218, 220–221, 241
Ross, Eva, 165
Ruffin, Josephine St. Pierre, 129, 149,
    173
Ruffin, Thomas, 87
Ruggles, David, 54
Rusk, Dean, 264
Rutland Weekly Herald (newspaper),
    101–103
Ryan, William, 236

Saint Augustine Normal School and
    Collegiate Institute, 143
St. Luke Herald (newspaper), 170,
    190
St. Luke Penny Savings Bank, 191
St. Luke's Hall (Richmond, VA), 190
Sanford, Rebecca, 66–67
Saturday Visiter (newspaper), 81
Savannah Tribune (newspaper), 184
school segregation, 206, 228–230
Second Conference of the International
    Woman Suffrage Alliance (Berlin,
    Germany, 1904), 159, 190
Sedition Act of 1918, 177
segregation. *See also* Jim Crow laws
    attitudes about, 123–124, 134–135,
        150, 246–247
    color line and, 12–14
    desegregation, 206, 228, 230,
        237–238
    enduring, 7, 12–14
    in government buildings, 177, 191,
        250
    of lunch counters, 6, 237, 250, 272
    in military, 228
    in schools, 206, 228–230
    surveys on, 246–247
    in theaters, 12–14
    of transportation, 230, 238,
        242–243, 250, 255–256

Wiley College, 263
Willard, Frances, 140
Williams, Fannie Miller, 3–4, 6–7,
  11–14, 12 (fig.), 215, 264
Williams, Frances Harriet, 183,
  214–219, 264
Williams, Frank, 3
Williams, John Sharp, 169
Williams, Mamie George, 184
Williams, Richard, 26
Wilson, Woodrow, 163, 176–179
Woman Suffrage Procession, National
  American Woman Suffrage
  Association (1913), 162–166, 179
"womanist" worldview, 7–8
Woman's Convention Auxiliary,
  National Baptist Convention,
  209–211, 210 (fig.), 214
Woman's ERA Club (Boston, MA),
  199
Woman's Journal (magazine), 128
Woman's Suffrage Club of Chatham
  County (GA), 183
Woman's Suffrage Club (Savannah,
  GA), 183
Women of the Century (book), 126
Women's Christian Temperance Union
  (WCTU), 140, 147, 194, 214
women's clubs. *See also specific clubs*
  club movement, 147, 183, 202, 209
  forming, 2–3
  naming, 173–174
  participating in, 9–11, 152–163,
    180–199, 209–212
Women's Missionary Union, Southern
  Baptist Convention, 214
Women's National Loyal League, 106,
  114
women's rights
  abolitionism and, 130–131, 254

antislavery and, 8–9, 101–102
churchwomen's rights, 60–63,
  124–134, 140–142
civil rights and, 202, 250, 267–268
conventions on, 81, 85, 115
debate on, 135–140
definition of, 94
endorsement of, 53–54, 82, 193
equal rights and, 7–9, 19–28,
  101–116
fight for, 8–11, 46–68, 75–94,
  130–147, 181–188, 193–202,
  244–255, 267–276
history of, 75–76, 245
human rights and, 222
intrusion of, 57, 140
philosophy of, 82, 265
racism and, 245
Women's Suffrage Party (New York,
  NY), 180–182
Woods, Mary Virginia, 110
Woolley, Mary Emma, 215
Works Progress Administration
  (WPA), 204–205
World War I, 177–178, 187, 224
World War II, 206, 224–229
World Antislavery Convention
  (London, UK, 1840), 57
Wright, Frances, 21
Wright, Joshua, 63
Wright, Samantha, 63–64
Wright, Zephyr, 262, 262 (fig.), 263

Young, Mary Sharperson, 181–182,
  200–202
Young Women's Christian Association
  (YWCA), 3–4, 183, 212, 215–216
Young Women's Christian Association
  (YWCA) Council on Colored
  Work, 4

 JOHNS HOPKINS UNIVERSITY

Martha S. Jones is the Society of Black Alumni Presidential Professor and professor of history at Johns Hopkins University. She is president of the Berkshire Conference of Women Historians, the oldest and largest association of women historians in the United States. Author of *Birthright Citizens* and *All Bound Up Together*, and an editor of *Toward an Intellectual History of Black Women*, she has written for the *Washington Post*, *The Atlantic*, *USA Today*, and more. She lives in Baltimore.